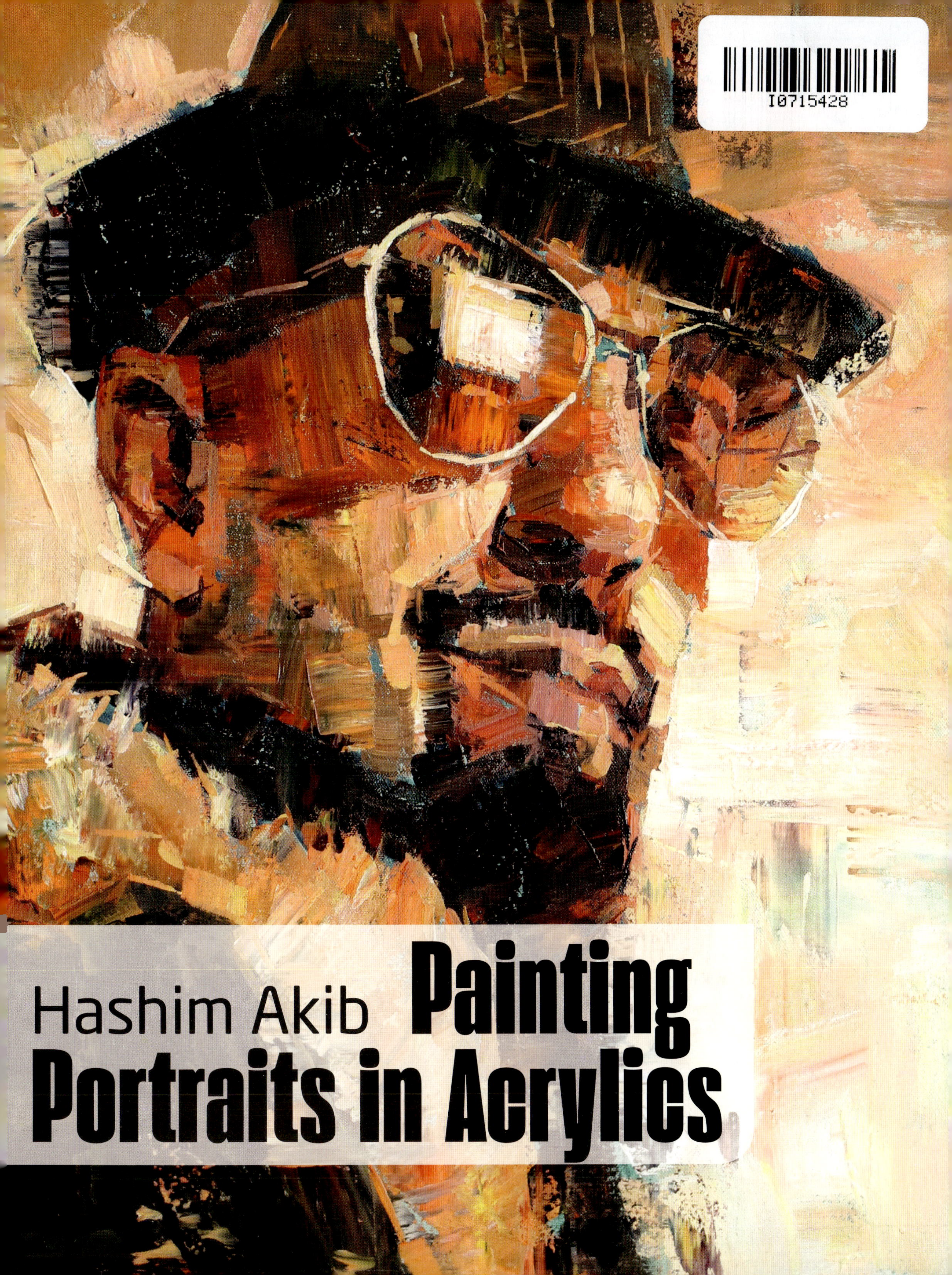
I0715428
Hashim Akib Painting
Portraits in Acrylics

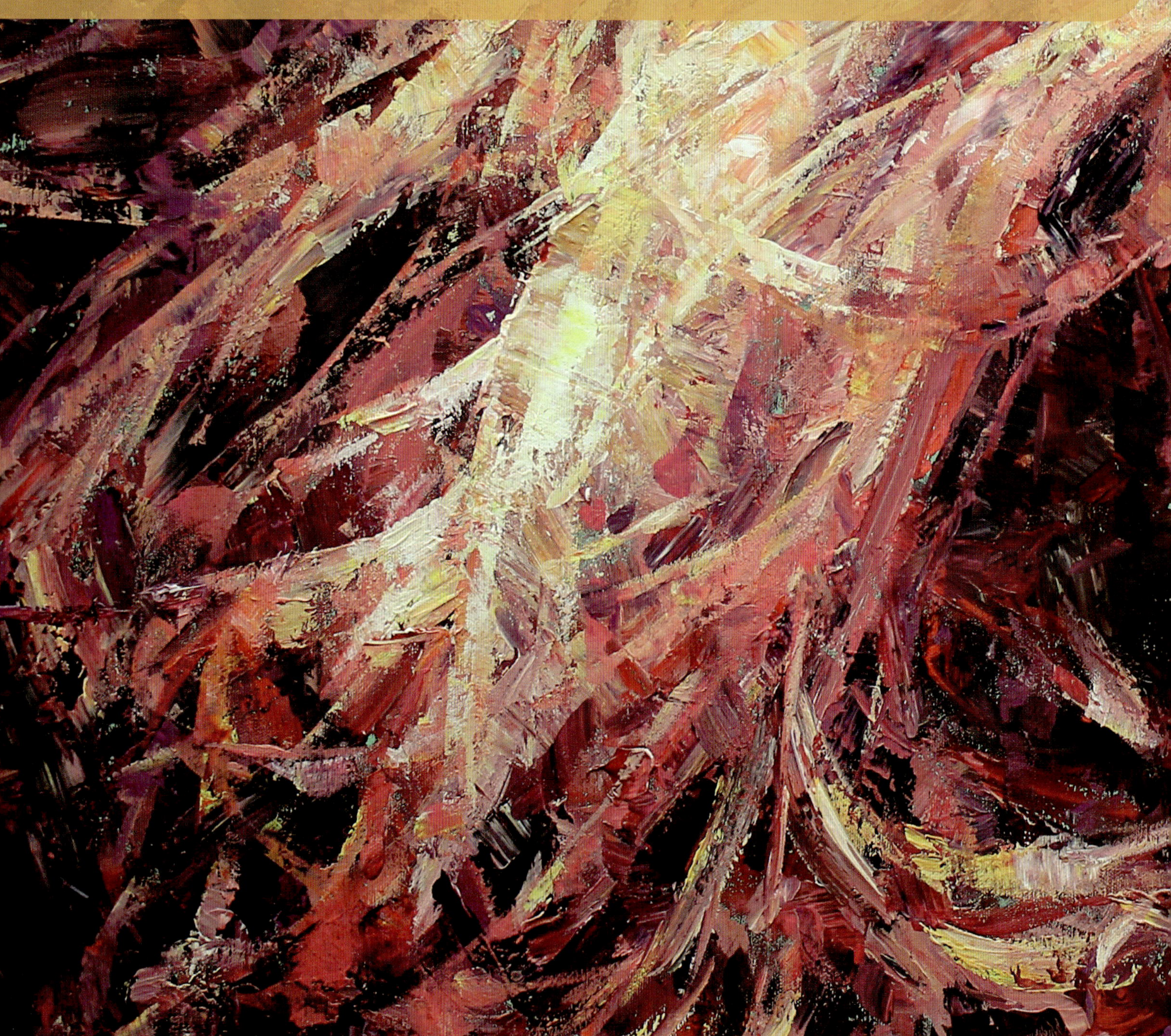

Painting Portraits in Acrylics

Hashim Akib

A PRACTICAL GUIDE TO CONTEMPORARY PORTRAITURE

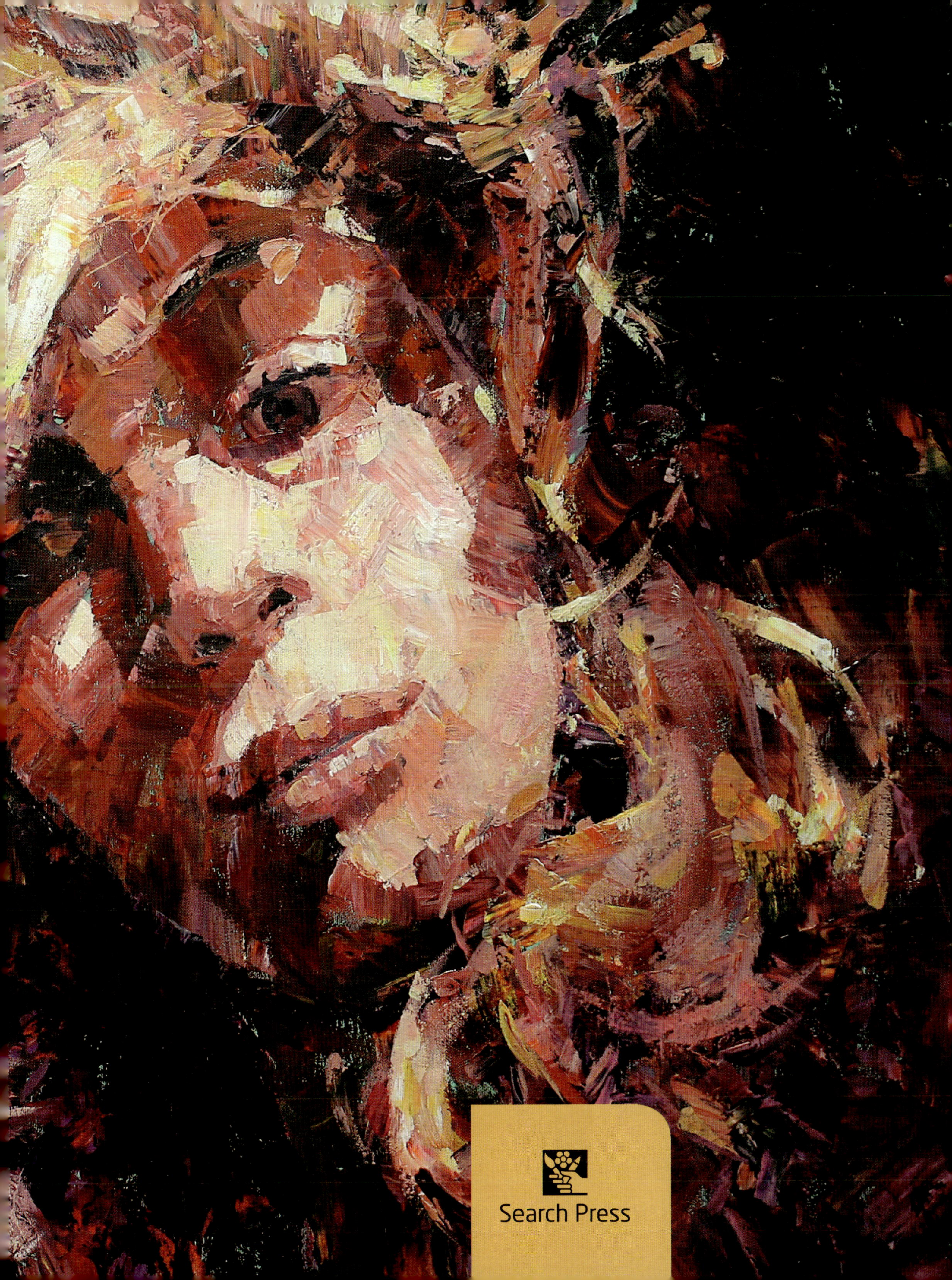

Search Press

First published in 2019

Search Press Limited
Wellwood, North Farm Road,
Tunbridge Wells, Kent TN2 3DR

8 9 10

Bookmarked Hub
For further ideas and inspiration, and to join our free
online community, visit www.bookmarkedhub.com

Publishers' notes
The Publishers and author can accept no
responsibility for any consequences arising
from the information, advice or instructions
given in this publication.

For errata, please visit our website
(www.searchpress.com) or the Bookmarked Hub
(www.bookmarkedhub.com).

GPSR information can be found at
www.searchpress.com
Printed in China, AP012026

Acknowledgements

Huge thanks to everyone who gave permission for
me to paint and include them in this book; sorry to
those who didn't make it in, but your contribution
was neverthless invaluable on my journey to
develop the ideas and processes contained within.

A special mention to Elena; Beth Reeks; Hasan, for
his amazing photographic portraits from his travels
around Africa (hasansoylemez.com).

To all at Search Press, especially Edward Ralph.
Special thanks to all my students, galleries that
support me, Natrah for being big sis, and Marie for
just about everything else.

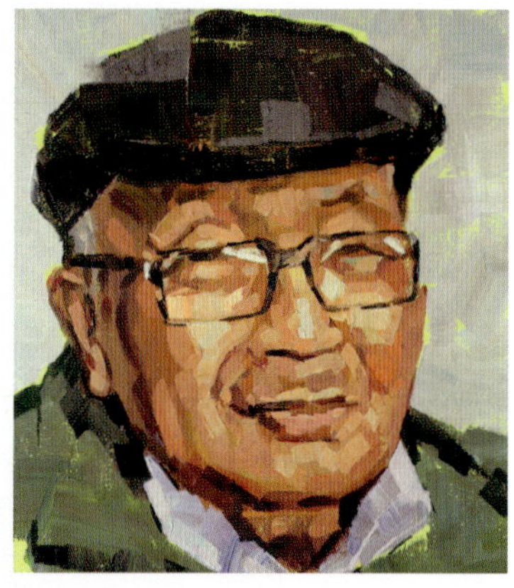

Dedication

For dad.

Page 1:

GEORGI 46×61CM (18×24IN)

Limiting colour and exploiting light and dark can produce
striking results. A cool-looking model also helps.

Page 3:

ELENA FLOWING HAIR 88×60CM (35×24IN)

Flowing hair that creates varying diagonals can be used
as a great compositional tool to lead you into the face.
In this case, angling the face into the hair creates a strong
underlying triangular shape.

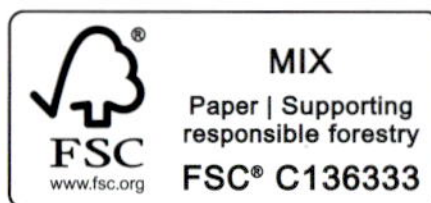

Contents

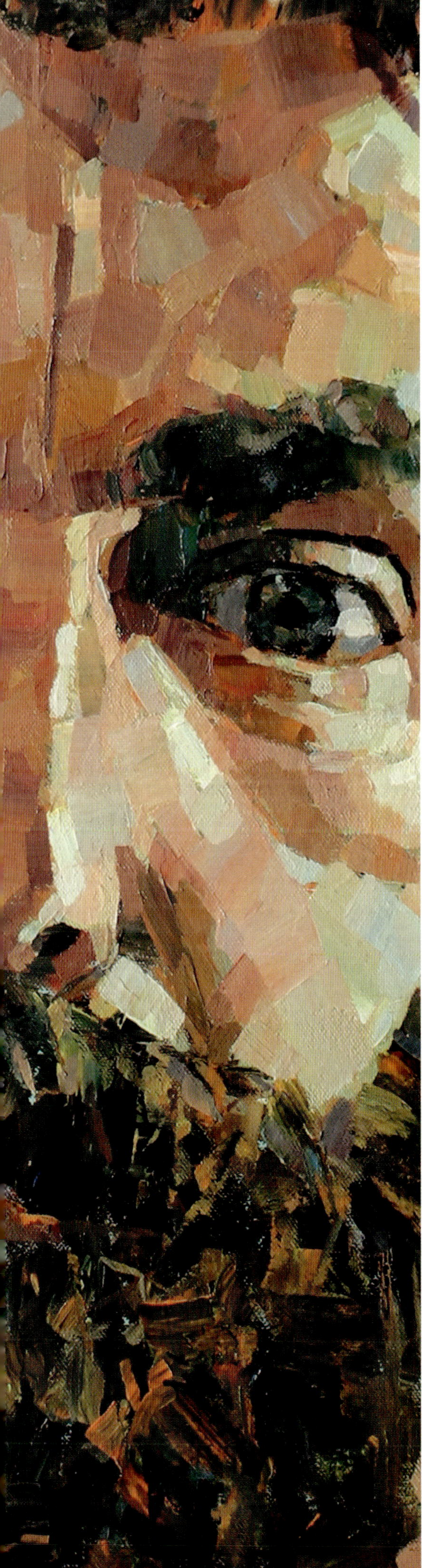

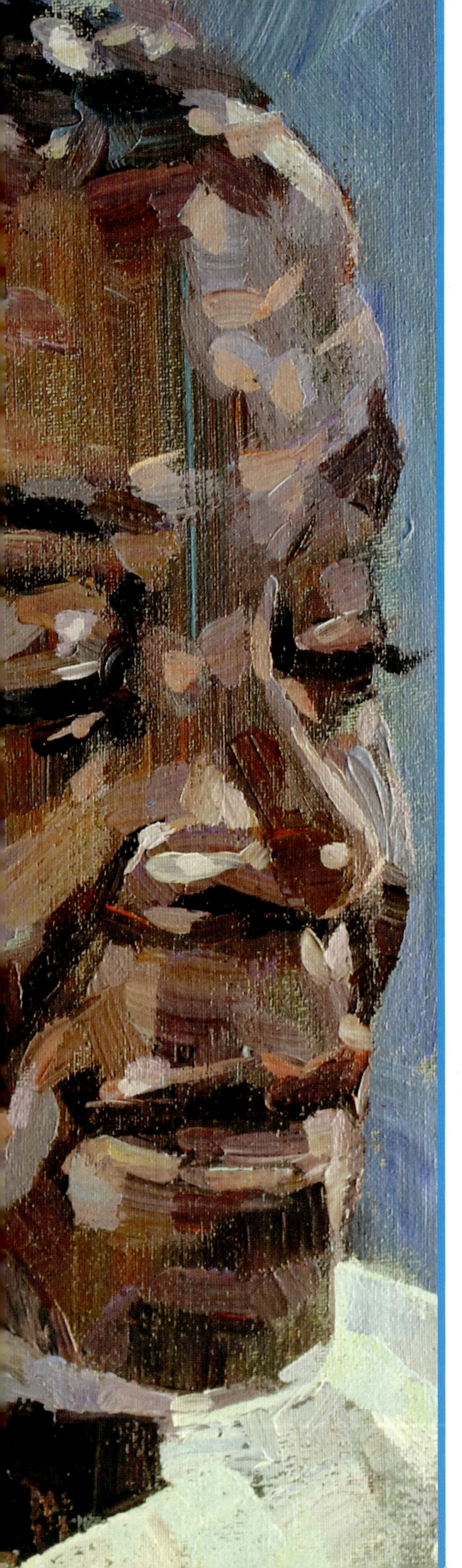

Welcome to *Painting Portraits in Acrylics*, and to new horizons in depicting the most challenging, exciting and intricate subject you'll ever draw or paint.

This book explores how we, as artists, can look at portraiture more creatively while maintaining the likeness of the sitter. If you are looking for a technical drawing manual on the physiology of the human face, or how to replicate the intricate contours of the *transverse nasalis*, then this is not the book for you. I avoid using small round head or rigger brushes, there's no generic flesh tint, and a photographic reproduction is absolutely not the ultimate goal. Instead, this book will take you through practical exercises with the overall aim of getting you to paint much more instinctively, allowing you to depict the essence of your model.

I paint with acrylics, which provide a wide scope for experimenting and offer the most diverse range of techniques one medium has to offer. Their quick-drying properties mean paintings can be completed in one sitting and their forgiving nature allows layers to be reworked or painted over. Mediums and enhancers can be added to create various effects, from thick impasto brushstrokes, to slower drying times and improved colour flow.

Whether you are a beginner, amateur or more advanced painter, or you picked this book up out of sheer curiosity, I hope you find something interesting and engaging that makes you consider painting portraiture in a new and contemporary light. Enjoy!

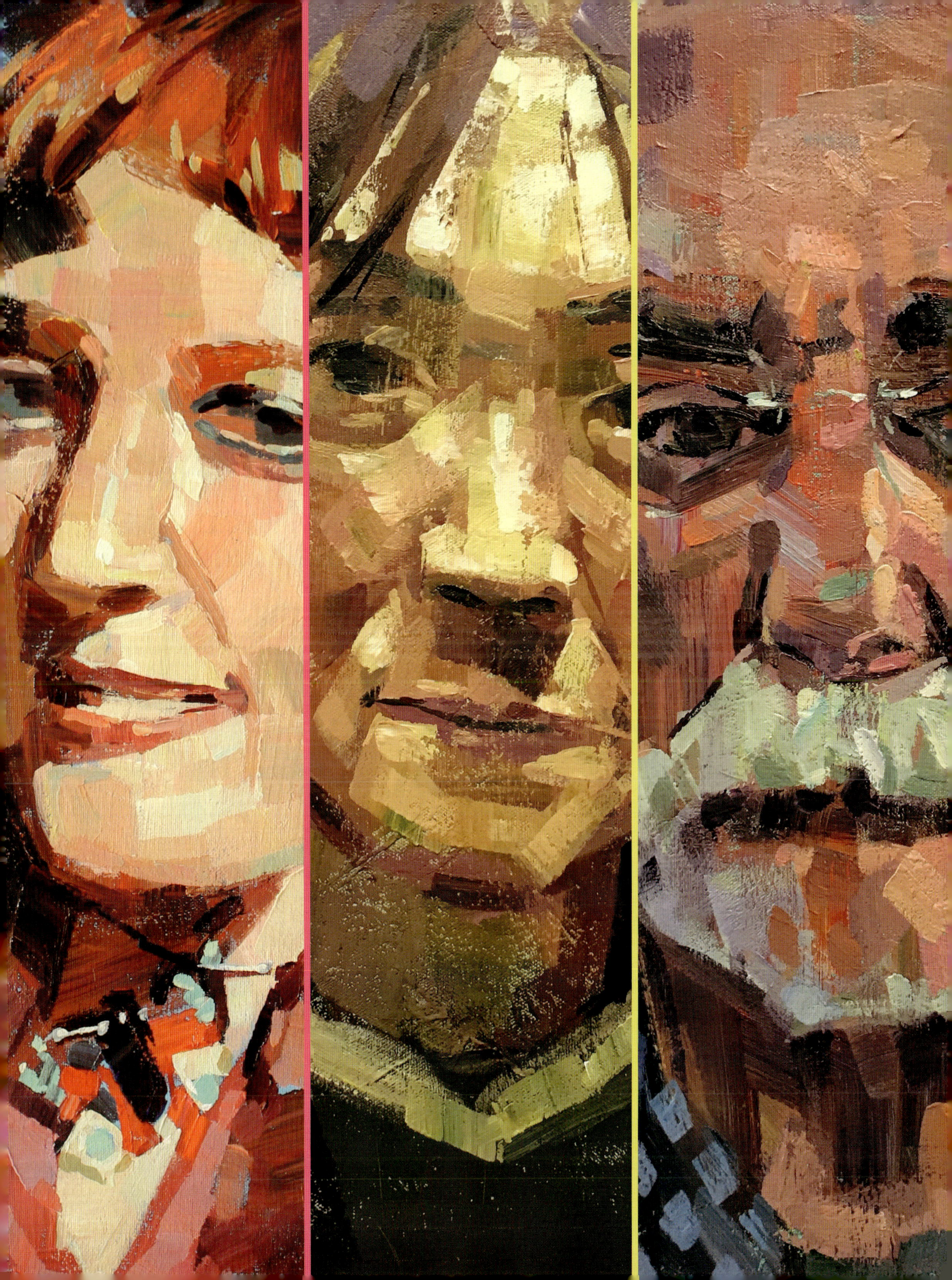

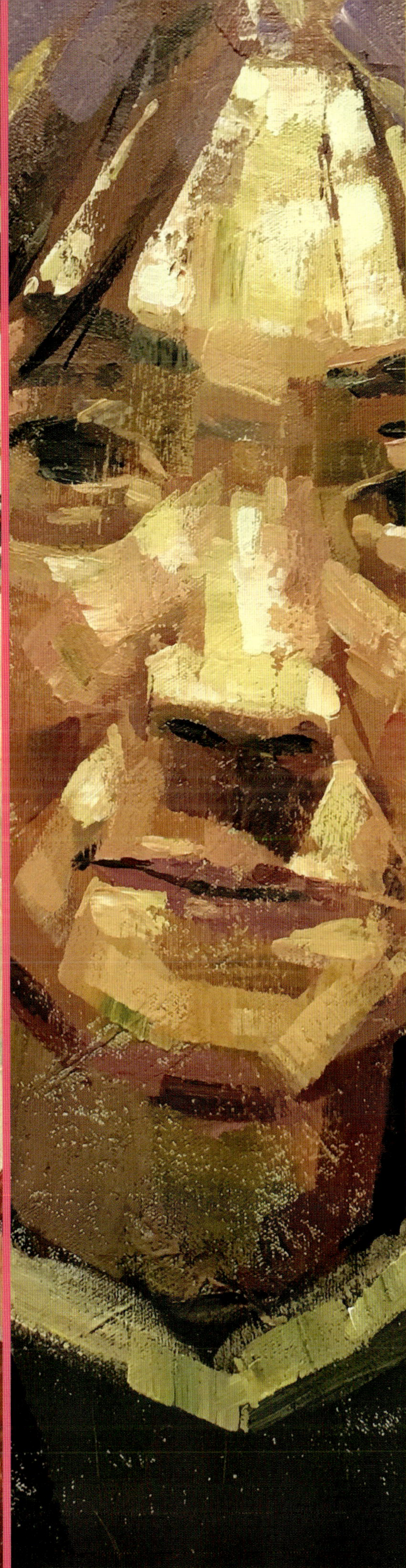
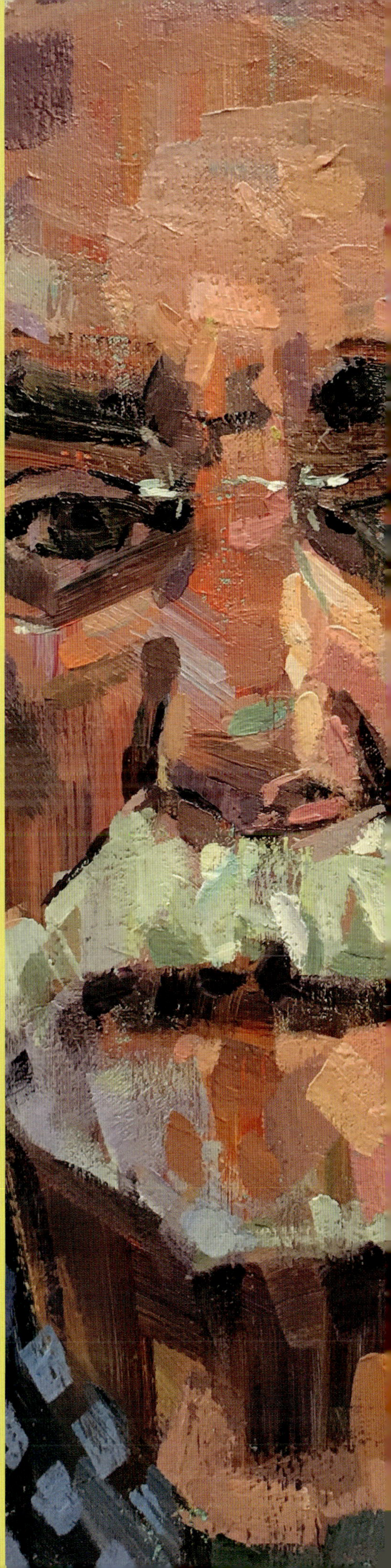

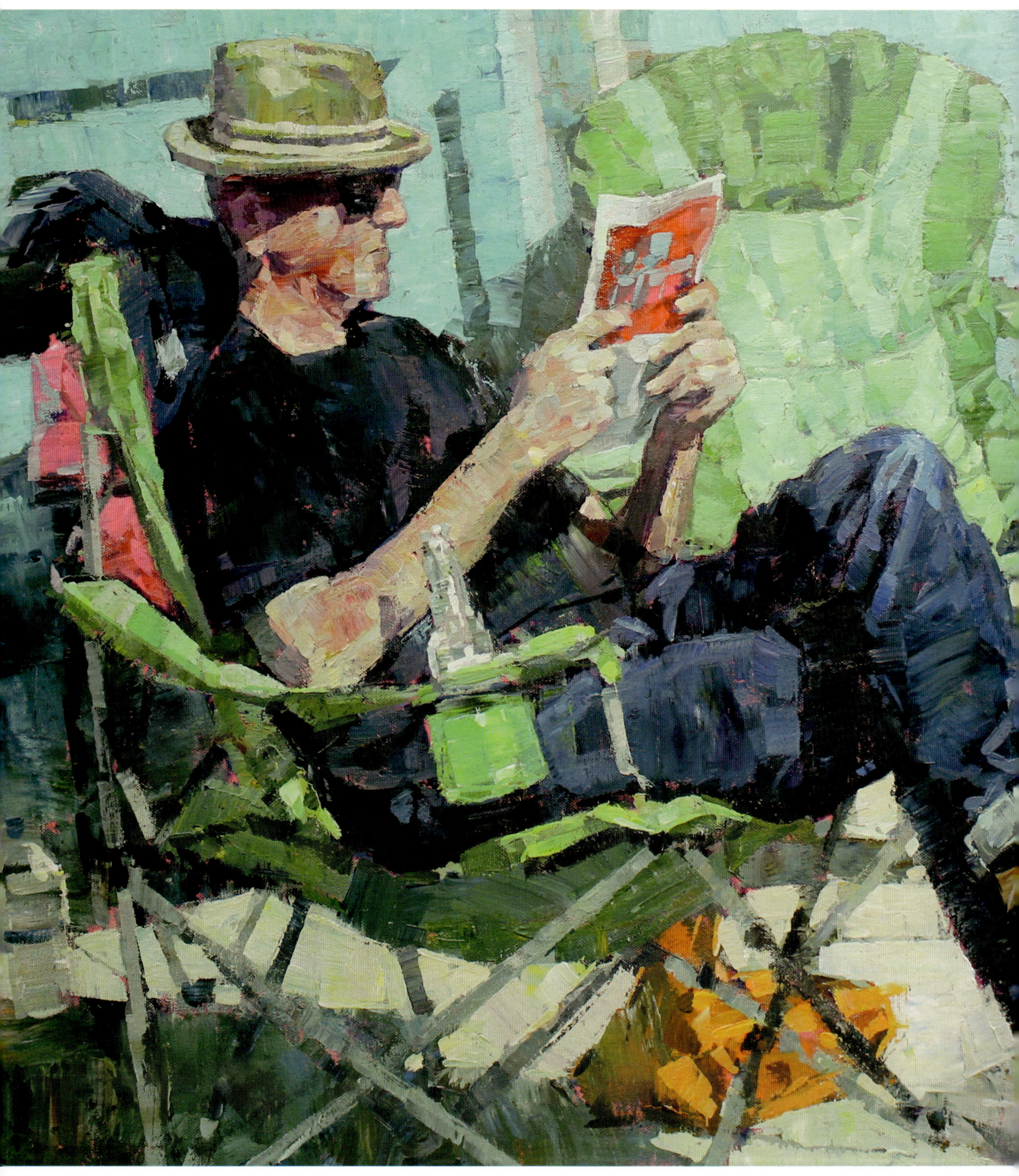

The problem with portraits

Portraiture has come a long way since the rigid depictions common in pre-Renaissance art. Traditionally, a portrait reflected someone's standing in the community. Aside from religious or devotional images, portraiture was reserved for the aristocracy, who could afford to commission artists. The sitters were surrounded by symbols of their wealth and influence; their props showcasing how well-travelled they were; their poses heroic and idealized. This period of portraiture resulted in formal, staged paintings showing the best sides of the sitter.

In the centuries following the Renaissance, portraiture developed, with artists beginning to capture more grounded, everyday images, and to portray the harsher realities of life through representations of the poor – either etched on the subjects' faces or through their environment.

Photography and the portrait

Relatively recently, the advent of photography provided the masses with the opportunity to have their own self- or family portraits. This has changed our perception of what portraits are. No longer necessarily idealized – though many are – they offer a personal view into our everyday lives.

Nowadays everyone takes selfies on their smartphones or digital cameras. The results are informal, showing us next to a celebrity or in a place we've visited. Some are intimate; capturing our dishevelled look straight from the shower, or collapsed on the sofa next to a beloved pet. Modern portraiture can be just as vibrant, dynamic, and self-effacing – even humorous – and provide a similar visual diary of our lives.

The contemporary portrait artist

Traditional portraiture tends to be formulaic – predictably angelic-looking children, or decapitated heads and shoulders with hazy backgrounds – or to ape photography through the creation of hyper-realistic, full-figure portraits showing every eyelash, wrinkle and skin pore. You can now easily find artists willing to paint or draw portraits at incredibly reasonable prices, and who vary wildly in the quality of their representations.

Over recent years, however, more contemporary artists – and individuals requesting portraits – are looking for fresher, more creative approaches. In order for a portrait painter to stand out, the painting itself needs to contain unique qualities that a photographic representation can't offer.

Portrait painting must evolve. Using the wealth of paintings and drawings from the past as inspiration, in combination with the convenience of modern technology to provide invaluable resource material, we can use our own interpretation to reflect portraiture for the modern era.

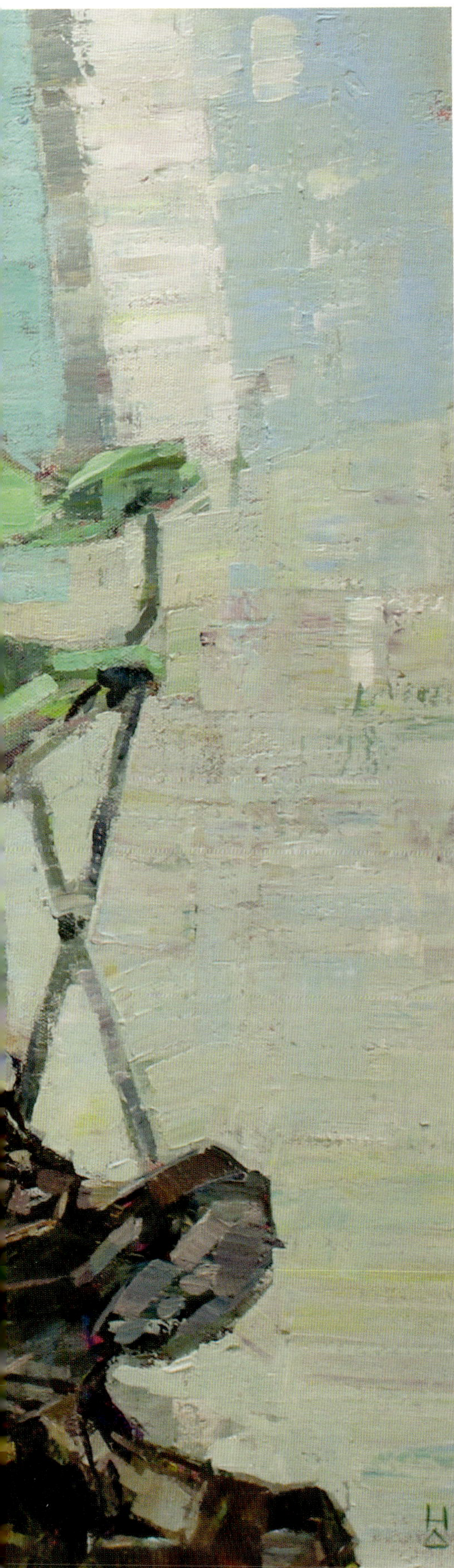

MAN SUNBATHING IN CHAIR 88×60CM (35×24IN)

Casual, everyday poses are great to make a portrait relatable. There's more of a narrative if the scene is set in a complete environment with weather conditions, props and fashion statements.

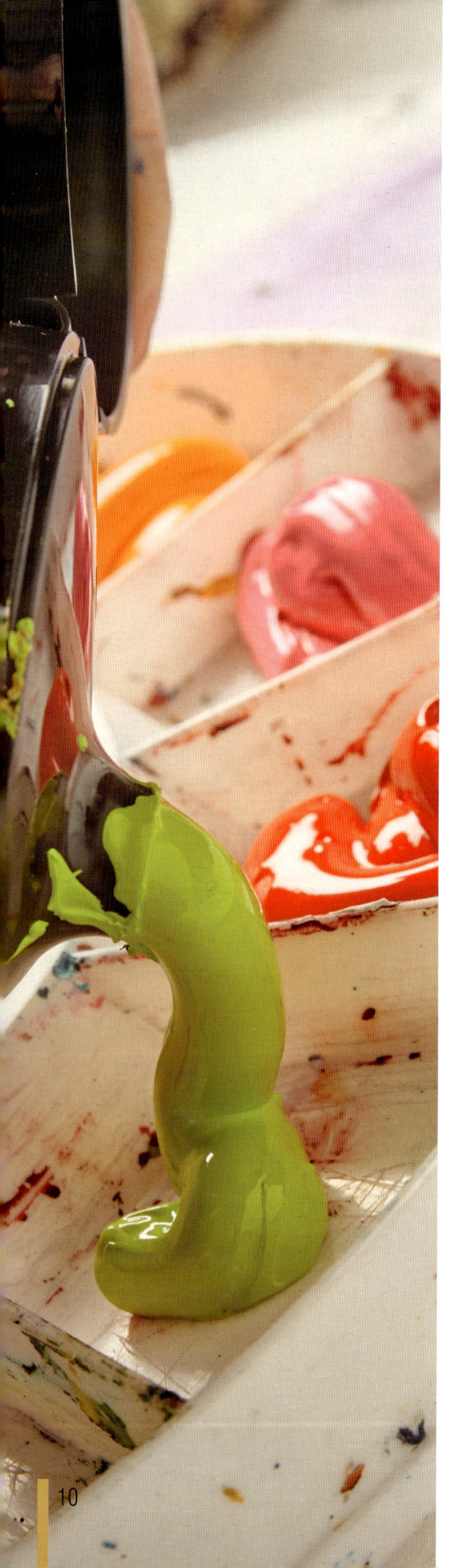

When it comes to materials, I keep everything as practical as possible. I lay out only what I need for a particular painting day and avoid cluttering up my work space. If you're a beginner, avoid huge purchases of equipment: keep to three or four brushes; a support such as a watercolour or acrylic pad; a mixing tray or old white plate; a water pot; and a small selection of acrylic paints, including white and the three primary colours: red, yellow and blue. Get to know these elements really well before expanding into new colours, brushes, canvases, art boards, mediums or spending more on expensive artists' quality materials.

The recommendations regarding materials here are intended to help you avoid becoming overly reliant on certain colours or brushes, in order to avoid creating predictable outcomes.

Acrylic paint

Portraiture has a long history and has been interpreted through many different types of painting media, including oils, pastels and watercolour. Only relatively recently has this expanded to include acrylics, which have been available only since the 1950s. Sitting somewhere between oils and watercolours, they were initially seen by many as jack-of-all-trades and master of none, never quite reaching the purity of watercolour washes or the smooth transitions of blended oils. However, taken on their own merits this water-based medium has many distinctive plus points: the main one being the rapid drying times, which allows you to complete a painting in one sitting. Acrylics are more durable than other painting media, as the colour pigment is suspended in a plastic binder which hardens when dry. Acrylics resist fading over time better than watercolours, are less toxic than oils, and only require soap and warm water when cleaning brushes after a painting session.

It is useful to know that most acrylic brands can be mixed together or used as a ground or base layer when painting in oils.

Today, the quality of the pigments and range of colours available has improved, while the expanding range of acrylic enhancers and mediums allows for greater colour retention when diluted, and altered painting times, making them high quality and hugely versatile. Even without these additives,

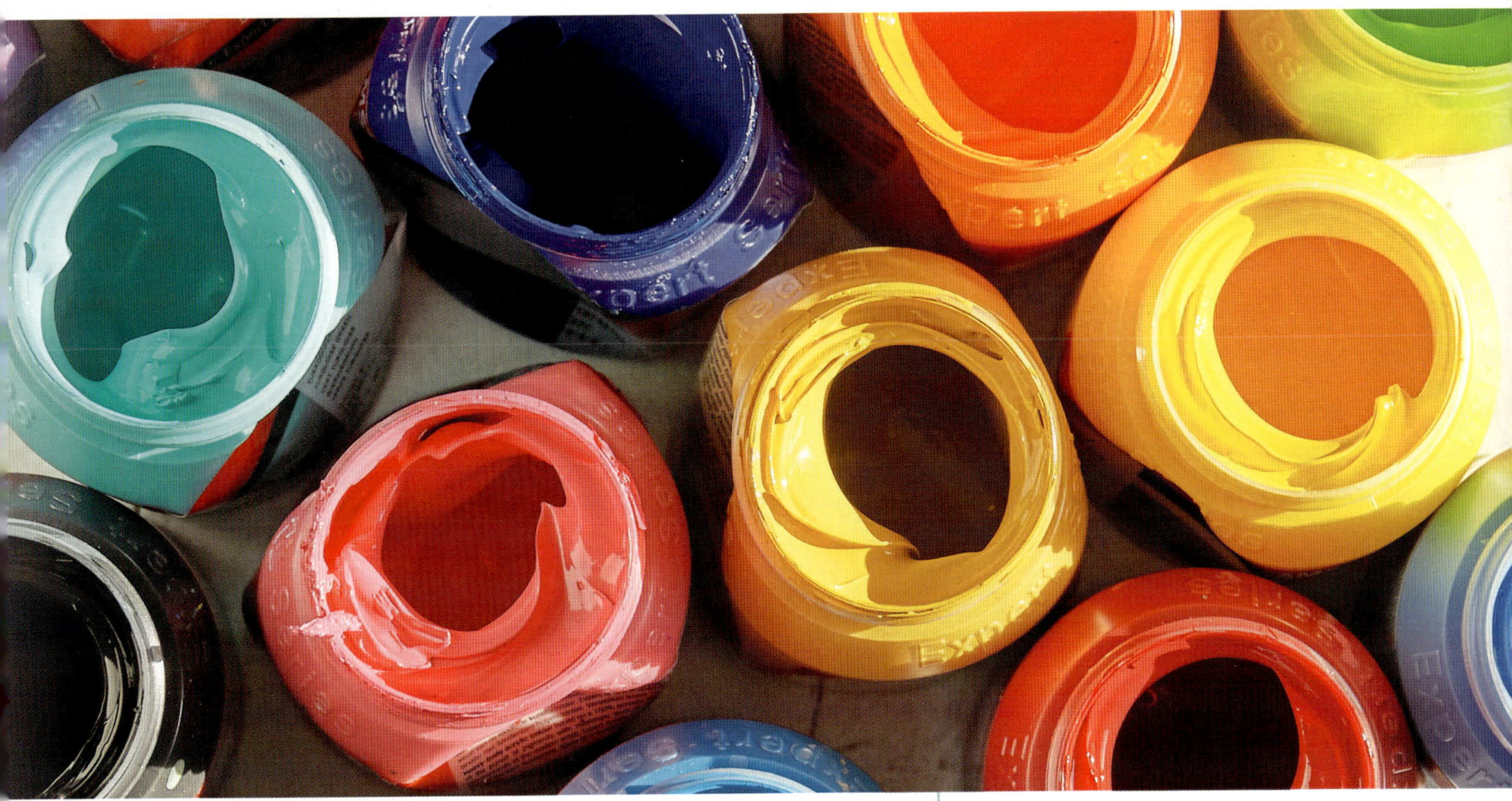

acrylics are available in lots of consistencies including fluid, soft, heavy and super heavy body versions – that is, from very fluid and watery to thick and gel-like – and also in spray cans.

When painting portraits, acrylics excel as the fast drying time means that you can add layers quickly, which helps to build momentum. They are also forgiving when mistakes need correcting. I use a heavy body acrylic range called Amsterdam by Royal Talens. This is available in Standard and Expert ranges, the latter being an artists' quality version that contains more pigment and less binder.

I do have a regular assortment of colours. My palette usually consists of twelve pigments or so, unless I am severely limiting my choices (we look at different colours palettes on pages 74–81). It is common for artists to stick very rigidly to the same palette as the outcomes are predictable and, as with most patterns of behaviour, this create habits which may be hard to break in the future. These comfort zones sneak up on you and can stifle artistic growth: be careful. To avoid colour-mixing complacency, I integrate new pigments on a regular basis. Alternating colours creates fresh learning curves and opportunities to surprise with new, dynamic colour schemes.

Drying times

Acrylics usually take roughly twenty to thirty minutes for thin layers to dry, and between one and two hours for thicker applications. Painting in warmer temperatures will speed up drying times.

Open acrylics

A new addition to the medium are 'open acrylics', which allow previously dried layers to be reactivated for additional painting time. Personally, I find the idea of returning to dried layers and reworking them less appealing, as our initial applications retain immediacy and a certain amount of energy and spontaneity. However, if you have come to acrylics from oils, they may appeal.

Brushes and applicators

I prefer large flat head brushes as these are ideal for loose, expressive and quick forms of painting with acrylics. You can cover large areas as the width means the brush carries a larger pigment load than a round brush. This cuts down on the need to constantly reload or clean the brush, which helps to keep you involved with the painting process for longer.

This recommendation may raise fears for beginners and some professionals who prefer ultimate control with smaller, round head brushes; but to reassure you, this is really a case of using the right tool. Start big, shape the forms with a medium brush, then end with the smallest for refinements. Starting with the smallest and ending with the same brush will give no contrasting effects. Small brushes also restrict the full flow of your arm, suppressing the gestural qualities of your marks. Flat head brushes are available with long to medium handles (or even handleless for ultimate expression) and are usually made with synthetic bristles.

The specific brushes I use are Daler Rowney's Sky Flow flat head brushes in sizes 50mm, 37mm, 25mm and 16mm (2, 1½, 1 and ¾in). I paint quite large so these are suitable for the size of my support. If your paintings tend to be quite small, adjust your brushes accordingly. Painting with oversized brushes helps to create uncontrived, interesting marks and over time dexterity will improve through the handling.

No handles

If you would like to try brushes without handles, Liquitex produce a range of paddle brushes for large, elongated brushwork. They come in four sizes: 25mm, 50mm, 75mm and 100mm (1, 2, 3 and 4in) and are the ultimate in free expression.

Palette knives and scrapers

A recent addition to my painting process is the use of plastic scrapers which have similar mark-making properties to palette knives. These can be used to drag neat paint to create various random, painterly effects.

There is a lot of improvisation with mark-making as there's no right or wrong way – the scrapers or squeegees I use are intended to clear air pockets from vinyl on car windows, for example. Some artists recommend old credit or store cards or bits of thin cardboard for similar techniques.

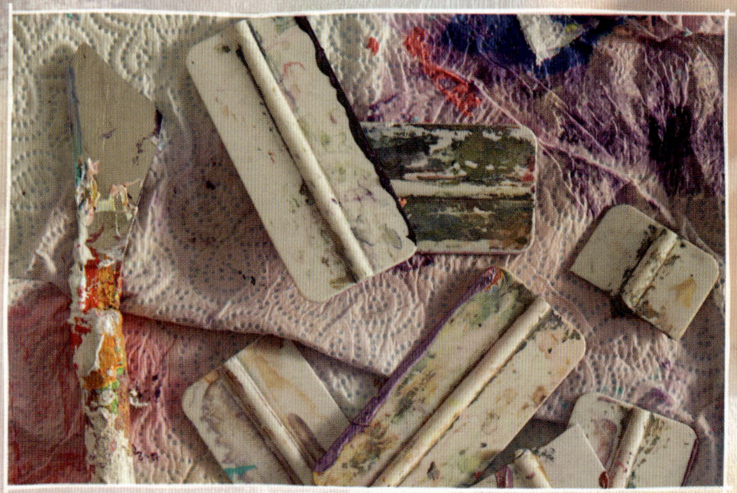

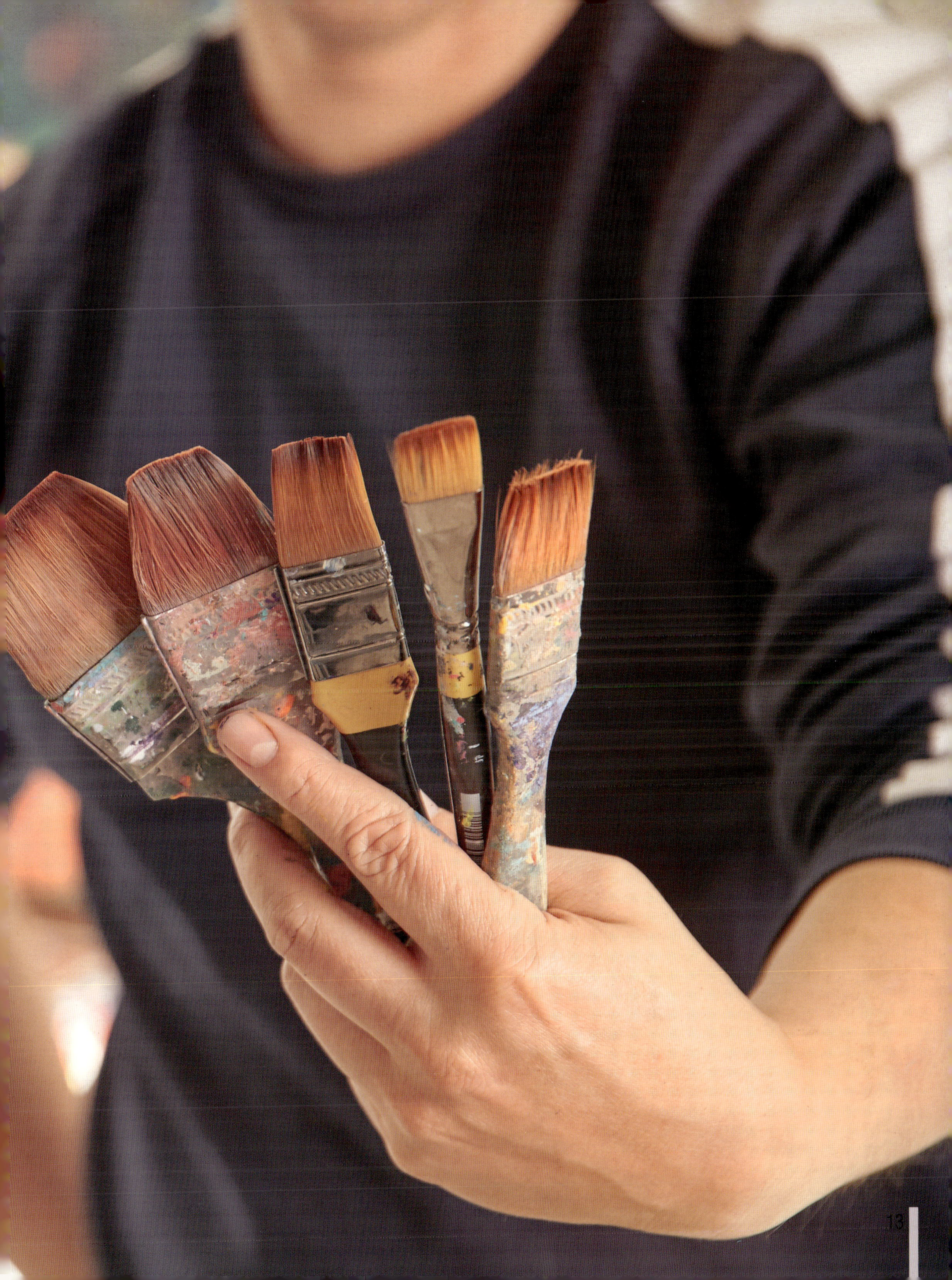

Supports

Canvas

Canvas comes in rolls or ready-stretched on board or blocks, in a range of sizes and available made to measure. Canvas can be found primed or unprimed, with smooth, medium or heavily textured surfaces. Canvases vary in price, quality and thickness. The most expensive canvas is linen, while cotton canvas is the economical choice.

Stretched canvas (canvas wrapped around a wooden frame) is my preferred support. Using these means that there is no need for framing: simply running a cord behind the finished painting will make it ready for hanging. You can tell a good quality stretched canvas by how tautly the canvas is wrapped over the stretchers. It should be drum-tight. If necessary, use the wedges provided to tighten the surface and avoid sagging. Canvas is great if you want to recycle or repaint several times over the same surface. I use quite thick paint and find two or three repaints is the limit before starting to lose adherence.

Avoid leaving canvas next to a heater or exposed to sunlight as the stretcher will warp. Warping may be rectified by using a thick frame but will be noticeable if left unframed on a wall.

If having multiple painted canvases creates a storage problem, cut the canvases from the stretchers and roll them up for stretching and re-framing at a later date.

Other supports

It's not necessary to work on canvas. Acrylics can be painted onto most surfaces – as long as they have not been varnished, as this will result in paint eventually cracking and peeling off. This also goes for previously used canvases which were painted in oils.

More straightforward supports include paper, boards, or panels. You can use watercolour paper but acrylic paint tends to drag and sink into the grain because the surface is unprimed. To avoid this, run gesso (another priming medium) or white acrylic paint over the paper to seal the surface before painting. When using thin paper and thicker quantities of acrylic, the surface of paper may buckle so it may be worth stretching the paper or using a thicker grade.

There are acrylic pads with a surface texture similar to canvas available. These are ready-primed so acrylic glides nicely over it.

Boards and panels are available in canvas, wood and aluminium. Boards offer rigid, lightweight support, and not prone to warping over time. Aluminium panels for painting will have been treated to take acrylic.

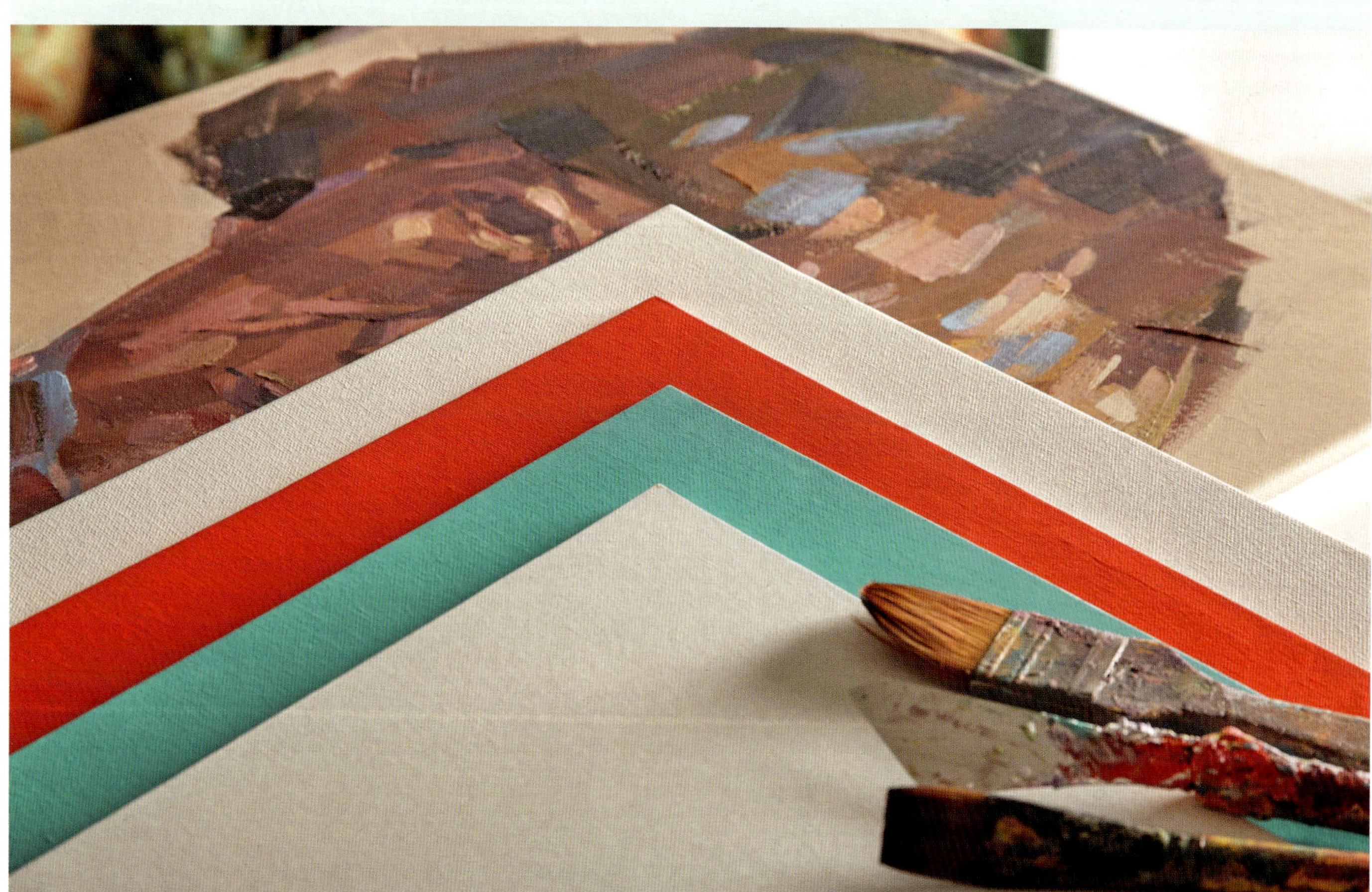

Additional materials

Plastic mixing trays I use two large white plastic mixing trays to try colours out. Being plastic, the large amounts of paint that accumulate on the trays are still usable over the course of a morning or afternoon's painting. Rather than clean the trays at the end of a painting day, I let the paint dry, then use a palette knife to simply scrape it away. You can instead pour warm water over the tray and scrub away dry paint.

Kitchen paper Kitchen paper or old rags are vital for drying brushes or mopping up mistakes – there will be plenty!

Free-standing easel I always paint at a free-standing easel so I'm more flexible. It allows me to stand back and view the painting as a whole. Finished portraits are generally viewed from a distance, so this provides a better impression of the overall effect of the artwork. Working upright is also kinder to my back rather than being slouched over a table. A table easel is another option.

Water pots It is best to have two or three pots especially when using large amounts of paint, as the water muddies a lot. Keep one pot with cleaner water for diluting paint, and use the others for rinsing.

Tips for looking after your tools and materials

- The acrylic brushes I recommend are made from manmade fibres and so are quite sturdy; requiring only soap and water to clean them after a painting session. Avoid paint drying on brushes as this will ruin them.

- Loading your brushes as shown on page 17 will inevitably muddy the wells in your palette. This can take the edge off vibrancy or strength of tone, particular on lighter colours. Darker pigments are easier to deal with and may just absorb the interfering colours unless a lot of white is used.

- When painting in acrylic you will find brushes will eventually lose their shape or flare out. Such brushes remain fine for applying base colours or large backgrounds but if you require a precision edge, look for a replacement.

- Acrylics dry quickly on your support and in your palette so I recommend using a palette with deep wells (see page 16). Stay-wet palettes are available, which use a damp surface to retain the workability of the paint, but if the base contains too much water there is a danger of the colours running into each other and becoming messy.

- Whichever palette you use, squeeze out slightly more paint than you need as the quantity will keep the paint fresh for longer. Heavy body versions of acrylic have a longer drying time so may be worth the extra expense.

- Once the colours begin to stiffen in the palette (generally round the edges of the wells), or pigment starts to run low, take the opportunity to clean your palette. Any leftover pigments can be used as a base colour.

- You can purchase retarder in liquid form to spray over your palette (see page 128 for more on mediums). This will slow down the drying time. Water can also be used but avoid spraying excessive amounts as colours will run and may dull the vibrancy of your colours.

- Cover your palette when taking breaks. I use a circular cake stand over the palette. If you still have large amounts of paint available for another day and can't place a flat cover over the palette, try placing the whole thing in a plastic bag. Prod the paint occasionally with a palette knife to keep the paint workable over time.

- To remove unwanted paint from your palette you can either scoop it out while it remains workable; or allow to dry. Once dry, your can peel it off with an old knife or pour warm water over the palette - once allowed to settle, the dry paint will become easier to peel away.

- If you are painting on a regular basis, you may wish to have a couple of palettes on the go at once.

- After a day's painting I skim away the top layer of any corrupt colour - mainly in the lighter pigments - and top up the paint if I need more the next day.

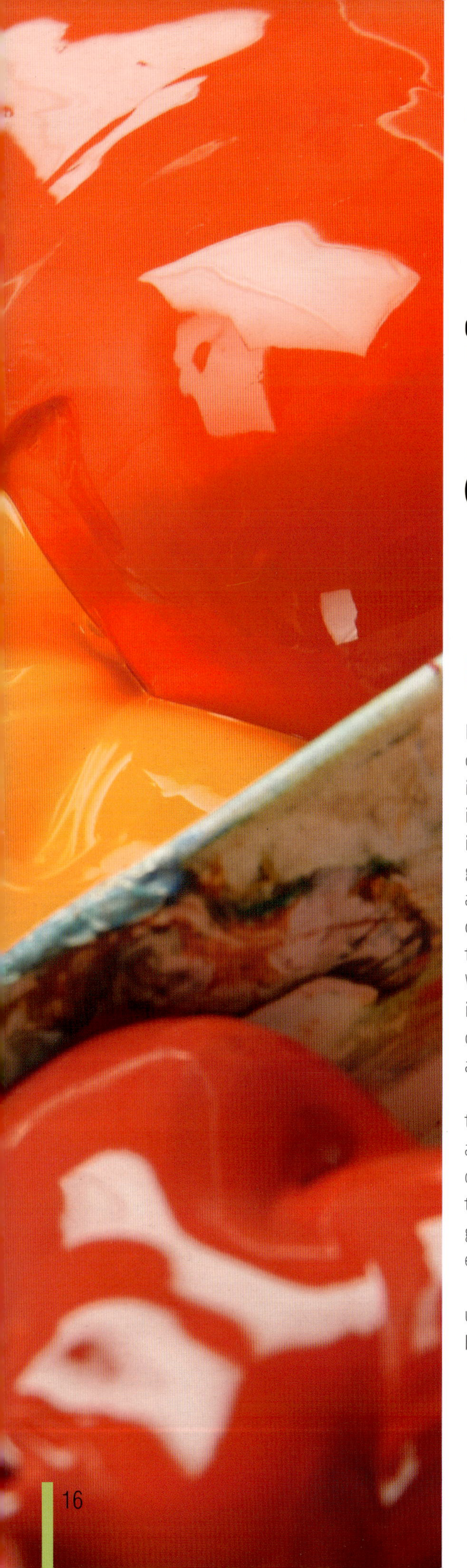

Finding the time to draw and paint can be tricky. Here are tips and short exercises to help you to begin your journey and show you the fundamentals of my painting techniques.

When you're ready to take the next step, the later chapters provide more challenging propositions. For the moment, let's look at a few approaches which go against the grain of traditional portrait painting. These reflect more contemporary attitudes to painting, and will help you to loosen up and start afresh.

Preparing your paint

In order to be completely focused once you begin painting, it is important to prepare what you intend to use beforehand. This includes filling your palette with generous amounts of paint – most amateur painters put out small dabs, which require topping up throughout the painting process. With more paint squeezed out there is a danger of quantities drying out, so the palette you choose is all-important (see right).

I normally have my palette on a table next to my large mixing tray, although the palette does have a circular groove underneath if I need to hold it. Every well contains a generous amount of paint, generally arranged from warm to earthy to cool. I also include plenty of white.

I use tubs of acrylic as it's more economical for the amount I use in painting. Another benefit is that I can return excess paint left in my palette back to the pot.

Use a palette that can hold a generous amount of each paint. I use a palette called a radial sorting tray, as its wells are the deepest I've come across.

Loading the brush

My technique often involves loading multiple colours on a single brush, particularly at the beginning of a painting. In order to avoid muddy or chaotic mixes I tend to ensure one colour dominates every mix.

Follow this loading process in order to minimize corruption when dipping in multiple colours.

1 If I'm looking for an interesting ochre-tinged skin tone for example, the largest quantity of pigment in the load will be ochre. However, I firstly dip the brush in a small amount of white, as light-hued paints are easy to corrupt with other colours. Only then do I load large quantities of ochre.

2 If I have more than one warm shade in my palette I'll be keen to use the others, such as magenta, pink or orange, as these will harmonize with the main colour (ochre). Again I can afford to pick up large amounts.

3 I next pick up some contrasting colours such as green. These are loaded in much smaller quantities.

4 Avoid too much colour corruption in your palette by dipping just once or twice from one well to another: avoid swirling or stirring the brush.

5 Once the pigments are loaded you can seal the brush off with another dip in your main colour (ochre). It can now be applied straight to the canvas or, for a flatter colour, blend a couple of times in the mixing tray, as shown.

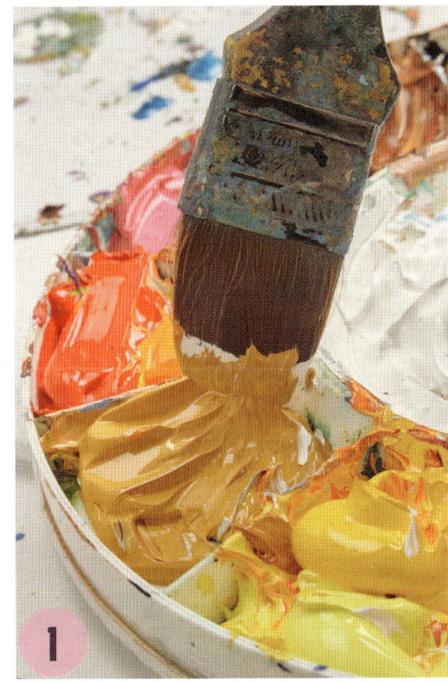

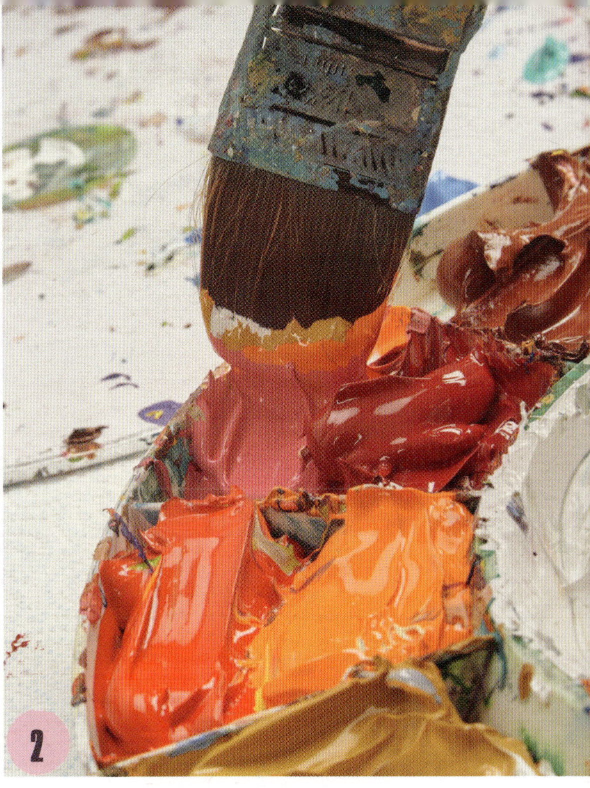

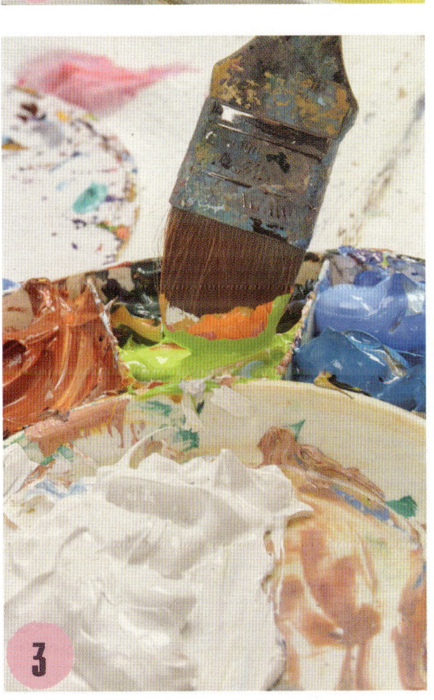

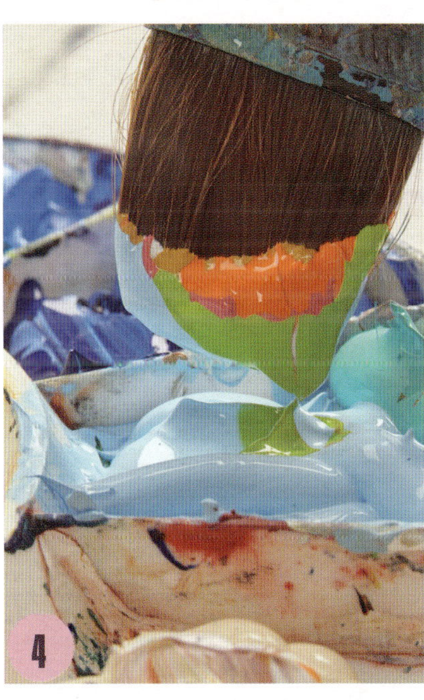

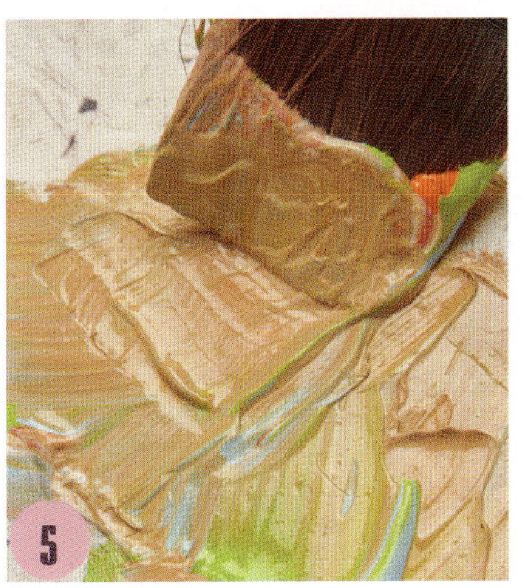

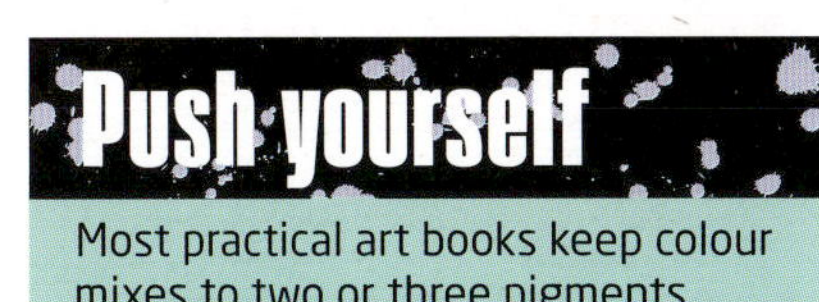

Most practical art books keep colour mixes to two or three pigments as this is easier for beginners to handle, but using more paints will help you extend your colour theory knowledge.

The more colours you use when mixing, the more risk there is, but you'll be rewarded with more sophisticated blends.

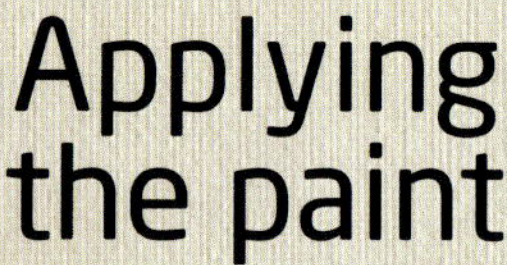

Applying the paint

Although I recommend painting with neat acrylic to retain colour strength, I do dampen my brushes at the start of a painting as this allows for a slightly easier flow when the paint is applied. The dampness also helps slow paint drying on the brush. Note that the brush is moist rather than dripping: too much water and loading several colours becomes messy or mixes into one generic colour.

Even with plenty of paint on your brush, the first application you make will be relatively short as the pigment will not have had a chance to embed into the brush. The paint will break up, creating a stroke similar to that shown here. You will need to load the paint several times and perhaps try a few strokes before you get a more consistent, elongated application.

Once the brush is sufficiently loaded you will find the paint glides off the brush more easily, and you'll be able to produce even strokes. The pressure you apply will have a bearing on the marks being produced: a lighter relaxed touch creates a granular, textured look, while applying more pressure will release more colour from the embedded pigment, giving bold, solid marks.

You might be thinking 'that's an awful lot of paint', but the basis of the technique is 'one stroke does more'. Rather than constantly building up layers, the first marks in certain areas will also be the last. The technique is thus similar to watercolour. More layers kill the initial fresh applications, while large singular blocks of colour next to each other knit together to create a clean, spontaneous look to a painting. This approach keeps the initial process sparse with more time later in the painting to develop and build up definition.

At times you might feel the urge to blend or feather colours together, but if you do, you'll discover your colours dulling down through the barrage of strokes.

It's worth reminding yourself that painting is an expression of you and how you feel about the process or theme you're depicting. A laboured, monotone brushstroke will reflect in the work, while enthusiastic applications will enliven the finished work. My boldest applications using my largest brushes tend to occur at the beginning of a painting as my enthusiasm takes charge.

The marks you make

Varying the pressure when you apply paint will produce either a smooth or textured finish. This depends on how damp the brush is and the quantity of paint loaded on the brush. Marks will also vary depending on whether you're holding the brush closer to the end or closer to the brush head. Try twisting the brush as an application is made to produce less blocky applications, too.

Even pressure A brushstroke with even pressure will produce a consistent layer until the paint begins to runs out.

Choppy marks Short, high-pressure strokes create full blocks of pigment.

Quick, loose strokes These incorporate both elements of smooth and textured finishes.

Heavy loading Loading more colours together creates interesting colour mixes.

Twisting Altering the angle of the brush as you apply the paint produces greater variety.

Using different tools Palette knives and scrapers produce interesting, uncontrived marks. The scrapers I use are ideal for both wide drags and more refined applications.

Dragging Dragged fresh paint over previously dried layers will produce interesting effects.

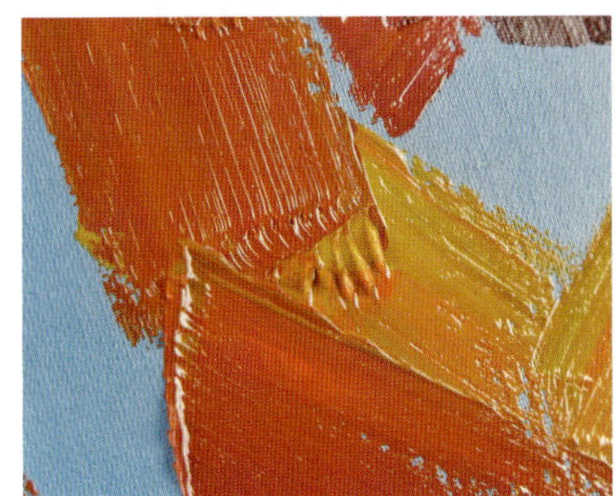

Choppy marks.

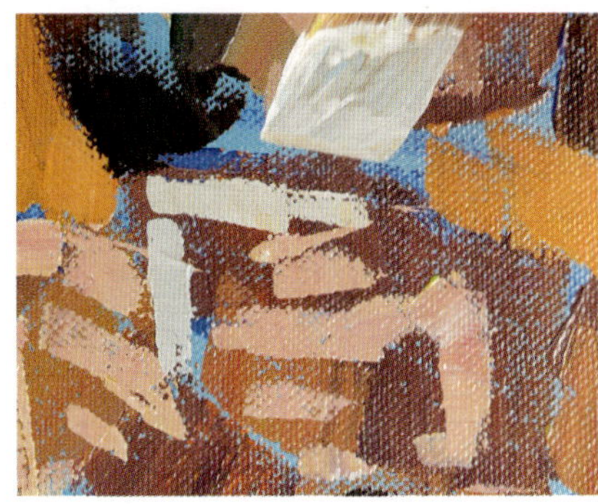

Fine lines with the edge of the brush.

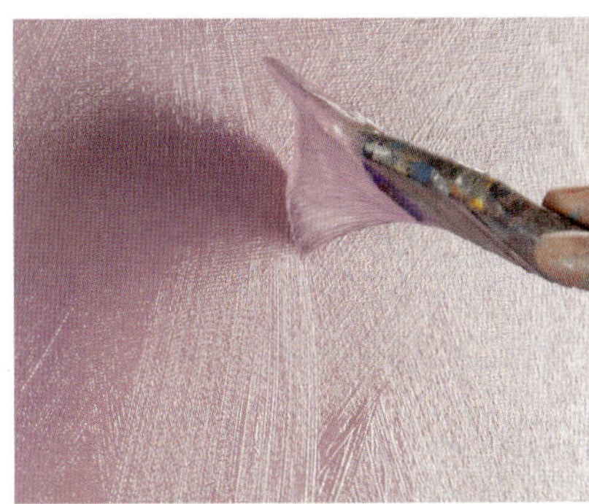

Twisting the brush.

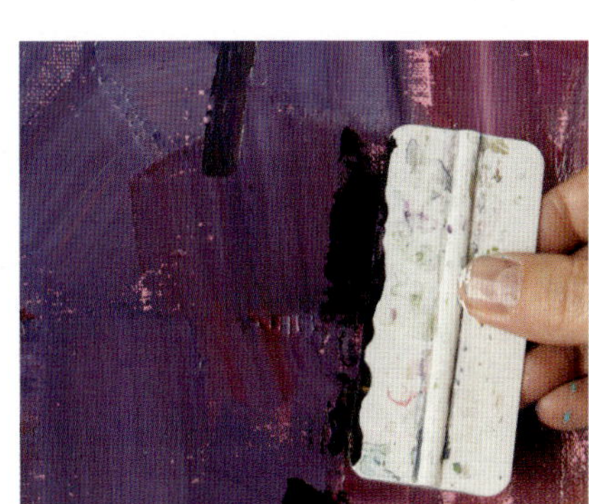

Using a scraper.

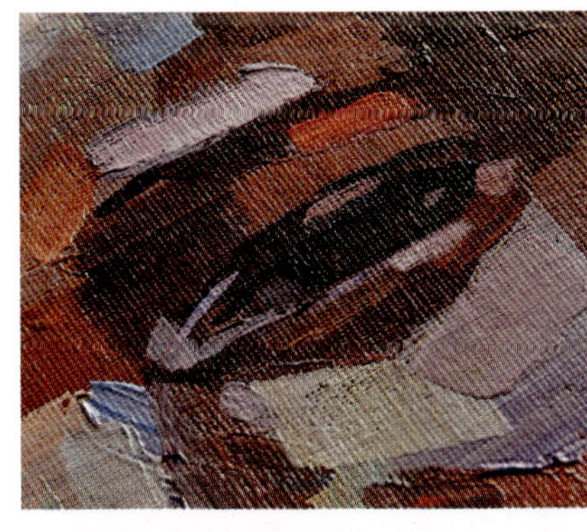

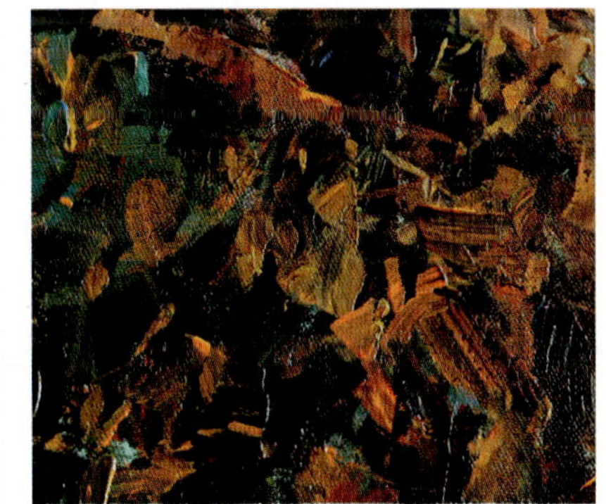

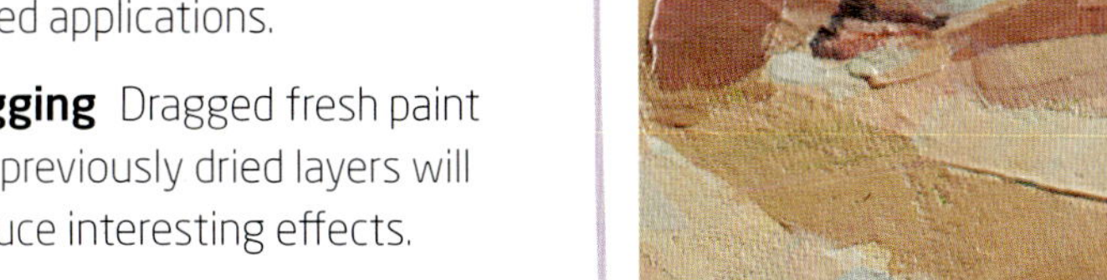

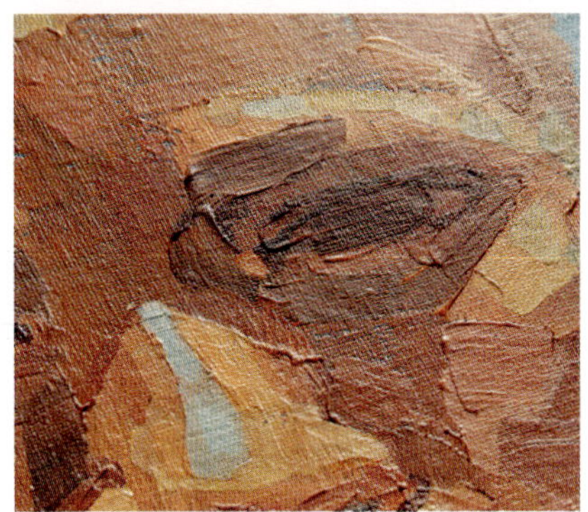

The details here show a selection or different marks, alone and in combination.

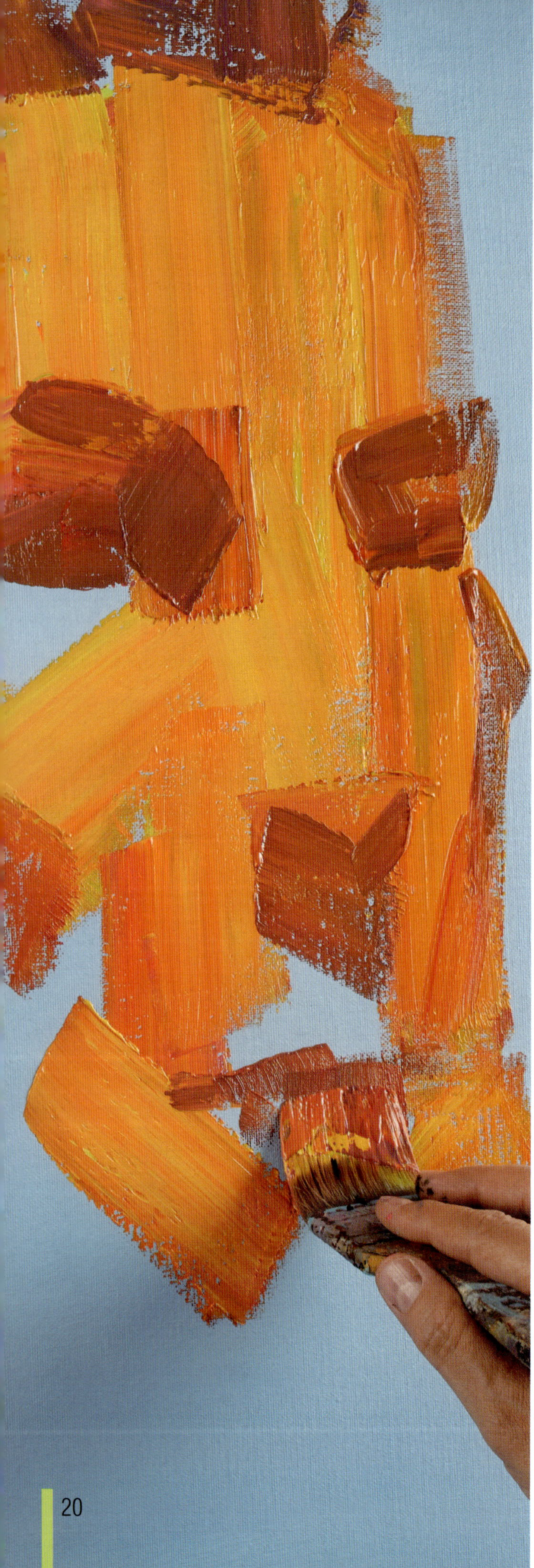

Building blocks for a portrait

Applying blocks of paint – as opposed to blending and layering – is a great way to begin streamlining your portrait painting technique. Making a few marks is also a good way to acclimatize to using a large flat head brush. It may seem clumsy at first, but dexterity will come with practice. For a beginner this may go against the grain, as smaller brushes provide more control, but they will also inevitably restrict your arm movements, resulting in less expressive marks.

If you begin with refined detail, it's extremely difficult to loosen up thereafter as your perception becomes fixed. Instead, begin big, moving your whole arm to find the overall shape with your largest marks. Next, turn to a medium brush and use pressure from your elbow to locate the main features; then end with your smallest brush and pressure just from your hand to add the final details.

How many blocks?

You will be surprised at how quickly you can imply a face with just a few blocks of paint. For this exercise use just one dark colour (anything will do – I'm using permanent blue violet) and white, plus a large and a small flat head brush. You can work on canvas or paper as you prefer.

1 Start by blocking in a rough silhouette of a head with random strokes of diluted blue violet. Allow to dry and add white to the paint. Apply a large block of the resulting light violet for the forehead.

2 Add another stroke above but slightly shorter in length.

3 Use the edge of the brush to produces a thin line for the top bridge of the nose and a larger block for the bottom. Add two small dabs for the nostrils.

4 Paint two downward angled strokes for cheekbones and a couple of marks to link the cheekbones to the forehead. Glide in one long relaxed stroke for the ear.

5 Add two small dabs within the corners of the eye sockets; then a large angled stroke on one side below the nose and a small drag next to it for the top of the mouth.

6 Add the cheek with a single angled block on one side of the face below the cheekbone.

7 Paint a small dab for the bottom lip and a larger angled block for the chin, then connect the two with a small downward stroke.

8 A large angled block for the neck finishes the structure. This simple framework provides the basis for you to develop the portrait further, allowing you to take it to a more finished conclusion, as shown on the lower right, opposite.

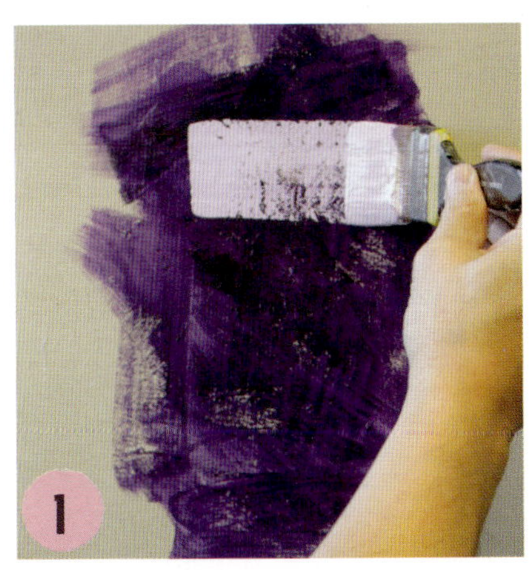

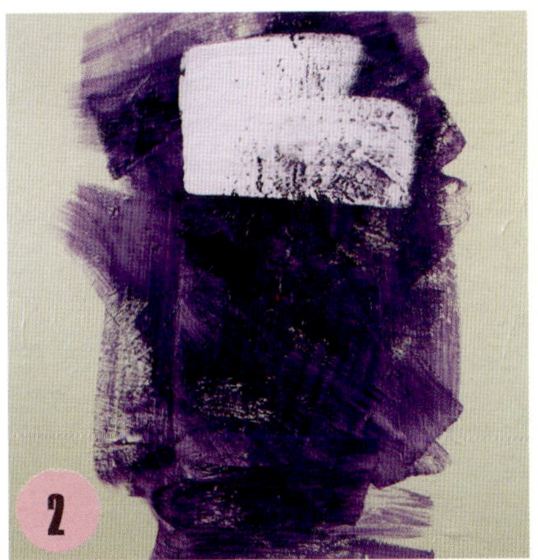

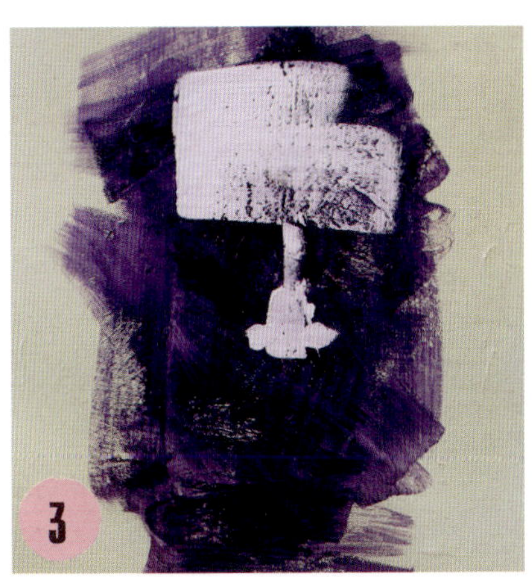

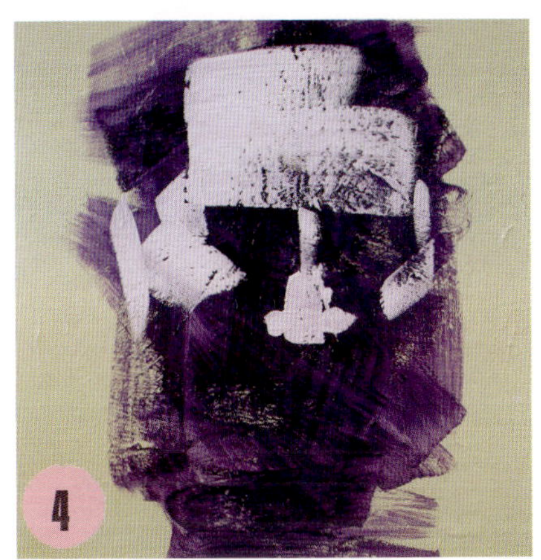

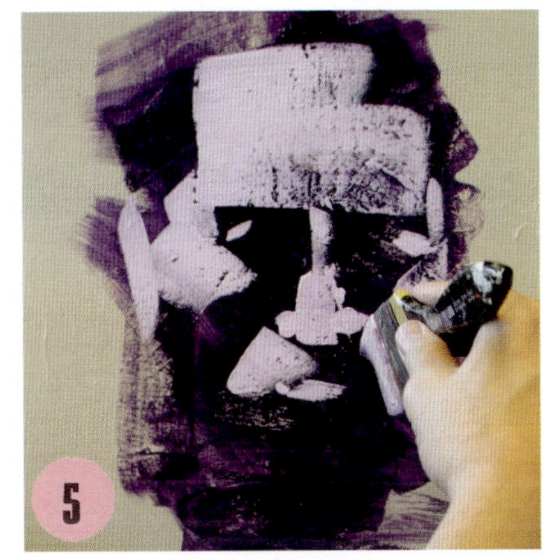

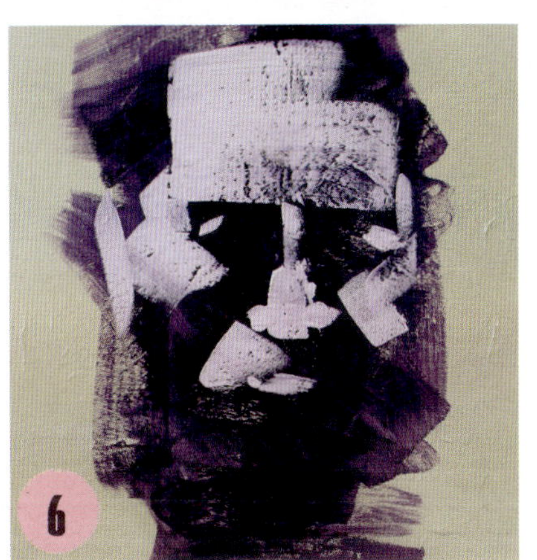

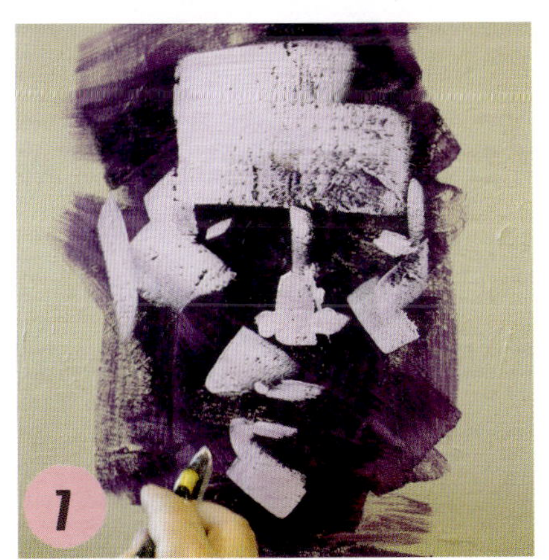

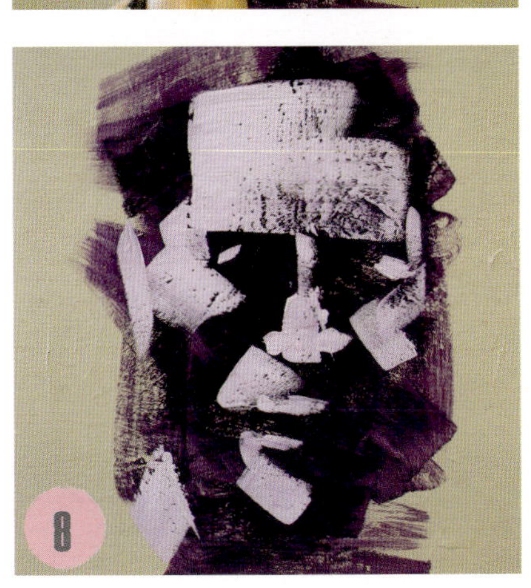

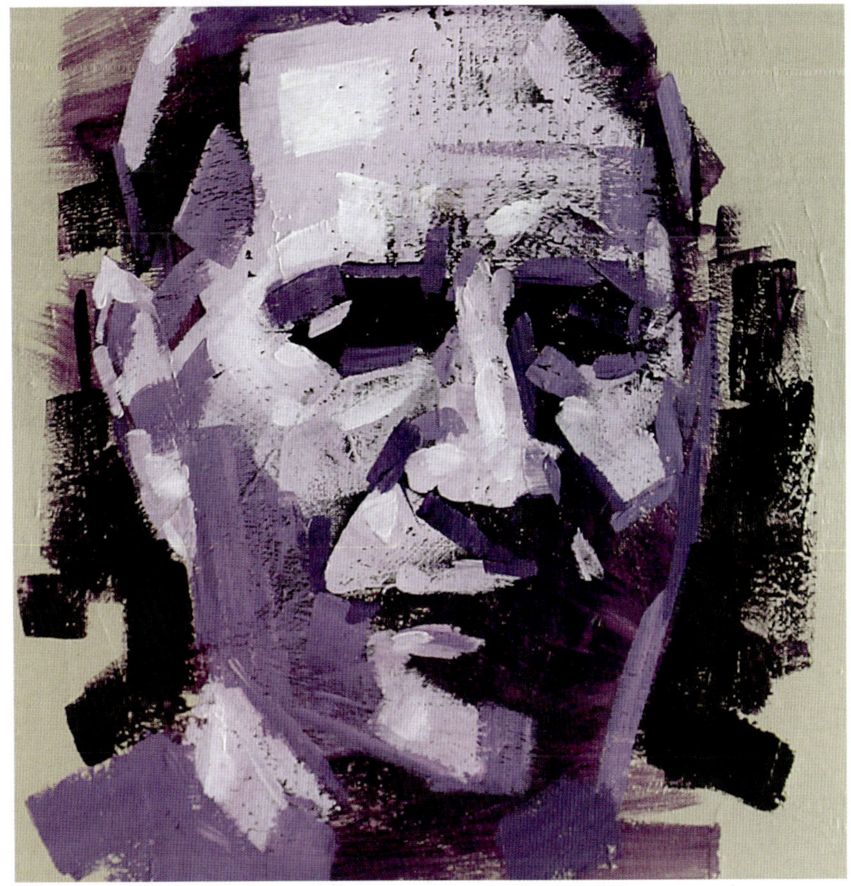

THE ROBOT

An approach I've developed as a way of establishing the overall composition and main features in a portrait is to begin with a 'robot'. This has many advantages. Firstly, even someone with very little drawing experience can replicate a simple robotic outline – think of it as a step up from a stick man by incorporating simple box and triangular shapes. This makes it easier to work out proportions as you have something simple to measure against. The other advantage is that it makes you more direct as no curvy lines are used. It's far easier drawing straight lines than circles.

This approach builds discipline and de-clutters your brain, helping you to avoid concentrating on every aspect of the face from the start.

Planning and preparation

When you begin drawing or painting a portrait get into the habit of looking at your subject for a few minutes in order to soak up what's in front of you. Has the individual a long face, big eyes, small ears, full or thin lips or any other distinguishing features? Coming to anything cold is difficult so these few minutes will make you accustomed to looking at the features more intimately.

This will help you decide on the shape or how big the robot face should be. You can also establish the composition, as to how the face fits on the paper or canvas. For convenience we will have the face looking straight ahead.

Brushes: 25mm (1in) flat, 16mm (¾in) flat

Paints: Oxide black, titanium white

Surface: Canvas board, 51×61cm (20×24in)

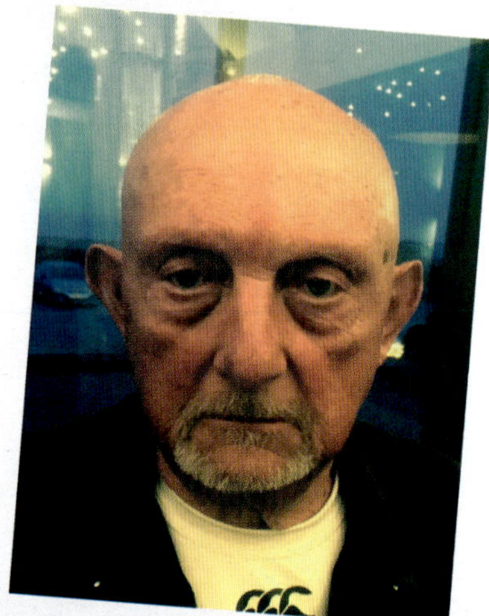

The source photograph.

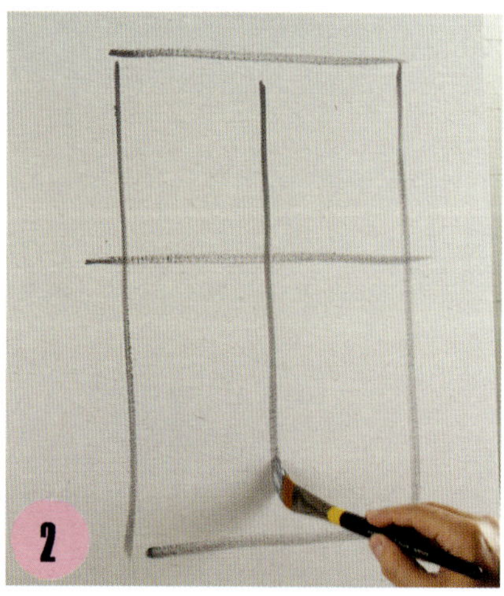

1 Prepare a midtone by picking up a little oxide black on your 25mm (1in) flat brush and combining it on the palette with titanium white.

2 Using the tip of the brush, paint a rectangle to frame the head. Use light strokes, just skimming the surface. Referring to your subject, add a horizontal eye line and a centre line.

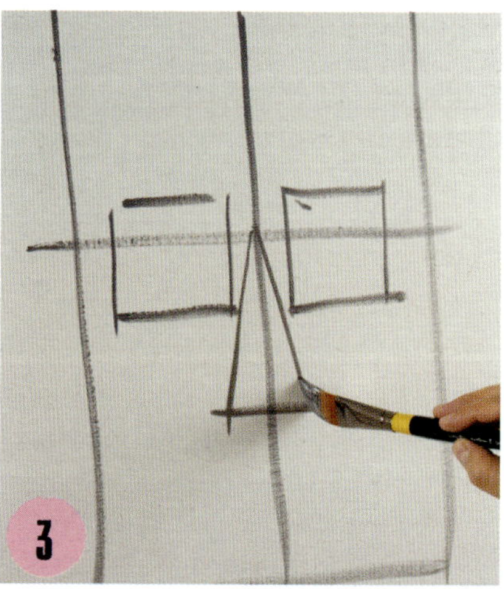

3 Establish the eye sockets with two rough squares. Don't be too precious – these don't need to be exact. Rather than try to find the eye itself, we're establishing an area where the eye can inhabit. Similarly, add a simple triangle – this will vary depending on your subject, but will tend to start near the intersection of the eye line and centre line.

4 Add the ears, which also sit roughly on the eye line.

5 Carve out the jawline with two lines, then do the same for the forehead. Still using only straight lines, add the shoulders and the subject's neck and clothing – in this case a T-shirt.

6 Starting with the eyes, begin to refine within the shapes you've established. Again, avoid the temptation to use curved lines – keep this instinctive and swift. Add bags under the eyes. You can start to use more pressure, which will broaden the lines you're adding.

7 Use the width of the brush to add the iris and pupils as single strokes.

8 Continue to build up the features within the areas you established earlier, building up the pieces like a jigsaw. Spend a little time correcting the jawline using diagonal lines leading to the chin. Get into the habit of avoiding rubbing out all the marks you apply, as these will create animation and give your sketch a sense of character.

9 Using varied strokes with the width of the brush, add some tone to the shoulders to help bring out some contrast. If necessary, you can start to fine-tune the overall head shape, going beyond the initial framework.

Hair and detail

If your subject has hair – including facial hair, as here – the temptation is to look too closely at individual strands or how hair flows. Instead, suppress logic and just box the shape in.

Portraits are incredibly technical. They will be resolved in the end with tiny adjustments, but early stages can be loose and quick.

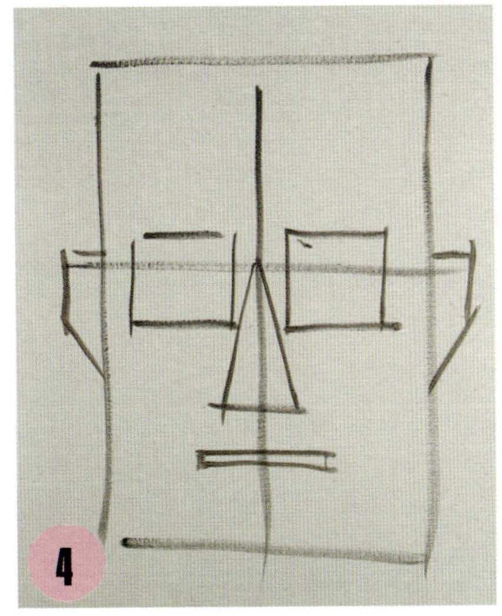

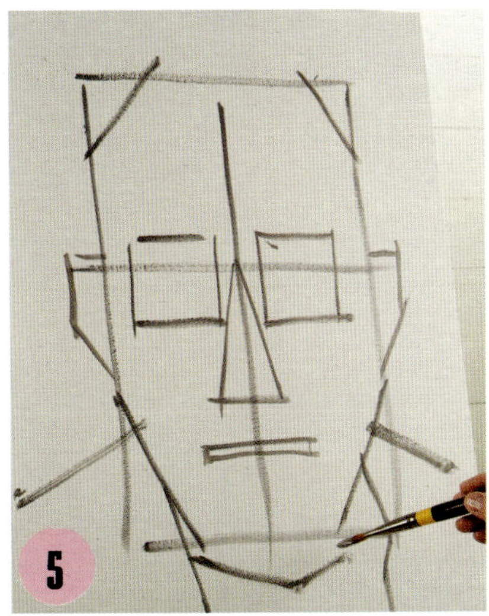

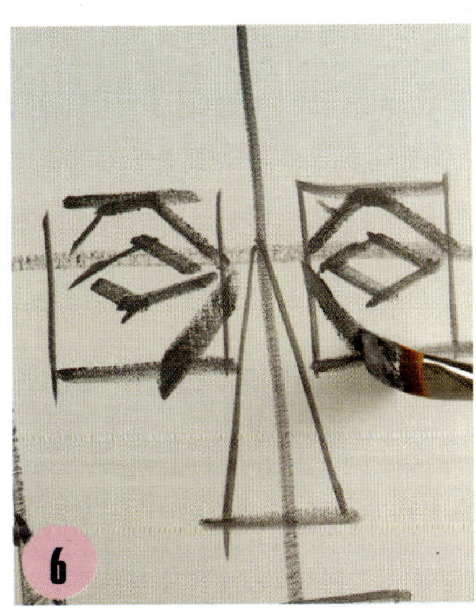

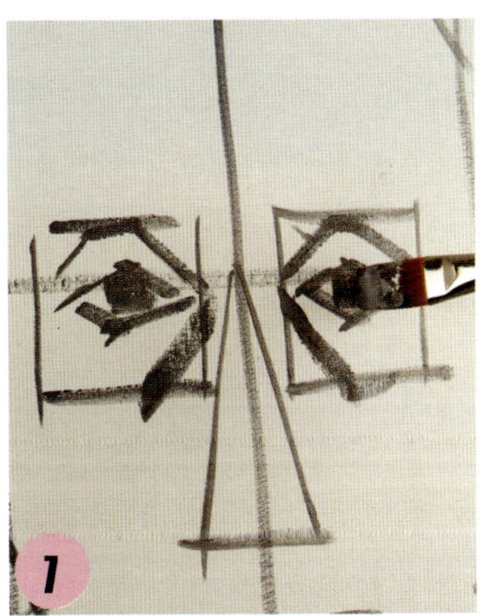

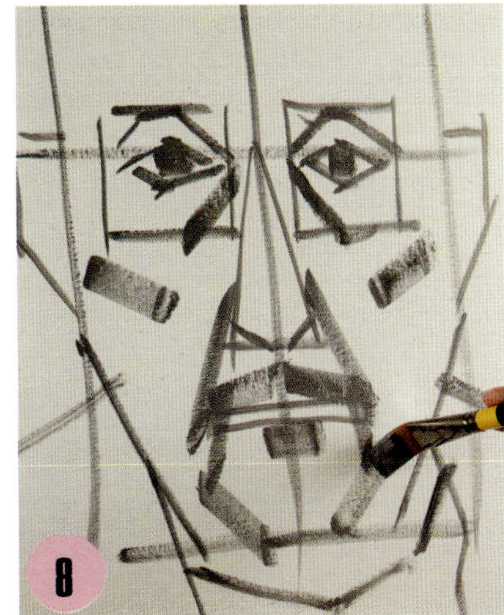

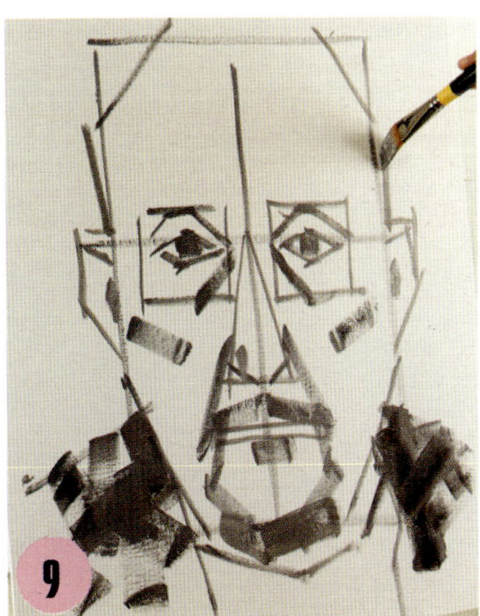

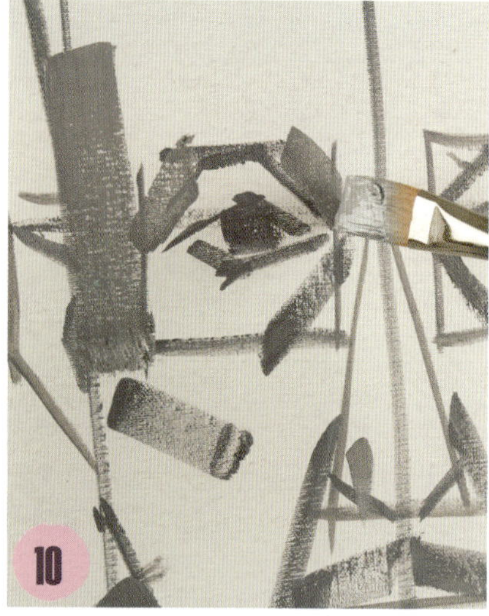

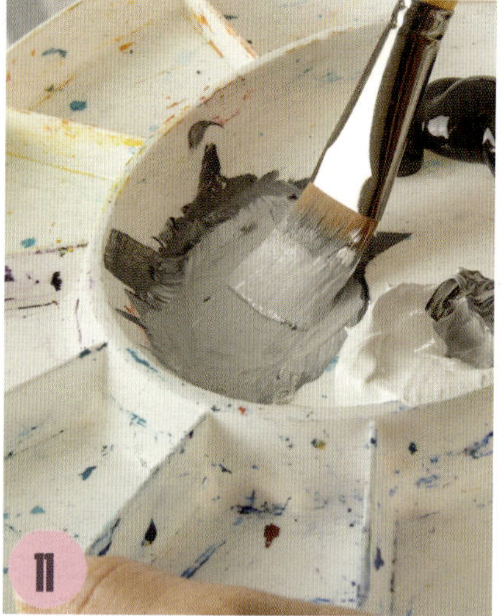

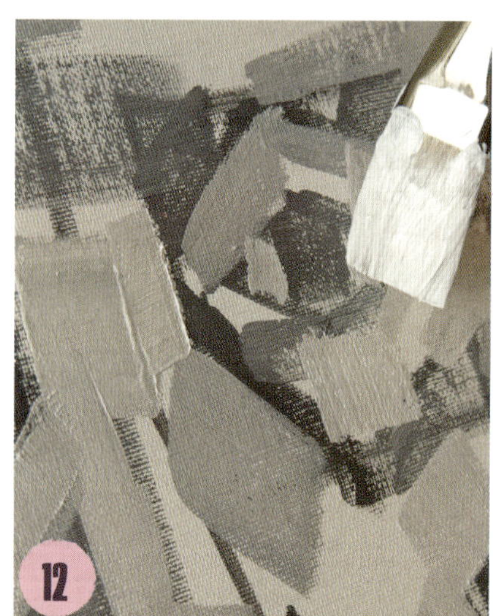

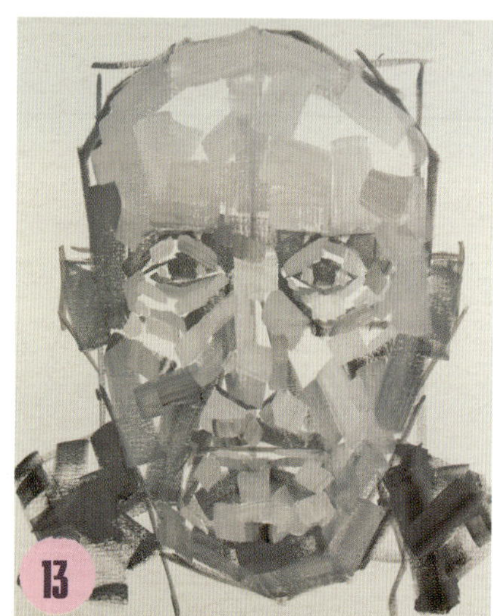

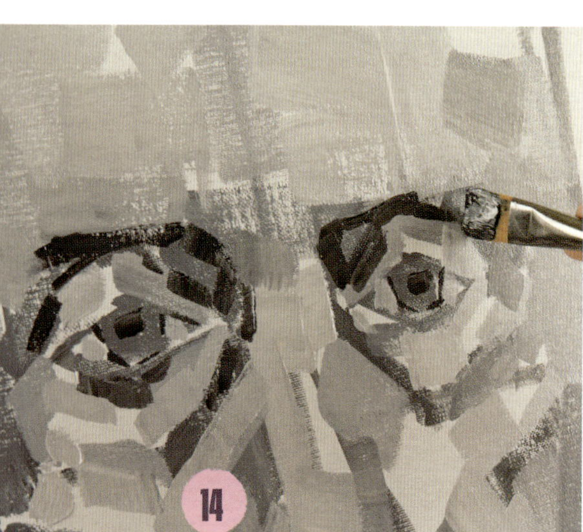

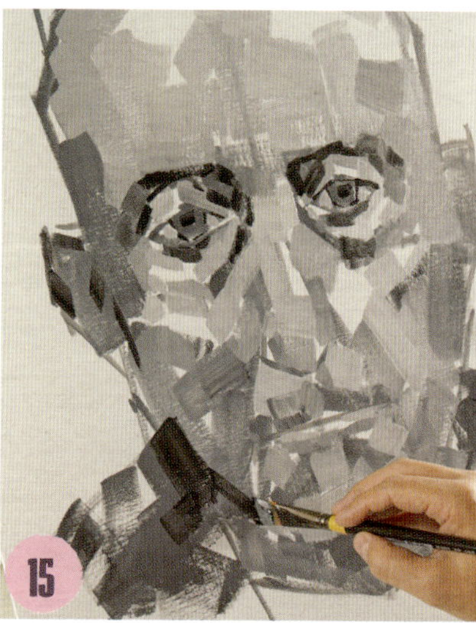

10 Shadow adds structure and shape, so use the flat of the brush to block in the midtone shadows – as earlier, keep your brushstrokes straight and simple. You can vary the pressure to alter the tone a little – letting more of the underlying surface to show through. This is the beauty of using larger brushes.

11 Add more white to the mix to give a lighter tone, and look for areas where this can be used. Use the marks you've established already to help guide you; but refer always to the subject.

12 As you work, the tonal marks will begin to replace the lines you've drawn. This is particularly noticeable around the nose and eyes. Use different parts of the brush – the width, the tip – to help you get the stroke you want. Be confident – you can always work over if necessary to refine.

13 After focussing on a particular feature, work on a larger area such as the forehead or cheek – this helps to ensure you don't get tunnel vision. With the basic shape established, you can now start to refine and adjust.

14 Change to the smaller 16mm (¾in) brush. Use a darker tone to refine the eyes. Pay more attention to the placement and angles of the marks you make now, bringing in slower curved marks if necessary.

15 In addition to refining the features, you can refine the overall structure of the portrait – altering or re-establishing areas such as the jawline and cheekbones. Leave odd marks to break the lines – they add looseness and dynamism to the portrait.

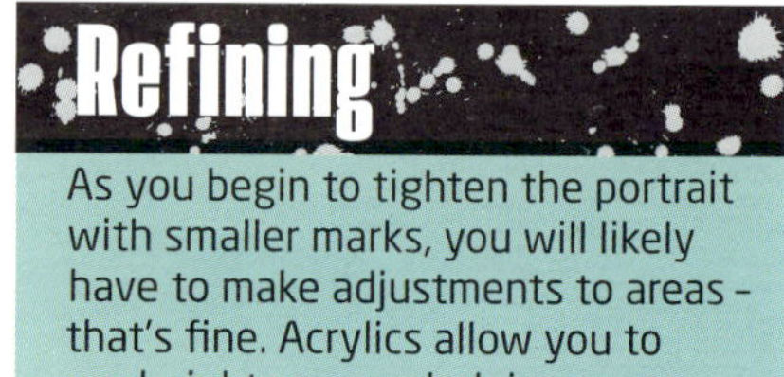

As you begin to tighten the portrait with smaller marks, you will likely have to make adjustments to areas – that's fine. Acrylics allow you to work right over underlying areas.

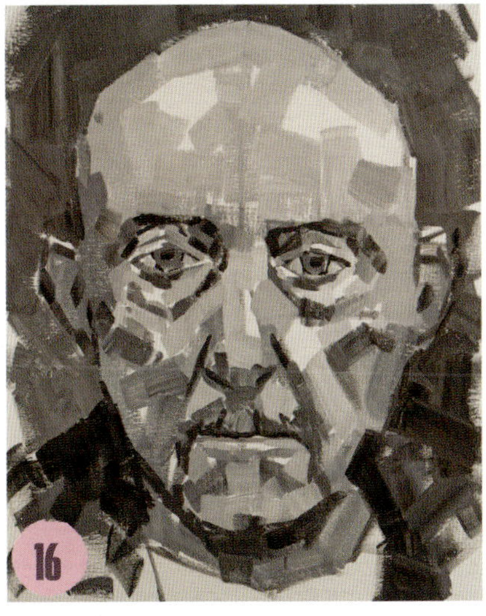
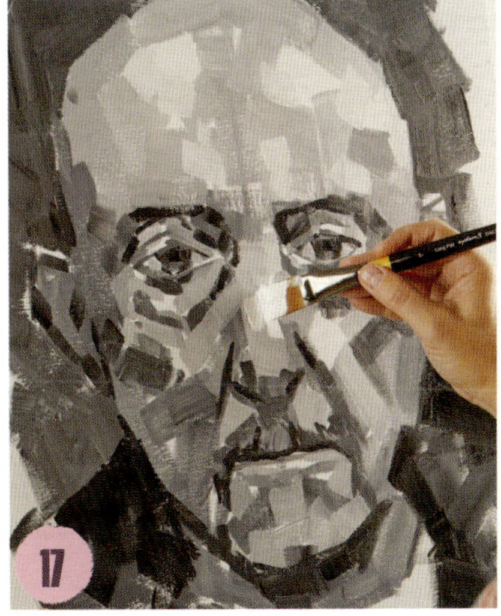
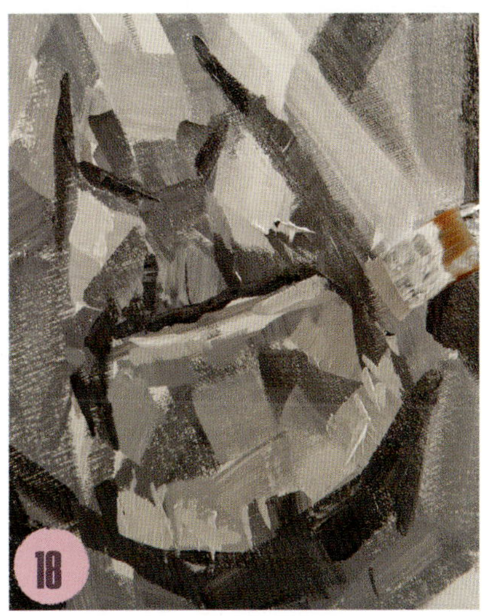

16 Adding the background (using a still-darker tone) allows you to obscure any remaining construction, and also to refine the shape of the head's outline.

17 As you reach the end of the portrait, introduce the strongest lights using a near-white mix. This helps to bring out the sculptural qualities of the painting.

18 When adding the final touches, don't try to paint every hair in the beard and moustache – instead, hint at their presence with occasional lines.

THE FINISHED PORTRAIT.

You can finish by adding additional curved lines to specify and fine-tune the portrait. Consider adding character lines and small curves added to enhance the eyes, nose, ears and lips. You will notice the contrast between the refinement of the curves against the harsher straight lines, a technique you may want to expand upon to create greater emphasis in the focal points, such as the eyes. By the end, the quality of your line and grip on your pencil or brush may tighten, becoming more pressured as you concentrate on detail – do leave some breathing room for the initial looser lines.

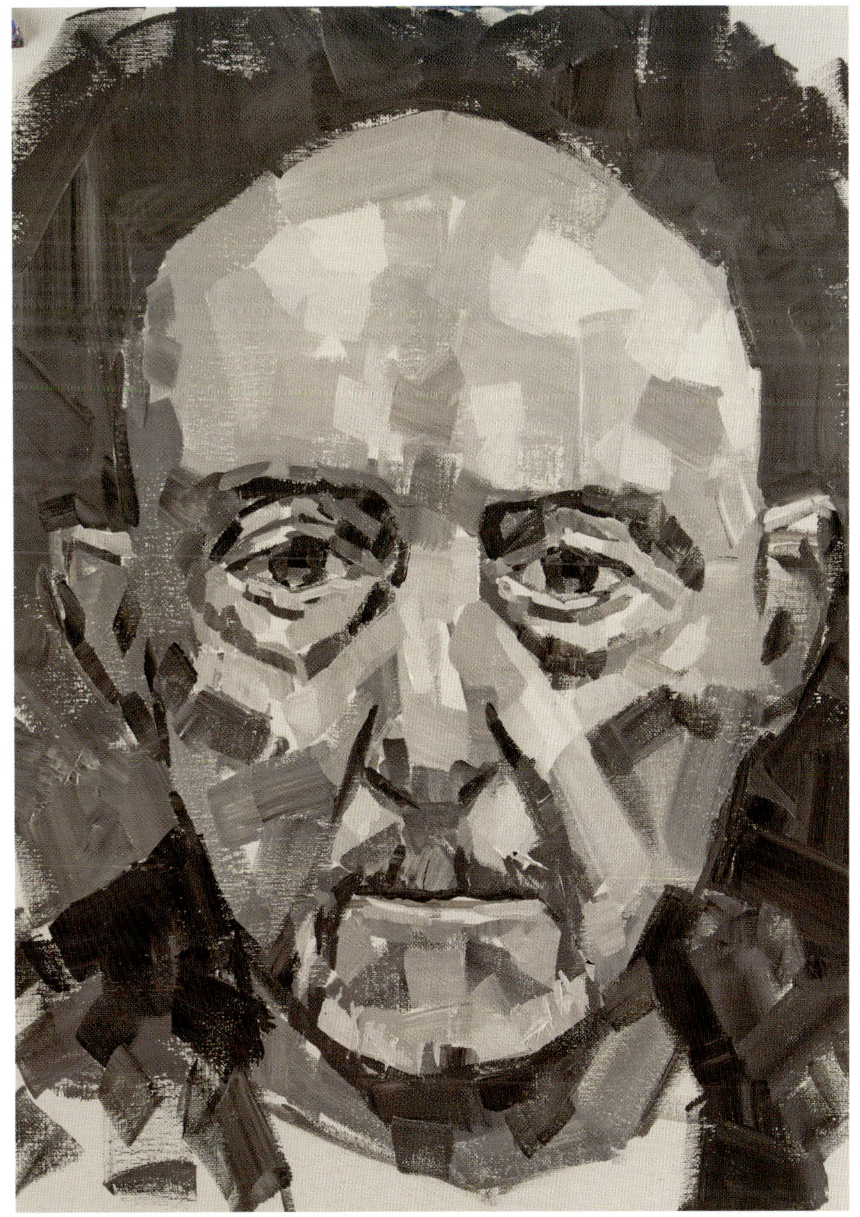

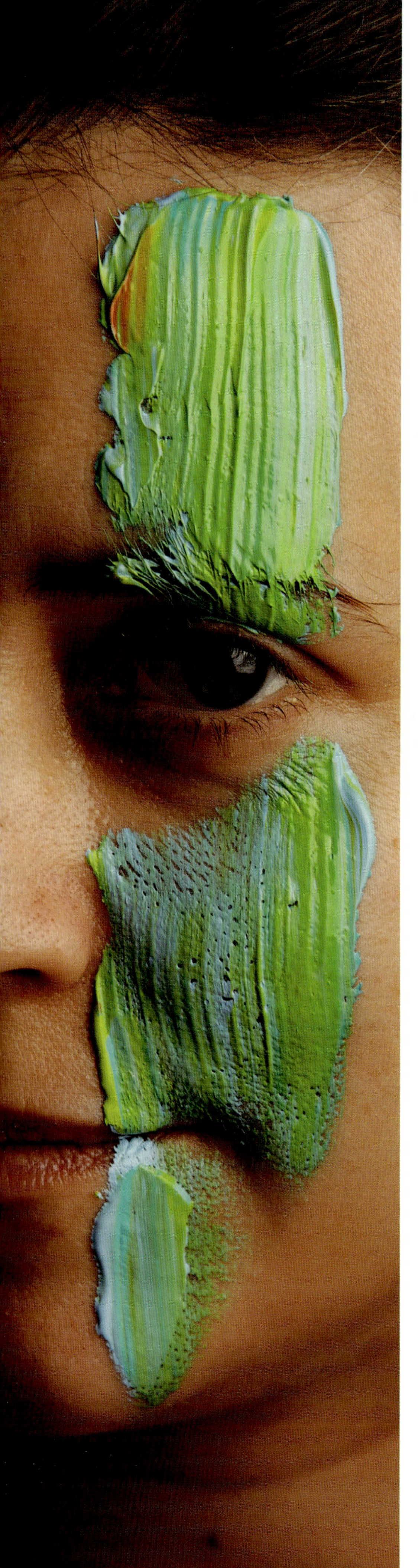

For some artists, diving straight in the deep end and seeing where the painting takes them is as much planning as they need. This is less intimidating and fun as there are no expectations. In a way this sense of chaos – just observing and being in the moment – is one of the key factors to any painting. Perhaps the biggest danger with any art instruction is the risk of the description of the creative process seeming rigid. By following a very prescriptive approach, you are at risk of losing sight of your own instincts.

Planning can sound quite clinical when making art, but many of the Old Masters planned and strategized so that each of their creations had clear goals to aim towards. Besides, there are downsides to no pre-planning: your enthusiasm and confidence can plummet if things don't go well.

For these reasons, I plan quite a bit and when things go right – or more importantly, wrong – I am analytical about why and when. This process is like solving a visual puzzle that sharpens you up for the next go. Pre-planning also saves on material costs if you can iron out potential issues beforehand.

Fundamentals of planning

I tend to prioritize elements of the portrait, starting with composition and how the space is being used. Each painting generally needs areas of interest and spaces of calm. Too much of either will clutter the image or make the eye meander around and lose interest. Next is the contrast between light and dark. This contrast helps to create three-dimensional forms, and the extremes of light and dark can establish the focal point. Finally – and more importantly for me – is how I plan to use colour. Again, I plan for opposites in order to create the most striking differences for maximum impact. On some occasions harmonious colour schemes are called for, but I tend to paint with more complementary colours for the extra visual punch (see pages 70–83 for more on colour).

My style is quite expressive so marks will come through naturally as I'm painting. I do keep a lookout for habits I'm trying to break like overworking details or avoid distractions from secondary areas. I'll then consider the details of the portrait itself, contemplating facial features and making choices on the main focal points. Generally, these are the eyes but my preoccupation not to follow the norm means that I'll look at other features as potential focal points, such as a distinctive nose, ears, jewellery, or brightly coloured spectacles or clothing (see page 110 for more on focal points).

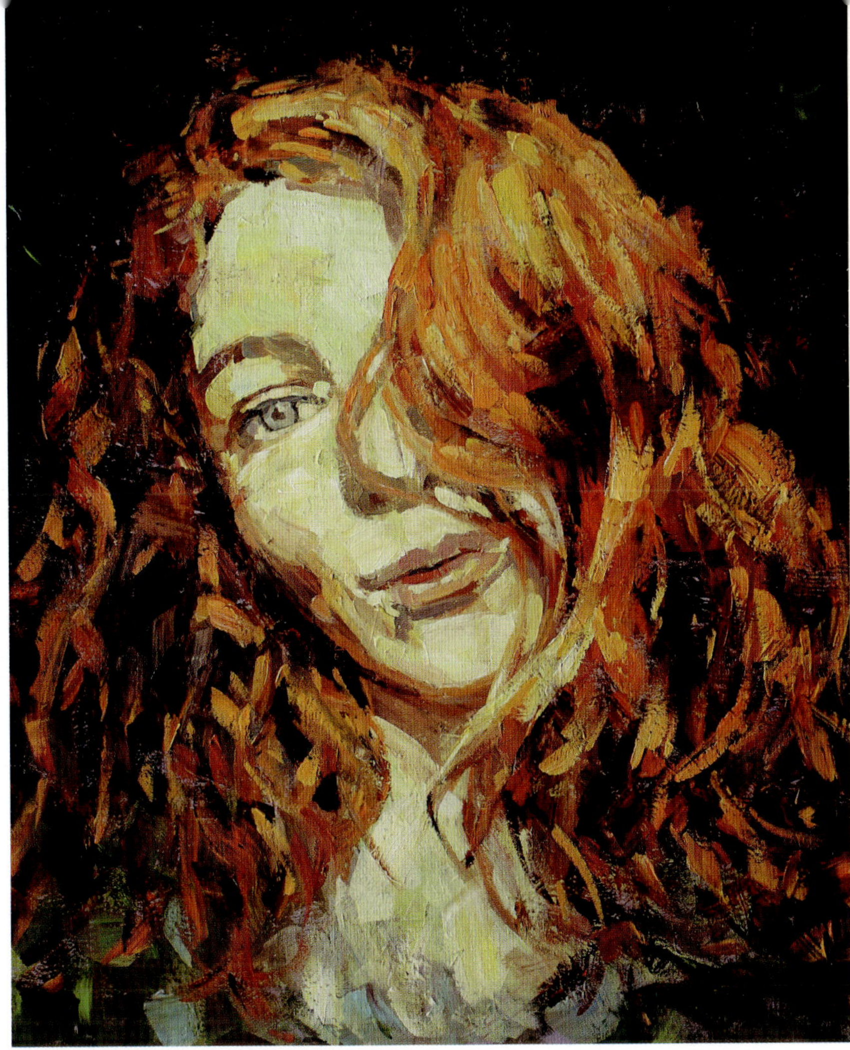

Aims and expectations

Whether you're a beginner or have drawn or painted for a while, practice is everything. Practical knowledge contributes to your pool of experience and over time will instil confidence. This is vital as the artwork you produce will reflect your mindset: your fears or insecurities and, when things are going well, your confidence. The more you can gain in self-belief, the greater the connection with a viewer; who will feel at ease with your creations.

You will definitely have both good and bad painting days, but as your confidence wavers, dig deep to shore yourself up. The other main ingredient to success is just to have fun; enjoy the exploration and, over time, the evolution of your new-found skills.

My advice is to avoid forcing any issues and set realistic goals. For example, the first few portraits you attempt will probably look a touch out of proportion or appear rigid. Rest assured that it takes some time to acclimatize to the act of drawing and how best to use a set of acrylic paints. The journey is everything; it should be one that you're keen to take every time you pick up a pencil or brush. Start simply by aiming at producing something that looks human, then move on to specifics.

For more advanced painters, with habits that have become ingrained over many years, there may be a harder task ahead. Question why you paint, draw or compose a painting the way you do. Perhaps you have stopped enjoying the way you paint as much, because the technique is dull, outdated, or has been saturated by other artists?

You will learn more by doing more. Despite your skill, avoid the lure of perfection. Stop fussing over one artwork, and instead do plenty of short drawing or painting exercises. If it helps, set simple goals for each individual study and see what happens. These goals could range from having a looser grip when drawing to simply avoiding cleaning your brush so much when mixing colour.

Try setting tighter deadlines for each portrait and stick to them; this way you'll develop an instinct to your painting rather than being overly self-conscious. Ignore the little voice in your head saying, 'I'll just do a little bit more'. Instead, stop and move on. Small changes like this will help you to produce more arresting, contemporary work.

The hook: make it relatable

A painted portrait is very specific. Unless the viewer knows the individual or it's a portrait of a celebrity, they're less invested. You need to find the 'hook' – that quality that invites a viewer to look – and keep looking.

One route to a hook is to find individuals with inherently interesting faces or eye-catching features like tattoos, jewellery, hats or brightly-coloured hair to add some dynamism. The other way to create a greater hook is in the way you paint your portraits.

Acrylics allow for a wide range of possibilities, but even if you're new to them, there is a lot you can do with the pressures you apply with a brush, or the use of your entire arm when painting. The less polished or refined a painting, the more visible the artist's hand. Flurries of marks, flashes of colours, and underplaying absolute realism opens up the image to greater interpretation. Exposed brushmarks are like the workings out of a maths equation; they show the viewer the journey you've taken to get to the answer – the finished painting.

Just like the contrast between light and dark, or between opposing colours, varying the scale of the brushmarks will create eye-catching contrasts that build up into a visual hook. Use expansive strokes with your largest brush at the beginning of a painting and reserve your smallest marks for the end to optimize the contrast. If you paint with a small brush throughout, you'll take longer in the build-up and layering, sap your concentration and underplay the contrast.

If each mark you make can play a more pivotal role, you will find you – and your paintings – will be fresher and much more energized.

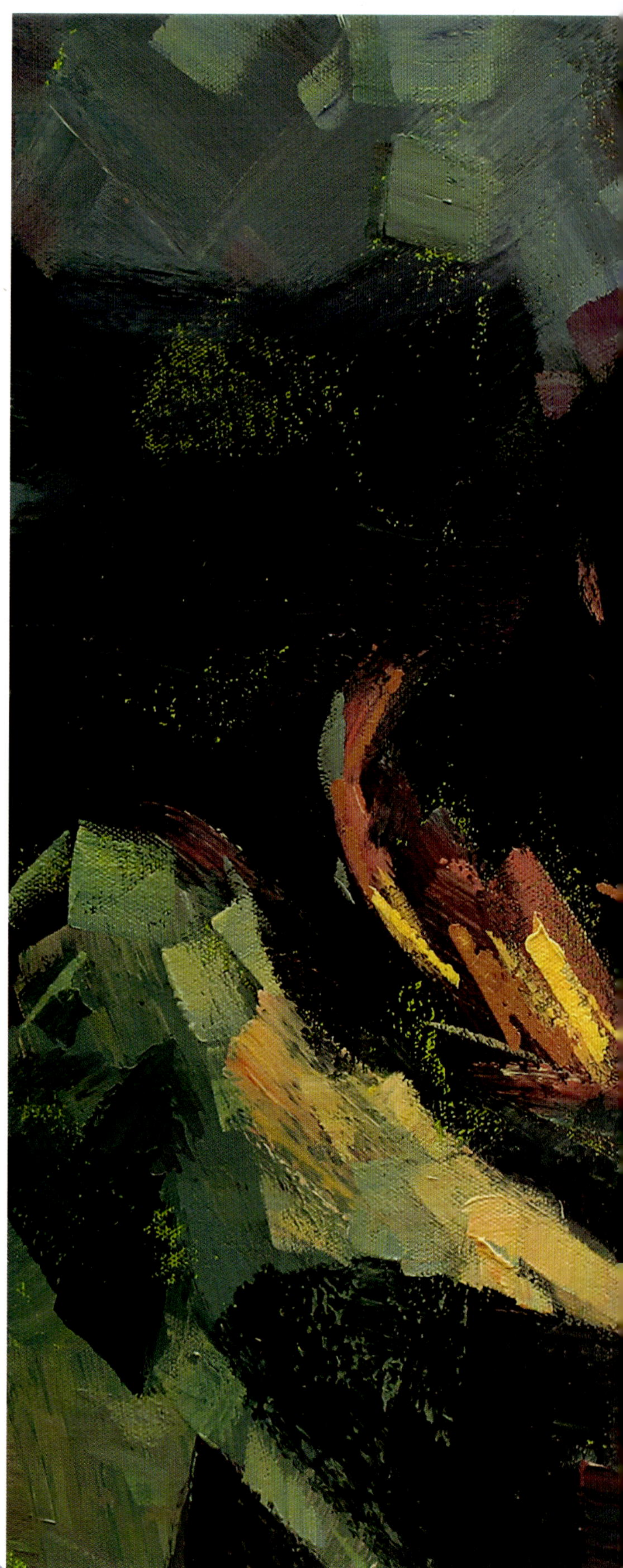

GLOWING LIGHT 60×46cm (24×18in)

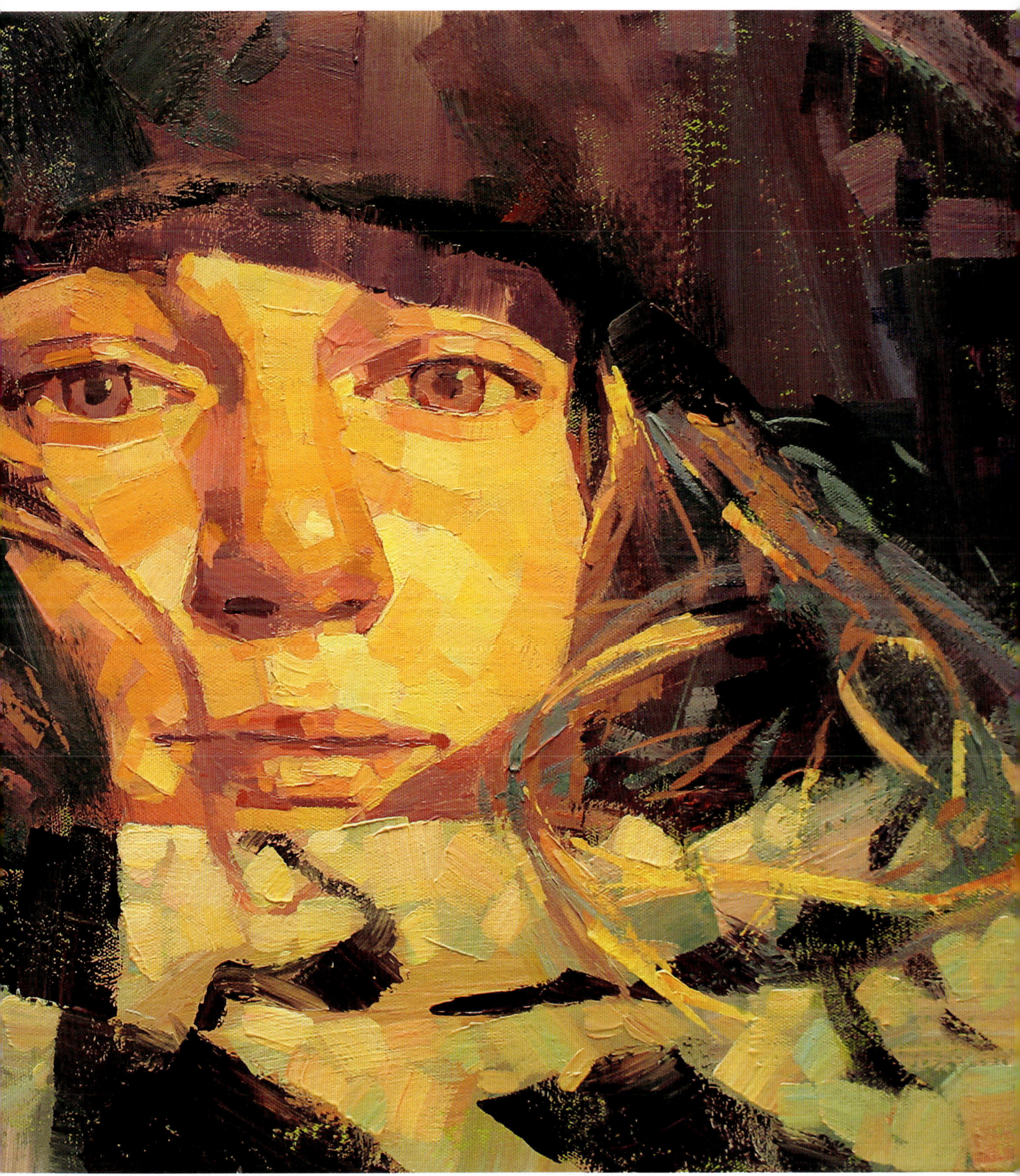

Drawing discipline

When I attended art college, life drawing or portraiture consisted of short, varied exercises which culminated into a longer pose. Accuracy was the absolute priority; making sure the figure looked in proportion and, when using light and dark, being aware of the main light source so that the shadows looked convincing. The hours of heavy concentration on realism this approach requires definitely pays off, as you develop a core skill which you constantly draw upon – even when painting expressively.

There are other traditional drawing techniques for portraiture including using a pre-drawn grid; using multiple circular guidelines as a foundation on which you can build; and drawing or painting with tonal values rather than line. All are valid and all will help with accuracy.

Put simply, however, if you want to improve your accuracy, just draw more! Place something in front of you, grab a pen or pencil and start sketching. The more you do, the better you'll become. Work with simple shapes and one main light source, and over time add more complicated and varied elements. Build towards sketching moving figures or animals. The quality of any of these exploratory studies is less important than the time spent just looking and contemplating how intricate these elements are. This is an incredibly important time for you to develop your creative mind and gain a greater understanding of how you perceive things.

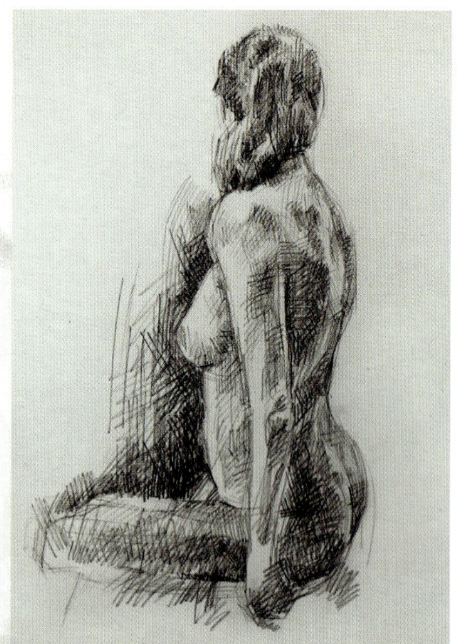

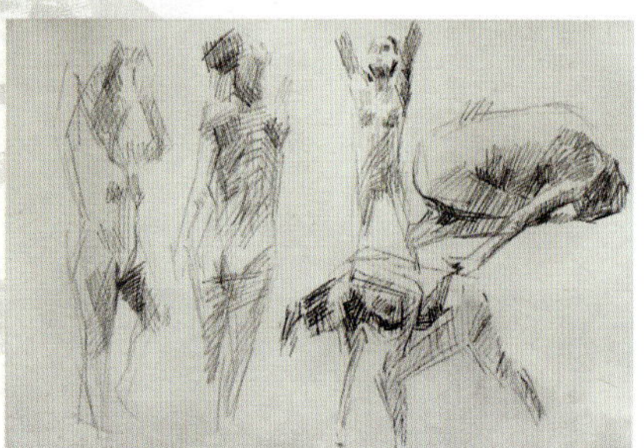

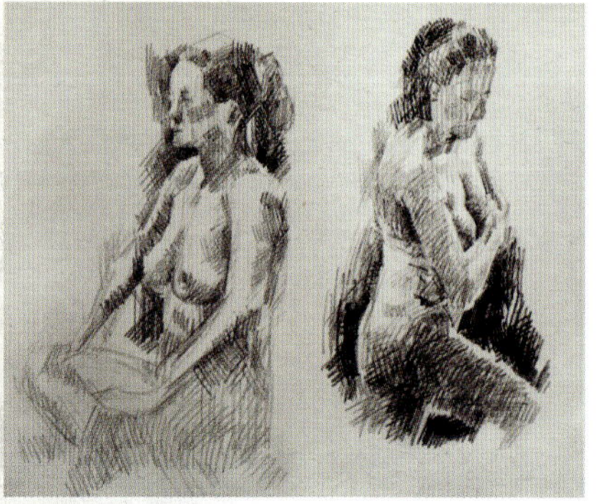

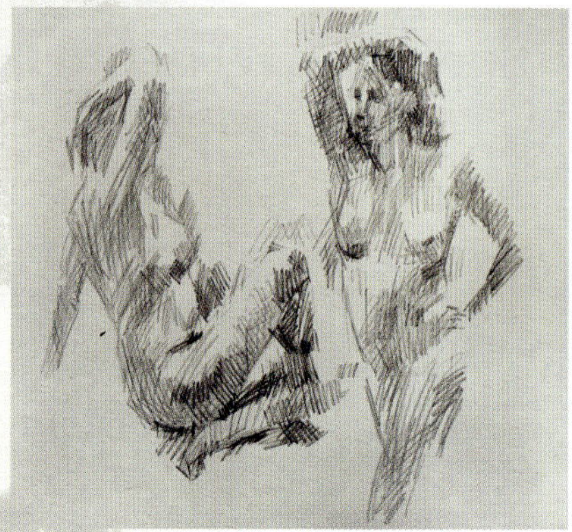

A selection of life drawings.

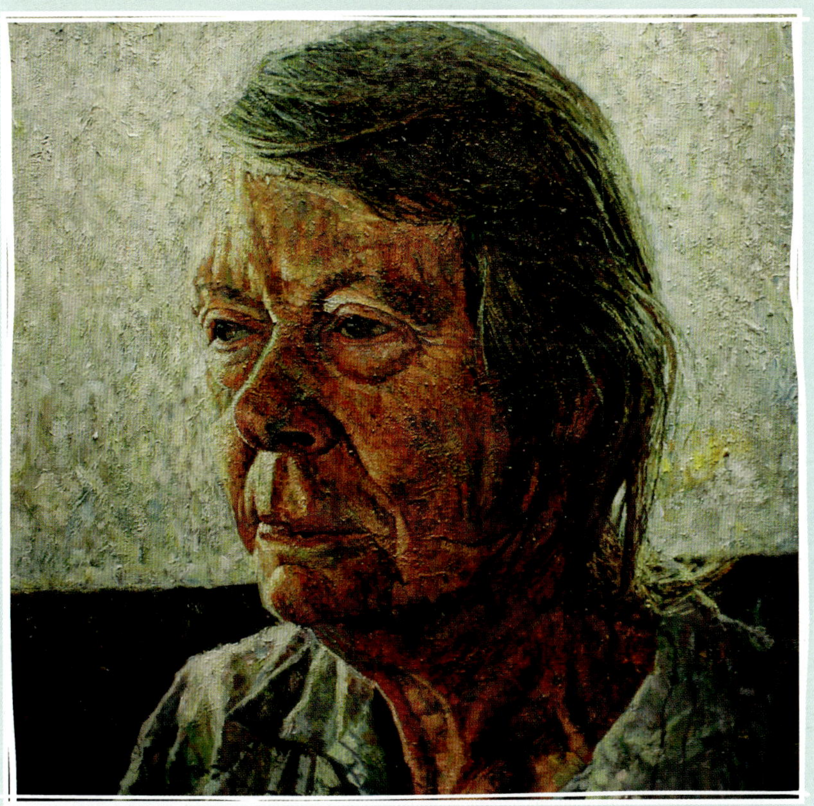

Traditional vs. contemporary portraits

Knowing what's gone before in portraiture does help in understanding what works and how to break the mould, so here's a brief outline of both traditional and contemporary portrait painting practices.

The formal pose in traditional portraiture is a slightly three-quarter view including the shoulders (or sometimes the full body), with the sitter thoughtfully looking at the viewer or out of an imaginary window. Light floods in from one corner, creating dramatic tonal contrasts. Colours are kept earthy with perhaps shots of vibrant colour in the sitter's attire. The main focal points are usually the eyes, generally picked out with sparkly highlights. Brushmarks are polished, and the background may be in soft focus with a greater emphasis on rounded shapes.

Contemporary portraits are much more confrontational, with dramatic colour schemes. They include exposed brushstrokes which may be much more angular. Palette knives, large brushes or scrapers provide these expressive qualities with some artists choosing to include diverse media such as spray paint or collage. Compositionally, angles are more dynamic with less static poses and expressions can be animated. Imperfections, distortions in the portrait, naïve interpretations and almost blurring or obscuring the face creates an edgier and raw quality.

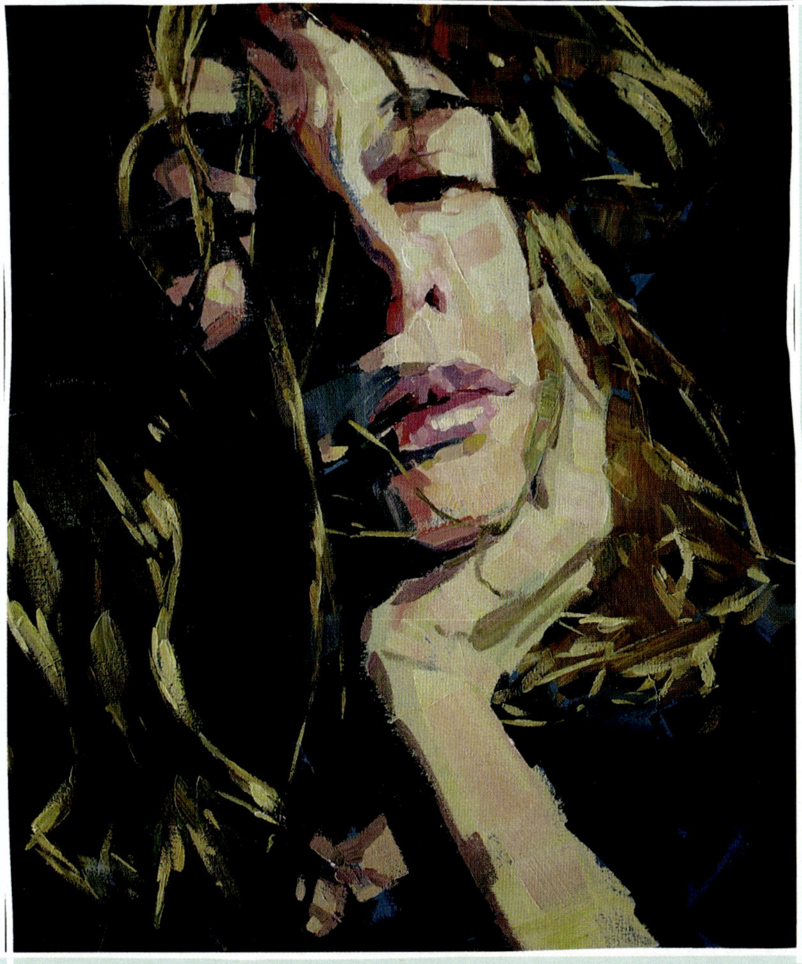

Top:
BRENDA 76×76CM (30×30IN)

This is one of my older portraits, painted as I made the transition from traditional to a more contemporary style. There's a lot more build-up with small brushstrokes and earthy colours.

Bottom:
ELENA LIGHT 51×60CM (20×24IN)

A more up-to-date approach here, using the minimal strokes and large flat head brushes I now favour. Less labour creates cleaner applications.

Accuracy and interest

One common concern with portraiture for both amateur and semi-professional artists is accuracy, and the idea that you ought to aim for photorealism from the outset. This drive for absolute realism can be counter-productive. Drawing one very accurate eyeball at a time, with all the lashes and reflections, moving on only when you are completely satisfied; then attempting the other with the same degree of scrutiny; moving on to the nose, mouth, ears and so on, was certainly how I used to paint (see *A change in attitude*, below). By the end, however, I usually felt drained by the process.

The final result often looks impressive as it has a polished photographic finish. The main difficulty lies in being able to sustain the high levels of concentration over long periods necessary to create an even consistency. This may be achievable over several painting sessions, but the longer you look at any subject, the less you view it as a fresh proposition. This obsessive part-by-part approach can thus lead to lifeless portraits with accurate individual parts that do not hang together as a whole.

Working on the overall image is the key to successful, arresting portraiture. Establish all the main forms to begin with – almost a blurry version of the portrait – then refine them. It is not until the later stages that you make the critical choices on detail.

A change in attitude

When I began painting I was keen to showcase a very technical approach in my work. This early self-portrait, painted from life, had me holding a mirror with my tongue sticking out, a spot light on the side of my face, while I painted with small round head brushes in acrylic on canvas. The painting process lasted for about a month.

The pose is confrontational but the style very conventional. At the time I assumed paintings should be representational and take an age to complete. This was partly based on my tastes in art at the time, along with inspiration from a couple of art lecturers from college who did far more superior technical work. Thankfully, a couple of decades' worth of evolution and several styles later, I discovered Impressionism, Expressionism and found other alternative ways to paint portraits.

Generally, I find both beginners and amateur artists just need the acknowledgement or even approval to try something different – including using bigger brushes!

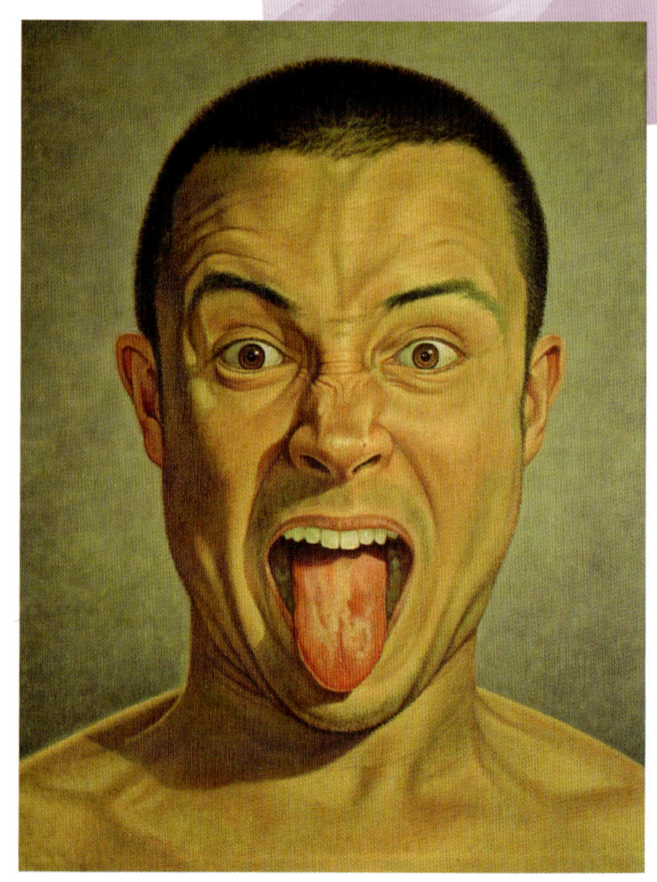

SELF-PORTRAIT, OLD STYLE 51×60cm (20×24in)

Think sculpture

I really like the idea of a sculpted painting. With this mindset, it makes it natural to look for shapes rather than lines. Lines can promote consistently hard edges, while there are naturally more variations when looking for shapes.

A sculptor begins with a slab of stone, wood or clay. They look to roughly shape the overall piece. Elements are merely implied early on, and refinements are only made towards the end. I translate this process into painting by using large supports, thick pigment and large flat head brushes. This idea best reflects my current painting ethos.

Sculpting with the brush

For this portrait, I imagined my initial flurries of colour and paint as slabs of clay waiting to be knocked into some kind of shape. These varied in size and direction but were are all applied with confidence. Painting a self-portrait provides no judgement or pressure to impress so I could simply use the exercise to realize an idea.

Mid-size blocks began to shape the features and a blocky pattern emerged. Realists would blend these together, but leaving them informs the viewer that this is a painting and not a photographic reproduction. I ended with some smaller brushmarks to add definition, but these aren't excessive.

Acrylics' quick-drying properties allow layers to be applied one after the other, with any mistakes quickly rectifiable. The process benefits from such fluidity. Using applications of thicker paint makes the next stroke easier to merge in, if you need to do so.

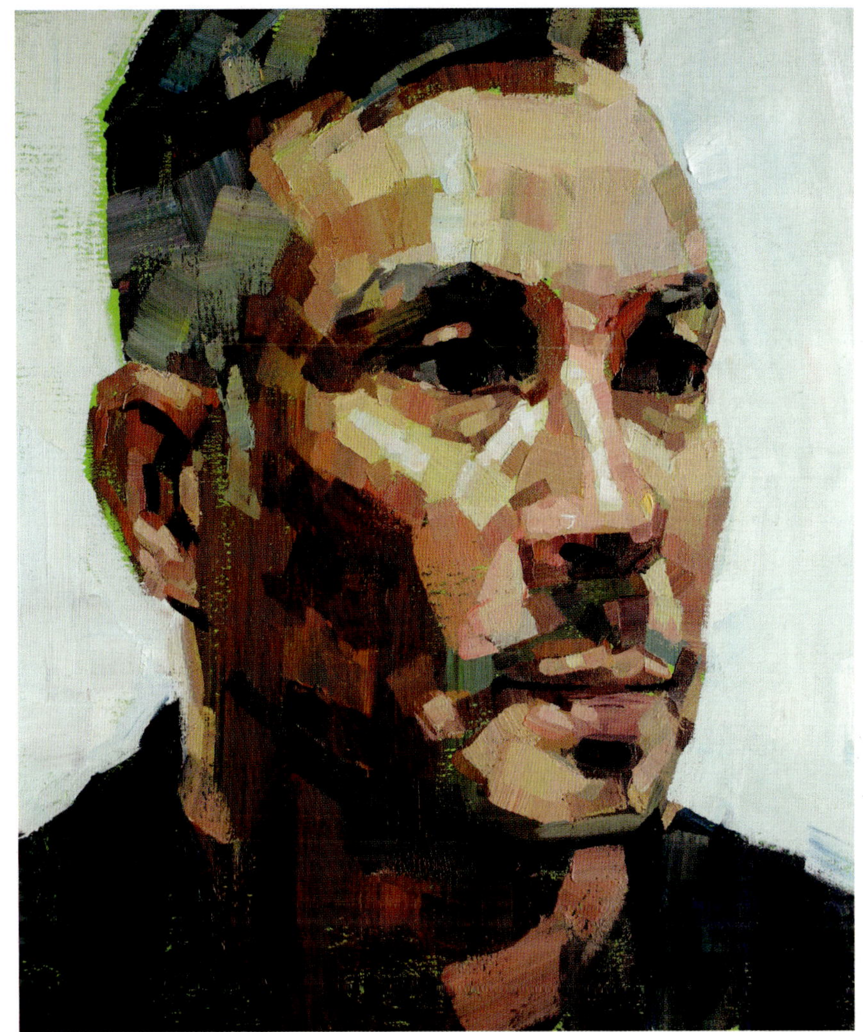

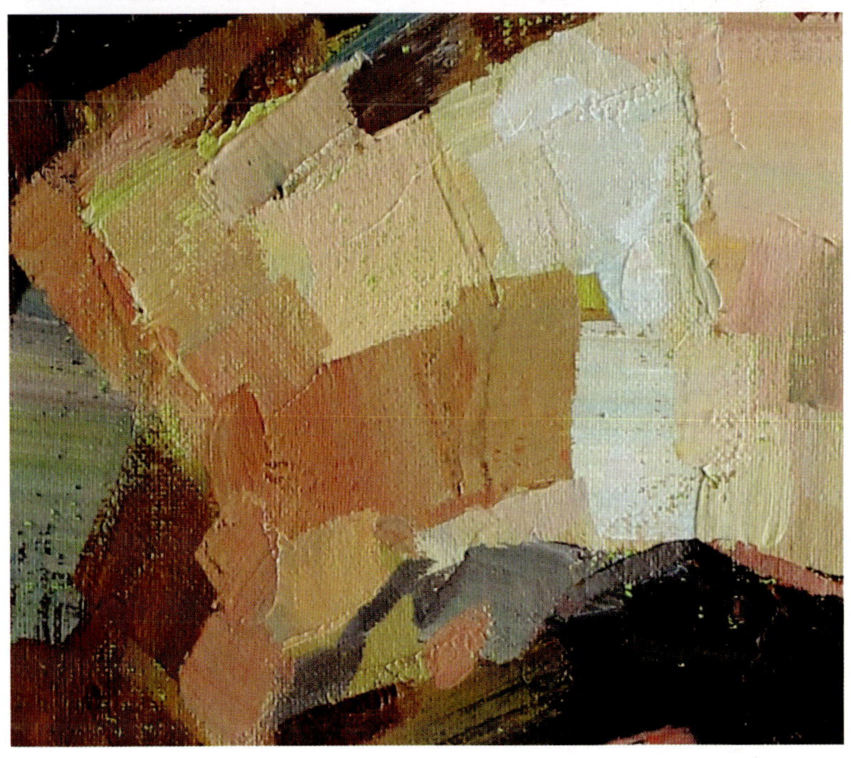

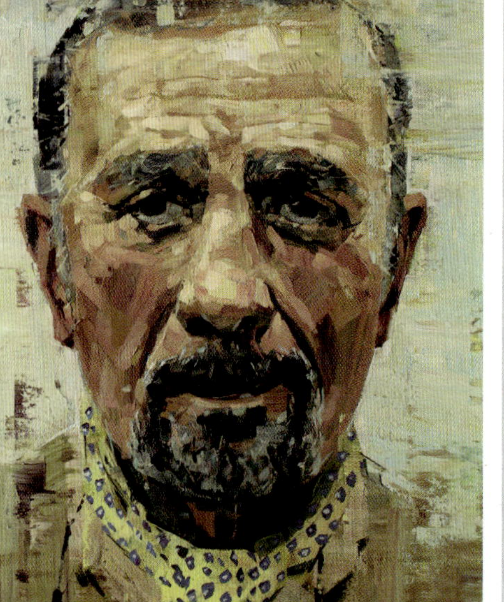

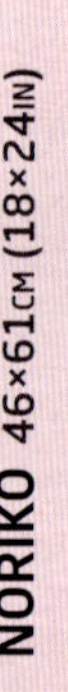

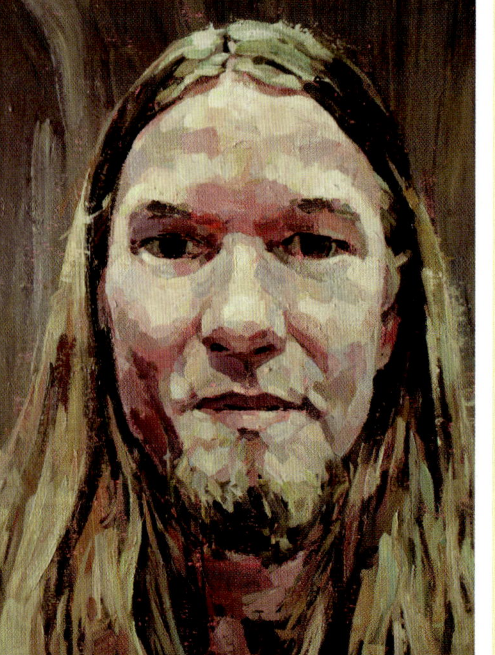

Choosing a face to paint

If you want to create an effective, characterful portrait, it's easier to start with a characterful face. The examples here show three subjects, each of which offered me some great – and varied – opportunities.

Contrast The portrait of Dr. Farid shows how important contrasts can be. Dark hair sits against areas of light-toned skin; while horizontal wrinkles lines are next to diagonals or verticals. The contrast of patterns next to plain areas is also on show, both through the beard against skin, and the patterned neckscarf against the doctor's collar.

Local colour If the model is wearing something bright, reflect variations of that colour into the face, background or hair to create a rhythm. Noriko's portrait shows this beautifully, with her neck picking up the hue on her clothing, and the pinks being echoed in her cheeks.

Warmth Lighter skin, as in the portrait of Walter, tends to showcase more red and this can be useful if most of the painting contains earthy colours. The warmth will draw you in.

Beyond the specifics, however, there are some universals to bear in mind when looking for a subject for portraiture, and that will help give you a sense of which subjects will suit your personal approach and style. These are, of course, generalizations, but they will provide you with some starting points from which you can expand and make decisions as an artist.

Gender

Traditionally, there have been plenty of advantages to painting female portraits: they're more popular as paintings, hair is a great feature to paint, make-up enhances eyes, rounded forms are more appealing to look at, and accessories such as jewellery create lovely sparkles of light to complement the face. Male portraits, meanwhile, have been far less adventurous: countless similar paintings reflecting a life in business or government; and at best a way to explore the gritty character of weather-beaten faces. However, don't be limited to stereotypes. Beauty is increasingly playing a part in male portraiture, especially as men have become more conscious of grooming. A well-maintained beard, tattoos, male jewellery or hats are all proudly showcased on social media and can add to the appeal when producing a male portrait.

Beyond personal aesthetics, there are general anatomical differences between the sexes. Females tend to have softer, more rounded, oval-shaped faces, they have thinner eyebrows, longer lashes, fuller lips, a more rounded chin, fuller hair and a smaller brow ridge.

Levels of difficulty in portraiture vary from face to face. However, it is easier painting traditional male portraits than female. This comes down to perceptions of beauty – coarseness generally adds to the masculine aesthetic, but detracts from traditional feminine imagery. This can dictate how the portrait is painted. Be careful, however. Too many exposed brushstrokes and you'll instantly age a face; too few and the portrait will look bland and reinforce stereotypes.

Bone structure

We tend to paint what's visible, so that's where most of the attention goes, but a consideration a lot of beginners neglect in portraiture is the underlying bone structure. As a result, faces appear flat or distorted. The skull and internal structure of the human head create the contours that provide more authenticity to the portrait. Having a sense of structure will also help guide you when features are disguised or obscured by facial hair, spectacles, hats or long hair.

Starting any portrait with a simple skull will create this foundation and also determine the face shape. You don't need to be a surgeon, but knowing a few basic principles will go a long way. For example, the length of the face from head to chin is generally the same from the tip of the nose to the back of the head. A lot of beginners make the forehead too small for the brain, or paint eyes that are too big for their sockets. Knowing the 'rules' will help you avoid such errors.

Eventually, you might like to play with these ideas – distorting features is actually a great way of adding personality and a naïve quality to the likeness, for example. Normally, however, an understanding of the mechanics of the face or figure is preferable before you distort them. Practising a few skulls will soon engrain the idea.

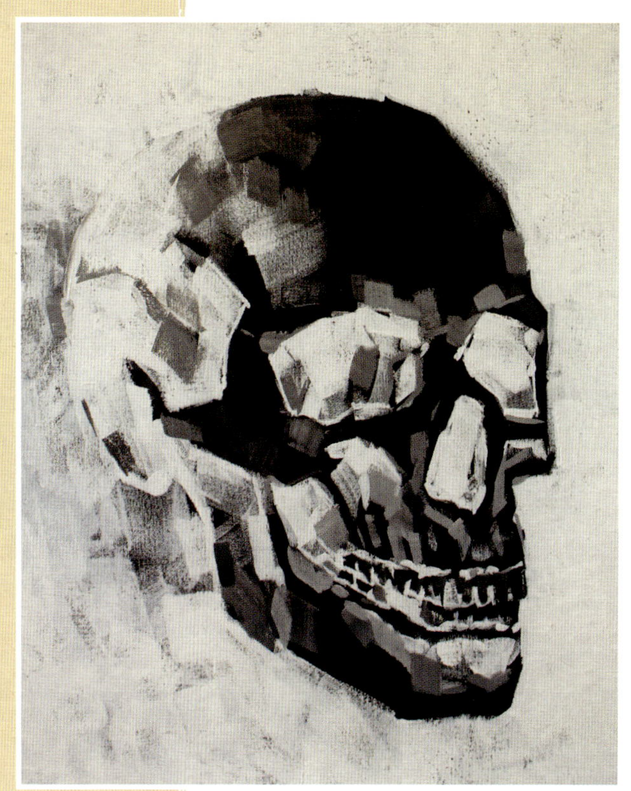

Making faces

Drawing or painting a made-up face is a great way to begin to create your own ideas – you might use the exercise on pages 20–21 as a guide, but with your own imaginary subject. Sticking to one or two colours will make the process much easier: if you're starting out, choose two contrasting colours and white.

Before you start painting, decide whether the portrait will be a close-up taking up the entire picture plane, or set back with part of a background. Consider where to place one main light source, which will cast consistent shadows. Next, choose any combination of colours (or perhaps just one) and paint the face; giving yourself a time limit of twenty or thirty minutes.

I love painting to a deadline: it's the single most important factor that stopped me fussing or overworking any artwork. When you set a deadline, stick to it. This creates momentum and you'll begin making decisive choices instead of wavering. They might even be the wrong choices but they'll make a positive mark.

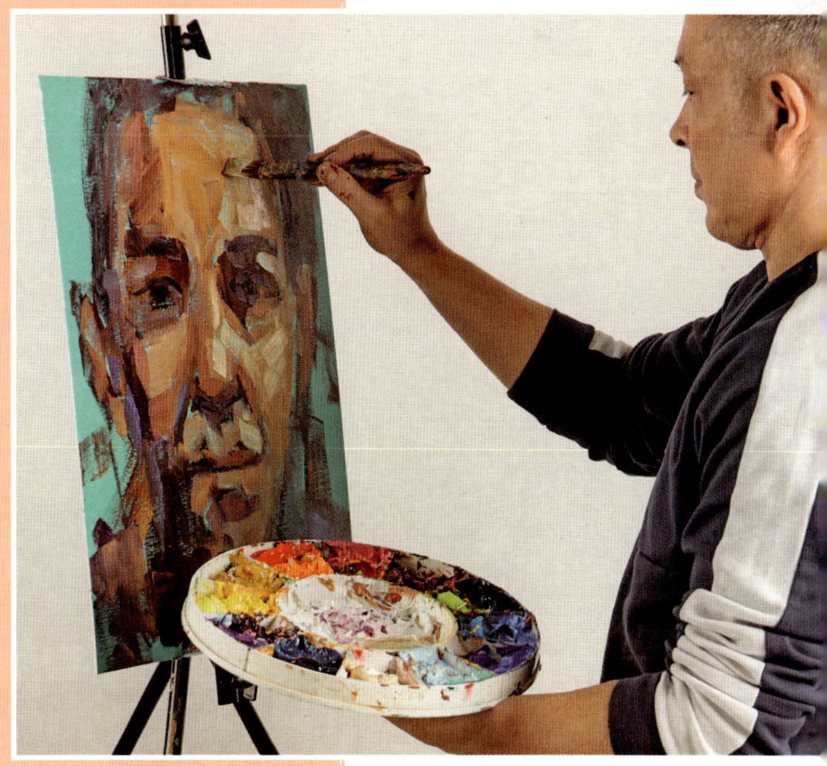

Finding a subject

Working from a live model (see pages 38–39) is more intimate and rewarding than from a photograph, but not always convenient unless you want to draw or paint endless self-portraits. Photographs are the most convenient way to get you started in portraiture.

Working from a photograph

Although high-definition photographs are incredibly detailed, the light, dark and colours they contain are still flattened when compared with the huge degree of subtlety our own perception can pick up on. There is also a danger that a portrait drawn from a photograph may look rigid if followed too closely. Using photographs is a compromise between adherence to the visual reference and incorporating your memory or imagination to make the image your own.

Ideally you want to work from photographs you've taken as you'll be more engaged. You'll have a better idea of the sitter's personality, that sparkle in their eyes or how animated they are. There are plenty of portraits in this book of individuals I've not met but found I've been drawn to. In these instances I've imagined their character or have used ideas about colours I've wanted to explore.

Getting your photograph

I invested in a Canon SLR camera a few years ago; I also have a smaller digital camera when I'm out and about for convenience. Even the camera on my phone produces pretty good snaps. I'm not too worried if the image isn't perfect as my style lends itself to interpretation and does not rely on absolutes. Too much information might lead to an obsessive painting. I don't tend to play with the image with any software beyond occasionally increasing the contrasts between light and dark.

You can source reference material with a quick internet search for interesting faces, which will provide plenty of opportunities to practise. Do note that there are issues with copyright when not using your own photographs, especially if the paintings produced are for sale.

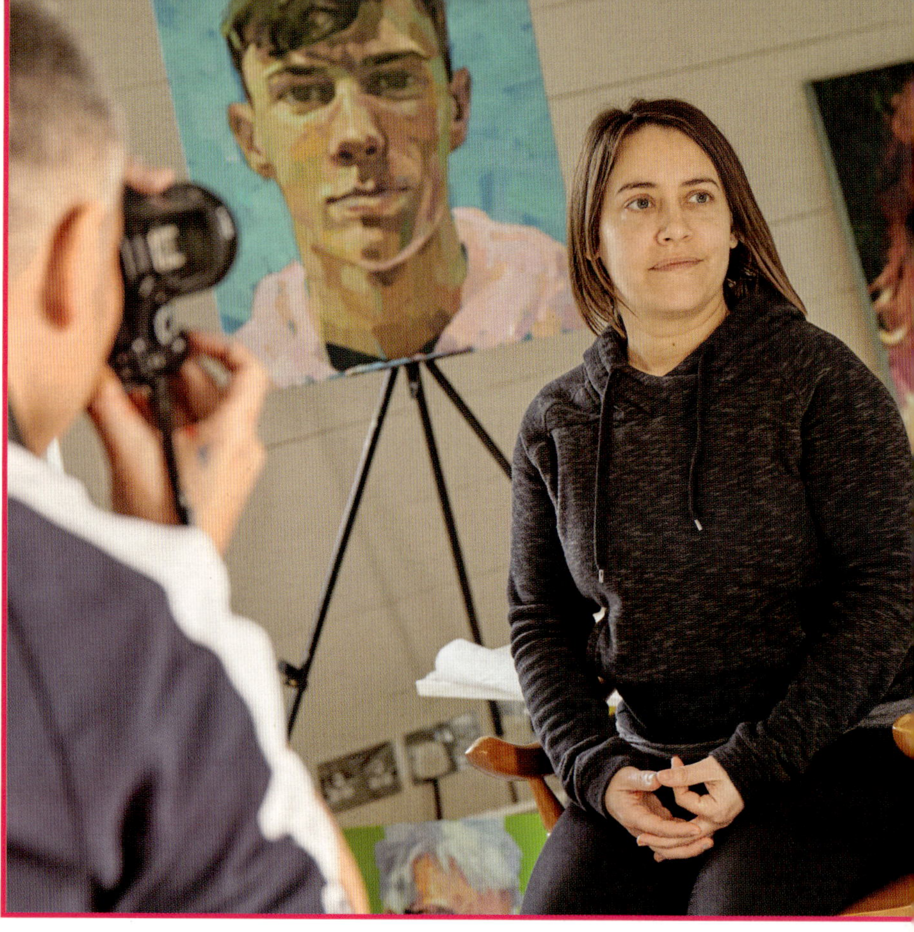

MARIE GREEN 36×46cm (14×18in)

Permissions

Sketching someone on a train, in a park or coffee shop at a relatively fair distance is less intrusive than sitting opposite them and dissecting their every facial detail. As a general courtesy, asking permission is not only polite but your unsuspecting model may even be delighted. If they prefer privacy, that must be respected.

To some extent using someone else's photographs has a similar issue. You must ask for permission, which may either be from the photographer or model. For many images I've used in this book I simply got in touch with individuals through social media and sent a message asking for permission. I mentioned how the final painting would be used and everyone I approached was more than happy to be painted or drawn.

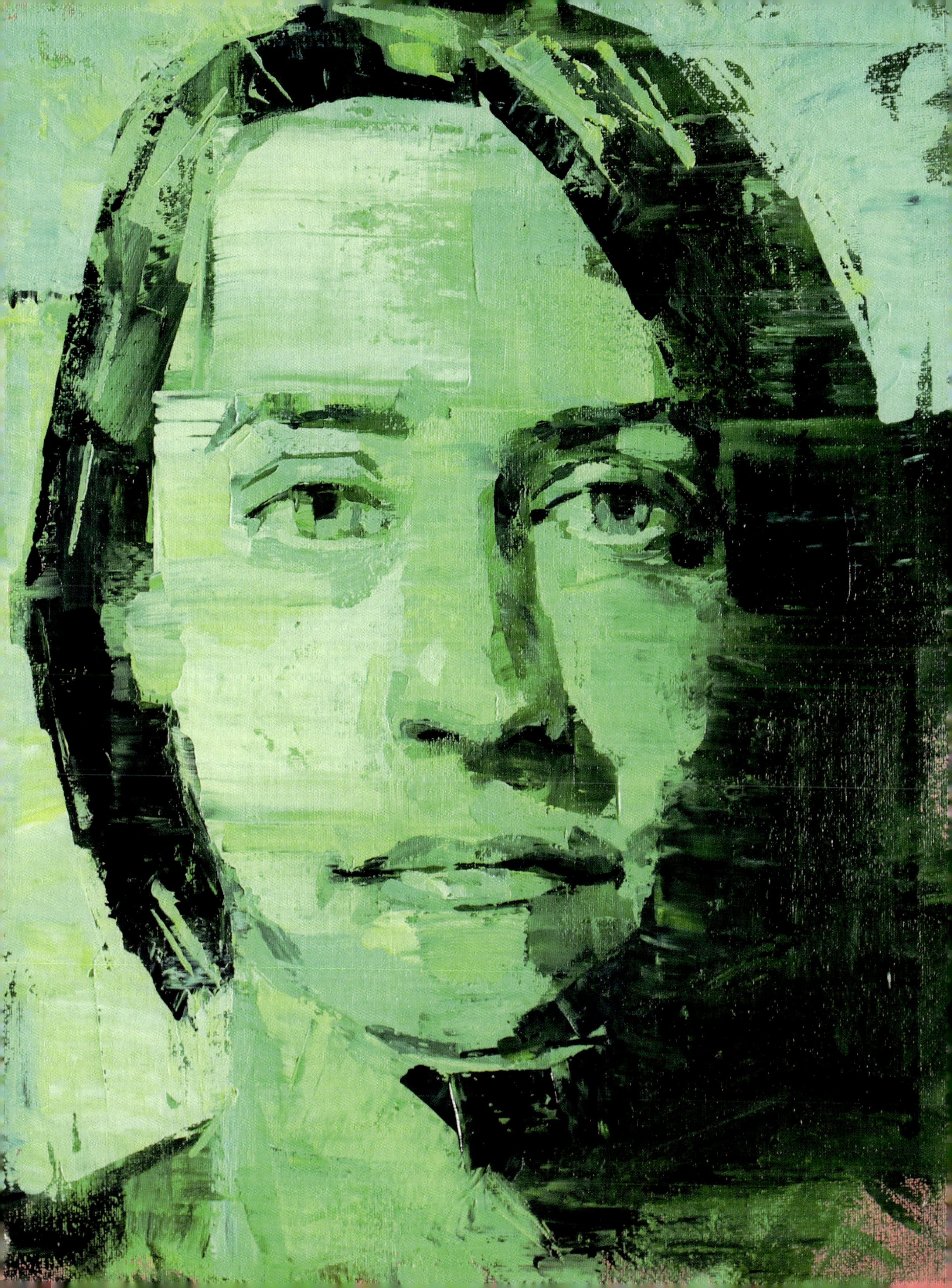

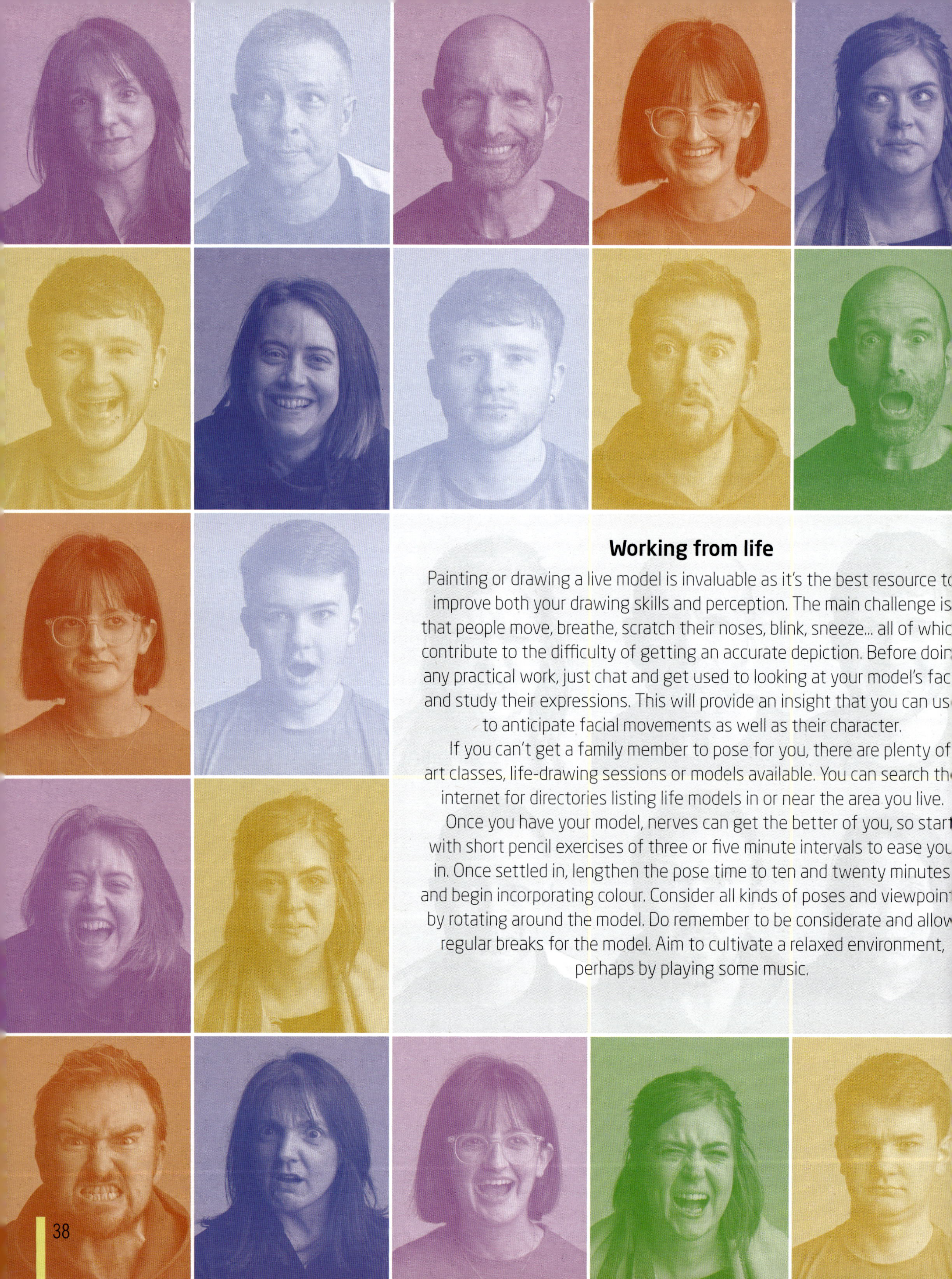

Working from life

Painting or drawing a live model is invaluable as it's the best resource to improve both your drawing skills and perception. The main challenge is that people move, breathe, scratch their noses, blink, sneeze... all of which contribute to the difficulty of getting an accurate depiction. Before doing any practical work, just chat and get used to looking at your model's face and study their expressions. This will provide an insight that you can use to anticipate facial movements as well as their character.

If you can't get a family member to pose for you, there are plenty of art classes, life-drawing sessions or models available. You can search the internet for directories listing life models in or near the area you live.

Once you have your model, nerves can get the better of you, so start with short pencil exercises of three or five minute intervals to ease you in. Once settled in, lengthen the pose time to ten and twenty minutes and begin incorporating colour. Consider all kinds of poses and viewpoints by rotating around the model. Do remember to be considerate and allow regular breaks for the model. Aim to cultivate a relaxed environment, perhaps by playing some music.

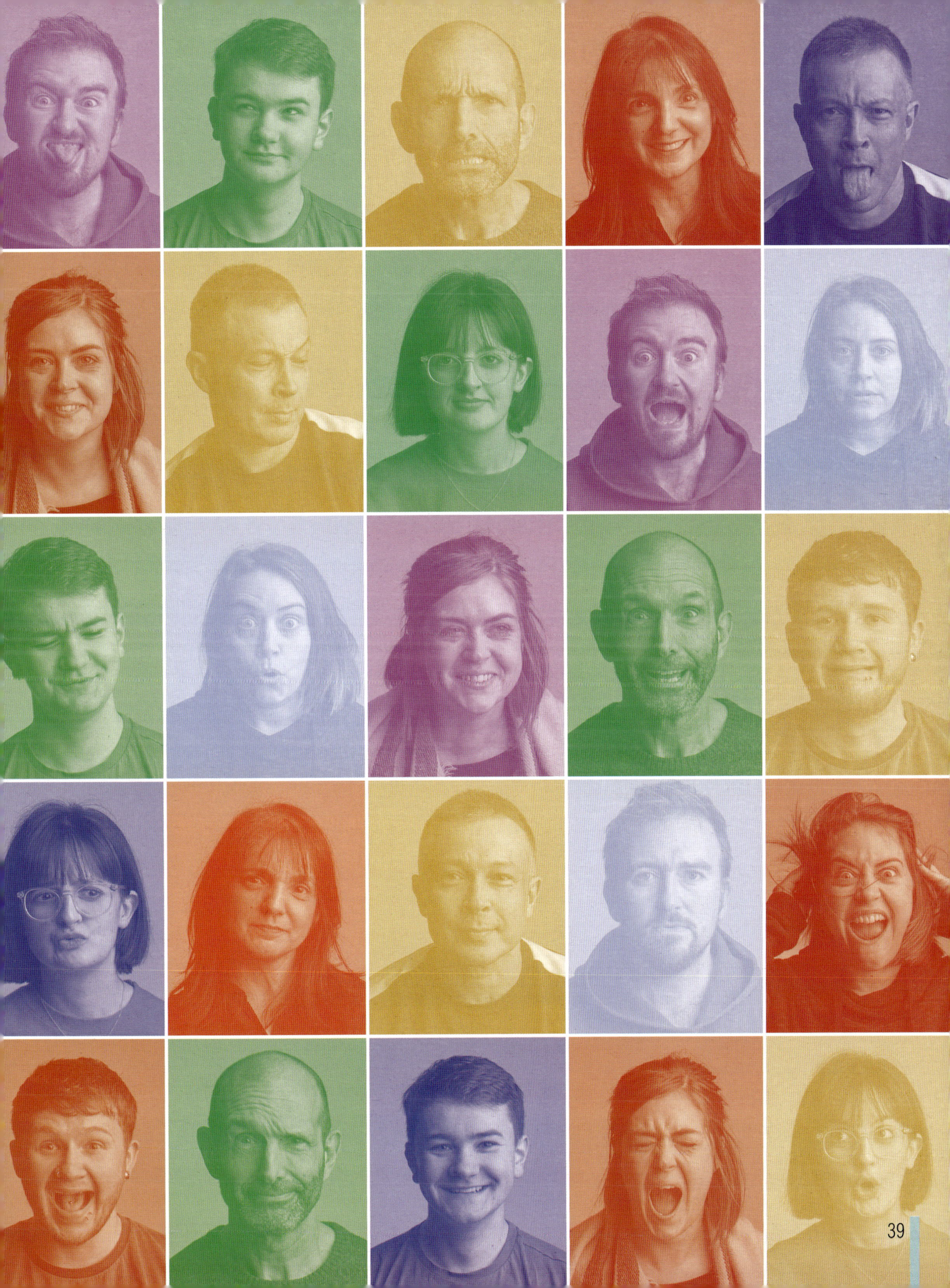

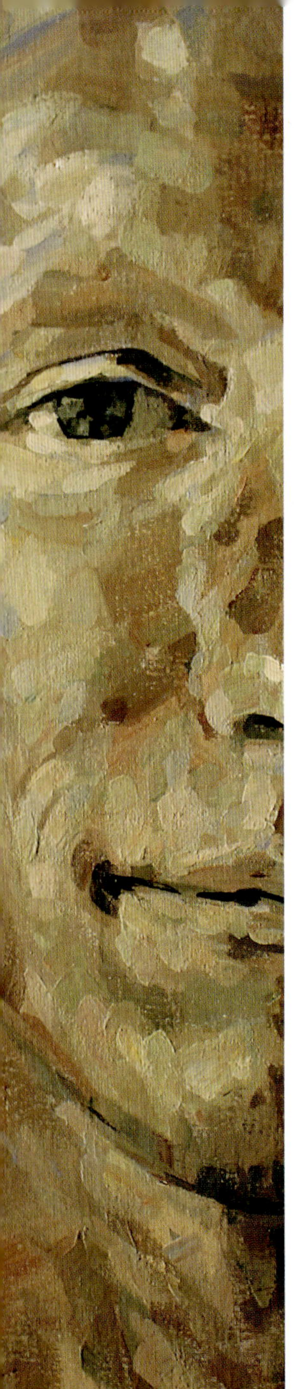

A face that tells a story

Part of the appeal of portrait painting is the story each and every face conveys. We can read the literal cues of skin, eyes, hair colour, proportions or levels of attractiveness, and we can make assumptions regarding what we don't see. Charisma is difficult to convey in a two-dimensional image, but we can get close to reflecting qualities such as a subject's shyness; emotions like anger, sadness, or happiness; and whether the subject is an introvert or extrovert.

When you begin taking up portraiture, you will find yourself scrutinizing faces a lot more closely. You'll latch onto particular features of interest – and it may not necessarily be the eyes. You'll take notice of face shapes or how elements like facial hair or spectacles can sometimes disguise interesting features.

It's not all about being young and gorgeous, either. Smooth, younger faces can present an expanse of colour which makes accuracy in locating the features a bit tricky, while wrinkles are an artist's best friend in portraiture: they help to create the line work to plot accurate measurements, in turn helping to create an effective hook.

Your imagination is important to nurture, so get to know the face and you can imagine the story behind it.

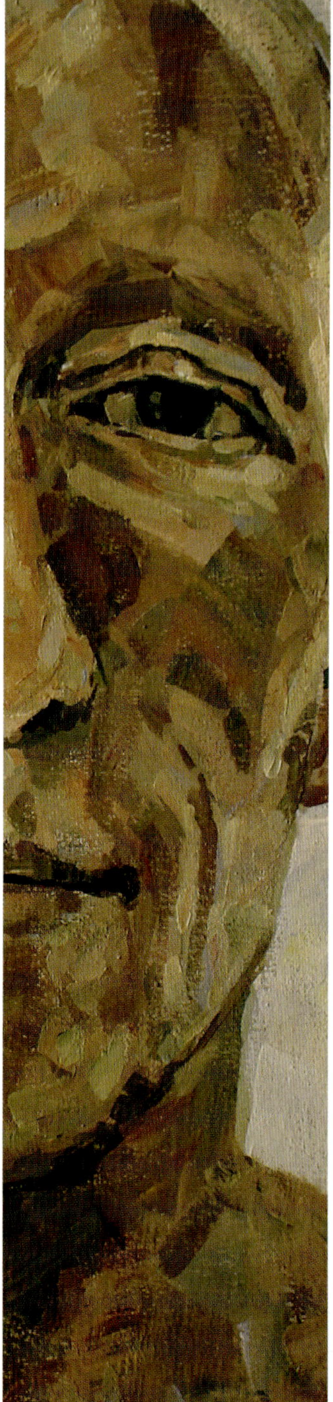

This is a quick study of Len, whom I met at an art group where I was demonstrating. Len has a great face for portraiture and his underlying confidence and easygoing nature added to the appeal. It's his handlebar moustache that was the main draw. At times it won't be an accumulation of things but one element of the subject's face that grabs your attention.

For the painting, I avoided any drawing and dived straight in with blocks of colours. His features were roughly implied and refined at the end. A dozen small lines suggest spectacles and the moustache creates an interesting semicircle in the lower half of the face. Less taxing portraits like this lift and build your confidence for challenges to come.

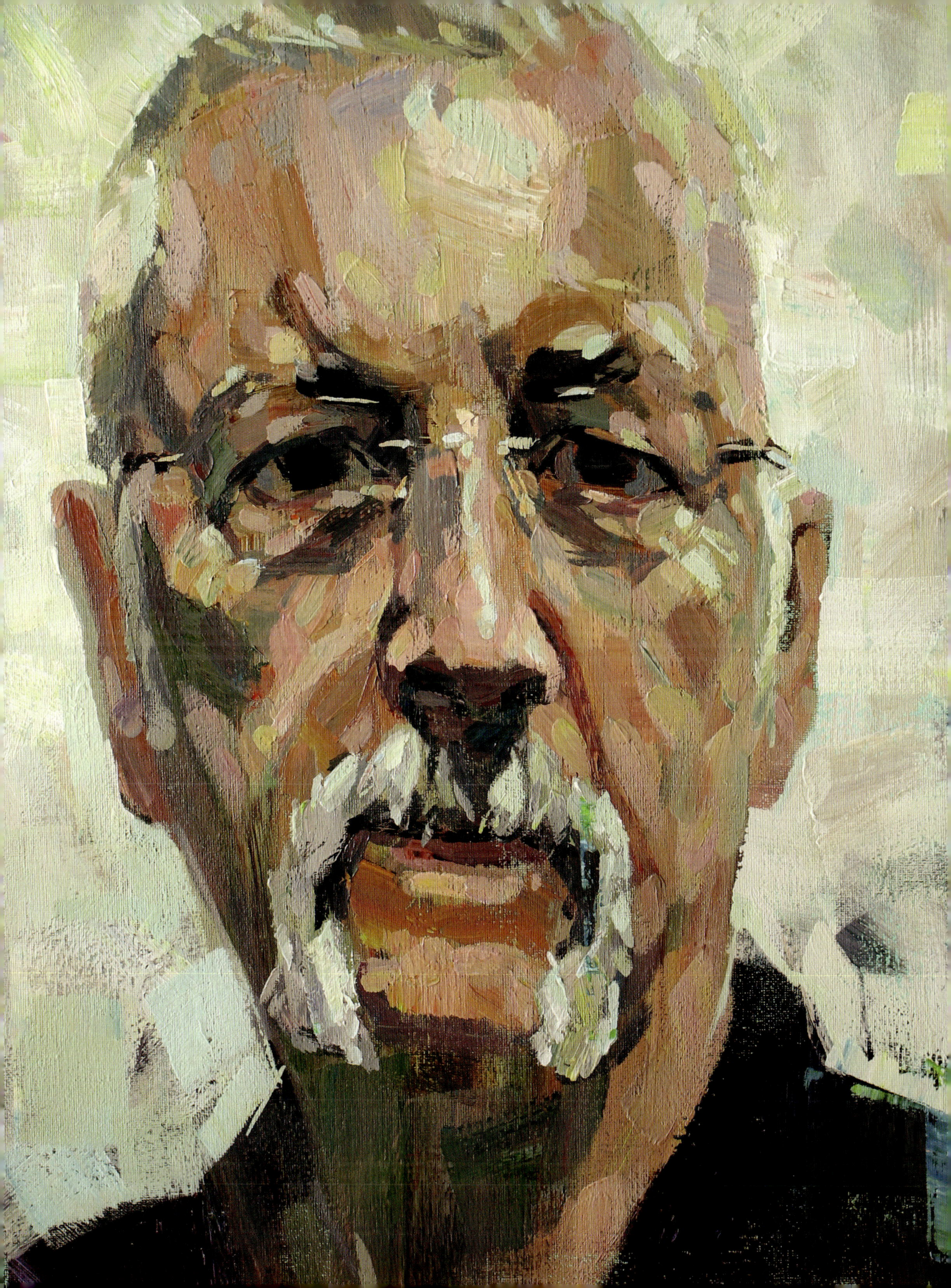

Skin, marks and character

Something with history or imperfections is always far more interesting to paint than a brand new thing – an old car, rusty boat, or derelict building will have a unique character. Being compared to an old rusty boat isn't the height of flattery, but the idea of reflecting history is also true of faces.

This is a tricky area for artists as a subject's facial quirk, disfigurement, blemish or wrinkle may be the element that draws you in. In my experience, it's no surprise that most models want what they consider their less flattering features underplayed. If you paint or draw realistically you'll probably soften the unwanted elements, and this can risk pandering to the sitter at the expense of the portrait. If the sitter has views on particular features, you are free to take them on board and make a choice to underplay them or to keep them in, as they add an historical dimension or characterful element to the painting.

See everything in abstract

I paint a multitude of subjects and the one thing they all have in common is that everything is seen and treated as an abstract. Whether painting a face, a cloud, a car or a bottle, everything can be reduced to shape, tone, line or colour. It's all the same.

In portraiture these would be the same considerations given to scars, birthmarks, moles or spots. Consider them as abstract forms that will enhance, diminish or add no value to the portrait.

A more expressive style creates the opportunity to integrate random marks. Mark making or colour can then be used to make creative statements or reflect a personality. It's worth mentioning that some of the most well-known contemporary figurative artists showcase human imperfections, including weight, scars and wrinkles.

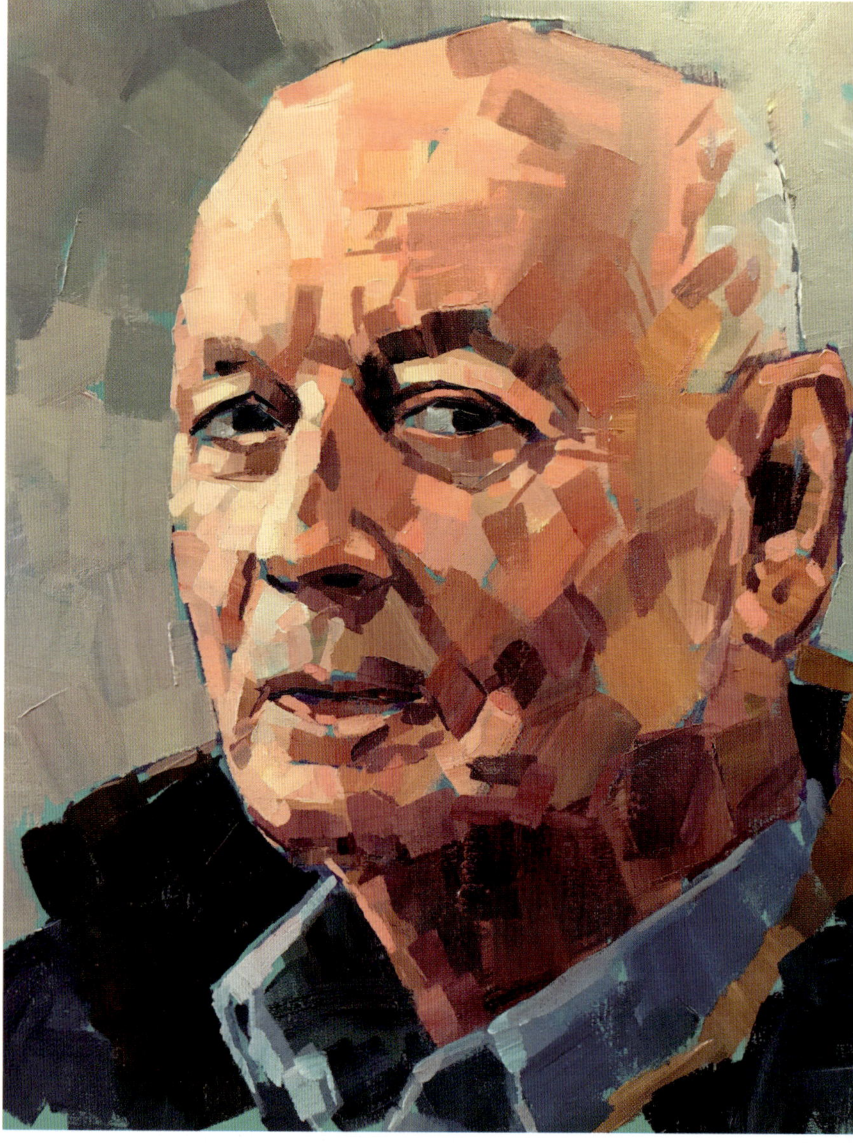

GORDON 50×70cm (20×27½in)

If you paint in a blocky or expressive style this will naturally create the appearance of age. Any refined mark or line in a drawing or painting is more pronounced than it appears in a photograph. Replicating every wrinkle will age the face excessively, so make certain choices and pick the most prominent. Avoid the temptation to blend lines in too much, and retain some rougher transitions.

To evoke the sense of age without picking out every line, apply your lines or blocks unfussily. Constantly reworking them draws unwanted attention and dulls the paint. When mixing colours remember that acrylics dry darker and what may appear correct initially will darken off.

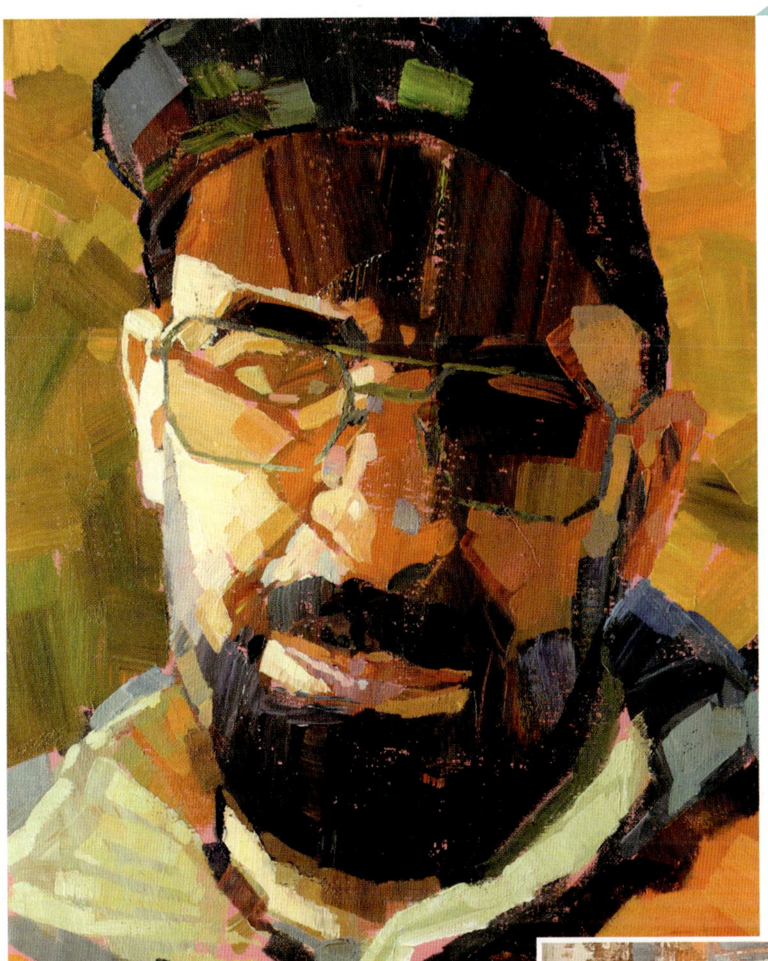

GEORGI #2 35.5×46CM (14×18IN)

This example simplifies the portrait into almost graphic blocks of colour. While painting, I stripped the details back to the highlighted areas, to avoid me scrutinizing the entire face. What information remained I tried to convey accurately, but I left the more abstract spaces open for the viewer to interpret.

BRIAN 61×76CM (24×30IN)

In this example the brushmarks in the face are balanced with even more dramatic applications in the background. This way the attention is spread outwards. Contrasting colours add to the interest.

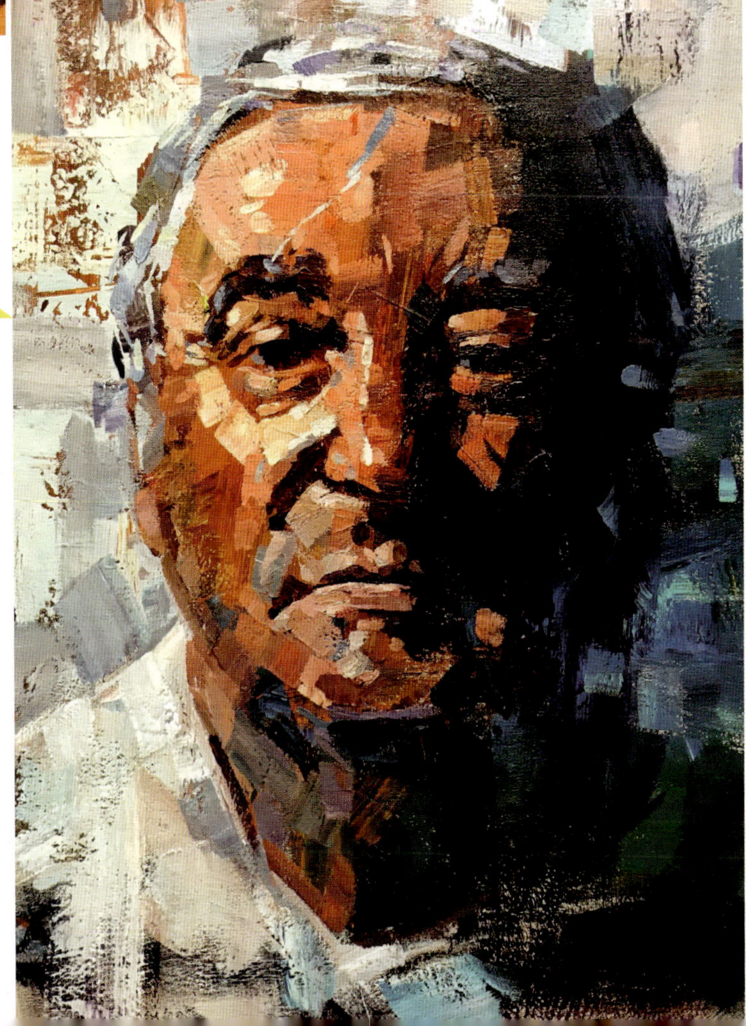

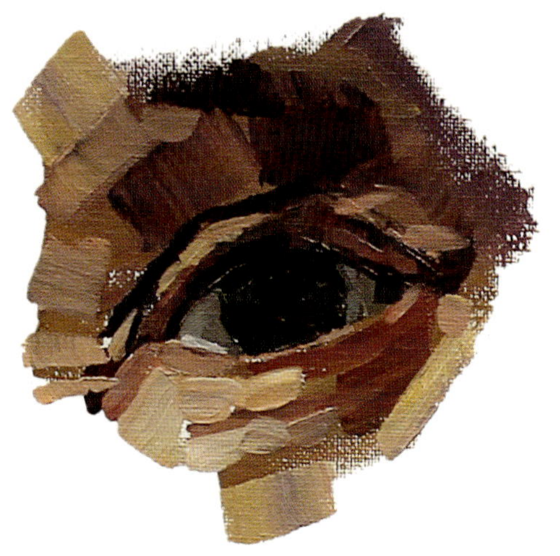

Facial features

The individual elements that make up a face can be tricky enough, so it's worth spending some time practising different component parts in isolation. Eye, ear, nose and mouth shapes differ between genders and nationalities, but avoid stereotypes which can make the creative process a lazy one. Contrary to cultural or marketing ideals, some women have thin, tight lips or hard, angular faces; some men have dainty little noses and large, appealing eyes.

The facial features of individuals from the same region can likewise vary dramatically, so treat every artistic endeavour as if you're seeing the human face for the first time. My own parentage is a mix of Malaysian and English, which creates all kinds of drawing and colour mixing challenges. Avoid logic's definition of what something is – whether it's an ear, nose, mouth or skin – and look for the creative definition in shapes, tones and colour.

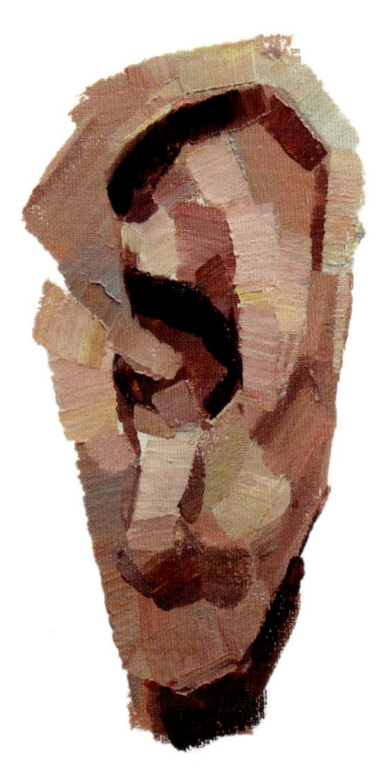

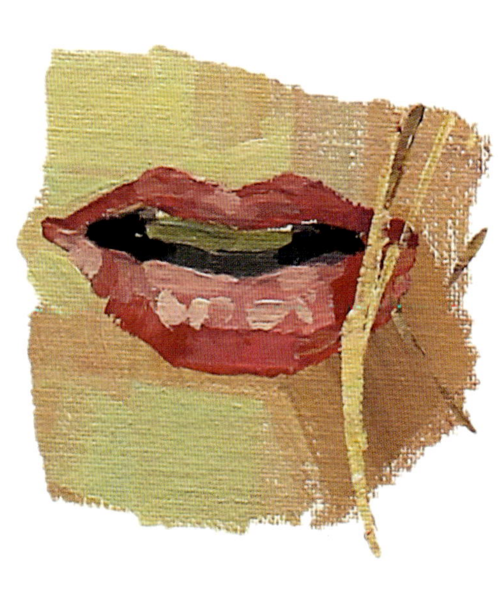

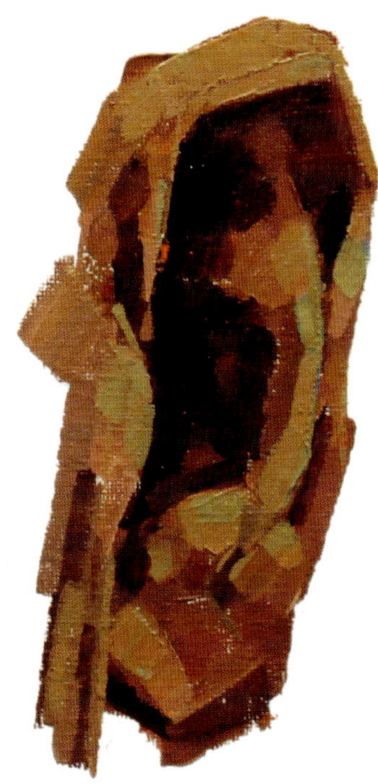

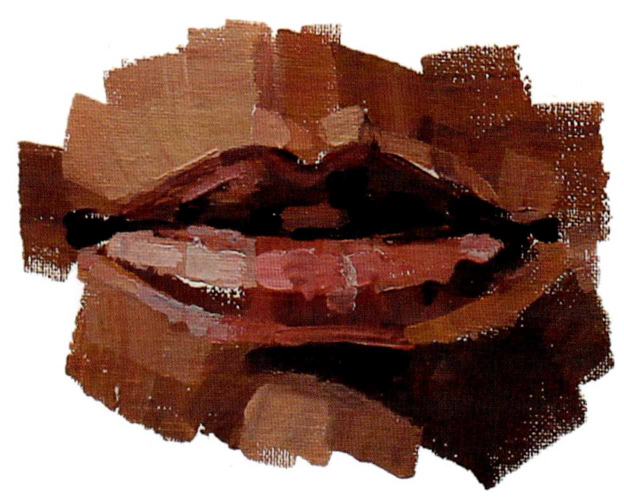

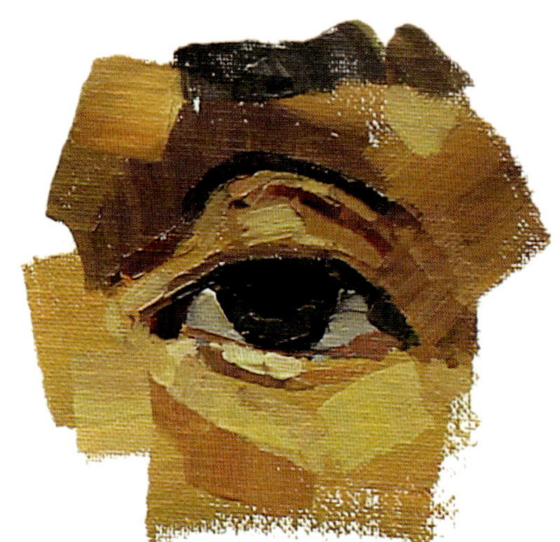

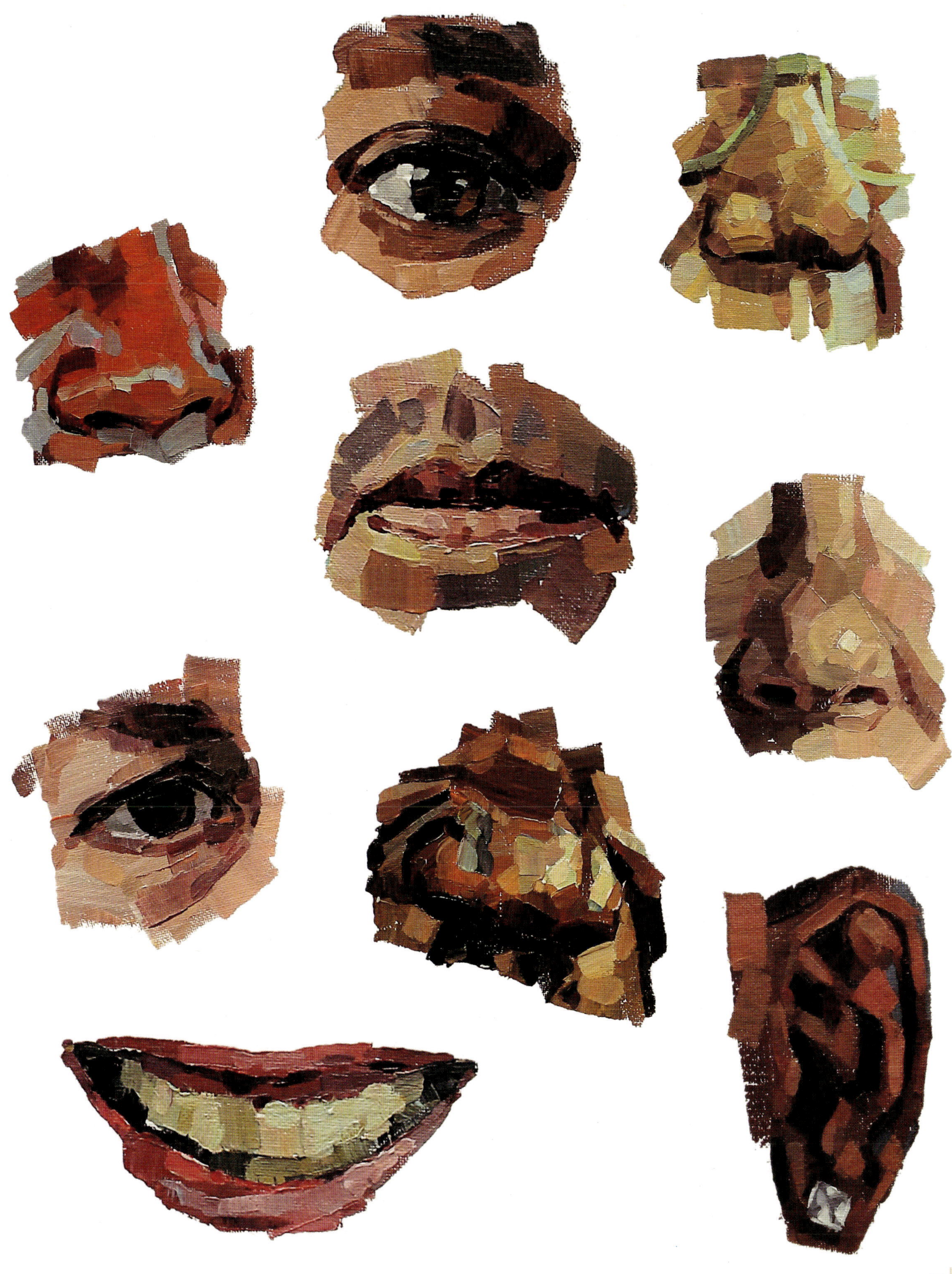

Mood and atmosphere

You need to make decisions about the way you'll represent your subject. Before painting a portrait, you need to consider the pose, light, environment and colours used. These make up the mechanics of each painting. The more you immerse yourself in portraiture, the bigger part each of the components listed will play. Sometimes you might feel that the reference material does it all for you, and your aim will be just to reproduce it, but there will always remain aspects that require personal interpretation. Mood and atmosphere are examples of such abstract concepts, quite separate from mechanics such as colour or pose, and less definable than concrete elements like how the features are arranged or mixing the right skin tones.

When considering any abstract element for a painting, remember an experience or something you've seen that triggered an emotional response similar to the one you want to include. This could be music you listen to, a film you've seen, or a book you've read. Painting is not just about visual ideas, but emotional ones as well. When painting or drawing anything, commit to both technique and emotion equally.

Painting *Csaba*

The portrait opposite looks relatively simple as there are no elements besides the figure's profile. It avoids flattery but elicits some kind of mood. The subject's determined gaze off-canvas implies that there's something more important than engaging with the viewer. The stark light produces strong tonal contrasts and, rather then looking into the light, the figure's gaze leads into the darkest area of the painting. This shrouds the face in shadows, adding to the mystery.

Colours automatically evoke an emotional response and traditional portraiture almost always veers toward warmer hues, as we find them comforting. In contrast, here a cool grey-blue background leads us to the light yellows and reds that light up the face, creating a slightly unsettling feel. Greys are also used in the hair and tattoos to unify the colours. The model, Csaba, is a young man, but I've avoided excessive blending of skin tones that might flatter a younger complexion and instead left exposed brushmarks to reflect a raw grittiness.

CSABA 46×61cm (18×24in)

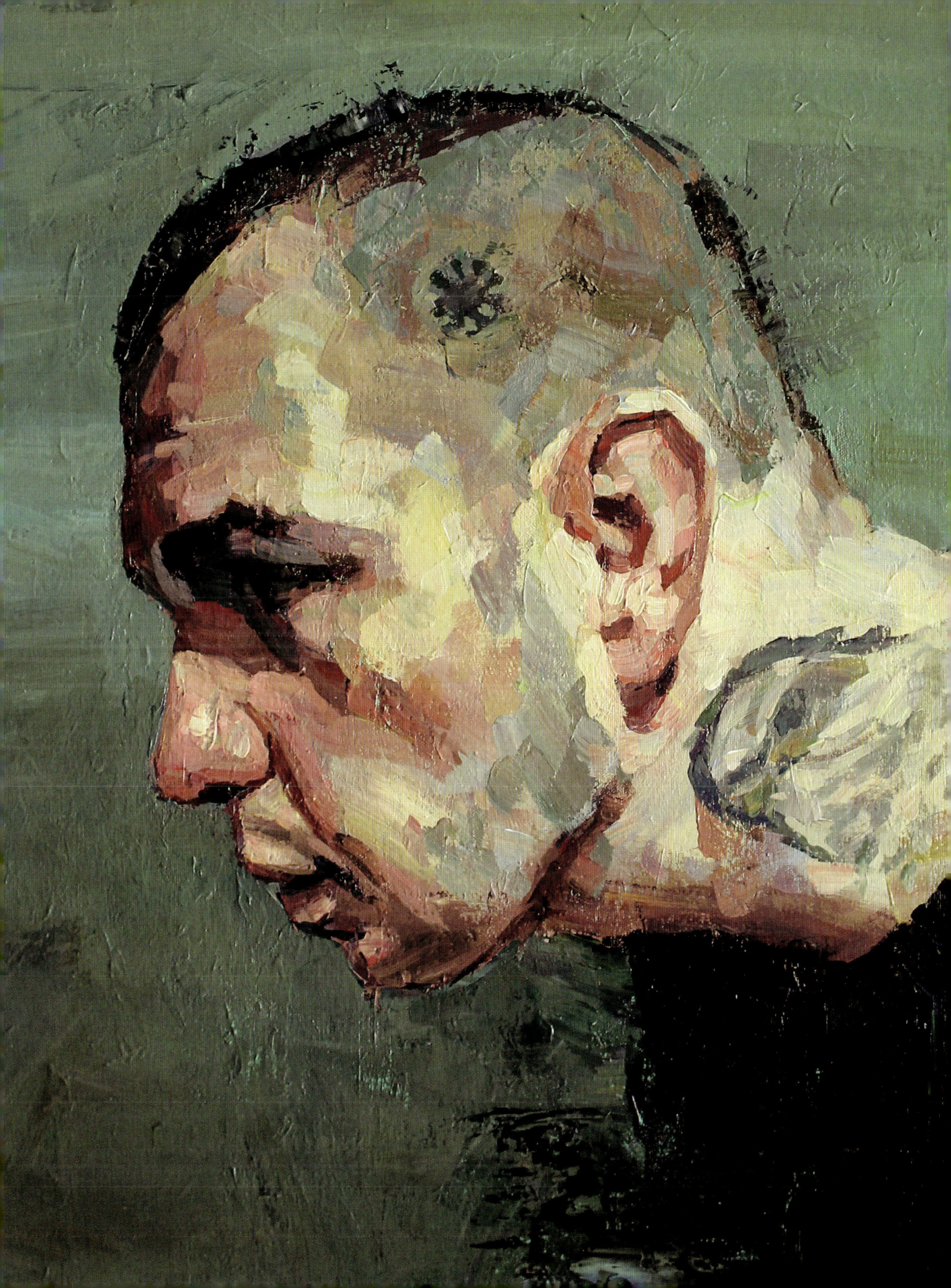

Your style

Generally speaking, artists find a process that suits them, rather than adapting their approach to individual subjects. This creates a consistency in the painting process and recognizable 'visual trademarks'. For example, I prefer very direct forms of painting, which is reflected in the way I apply paint and my use of strong colour. Although my paintings are representational, details are kept to the minimum; and the portrait relies on the viewer to interact and finish certain visual sentences. This way of painting suits my temperament and echoes my artistic influences.

Finding your own personal statements begins with your understanding of the basic mechanics of drawing and painting. This is the base on which to build experience and confidence for more personal interpretations to flourish later on. It is difficult to resist influences from other artists whose perfected style would be easier to adopt. I'm all for trying to mimic other artists' work for a period, as you'll gain invaluable insights into working methods, but avoid permanently becoming a carbon copy. Think of any well-known artist and it's their unique creative outlook that makes the art stand out.

One reason why personal style is important is the well-worn tropes in portraiture that flood galleries and art books: young women in red dresses looking forlorn, clasping hands, or numerous ballet or flamenco dancers. These are extremely popular scenes to paint but so overused they risk being dull or clichéd. Developing your personal style is a way to add a few fresh twists to a composition or technique and make it something striking and effective.

Tell me

In order not to be overly reliant on any reference material or overly influenced by another artist, make sure your paintings say one or two things about the subject or process that are personal to you. That way your art will start to become recognizable and a style will emerge. For some this is quite difficult, as it's always easier following a guide rather than carve your own path, so here are some starting points:

- Add odd shots of colour in less important areas
- Incorporate marks which are less blended or polished than the rest
- Change a background colour
- Leave a sketchier feel to a painting
- Look for elements in a scene that you want to add or take out.

Remember that it is your interpretation, so start establishing a greater creative foothold.

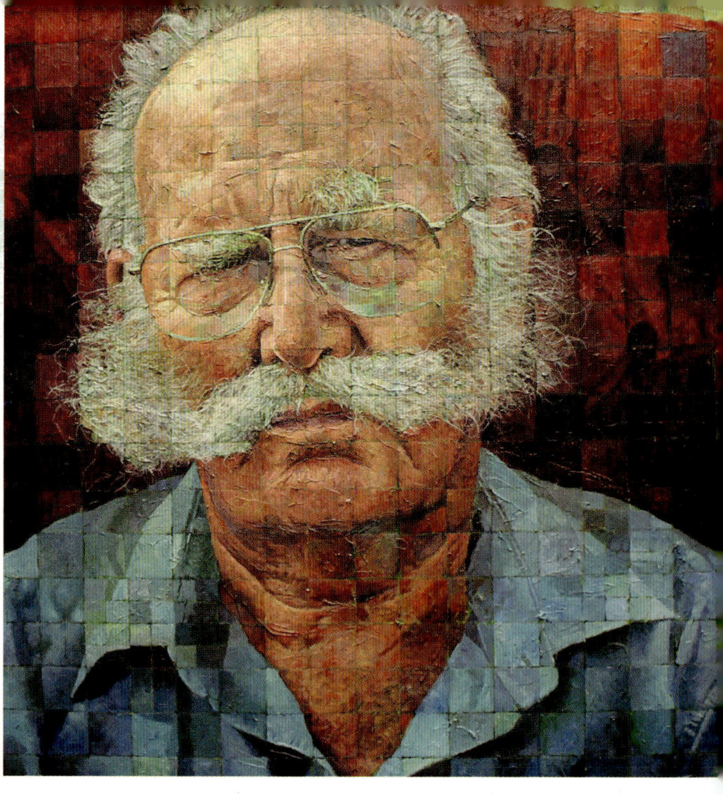

BRUCE, OLD STYLE 76×76CM (30×30IN)

Painted early in my career, at a time when I was preoccupied with detail. Every section of canvas was broken into small squares, each given the same level of scrutiny. This process was less about enjoying the act of painting and more about the relief in finishing it; and is part of why my style developed.

FRANK 36×46CM (14×18IN)

This painting shows my current loose, expressive style. The exposed and varied brushmarks reflect the process as well as the subject. The sketchy feel reflects the hour or so I spent painting it and exudes more vitality than one obsessed over for weeks.

With that said, the time spent agonizing over drawing and painting mechanics did help me build a firm foundation on which to develop a new, more personal style later on.

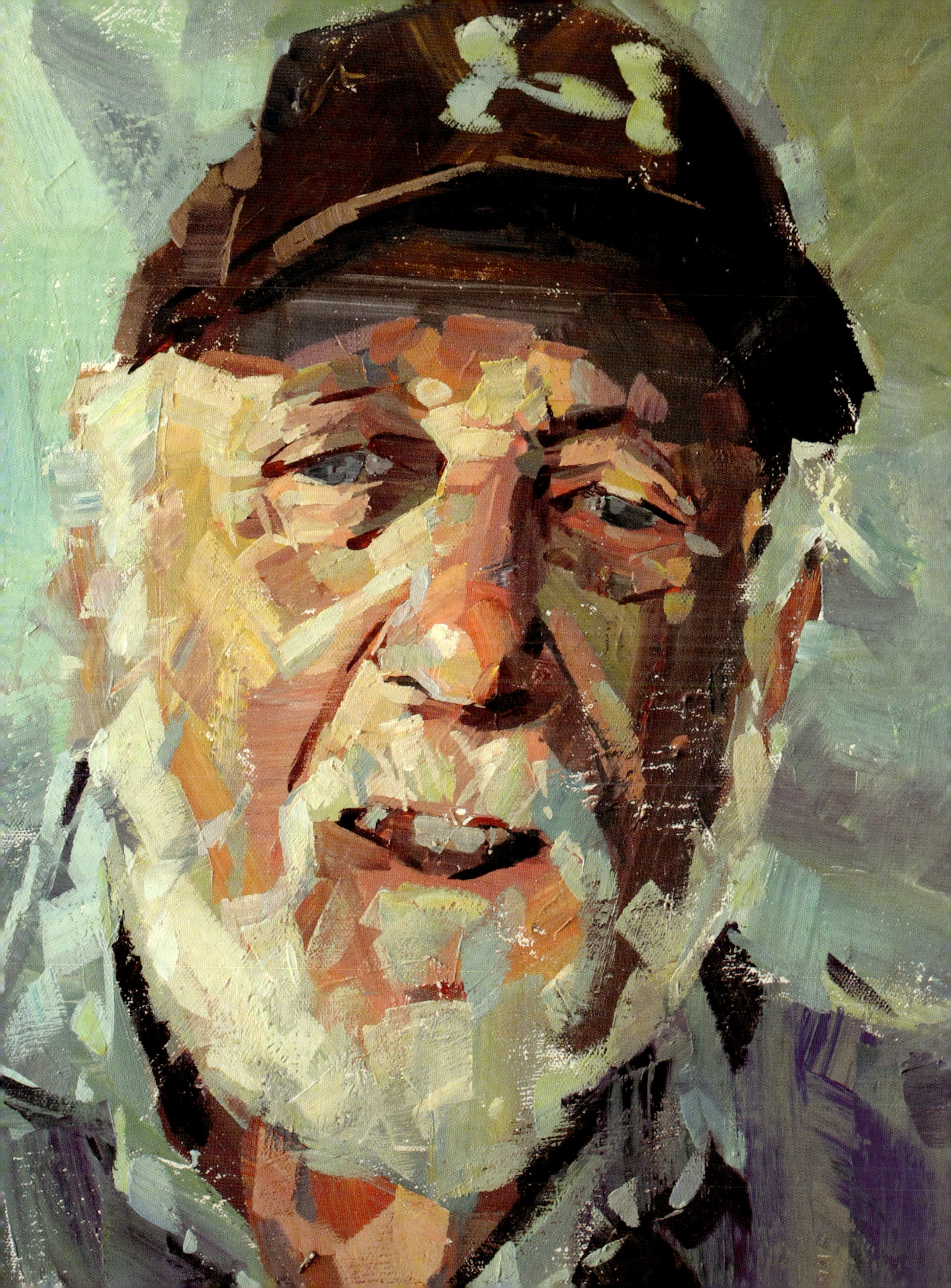

Older faces are such a great place to start with portrait painting. There's so much more interest with character lines and variations in colour.

The large flat head brushes that I recommend provide a sculptural feel and almost showcase a face moulded over time. Grey hair is an interesting challenge and reflects surrounding colour more than just mixing black and white.

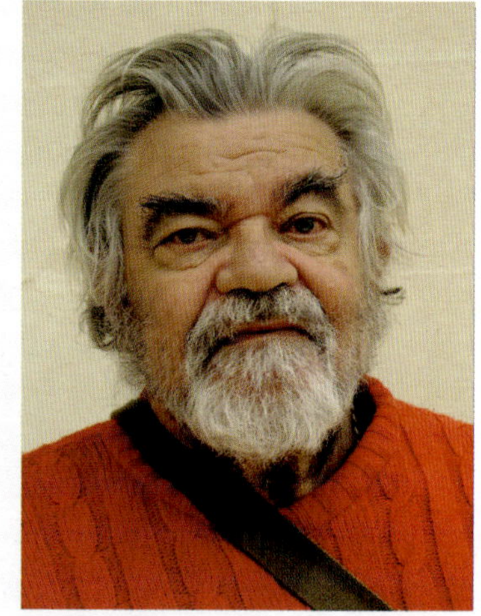

The source photograph.

YOU WILL NEED

Brushes: 50mm (2in) flat, 37mm (1½in) flat, 25mm (1in) flat, 16mm (¾in) flat

Paints: Titanium white, sky blue, permanent lemon yellow, permanent yellow medium, permanent lemon yellow, king's blue, pyrrole red, burnt sienna, yellowish green, cadmium orange, permanent blue violet opaque, permanent blue violet, sap green, phthalo blue, quinacridone rose, quinacridone rose opaque, turquoise blue, turquoise green, cobalt blue, yellow ochre, Prussian blue

Surface: Canvas board, 51×61cm (20×24in)

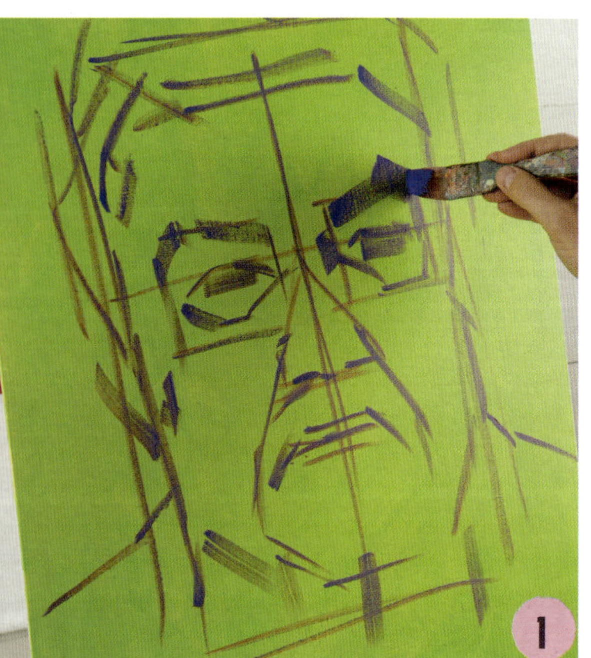

1 Starting on a field of yellowish-green, use a 25mm (1in) brush with permanent blue violet opaque to establish your framework. Make sure you get the subtle angle of the head correct. Older faces tend to have stronger features and more obvious lines, which gives you a good route into the portrait.

2 Using a damp 37mm (1½in) flat, pick up titanium white on the tip. Dip the loaded brush successively into yellow ochre, pyrrole red, cadmium orange, quinacridone rose, quinacridone rose opaque, creating a multi-layered mix on the brush itself. Pick up small amounts of cooler colours – sap green and yellowish-greens, along with King's blue.

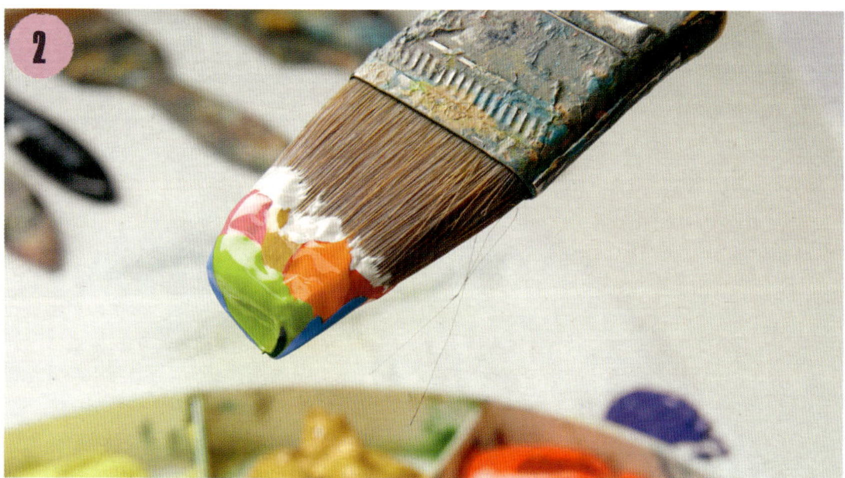

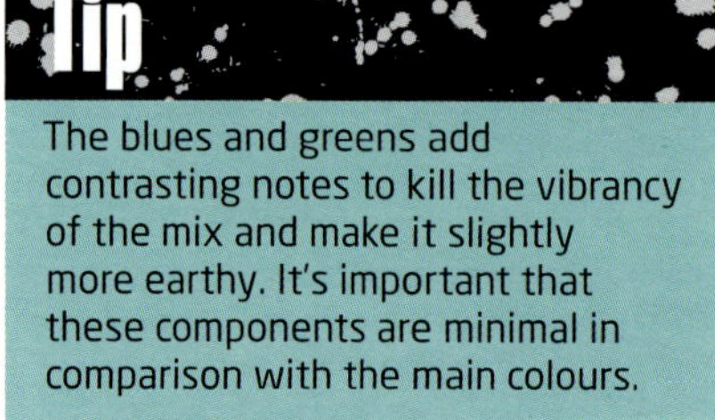

Tip

The blues and greens add contrasting notes to kill the vibrancy of the mix and make it slightly more earthy. It's important that these components are minimal in comparison with the main colours.

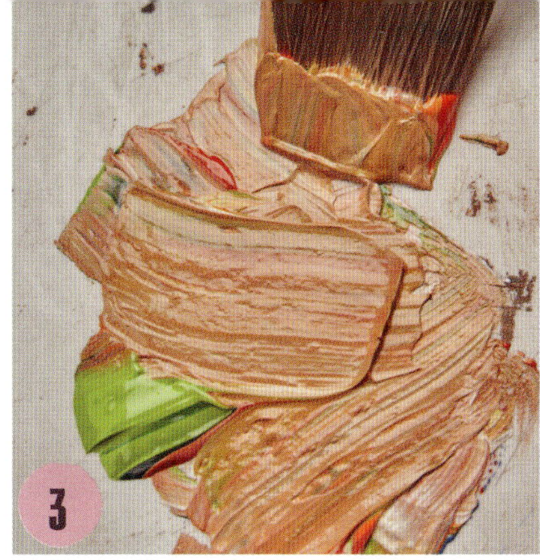

3 Make small, light marks on your palette, drawing the brush a short way to see how the colours interact. We're looking for an overall pinky-ochre tint to the base skin mix. Reload the brush with the same balance of colours and build up a good well of the mix on your palette. Do not mix the colours if possible; use light touches to deposit the paint on the palette.

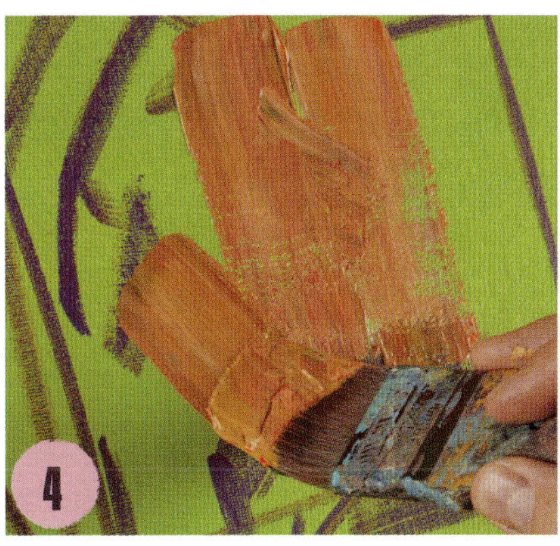

4 Look for large areas to fill in and begin to paint with this base flesh tint. Start by using the paint on the brush to block in the forehead with clean, angular strokes.

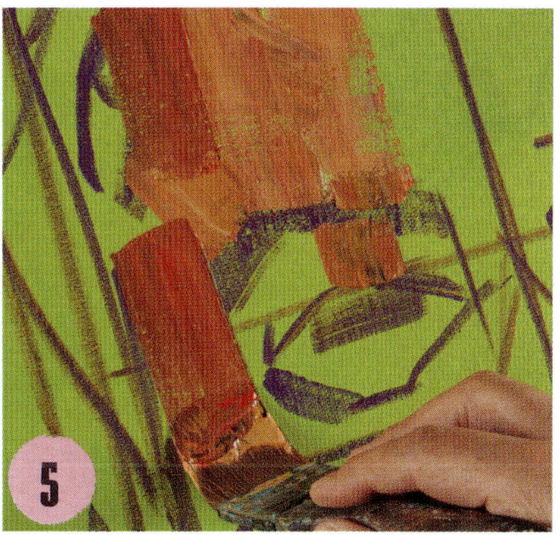

5 As you work into the shadows on the left-hand side, add permanent blue violet opaque and permanent blue violet to an area of the pool of colour, keeping most of the pool the original colour.

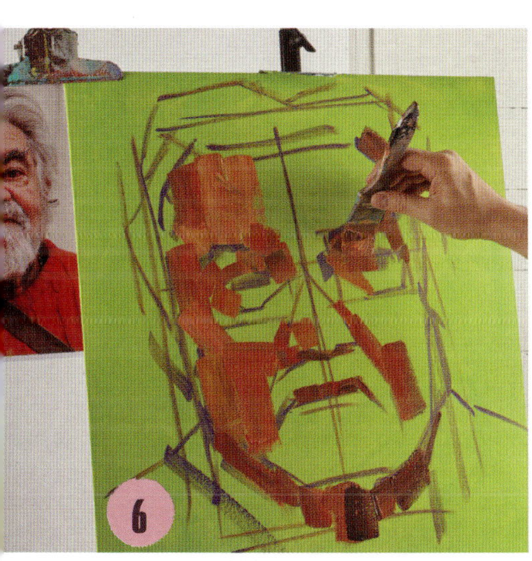

6 Continue to build up the skin tone across the face with broad, confident strokes. Use plenty of paint. Each stroke should almost completely cover the green underpainting, and the individual colours blend together as you move the brush. Still using the 37mm (1½in) brush, block in the eyes as pools of the overall colour – a reddish-brown here.

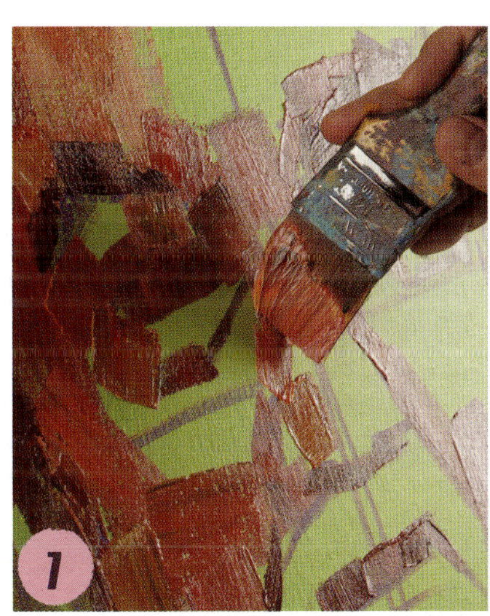

7 Using the features for reference, look for particular hues coming to the fore. The bridge of the nose, for example, is redder that the surrounding skin, so use an area of the pool on your palette that contains more red – or pick up more red hues (such as pyrrole red) as you reload your brush.

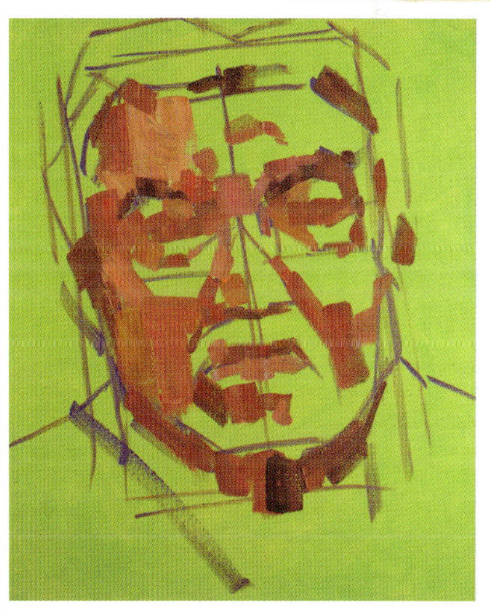

The portrait at the end of this stage

This way of painting will naturally cause certain isolated touches of colour – that is, the component paints – to emerge here and there. Embrace this – they will add to the overall harmony of the painting and make sure it hangs together as a whole. As you work, jump around the face. Where similar colours and tones appear on different areas, use the same load of paint. Again, this helps to ensure that any variation in hue that occurs isn't isolated to a particular area.

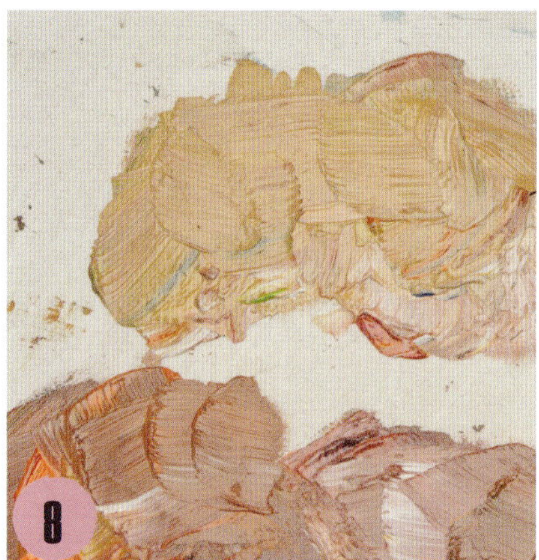

8 With most of the midtones across the face in place, begin to build up the highlights. Create a new pool nearby on your palette, as described earlier. Use the same colours, but this time with more titanium white and yellowish green. This bright green is important to diffuse the red and also to tint the hue: as it has a yellow component, it brightens the mix.

9 When applying the paint, use dynamic marks to create big, blocky strokes at different angles – this helps to create a sense of age and texture to the skin, rather than the smoothness of youth.

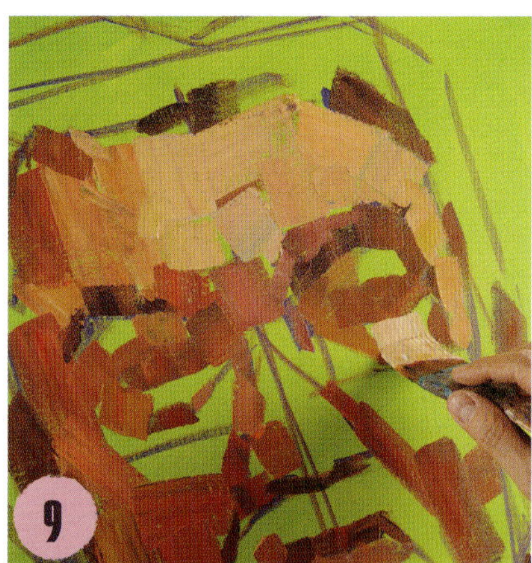

10 Once the initial highlights are in place – mostly in the upper right-hand side of the painting, but remember to dot some of the same mix elsewhere – begin to bring in strokes that use a combination of both main pools: the base skin pool and the highlight pool.

11 Utilizing what you have on your palette, use any areas with grey-blue accents to bring some colour into the areas of hair. This will act as harmonizing shadow.

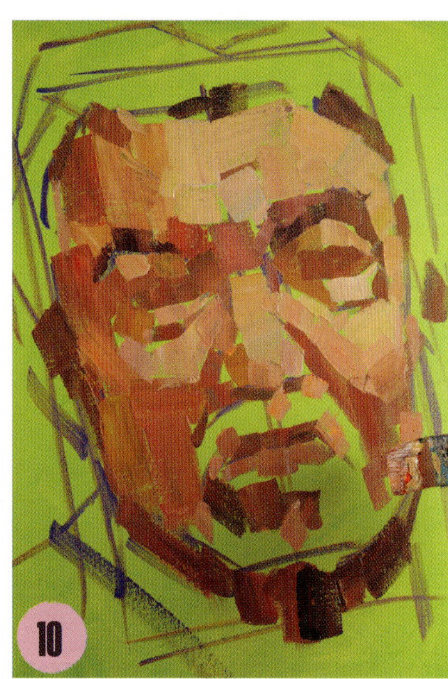

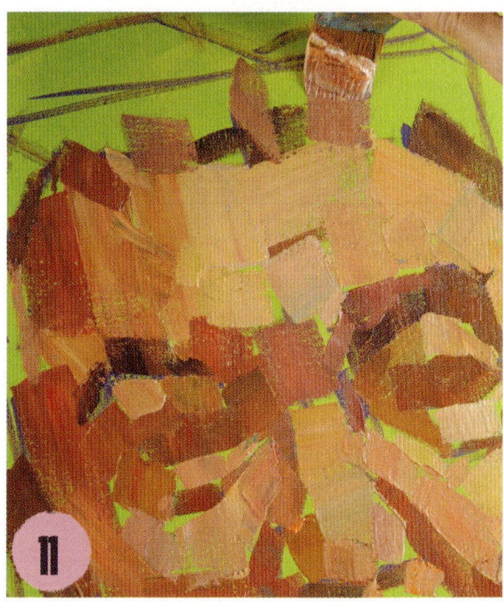

12 Without cleaning the brush, prepare a third pool that uses titanium white, king's blue and sap green for the hair.

13 Build up the mass of the hair using this pool. Aim for a patchwork of strokes that creates texture without necessarily indicating the direction of individual strands or locks of hair. Include the beard and eyebrows. To darken the hair pool, introduce more sap green and permanent blue violet as you reload the brush and refill the pool. Use this to develop the hair; chopping and changing the angles of the brush to get as much variation as possible.

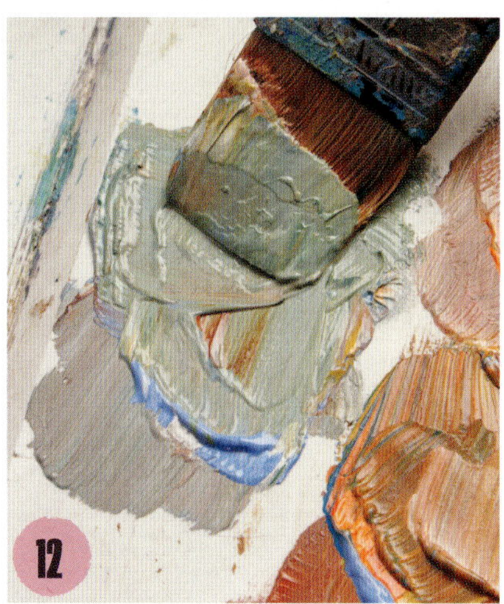

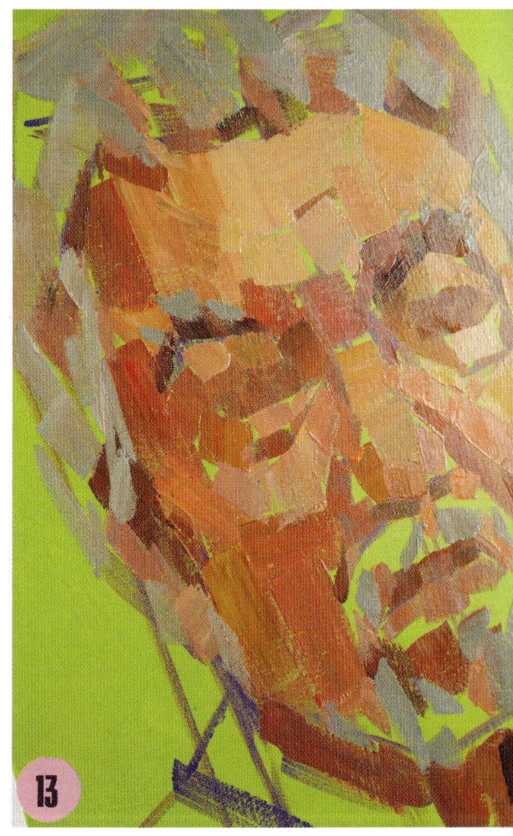

14 Make a new hair highlight pool from yellow ochre, titanium white, king's blue and yellowish green. Use this to develop and start to shape the hair – particularly the beard.

15 Add some small harmonizing touches to the skin using the hair highlights and skin highlight pools. These bridging marks help to soften the gaps between the main marks, and also cover more of the underlying green base layer. They can also be used in the background. These will mostly be covered, but will subtly help the background and face work together.

16 Block in his clothing with pyrrole red combined with a little sap green. Use a 50mm (2in) brush. Add king's blue for shading on the left-hand side, and hints of yellow ochre and titanium white on the right-hand side for highlighting.

17 For the background, use titanium white, yellow ochre and king's blue. Continue using the unwashed 50mm (2in) flat brush and dynamic marks. Introduce a little permanent blue violet opaque to the mix to give a subtle shift to the background on the left-hand side.

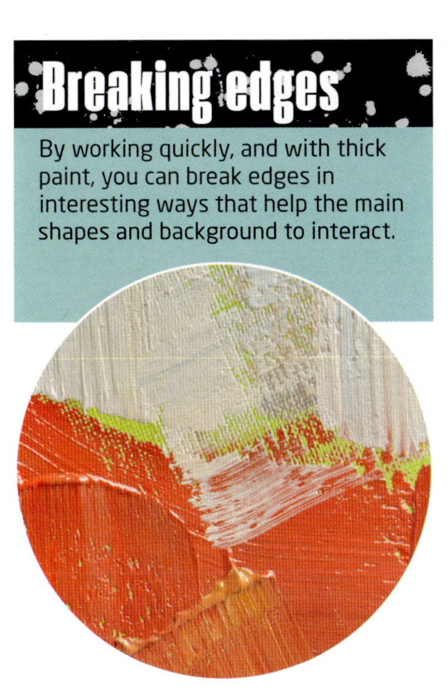

By working quickly, and with thick paint, you can break edges in interesting ways that help the main shapes and background to interact.

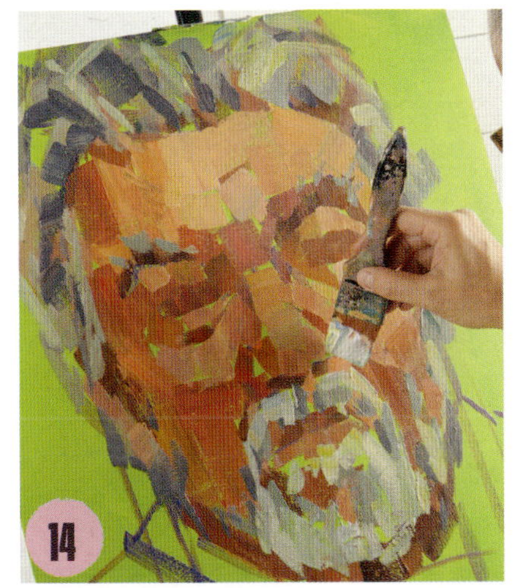

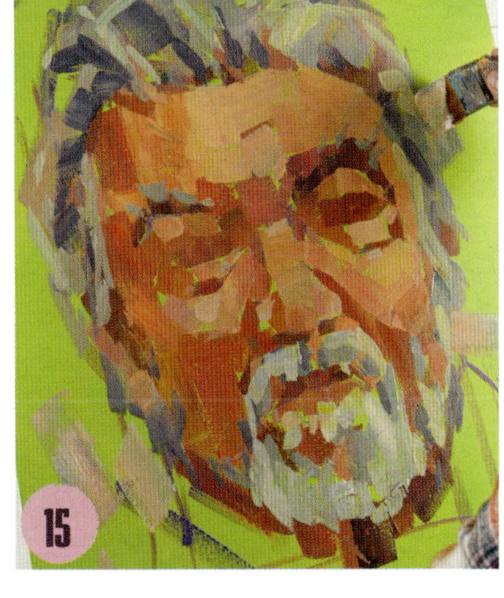

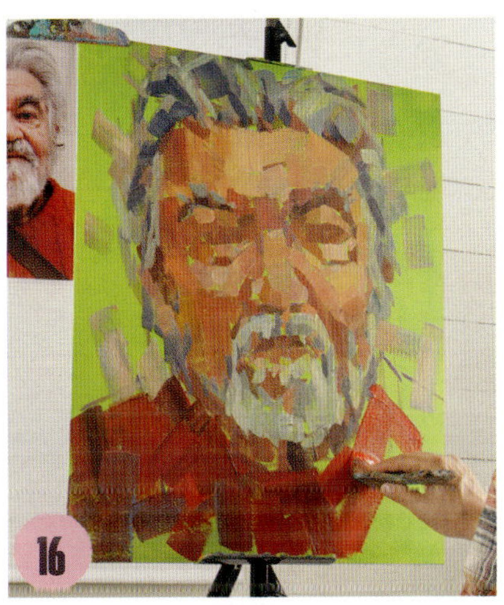

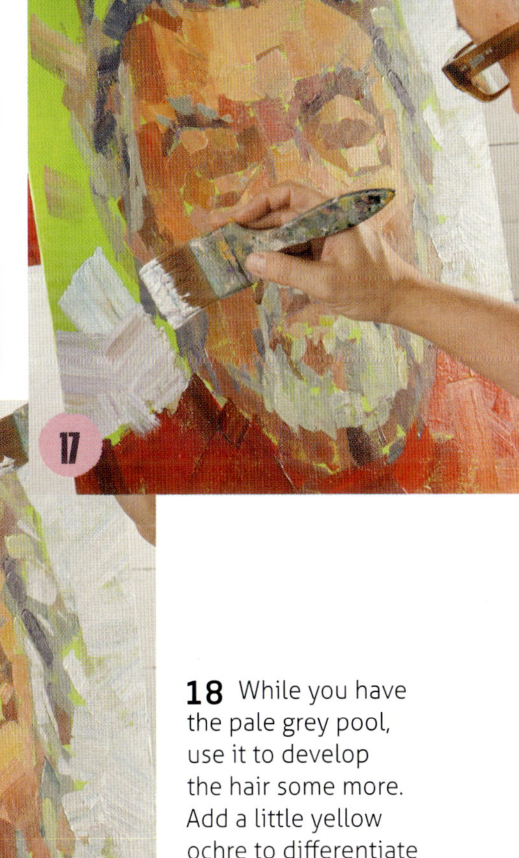

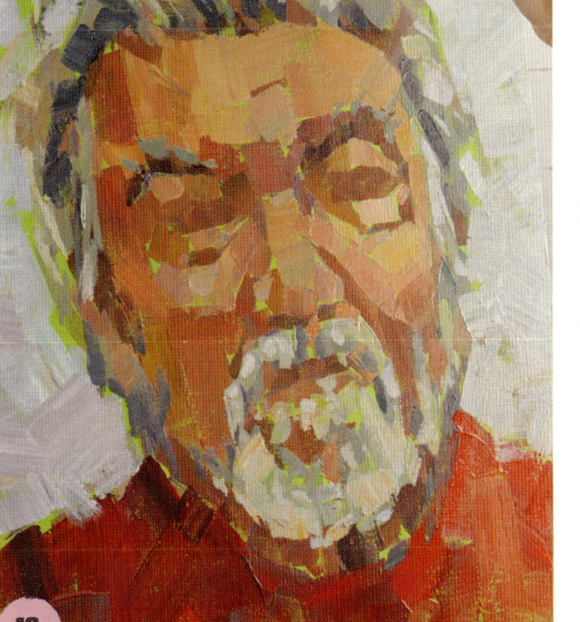

18 While you have the pale grey pool, use it to develop the hair some more. Add a little yellow ochre to differentiate the marks from the background.

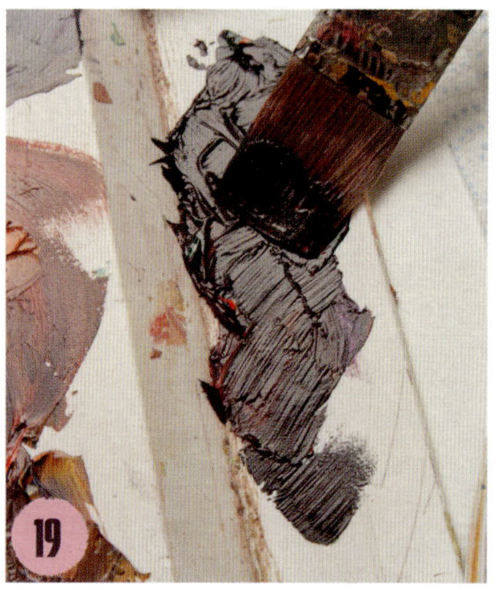

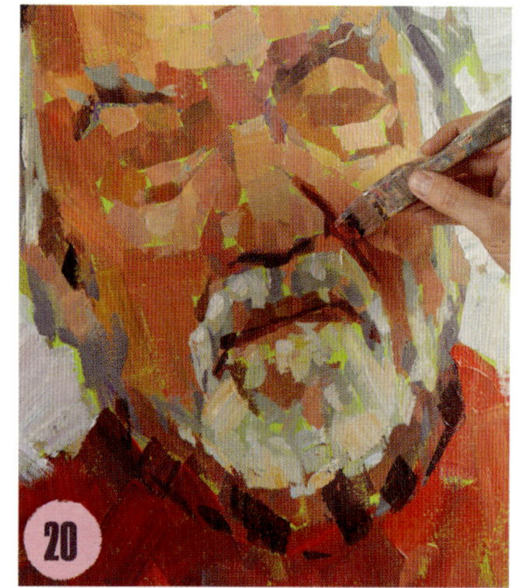

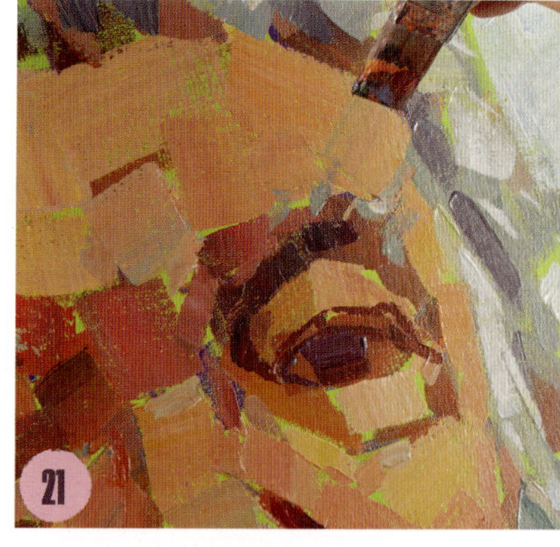

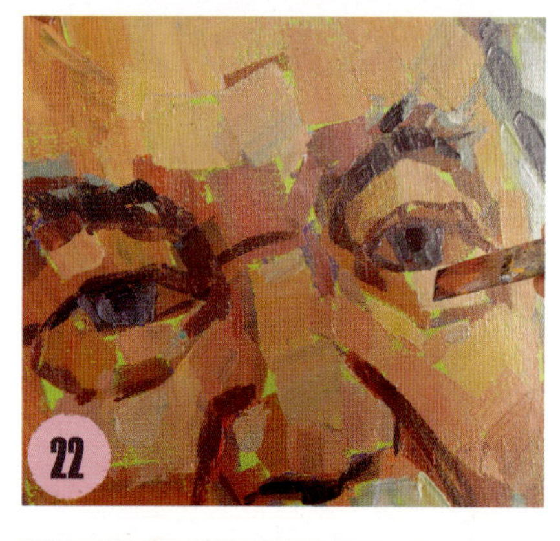

19 Swap to a 25mm (1in) flat brush. Using permanent blue violet opaque, sap green and burnt sienna, create a dark neutral pool.

20 Working slightly more slowly, add smaller, more considered marks to develop the dark areas. Step back every once in a while and check your reference. Warm the dark with pyrrole red for use in warmer shadows, such as those around the mouth.

21 Develop the eyes and bridge of the nose. Use the edge of the brush to establish the eyelid, then draw it down to place the iris and pupil.

22 Using a 16mm (¾in) flat brush, add a little king's blue for the subject's irises, and a combination of permanent blue violet opaque and sap green for the pupils.

23 Create a new highlight pool of titanium white with a little yellow ochre and a hint of quinacridone rose opaque. Refine the skin with bridging marks using this new highlight pool in concert with the other pools on your palette.

24 Develop the area around the eye on the right-hand side using the highlight pool. These marks should be understated. Because they are relatively detailed, they will draw the eye; so it is important not to overdo them.

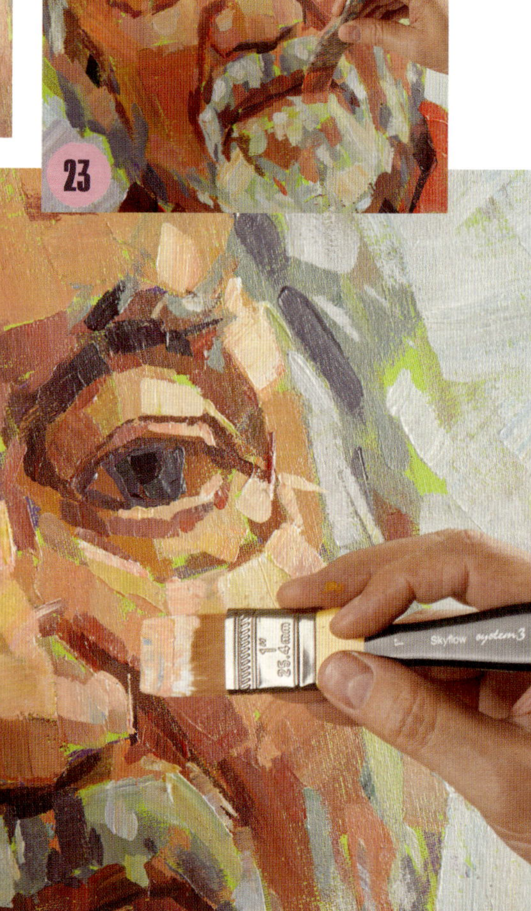

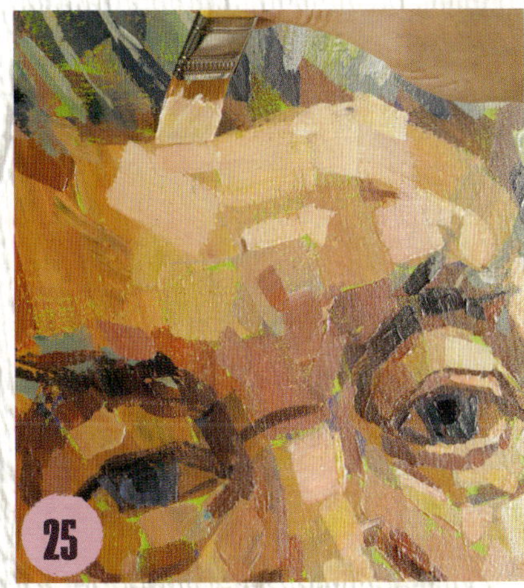

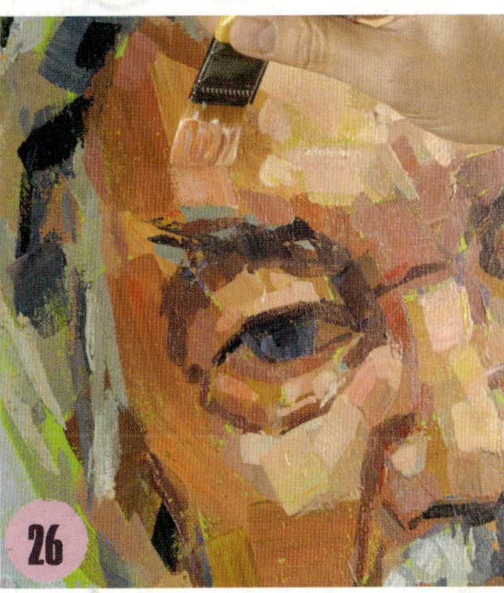

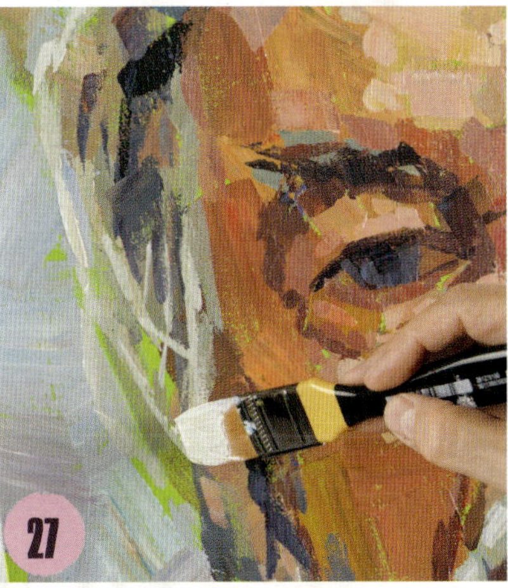

25 Build up the forehead using thicker, blockier strokes. Leave some more pronounced than others, and use the placement to suggest the wrinkles and lines in the skin. Avoid over refining these marks, or you'll lose this effect.

26 The nose and left-hand side of the face are redder than the yellow-tinged highlights on the right, so combine the highlight pool with more of the redder areas on your palette – or simply add hints of cadmium orange or pyrrole red to the brush.

27 Use titanium white, with tiny touches of king's blue, yellow ochre and sap green to add the highlights to the hair. Use these to help catch and direct the viewer's eye and suggest the direction of the hair.

THE FINISHED PORTRAIT.

After adding the final highlights using a very light pool of titanium white, permanent lemon yellow and quinacridone rose opaque, you can make any adjustments you feel necessary.

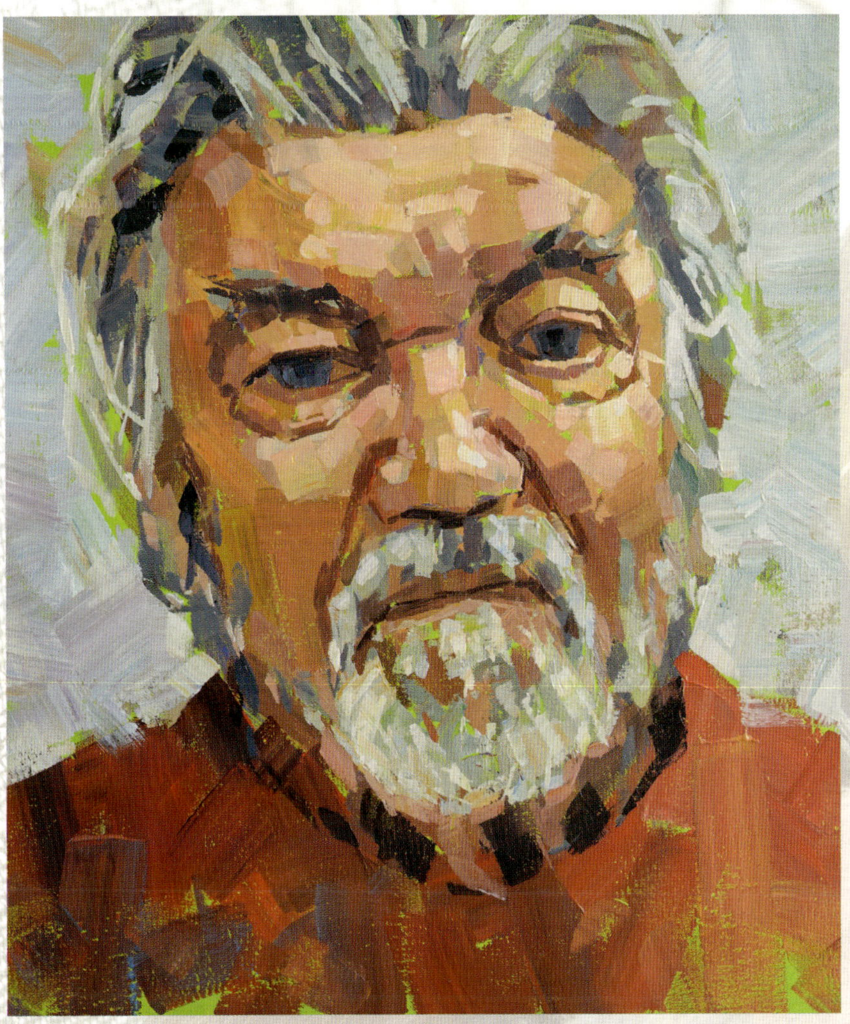

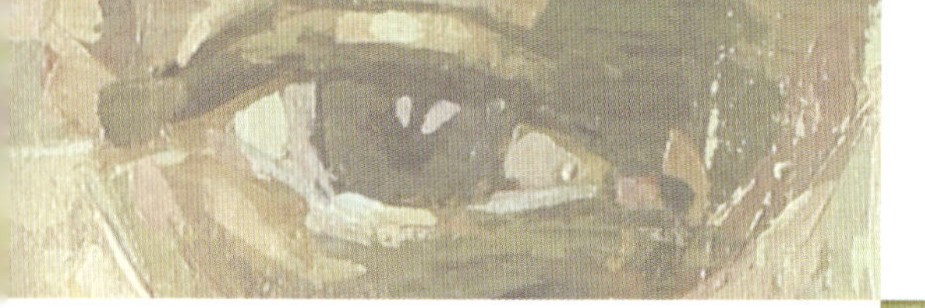

Painting *Suneel*

Drawing or painting a male subject has less reliance on refined beauty so the brush arm can relax into more expressive strokes. Too many exposed brushmarks or streaky colours can instantly age a face. Compared with females, male faces are generally more angular, with a larger skull and cheek bones, wider chins, thicker eyebrows; they might be bald but have more facial hair.

I find that faces from subjects with a different ethnicity to my own have a very interesting story to tell in portraits. It may be a result of my own heritage, or just curiosity. I've learnt a great deal from the history of Western portraiture and would simply like to reflect the variety of cultures we share the planet with. It's a huge advantage to have such accessibility through travel and social media and this should be included in contemporary portrait painting.

Darker skin colour does provide more scope for colour as there is less reliance on pastel tints.

This portrait veers towards an earthier palette, with the warmest tints in the face to draw you in, while darks create a frame. I always use plenty of paint for depth and vibrancy but here I used the background as an opportunity to drag some applications. This creates a few more variables that the viewer can appreciate and not just the same collection of marks.

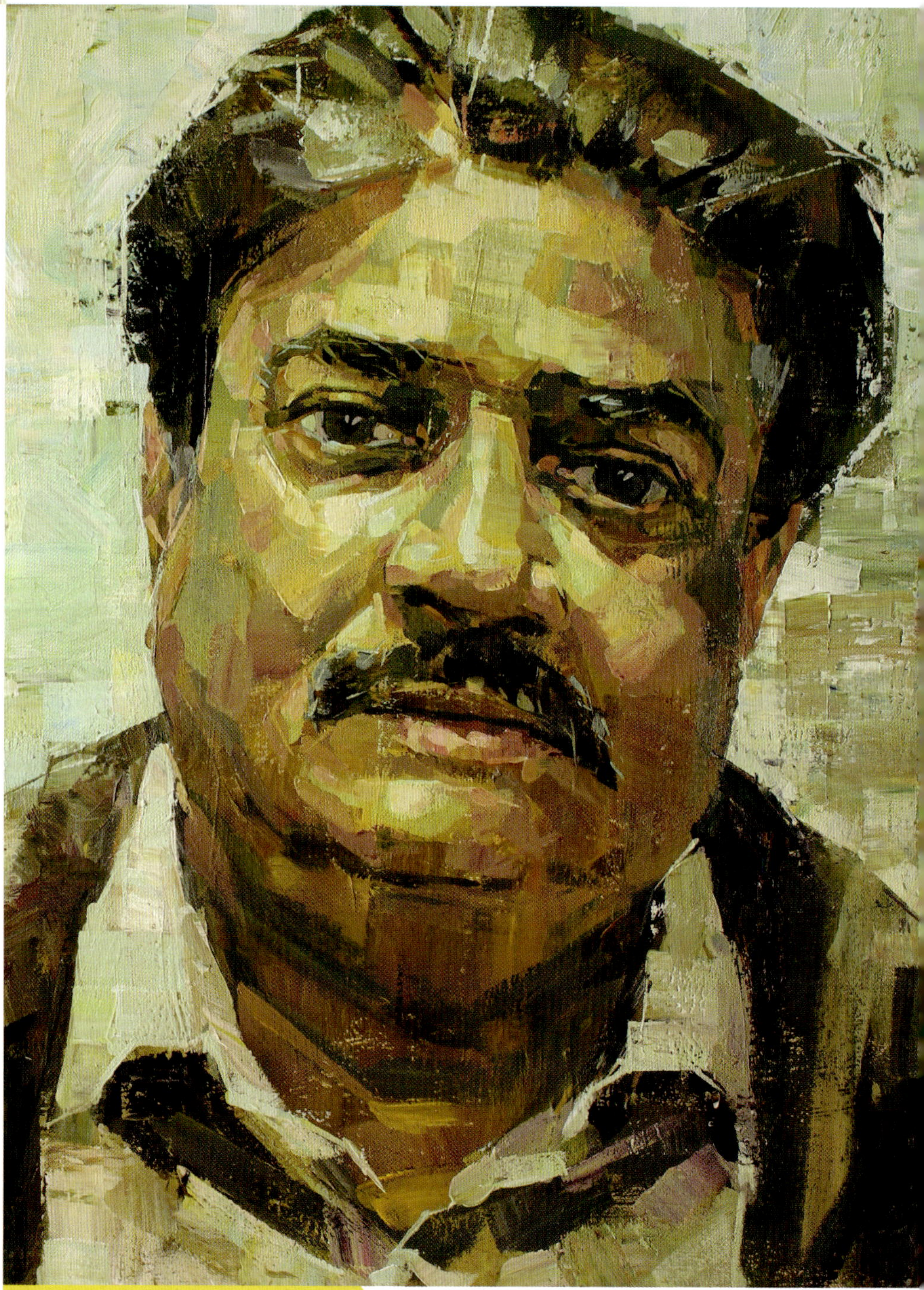

SUNEEL 51×60CM (20×24IN)

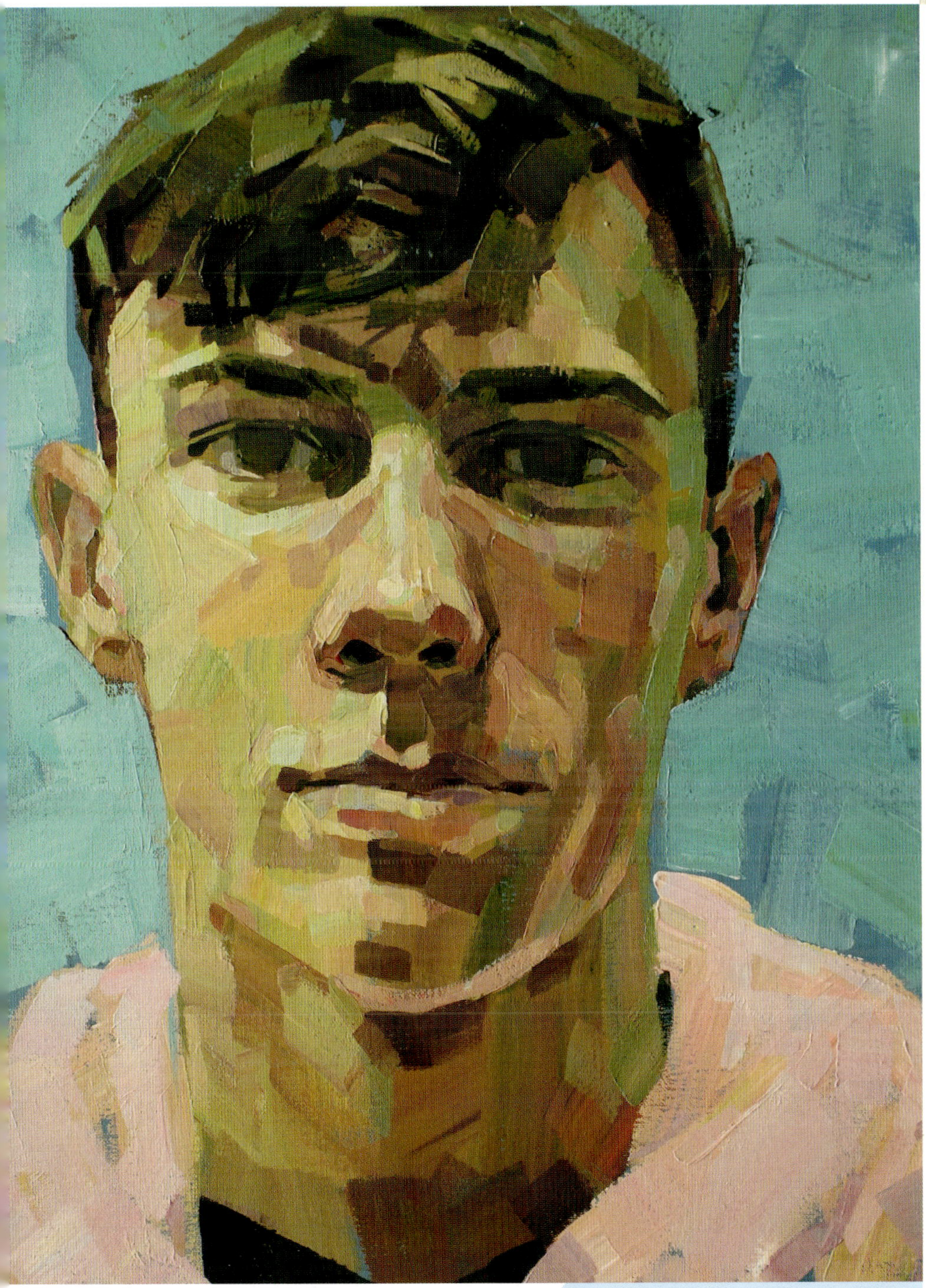

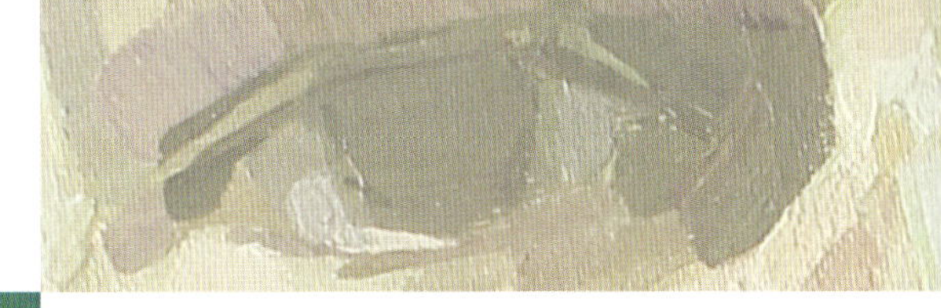

Painting *Harrison*

Younger male faces generally have more pronounced jaw lines, cheekbones and clearer complexions. For an artist this can be less interesting than a mature face like the one in the preceding demonstration (pages 50–55), but equally this can provide the challenge and inspiration to show what you can bring creatively to a less obviously promising subject.

I'm always keen to use rich colour, and especially with younger portraits as this reflects the vibrancy of youth. The reference photograph I worked from wasn't great, and had a plain beige background which did nothing for the portrait. I opted to swap this for light blue to contrast with the flesh tints and pink hoodie.

It's important to echo bright colours, even in subdued forms, around a painting in order to bridge one area to another. Blues have thus been mixed in with the flesh colour and applied to the shaded parts of the face, which also contain more exposed brushmarks. I used an even mix of tints for a smoother complexion in the highlighted side.

I was also very keen not to overplay the highlights in the eyes. I associate the typical 'beacons' of stark glittery highlights with cute or cheesy portraits of children or pets. The eyes are thus areas of potent darks, mirrored in the hair and echoed as a hint in the T-shirt.

HARRISON 51×60cm (20×24in)

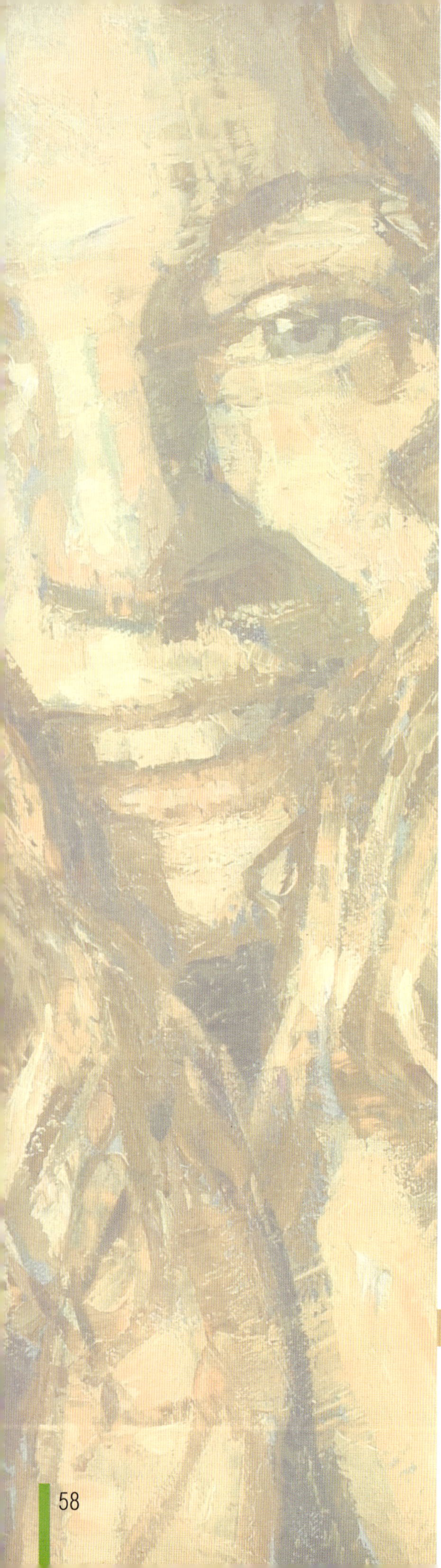

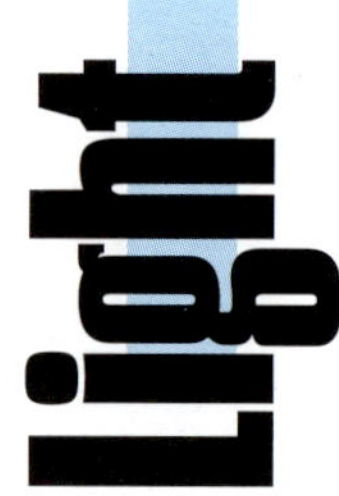

light

As I mainly work from photographs, I do spend time considering the lighting in a portrait. Light can compliment and flatter, or illuminate every blemish or imperfection. Depending on the nature of the portrait and what you want it to say, you'll need to light it accordingly. Light can be used to create compelling narratives or set the emotional tone by incorporating colour.

If you are working from photographs, you can obviously change lighting settings prior to printing the reference material, but lighting the scene with a plan in mind beforehand is much more organic.

Natural and artificial lighting conditions can vary. You will get a very different impression painting or photographing a face at midday than from warm, glowing evening light. Standing next to neon signs at night floods the face with bright, vibrant colour compared with one stark, overhead street lamp, for example.

Of course, light – and darkness – in a portrait have to be represented with paint, so in this chapter, we explore some ways to use light and tone in your artwork to give the most arresting results.

INTO LIGHT 51×71cm (20×27½in)

This limited colour portrait is about light and darkness, and the dramatic value they add. As you can see, lots of details can be eliminated by simply highlighting the most important aspects of the figure. Shadows can also be used to explore creative mark making and textures instead of voids of flat tones.

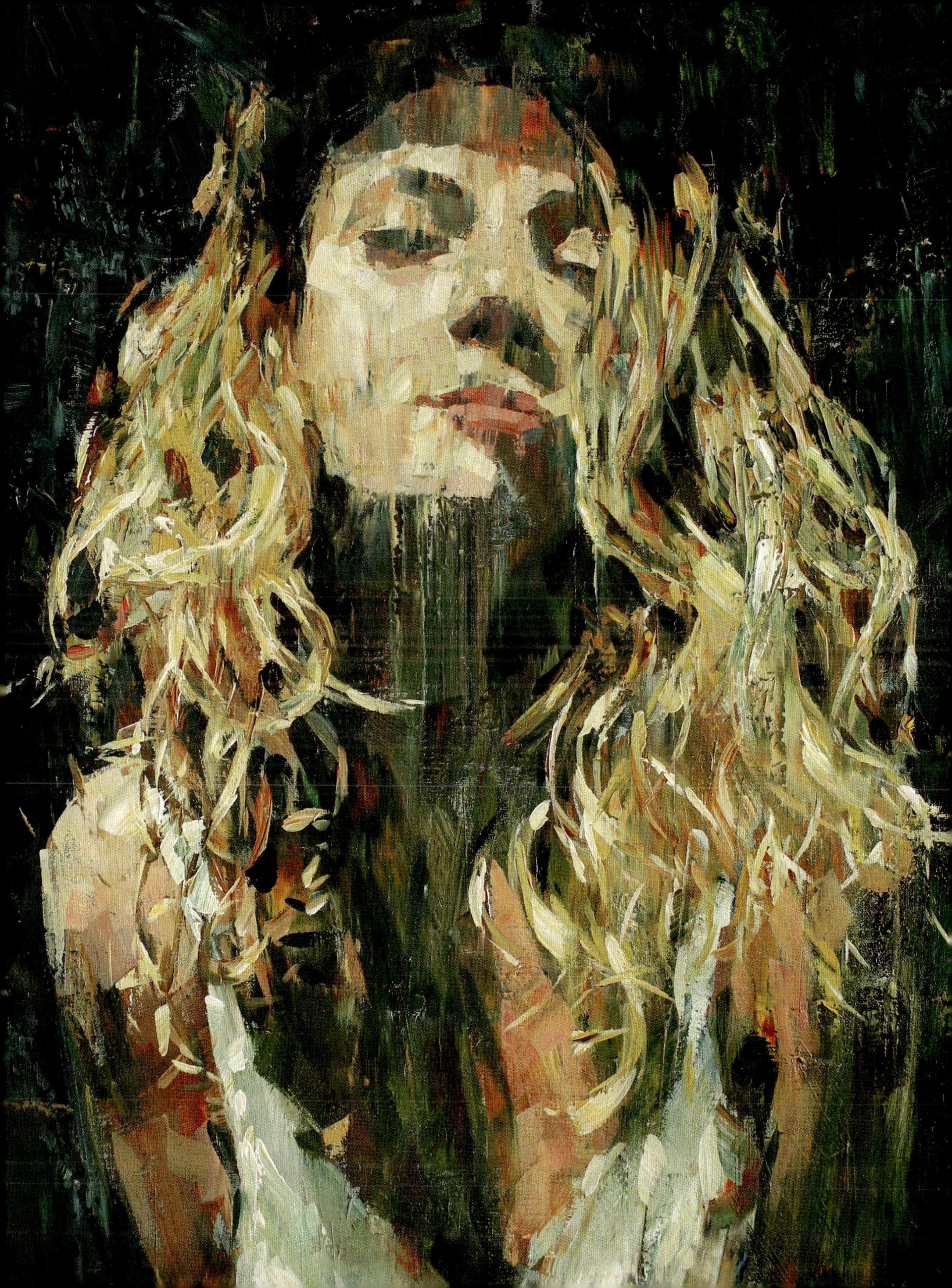

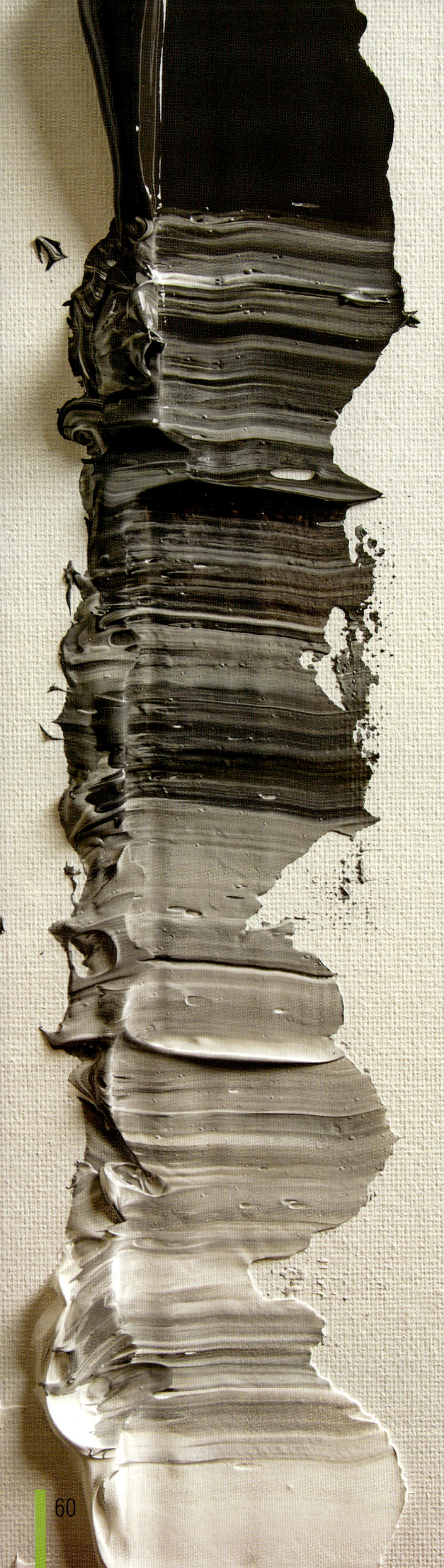

Light and dark

Tonal range

Achieving the right tonal balance in any painting is imperative if you want to create the illusion of three-dimensional forms. This provides the realistic hook that most people can relate to.

In painting we use the tonal range to locate the appropriate lights, greys and darks, sometimes called tints, tones and shades respectively. Put very simply, a tint is white mixed with colour, tones are greys mixed with colour, and shades are black mixed with colour.

Why work in monochrome?

When working from photographs, the subtlety in the tonal range is sometimes lost as darks and lights appear too consistent. The same strong darks appear equally as dominant in the background as they do in the foreground, and the same is true of lights. In reality, the potent lights and darks happen in the foreground and recede into softer variations in the background. Being aware of these differences will make your paintings more insightful, and more related to the real world as opposed to a two-dimensional photograph.

If you've painted for a while and find your full-colour paintings lack impact, try photographing them as black and white to reveal the relative strengths in your lights and darks. You can then use that knowledge in the future to adapt your tonal work.

Beginners to acrylics may find painting using black and white is a valuable gateway into understanding the qualities of the medium. With no hue to worry about, you can fully concentrate on the balance between the tonal values. The 'robot' demonstration on pages 22–25 uses this approach.

Which black and white?

It is worth considering which white and black to purchase as they can vary in opacity and even colour. I use titanium white for all my paintings as it's an opaque white, a quality I need when mixing with dominant colours. Some portrait artists prefer a more transparent or creamier coloured white, such as mixing white or zinc white. The options with black are less obvious; my preference is oxide black as it's more readily available but carbon black is considered the darkest for its refined pigment.

THE TONAL RANGE
Here's an illustration of the numerous acrylic tints, tones and shades available from mixing oxide black with titanium white.

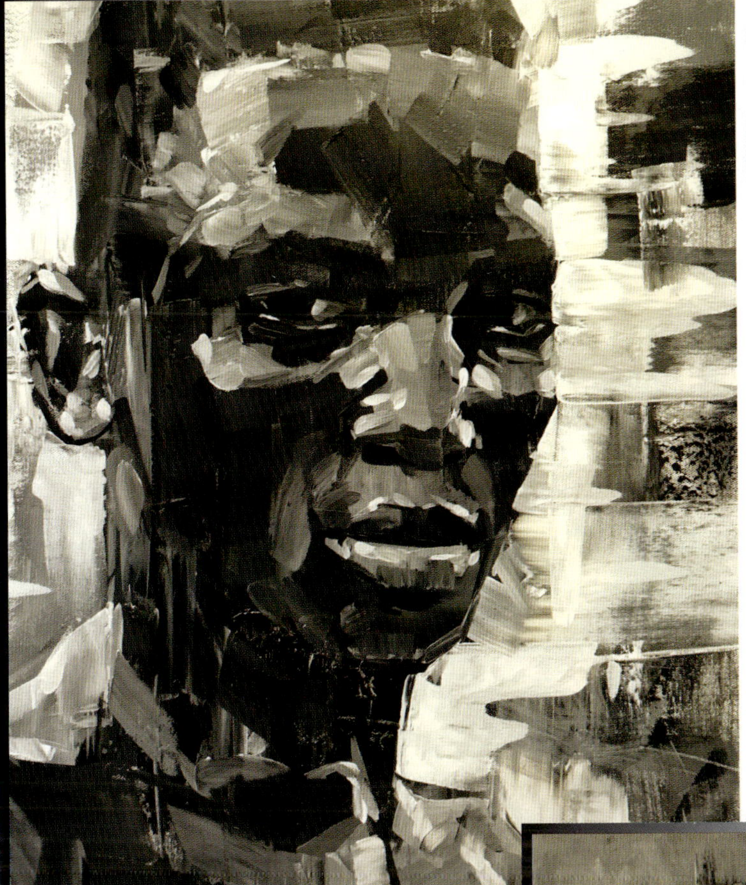

PORTRAIT WITH MARKS 46×61CM (18×24IN)
Black and white provides lots of opportunities to be creative with different forms of mark making. For this portrait, I made random applications of black and white with my brush then used scrapers to create large drags of paint. I blocked in the shape of the face and used a few variations of tints to add definition.

CLIVE 51×61CM (20×24IN)
I began with a simple sketch and applied dabs of paint with my brush. I did this fairly quickly so the paint was still workable, giving me the opportunity to use my scrapers to lightly drag some of the paint from one dab into the other. This created diffused edges, resulting in a softer feel to the portrait.

The power of notan

Using the extremes of the tonal range in your painting is a great way to create a strong, harmonious composition. As artists we are used to looking at large anchoring shapes in composing a scene: in a head and shoulders portrait, the shape the form creates is triangular – the shoulders the base which leads to the point at the top of the head. Another approach is to ignore the form and instead look at the balance between areas of darkness and light.

This is well-demonstrated by the Japanese design theory known as *notan*. The concept behind notan is to reduce a scene to a very limited range of tonal values, ideally black and white, with midtones included only if necessary.

By simplifying the image into dark and light patterns, you can better gauge the core structure of the composition. There may be too many dark areas. A line of light leading to the focal point may be interrupted by too many additional forms. Shapes may be too horizontal or vertical and the inclusion of diagonals may be needed.

A standard head and shoulders portrait may need less composing but when you incorporate a setting then creating a clear path of light is paramount. Notan is a great tool to help you identify what you may need to change in a composition to improve it.

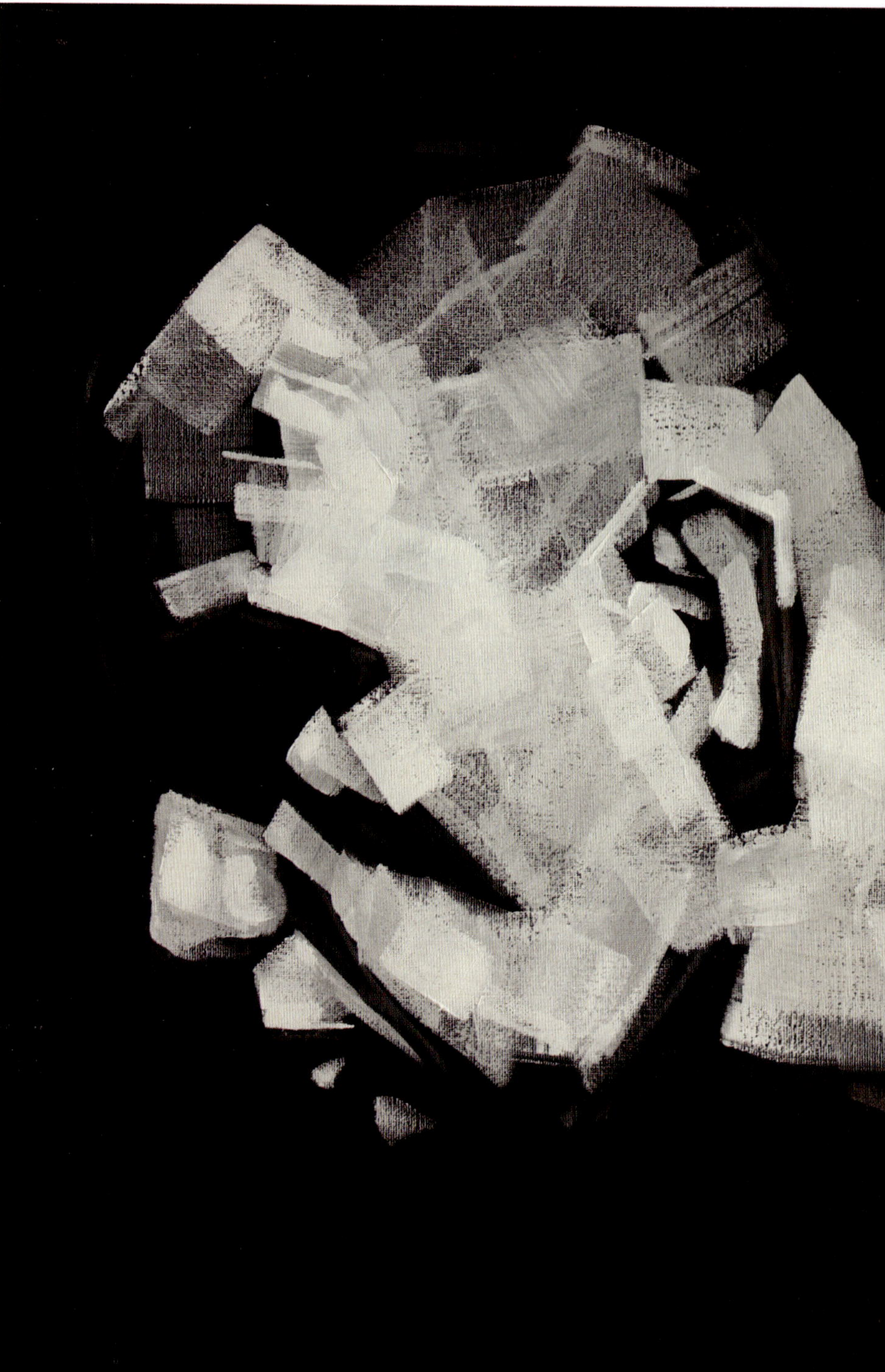

Introducing colour

Before diving into a palette full of colour it's helpful to add just one or two to your palette of black and white. This way your first steps into colour aren't fraught with clashing or messy colour mixes.

When choosing a couple of colours to practise with, try to look for something with striking differences in tone (light and dark) or warmth (cool and warm). A few effective combinations include phthalo turquoise blue and burnt sienna; orange and permanent blue violet; or yellowish green with cyan blue. Use white to create tints and black, if needed, to add impact for darks.

For the painting to the right, I used a green base colour (see page 82) and choose magenta to create strong contrast. Having applied the green base and allowed it to dry, I dragged mainly horizontal brushstrokes over the canvas. White was used to create a soft pastel magenta, while small amounts of black allowed me to darken the colour. I left some green visible at the bottom of the image to spark against the various tones of magenta.

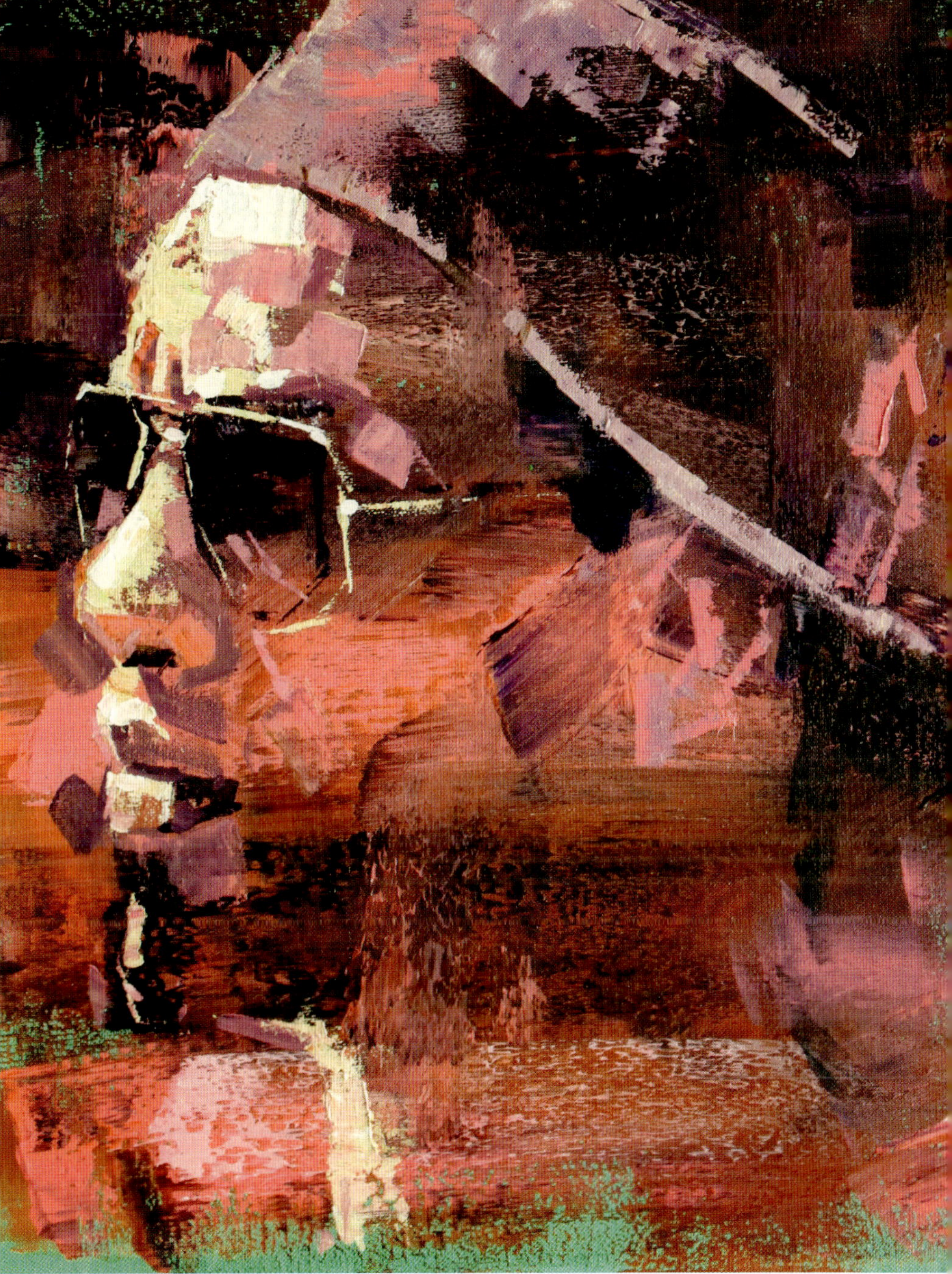

PINK MARKS 36×46cm (14×18in)

Once dry I used a combination of my 25mm (1in) flat head brush and scrapers to define the profile. The progression from using just white and black is simple. It's essentially the highlights that provide the clarity, with a few carefully placed darks and blocks of light magenta.

Chance encounters from the initial large applications next to more controlled ones provide the differences between order and chaos. This also shows how you can do so much with the most sparing of drawing and painting.

Painting with light and dark

Beginning any painting by simply applying random marks may seem undisciplined but if you locate a light source and bring out a few facial features using light and dark, suddenly our perception changes to something relatable.

This is a great exercise to try and I guarantee you will get at least half the painting right even with very little experience.

Using light as a guide

Start by choosing a face to paint with contrasting lights and darks. To keep things simple we'll use just black and white. Before considering the portrait, we will just make marks, the more random the better.

Using a large flat brush with oxide black and titanium white, apply verticals, horizontals and a few diagonal strokes using an under-mixed grey so that some uneven streaks of black and white emerge.

Next, add purer blacks and whites with slightly thicker paint to create certain drag effects. The most important consideration is not to overpaint the layers as the applications will mesh together, creating dull, flat greys. You're looking for dramatic leaps of light and dark with some midtone greys. The joy of this exercise is that there's no right or wrong way: just enjoy mark making, and feel free to employ a scraper or palette knife for variety. Allow these layers to dry before moving on.

The next stage is the portrait which does require some technical thought. Roughly sketch the face over the initial marks. Hopefully, you'll find that the random layers built up suggest the natural lights and darks in your photographic reference. Once you've sketched in the features, start by adding tints, tones and shades to develop the portrait.

The focus for most portraits are the eyes so spend some time developing these features and you can be less polished about the others. As the face emerges, avoid overstating the portrait with detail by leaving some of the early flurries to add an uncontrived, energetic feel to the painting.

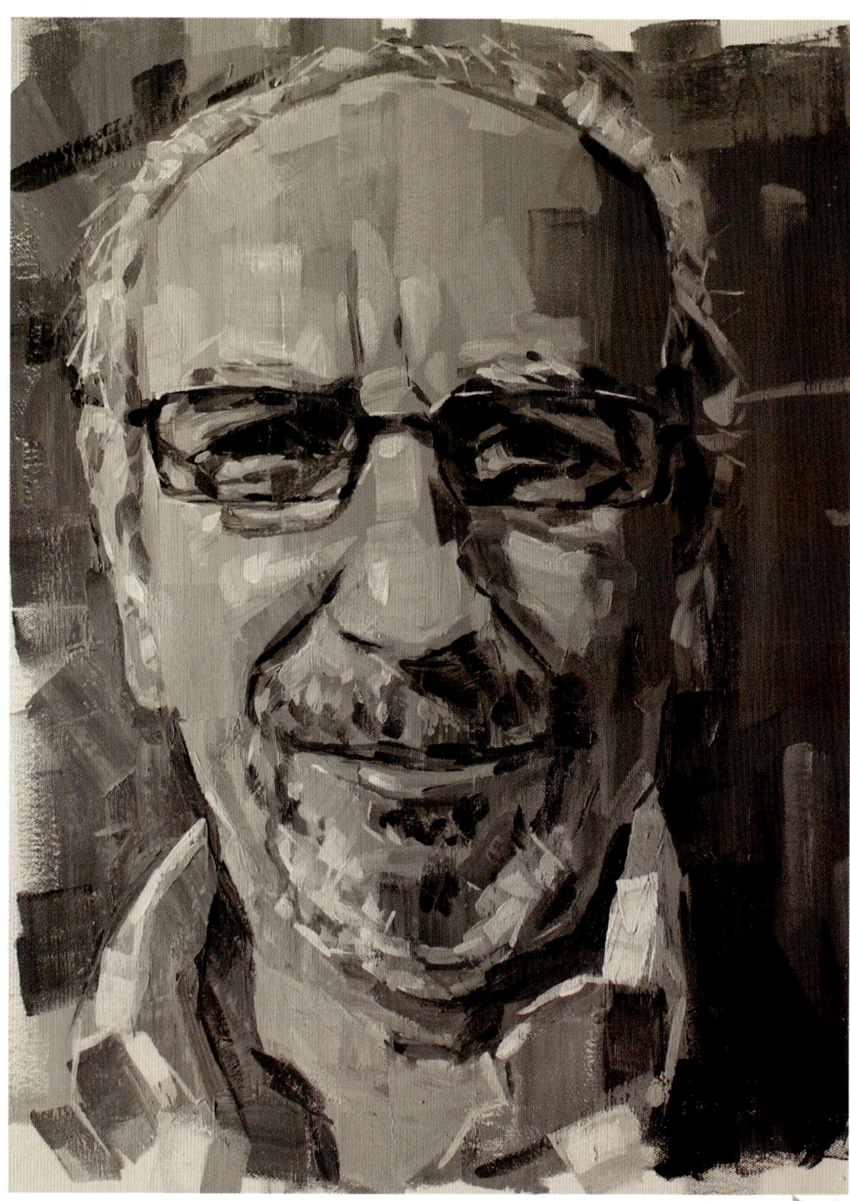

For the example here, I diluted the initial layers of paint to provide better coverage while keeping the pressure on the brush quite varied, from fairly firm to a gentle skim.

JOHN JOANNOU 46×61CM (18×20IN)

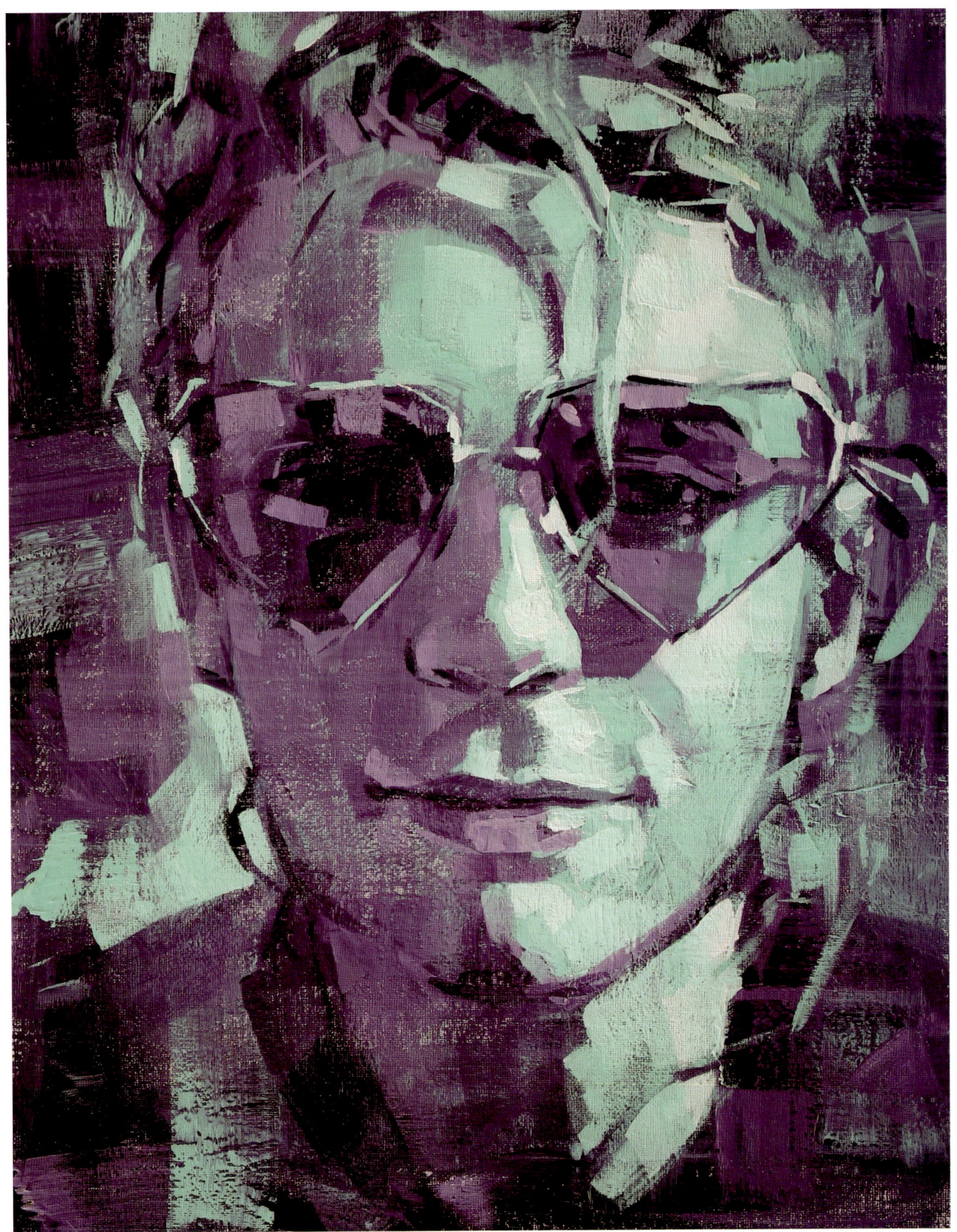

SUNGLASSES 36×46cm (14×18in)

Here's another example of a chaotic start resolved using light. The palette was restricted to turquoise green and permanent blue violet, with titanium white used to vary the tone.

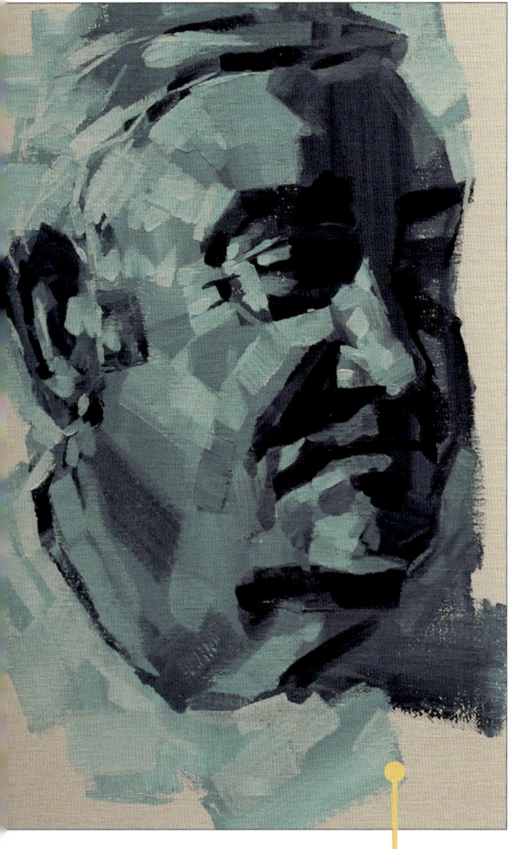

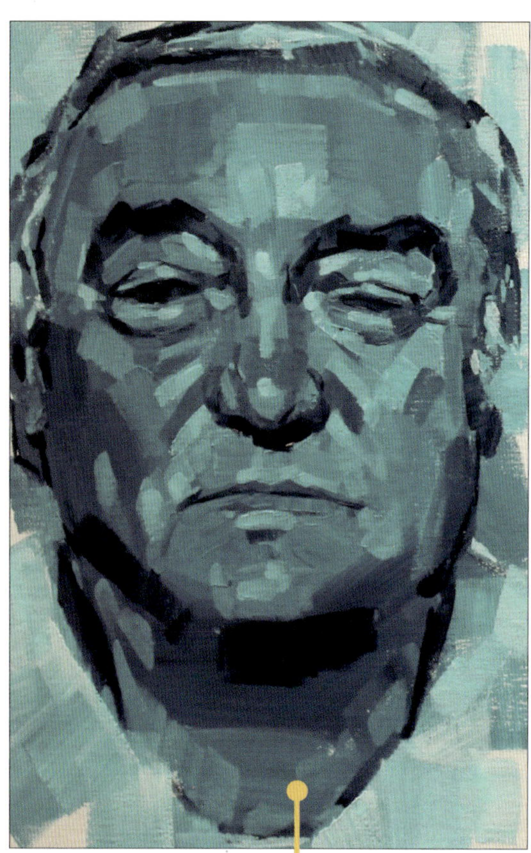

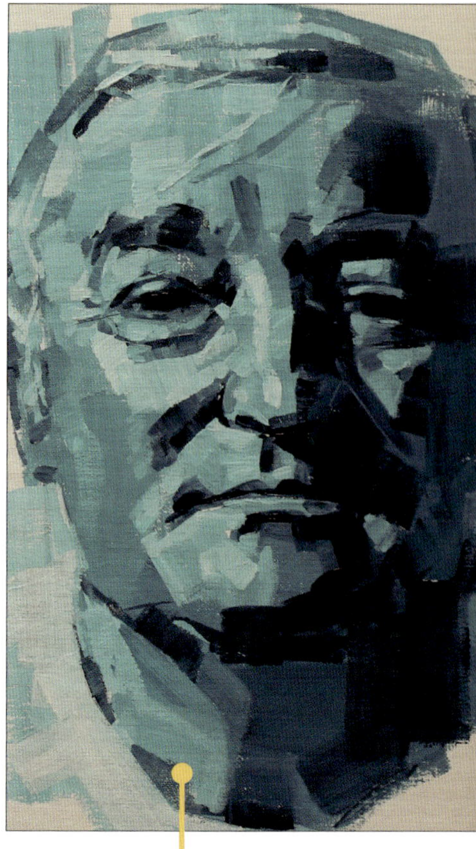

BROAD AND SHORT LIGHTING

The light is set up high to one side while the face is angled either into (for broad lighting) or away from (for short lighting) the light source. Short lighting is more complimentary, as you have less of the face lit, which creates a slimmer appearance.

PARAMOUNT LIGHTING

This extremely complimentary approach creates pronounced cheekbones and a strong jawline. The light is placed high above the camera and is so-named because this approach was used to light lots of Hollywood actresses during the 1920s.

REMBRANDT LIGHTING

Named after the great artist who used strong contrasting light on his subjects. It is distinguished by the small inverted triangle of light on the darker side of the face, while the other side is brightly lit. The light is placed in front and to one side of the sitter, above the eyeline.

The light source

From a technical perspective, establishing a light source is imperative in creating naturalistic lines of shadows. Light draws out solid forms, illuminating pockets of interest, while darks sit back to frame the highlighted elements. One main light source creates a definitive focus, while multiple light sources dampen each other, creating a flatter, calmer impression. The positioning of the light will also determine that sparkle in the eyes as the light is reflected. I never use a flash, even in low light conditions, as their use tends to flatten the features.

For the portraits above, I have used one main light source – sometimes called a key light – from different angles to create varied effects. Some of these approaches are common practice for professional photographers and they can also be utilized by painters.

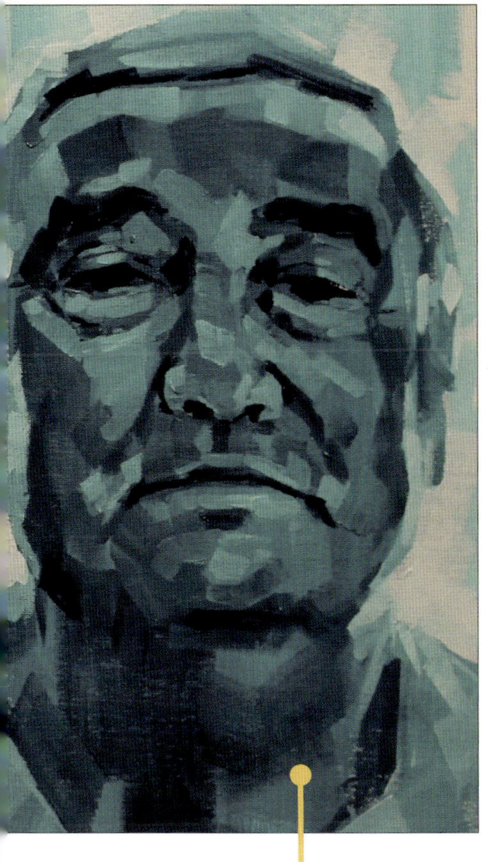

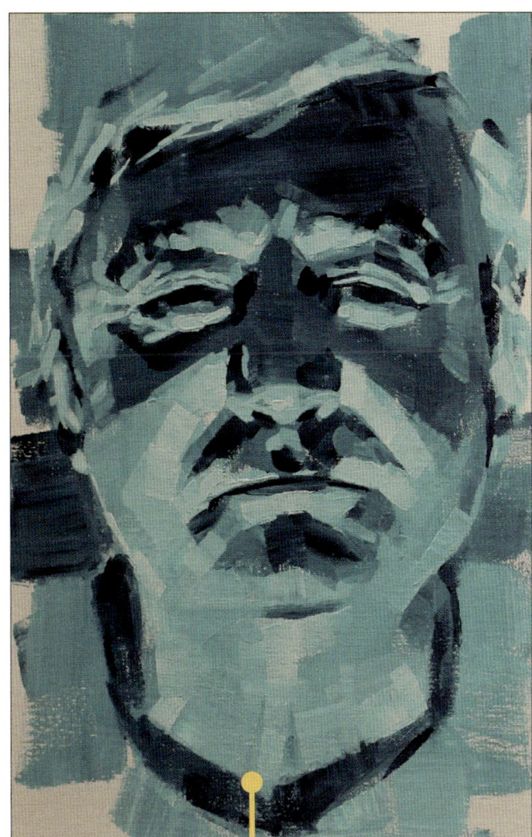

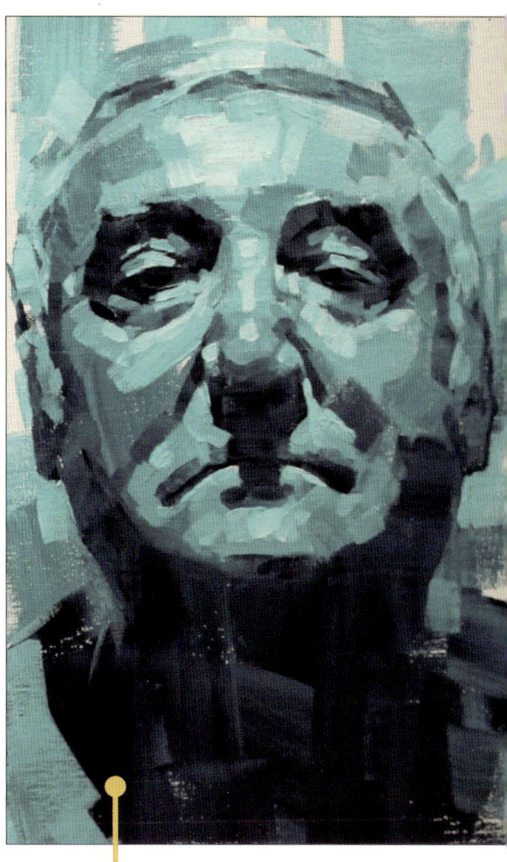

BACKLIGHTING

When the main light source is behind the model, this creates a certain glowing effect and throws the model into silhouette. This can add mystery and is a relatively unusual choice in painted portraits.

UNDERLIGHTING

Any unusual light source, such as lighting a face from below, conveys something sinister – here it suggests a figure over a fiery cauldron. It isn't particularly complimentary, but is great for dramatic value.

DIRECT OVERHEAD LIGHTING

Similar to underlighting, a light source directly overhead can evoke something sinister or an authority figure.

Other lighting

Accent lighting Lighting focussed on a specific area. Typically used to spotlight important elements or features, in portraiture you can use accent lighting to draw the attention away from the eyes for less obvious focal points.

Ambient light Pre-existing, unstaged light such as natural light – whether outdoors or streaming through windows. It can also refer to artificial light from normal room lights. Most portraits you paint will be under these lighting conditions.

Split lighting This lighting divides the face into light and dark, creating dramatic shadows.

Task lighting This sort of lighting tends to be for practical purposes – examples include the light created by lamps set up to help you work, or security lights for gardens. For portrait painting task lighting may be useful to illuminate elements in the background to create more interest or fill empty spaces.

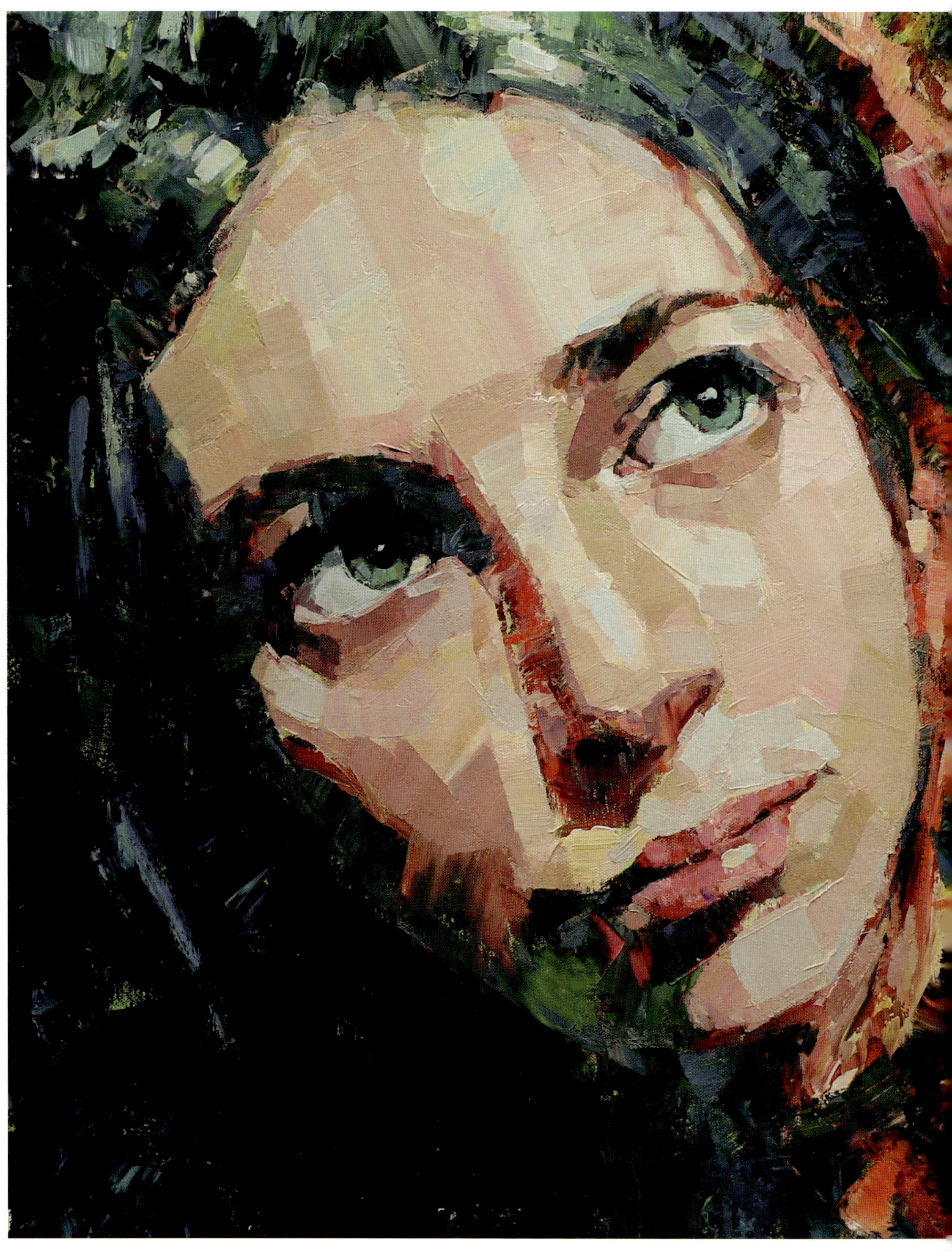

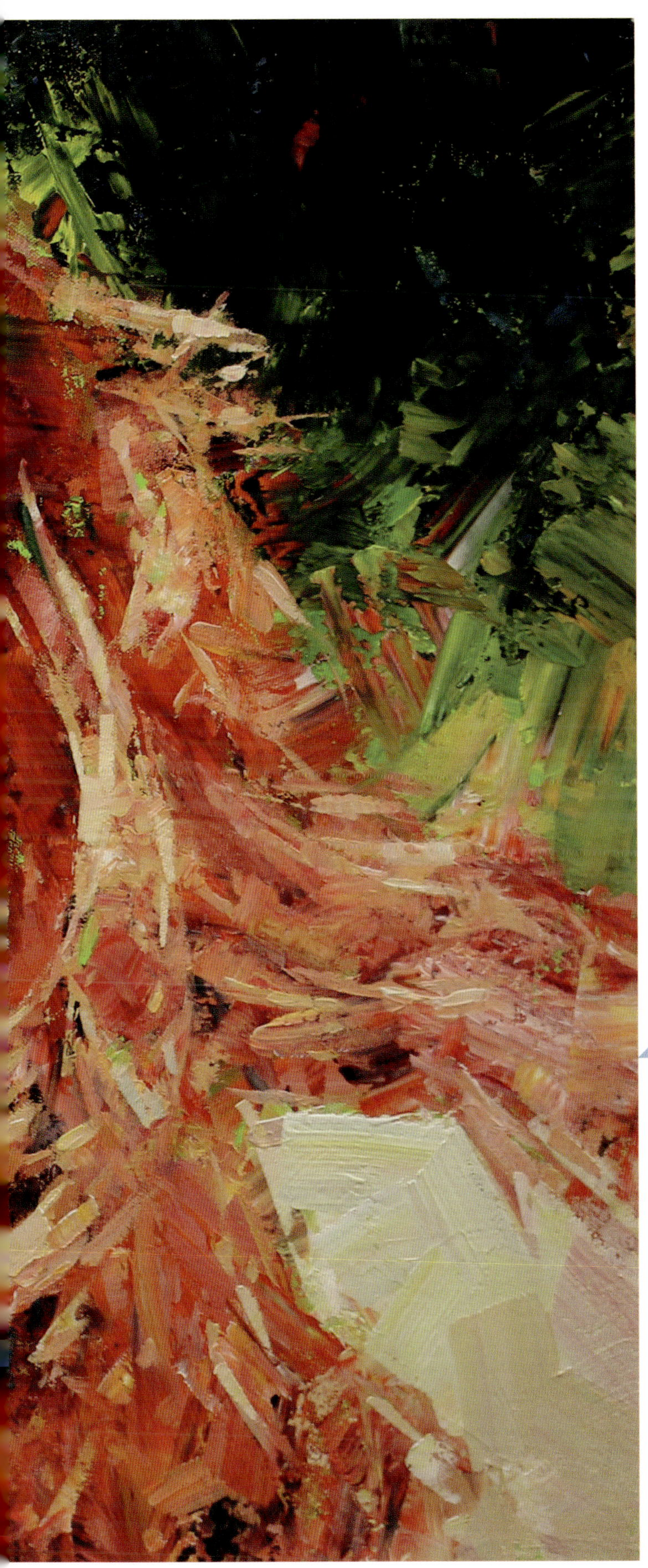

Colour lighting

Colour adds another component that can elicit a mood. A cool blue light or fiery red superimposed onto someone's face instantly changes our perception. In scenes where multiple colours make things tricky to navigate, as they interact and produce a multitude of shadows, one dominant coloured light source can help to create a consistent look to the portrait.

There are several ways to achieve coloured lighting effects with task lighting, including coloured gels or transparent filters you can purchase to cover over lights. For my portraiture, I use a 30 watt garden light that changes colour and includes a remote control.

The colour of the lighting you should use is a question helped with some knowledge of colour theory, which we cover in the next chapter. A good starting point is to find a light in a complementary colour (see page 72) to an element of your subject. Complementary colours always spark off each other and appear brighter when placed side by side.

Experiment to find unusual lighting combinations or look for inspiration from photographers and artists. Explore photographs on social media, too, where random, dynamic lighting conditions are abundant.

RED AND GREEN PORTRAIT 76×61cm (30×24in)

Lighting can illuminate aspects of a painting and dramatically change the outcomes. The model already had red hair and the intense light enhanced the colour and created dark shadows. A touch of lime green next to the red plays two complementary colours against each other; while subtle pastel tints in the face balance out the vibrant reds.

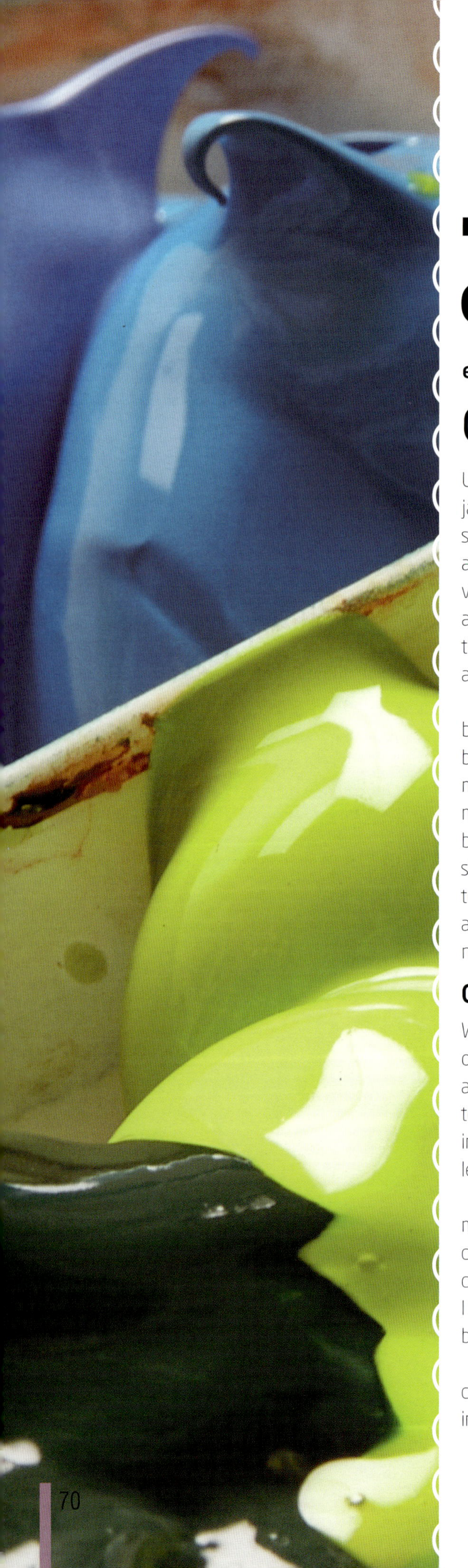

A simple way to start thinking about colour is through temperature. Take a black-and-white photograph and imagine the lightest areas as warm, eye-catching colours such as reds, yellows and oranges; and dark areas as cool, receding colours like blues, greens and violets. Hot colours grab the eye, while cool colours recede into the background. You can use this effect to give impact and dynamism to your paintings.

Colour and paint

Using pure warm and cool colours in a painting may produce a garish or even jarring image, so in order to create a naturalistic look we usually need to subdue, or neutralize, pure colour into an earthier pigment. Many artists mix a neutral colour, such as brown or grey, into brighter hues to soften their vibrancy. Mixing can also be used to link one pigment to another, or to create a darker version for shadows. In the same way we use white to create tints; the challenge when mixing neutrals with colour is in the quantities used to avoid overly chalky or muddy mixes.

Your palette should contain the three primary colours of red, yellow and blue. From here you can mix all the colours you need to get going. Yellow and blue can be mixed to make green, for example. You can purchase a ready-mixed brown for your neutrals, but you'll create a more varied pigment by mixing green with red. Depending on the quantities you use, the result will be a reddish- or greenish-brown. Equal quantities will provide a more even shade. If you'd like to try a grey, just mix this brown with blue and add white to lighten. These simple exercises are very much the start of colour mixing, and once you've build up your experience you can explore much more complex neutrals by using complementary colours.

Other qualities of paint

When choosing which colours to mix, you will find some of the same family of colours veer towards cool or warm variations. For example, lemon yellow is a cool yellow, while cadmium yellow is warmer. Mixing pigments of the same temperature will produce a cleaner colour mix. A warm range of primaries may include pyrrole red, permanent yellow medium and ultramarine blue, while lemon yellow, quinacridone rose and cyan blue form a cool starting trio.

Each paint colour also has properties that make them more transparent or more opaque. This makes certain colours suitable when creating flat areas of colour or more versatile for mixing with other colours. Information on opacity can usually be found on the side of each tube or tub of paint. The acrylics I use have a small box left blank to signify a transparent paint or a full dark block for an opaque one.

If understanding these nuances – let alone learning the names of each colour – seems daunting, let me reassure you. You can just start painting and instinctively you'll pick up on these values.

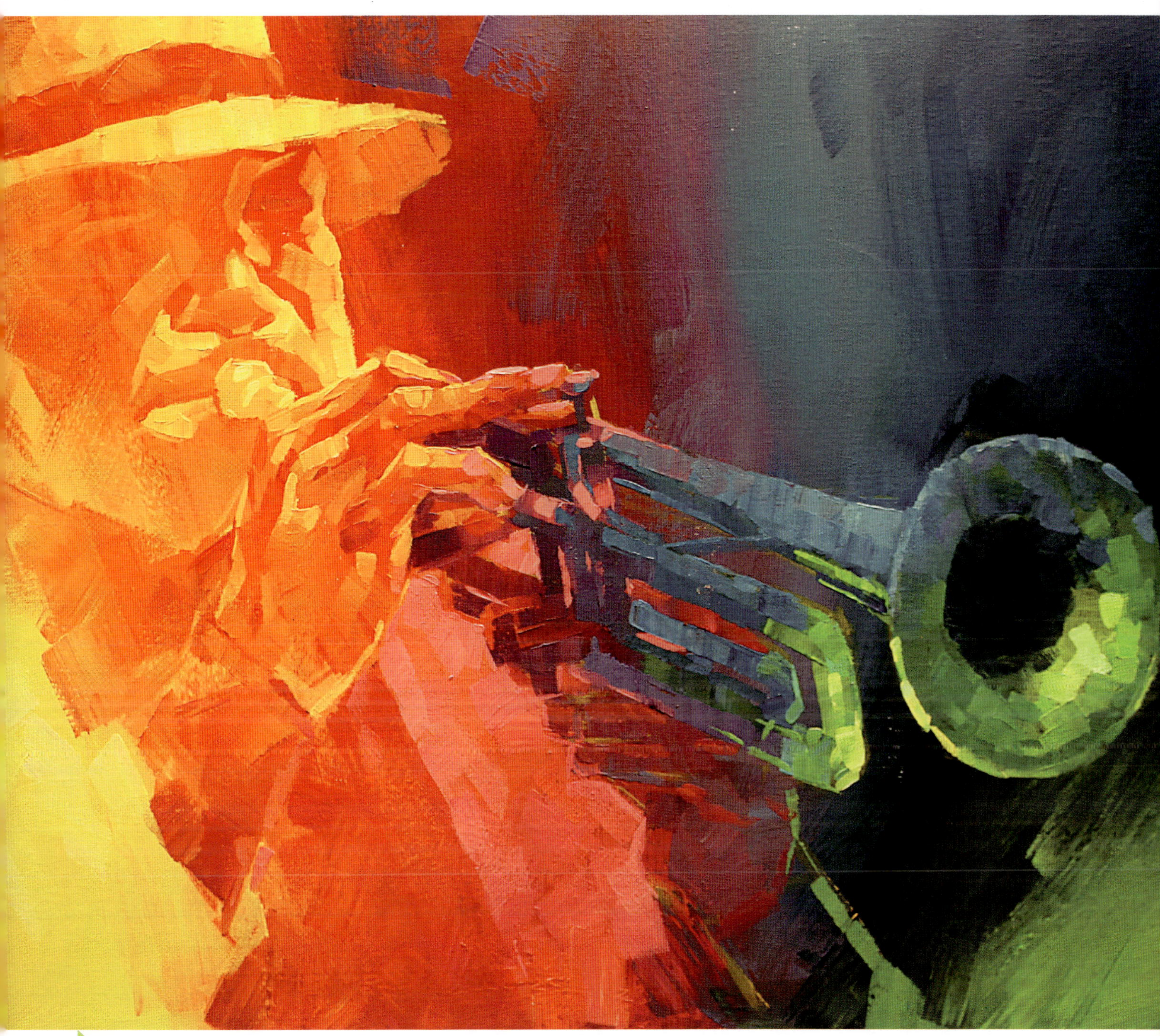

JAZZ 61×51cm (24×20in)

This painting gives a good example of how colour temperature can help to lead the viewer around a portrait. Your eye is immediately drawn to the warm reds and orange of the figure; and then to the yellow tip of the trumpet. Only then does the eye move on to the cooler surroundings; before returning to the figure.

Complementary colours

Complementary colours are colours that create neutral, earthy shades when mixed together (depending on the quantities). When placed side by side they work together and both colours appear brighter.

Examples of complementary pairs of colours are reds and greens, oranges and blues, yellows and violets. When mixing these combinations together, it's best to have one colour that dominates more than another; this will avoid lifeless, dull mixes. As certain colours are considerably lighter than others, such as yellow against violet, you'll need a lot less violet in the mix and may need to utilize an opaque white to strengthen the yellow.

When showcasing complementary colours in a finished portrait, always have one colour in the scene that dominates or is echoed throughout. You are in safer hands when employing harmonious colours which are all related with very little conflict. These may be a range of either warm, cool or earthy shades. Harmonious colour schemes can be predictable, but complementary colours – while tricky to balance – provide more scope and greater understanding of the boundaries in colour mixing.

This portrait plays off two complementary pairs: red and green, and orange and blue. When working with several dominant colours, there is a danger of these clashing, which is why the addition of light and dark tones along with more neutral earthy hues helps to counteract the vibrancy. The distribution of colours needs to be balanced, with one dominating in its purest form: to enable this, keep other colours more subdued or reserved for smaller areas of the painting.

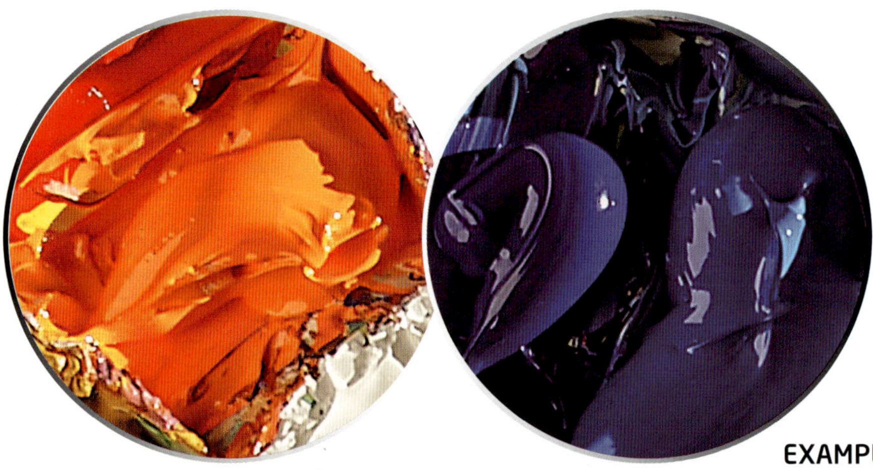

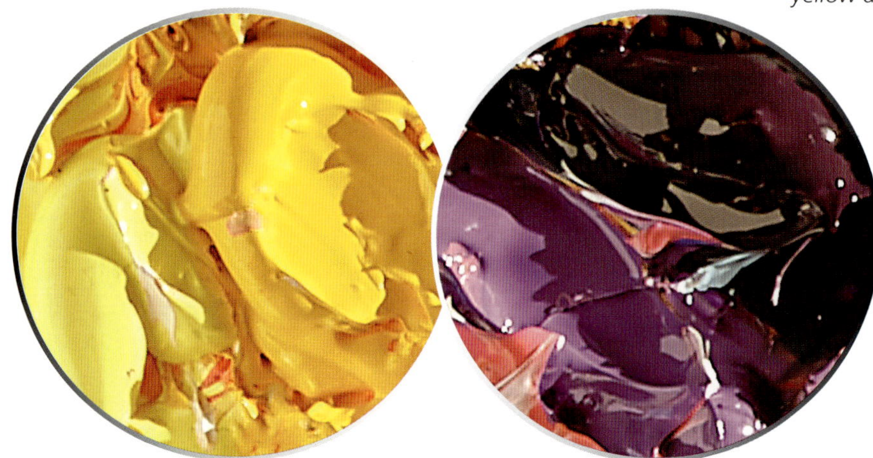

EXAMPLES OF COMPLEMENTARY PAIRS

Orange and blue are complementaries, as are yellow and purple.

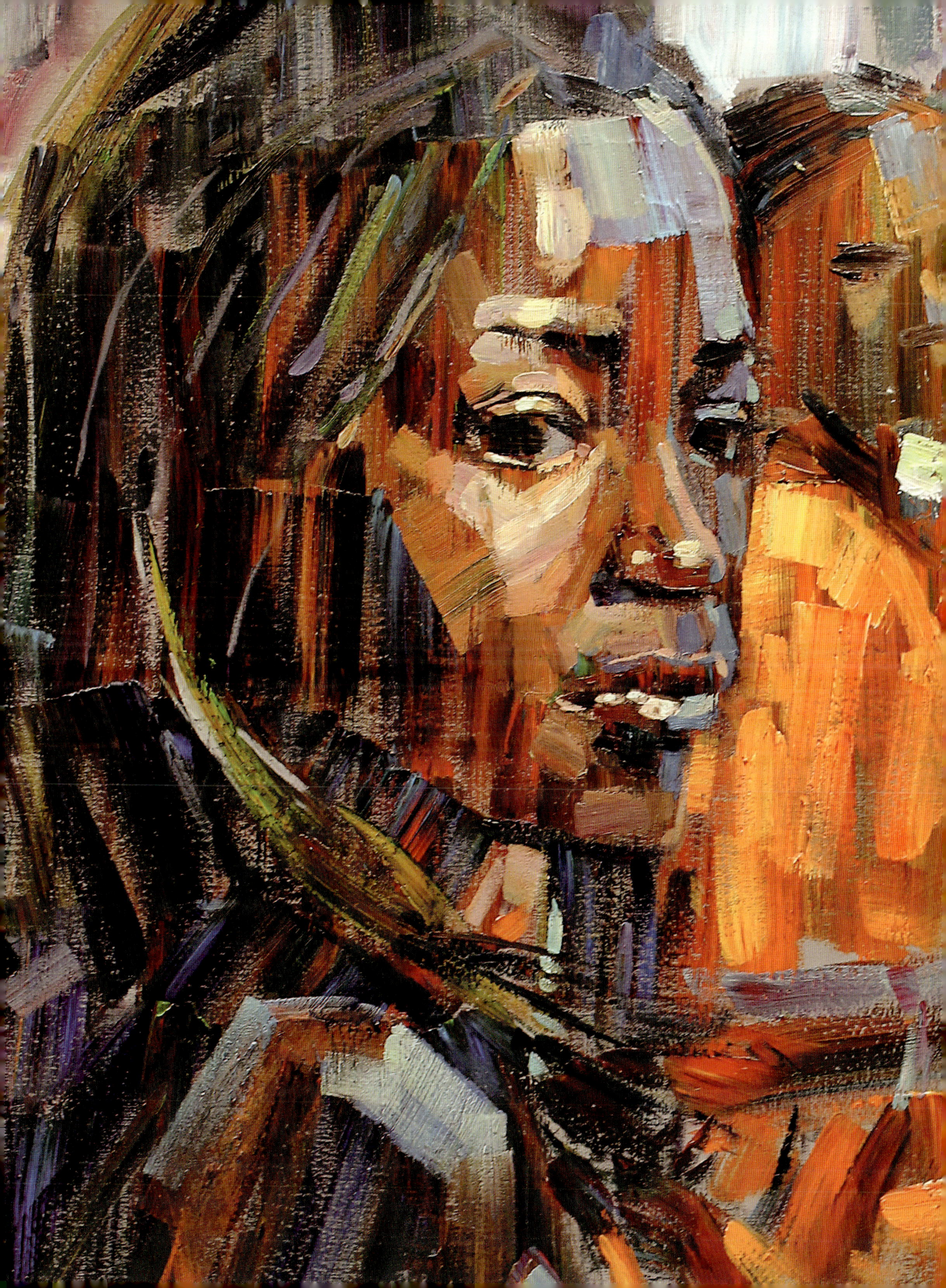

Colour palette

Each colour in my palette does a particular job. I have colours which do the heavy lifting, such as white, red, violet, blues and a couple of earthy pigment. I go through tubes of theses fairly rapidly. Others are used more sparingly to add a touch of sparkle to the finish.

My core palette consists of the following colours available from the Royal Talens' Amsterdam Artist Acrylic range. Similar colours are also available in the students' quality range. If you choose a different brand, look for the qualities listed below.

Cadmium yellow lemon A warm primary, this is great for zingy, sparkly highlights.

Permanent yellow medium Versatile when mixing with warmer colours and lifting flesh tints.

Yellow ochre An opaque, light, earthy pigment, it is great for adding subtle warmth when mixed with other colours. Avoid using large quantities as it can overwhelm other colours very easily.

Pyrrole red A must for portraits, this hot primary mixes with most colours for skin tones.

Quinacridone rose This is a great bridging colour between red and blue. It creates useful 'sparks' amongst other colours, both warm and cool.

Burnt sienna A transparent warm brown, this is extremely versatile and I often use it to divert rich colour into an earthier pigment.

Yellowish green A zippy green, this injects life into dull tints and provides good value next to reds.

Sap green A versatile green. Ideal for mixing browns when added to red, or used on its own terms as an earthy green.

Cobalt blue Ideal for harmonious mixes with magenta, rose or violet. Lovely to use with other cool colours in shadows.

Cyan blue A dominant dark blue even as a light tint. A small amount goes a long way. Note that cyan blue is not available as an Amsterdam's artists' quality paint, so try the primary cyan in the standard range or a similar Artists' quality colour from a different brand.

Prussian blue Depending on the level of depth I am creating, I sometimes use this very dark shade in place of oxide black. I use it sparingly towards the end of a painting or when mixing with other colours.

Permanent blue violet An essential all-rounder for mixtures of shadow colours, as a lighter tint, or to bridge warm and cool colours together. This comes in both standard and opaque.

Phthalo turquoise blue One of my favourite colours, this is great when used on its own for tonal studies or when mixed to create potent darks.

Titanium white No other white will do. Titanium white's opaque qualities are needed when mixing with dominant hues and for creating your ultimate highlights.

Ivory black A quick word on using black in paintings, which I am happy to embrace. Black can dominate and suck the life out of other colours, but in small doses it can provide a potent shot of dark. This extreme helps to crisp up certain forms, it's less abrasive against dominant colours and the contrasts with lighter tints are greater.

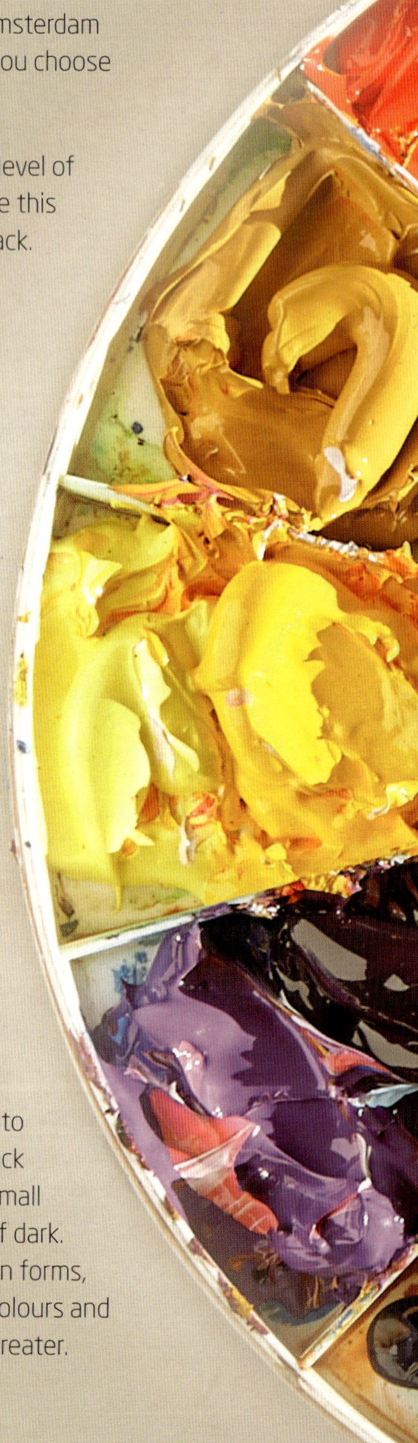

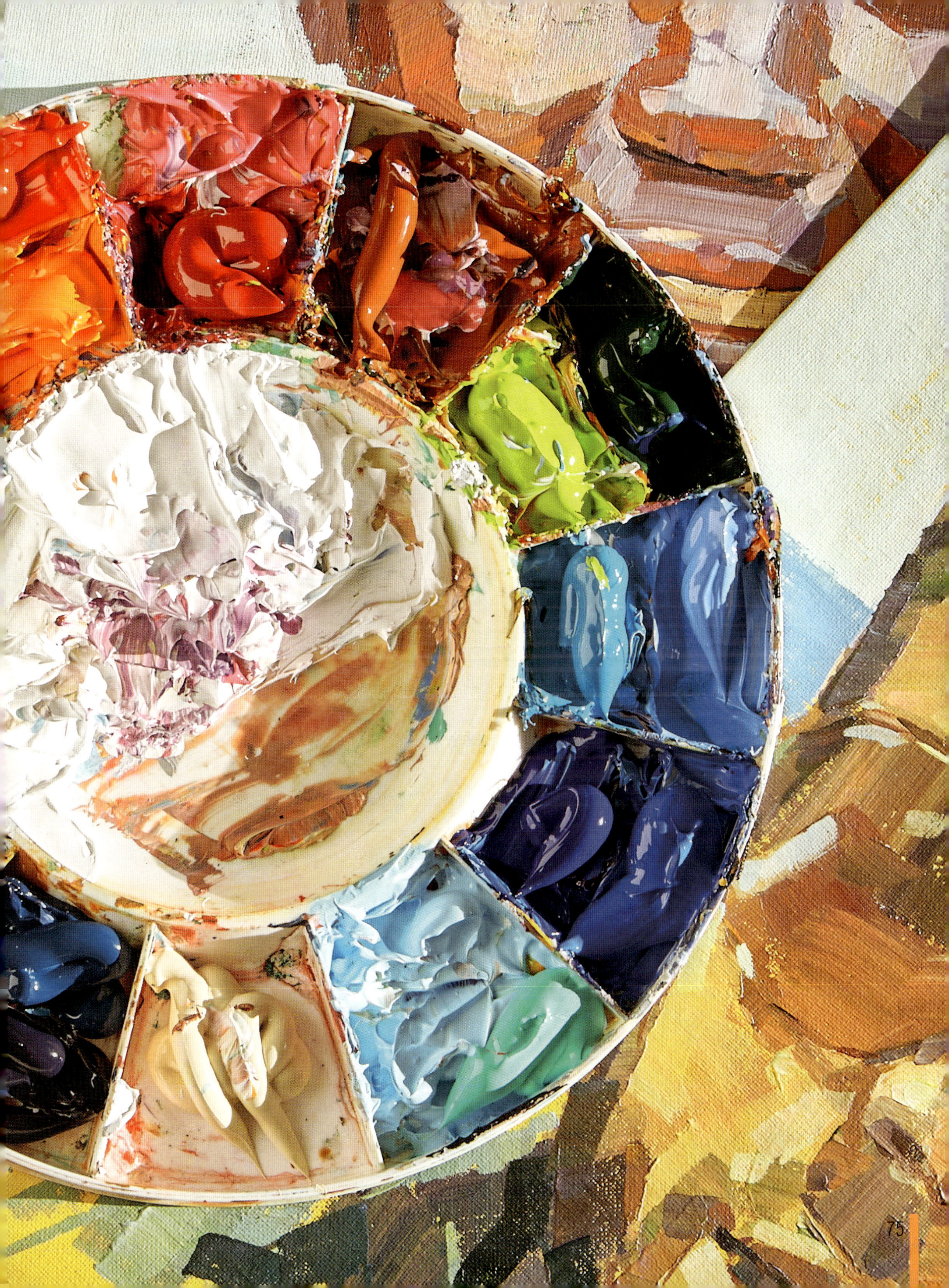

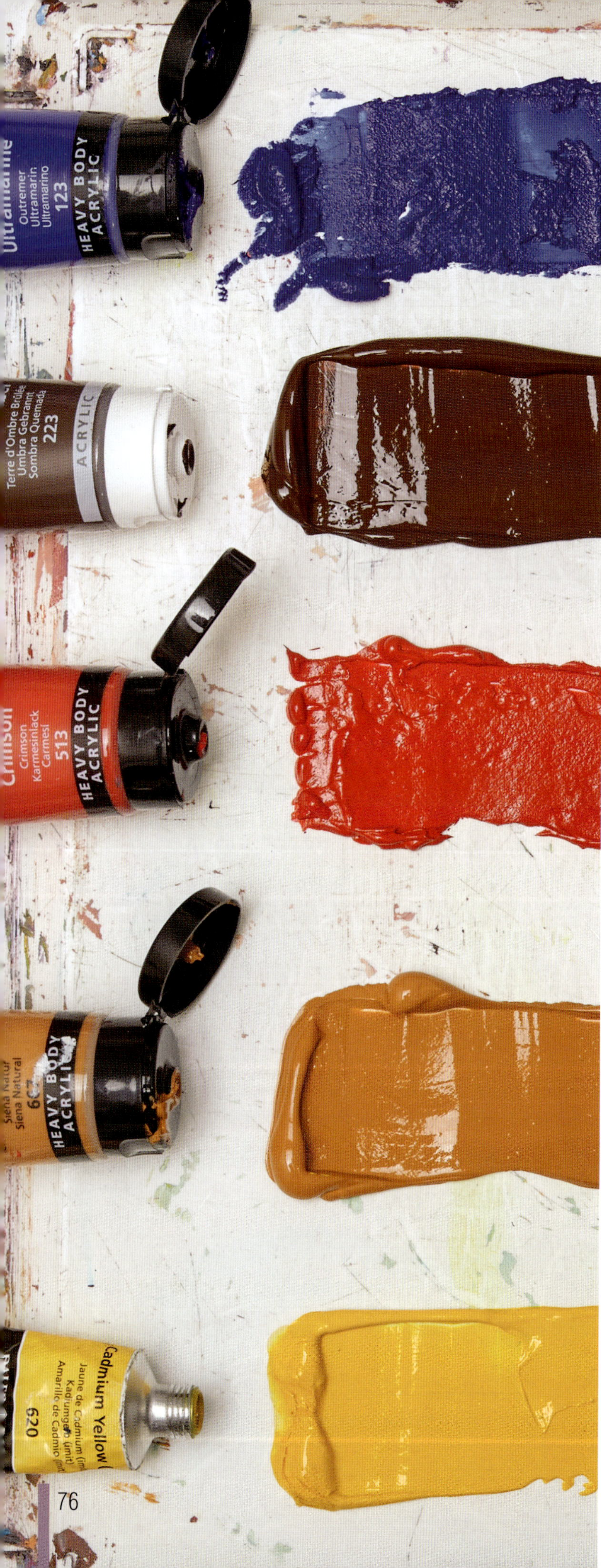

Varying your palette for effect

My core palette, detailed on the previous page, is not fixed. I vary it from painting to painting by adding, removing or swapping colours. If I have a particular effect or mood in mind, I might pick a more limited selection, such as those described on the following pages. Experimenting with the different palettes will help you to find your own preferred combination.

This fairly conservative set of standard colours is particularly suitable for beginners as the colours are easy to work with.

Traditional palette

- Burnt umber or raw umber as a neutral mixing brown

- Ultramarine blue

- Hooker's green

- Crimson

- Raw sienna

- Cadmium red

- Cadmium yellow

This is a very versatile palette with passive colours making them easier to mix. I tend to reserve the stronger colours for isolated features or to create a striking focal point.

Many of these pigments are cheap as the ingredients are more readily available and easy to manufacture. Using these traditional colours does produce pleasing outcomes but remains a safe and relatively predictable option.

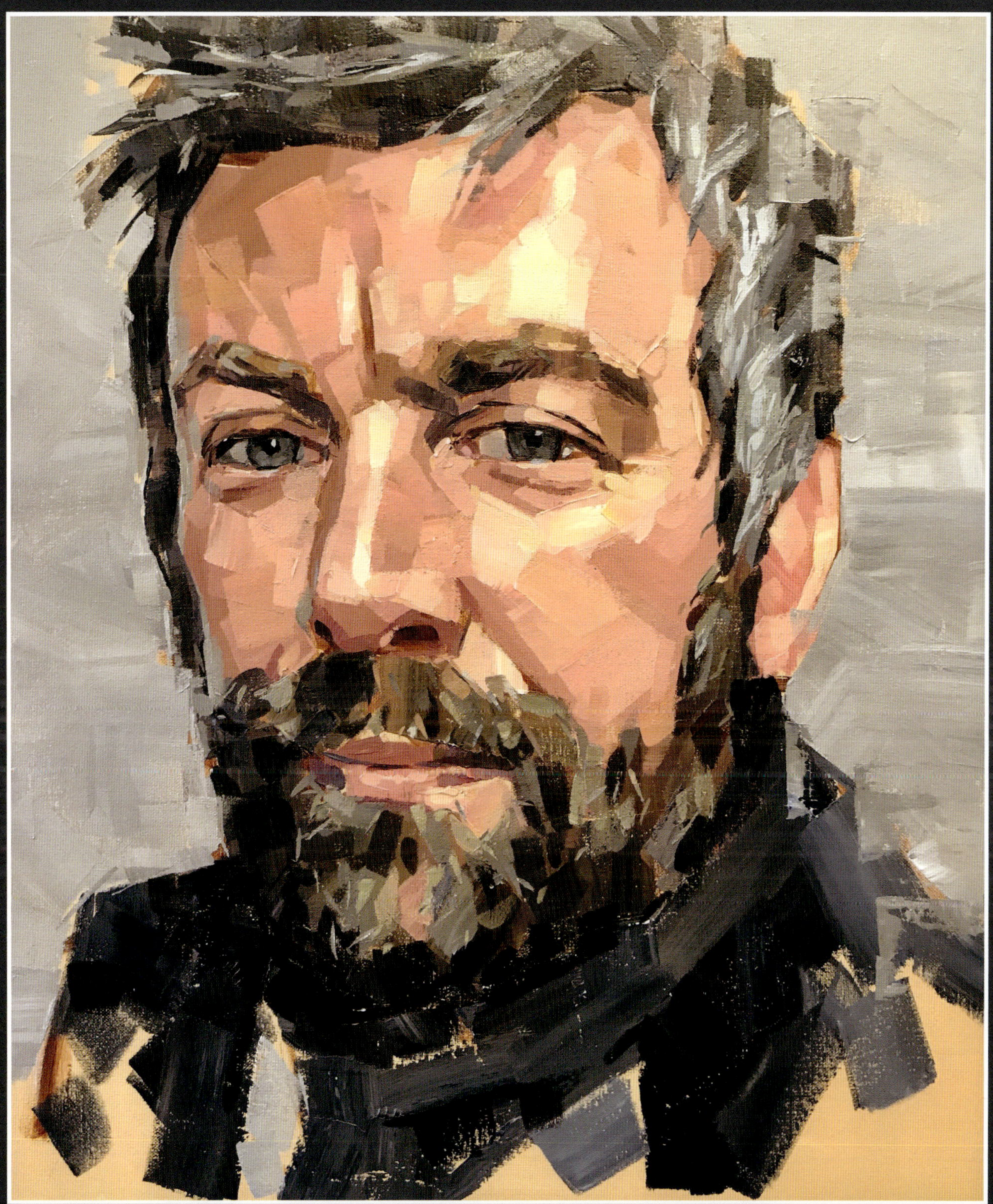

ANDY 61×51CM (24×20IN)

I began my painting career with the pigments in the traditional palette listed opposite, and this painting reminded me of the ease of mixing such versatile colours. The portrait veers towards earthy and dark neutrals which frame the warmer colours.

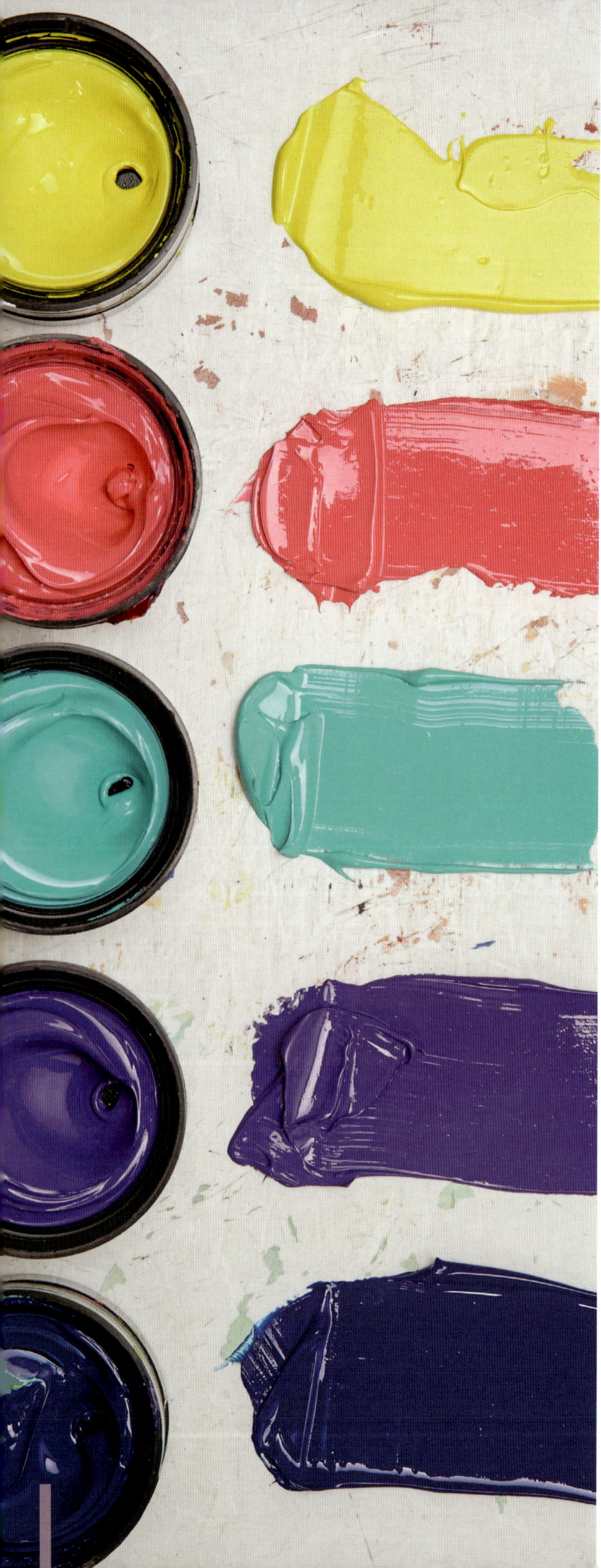

Vibrant palette

Today we have access to a huge range of colours with new additions continually being added by different manufacturers. This palette consists mainly of very saturated, dominant pigments, made using more modern synthetic materials than the traditional palette on the previous page. The range of colour mixing possibilities is widened by the added saturation, as is the scope for learning and discovering unusual combinations.

- Cadmium yellow lemon
- Quinacridone rose deep opaque
- Turquoise green
- Permanent blue violet opaque
- Cyan blue

Your first forays into mixing with such dominant hues will likely result in garish paintings owing to the strength of the hues. Cyan, for example, is incredibly potent even as a tint. Its equivalent in a more traditional palette, ultramarine, will always be a mid-range blue in comparison. However, as your perception calibrates to richer hues, you'll produce something less manic.

A vibrant palette like this offers greater choice as earthy and neutral hues are still mixable, but you'll have the option of added saturation: great to heighten the contrasts in colour.

When you paint professionally you always look for any kind of impact. This is normally judged by stepping back a few feet. Beginners often judge a painting from the distance they are working from, but it's worth taking into consideration how it may look from a room away, in a gallery full of paintings, or hung in a low-lit room. Lifting the colours guarantees some impact in all conditions.

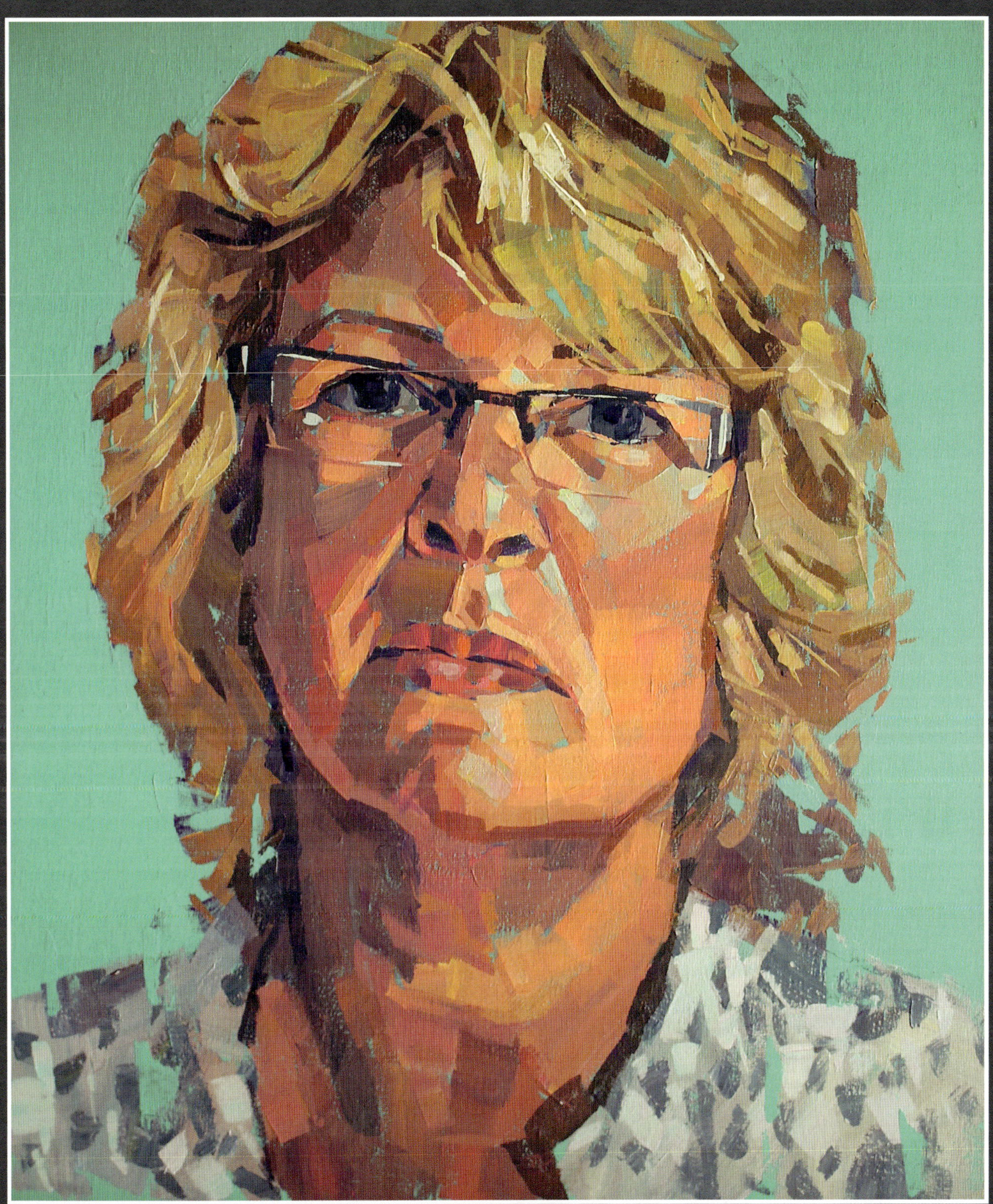

LYNN 61×51CM (24×20IN)

I like portraits with a strong background colour. The portrait itself can remain naturalistic but the colour adds vitality. It's all too common to find dark, moody backgrounds, and colour celebrates the portrait.

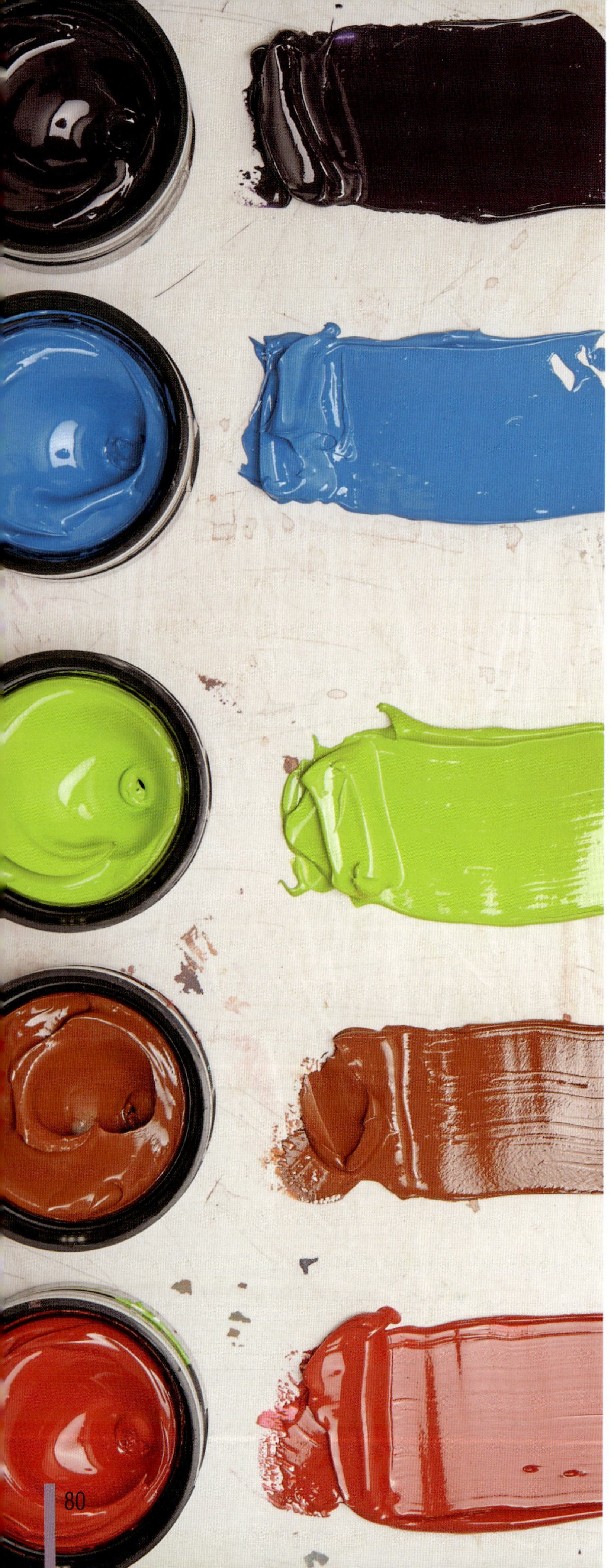

Contemporary palette

Recently I've been more conscientious about designing colour schemes in my paintings, and this reflects in my palette. I have read countless books on colour mixing and swatches to explore these ideas, and made some interesting discoveries such as a traditional western palette of watercolours being different from a Japanese set. Being aware of different ideas like this will provide the inspiration to vary your choice of pigments.

- Permanent blue violet

- King's blue

- Yellowish green

- Burnt sienna

- Pyrrole red

The inclusion of both vibrant and earthy hues in this palette provides the scope to maximize all options, and is a combination that can be seen in lots of contemporary portraits: a huge accent of orange or red in amongst rich darks or plain cream backgrounds, for example, or a random splatter of turquoise over neutral greys. The sense of experimentation is visible and sits alongside the representational aspect of the portrait.

In acrylics, your choice of colours may also be a way of enriching others. In portraiture I particularly like mixing yellowish green with white for highlights, as it provides more contrast with the reds than a more traditional yellow such as lemon yellow. Similarly, permanent blue violet can produce more variables to enhance darks than burnt umber.

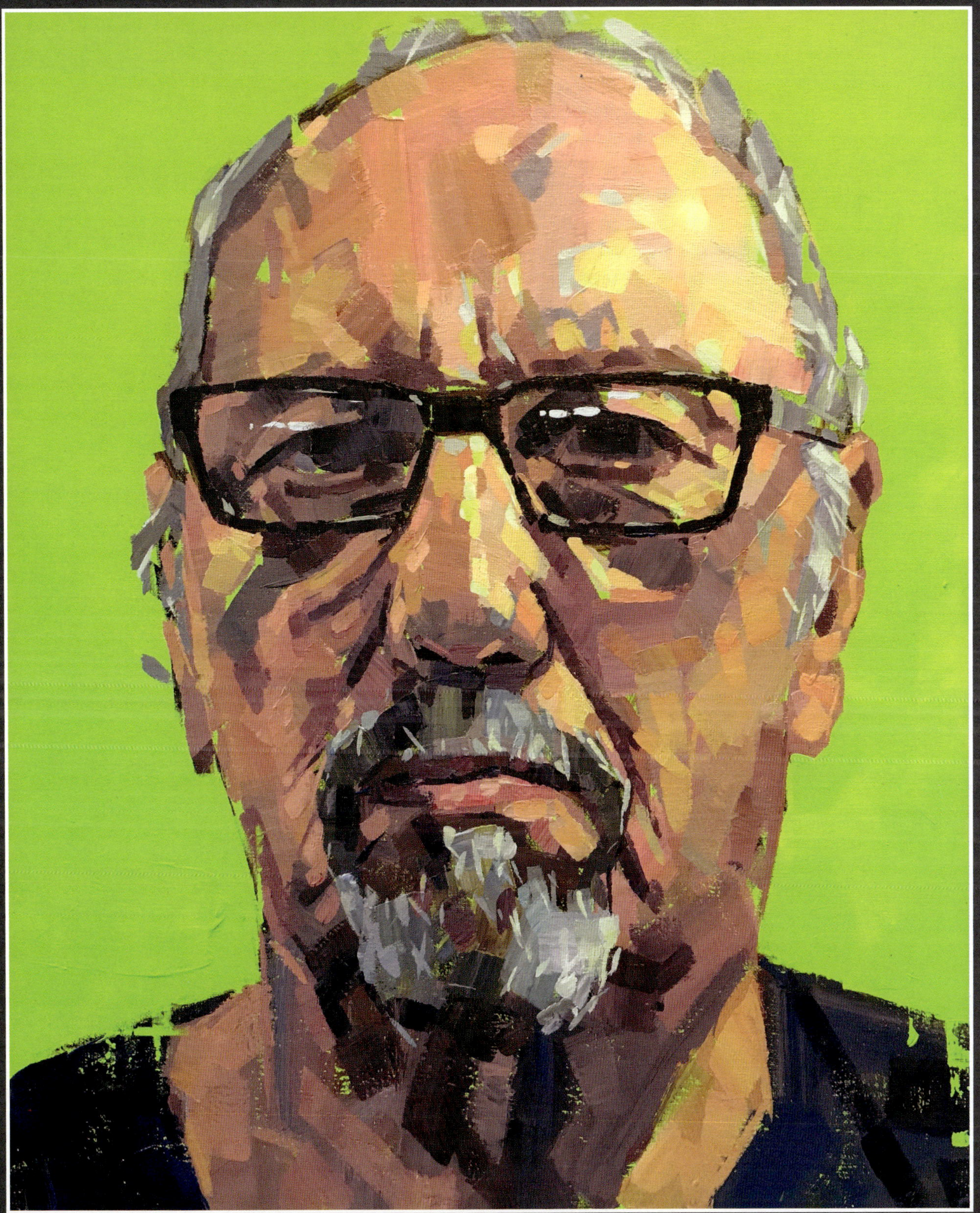

ROY 61×51CM (24×20IN)

Roy has a great face for portraits; his stern gaze disguises a great sense of humour and a real warmth as a human being. The use of vibrant colours goes some way to contradict the expression and suggest the underlying character.

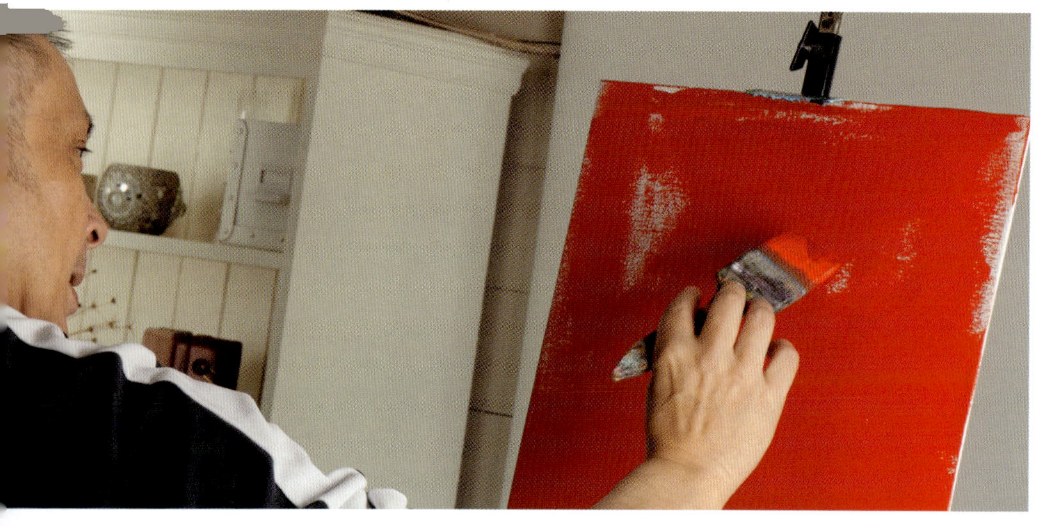

Base colours

I begin all my paintings with a base colour, which provides a tone or tint to create potent highlights and also acts as a simple warm-up before proper painting begins. Any base colour will affect subsequent applications of paint, usually darkening the mix, so layers of colours will appear richer if you use a white ground. However, a base colour establishes a tone and, as light tints that are applied have less competition from the white surface, they really pop. A blank canvas can be intimidating to a beginner, too. On balance, I think the advantages of any base colour in acrylics outweighs the downsides. The choice of colour can also play a part in the outcome if certain areas are left to flicker through. A warm base colour, such as a soft pink or earthy brown will harmonize with most skin types, but a complementary blue or green will create more dramatic effects. The base colour you choose will depend on the elements you want to dominate, which may be the background or the subject's attire – not necessarily the model's skin. A muted neutral base may be the best choice to create an understated feel. Whichever colour you choose, avoid making the base too dark as it may be difficult for any of the forthcoming colours to dominate.

Painting a base

1 Dampen a 50mm (2in) flat brush and load it with the base colour of your choice. Use this chance to warm up your arm with large, expressive strokes, covering the board.

2 Once you have covered the board, work back over with the brush to help smooth out any particularly obvious brushstrokes. It's good to have some subtle movement; the important thing is to completely cover the white, including any in the grain of the canvas. Don't let any speckles show.

3 Allow to dry – then start painting!

Painting different base colours can be fast – use a large brush and big, quick strokes to block in the field. Vary the angles of the strokes (see left) to create a dynamic, interesting surface on which to paint. The important bit is to cover the whole surface completely.

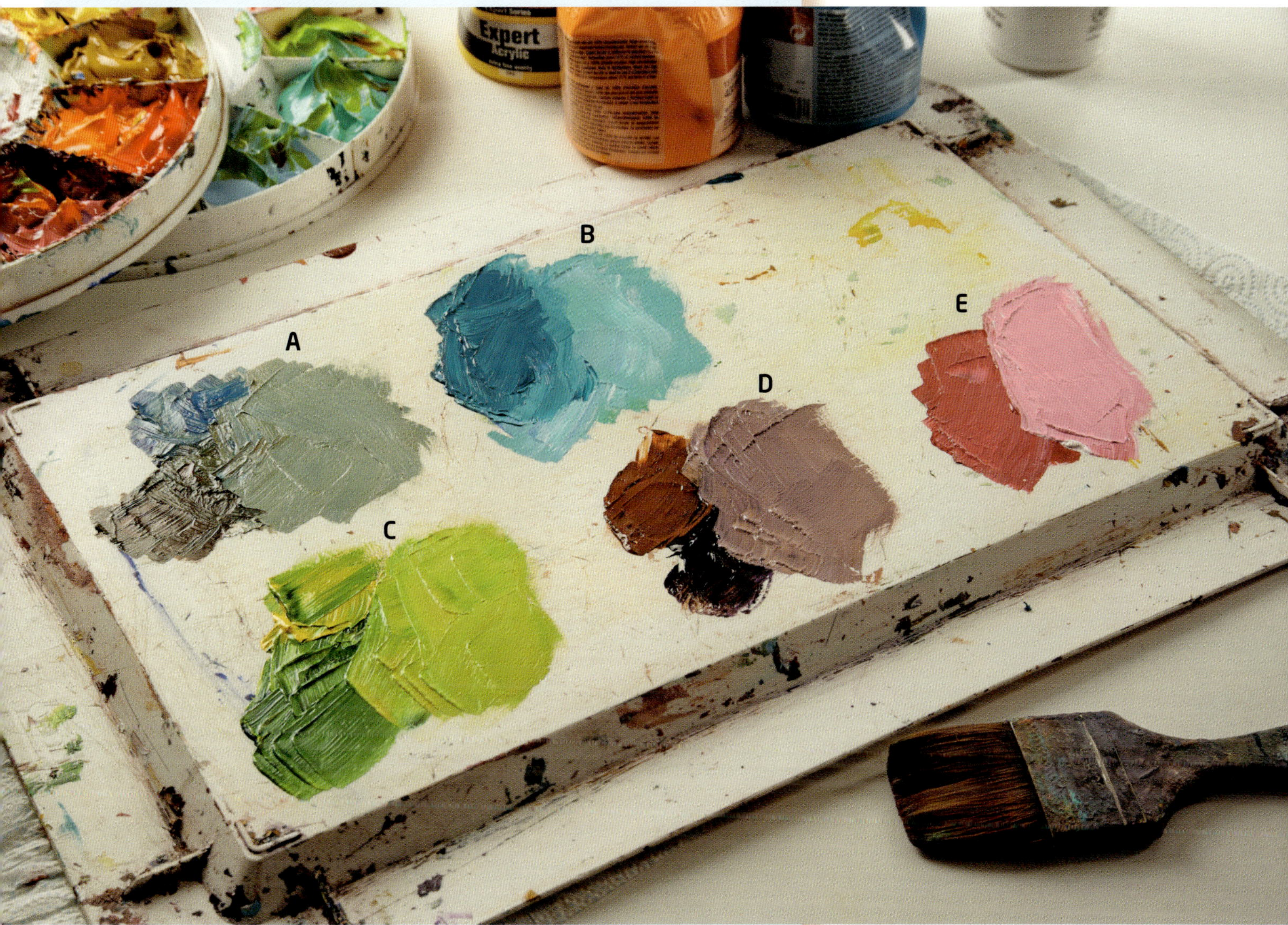

My top five base colours for portraits

A - Blue/brown grey A mix of phthalo blue and burnt sienna with titanium white, versatile enough for any portrait.

B -Turquoise Phthalo turquoise blue mixed with titanium white. This is an ideal contrasting colour for a warm skin tone.

C - Light green Sap green and cadmium yellow medium mixed with titanium white. This is an almost fluorescent base colour similar to turquoise, but with richer contrasts against reds.

D - Plum violet Permanent blue violet and burnt sienna with titanium white makes a harmonious base colour with earthy qualities.

E - Magenta pink Quinacridone rose with titanium white is one of my all-time favourites. It is versatile and harmonious against skin tone and contrasts against dark backgrounds, cool shadows or cool-coloured clothing extremely well.

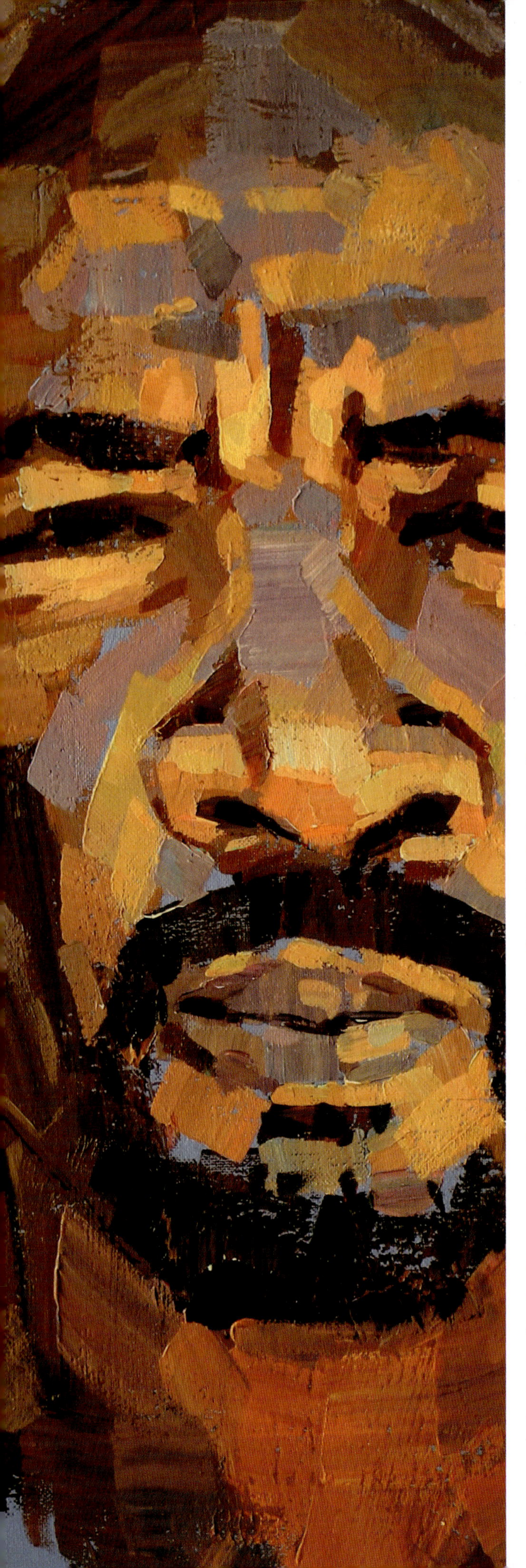

Painting skin

This is an important part of portraiture and one that a lot of people struggle with. A paint you can buy called 'flesh tint' has been the cause of many a failed portrait. Skin is both luminous and varied in colour, so any single hue will always fail to do it justice.

There are all kinds of different skin tones. The most apparent difference might be between ethnic groups, but the age of the figure, the weather conditions and lighting also create huge variation in how a complexion appears. Changes and variation are also caused by illness or environmental factors, such as heat or cold. Nevertheless, in most representational portraits all skin types will appear relatively consistent in colour. It's the external factors, such as lighting and environment, that draws particular hues forward.

Colour can be used to subvert our own expectations. A tattooed face with studs and a shaved head will conjure up a certain impression, and suggest a predictably gritty palette of dark or bold colours. Painting this portrait using pastel tints would play with that expectation, as would an unassuming portrait of someone's grandmother painted with vibrant or garish colours.

Equally, you might decide to completely ignore convention and re-imagine the portrait in your own chosen colour scheme. Realists can turn off now! Colour is a powerful tool in implying mood or to elicit emotion based on our common interpretation of what certain colours mean: a portrait with lots of fiery red implies passion and danger, for example, while purple suggests royalty. Blues imply a cool and calm persona.

There is nothing that forces you to copy the colours in front of you. Many modern artists explore these options in order to simply create arresting images. Art can sometimes be less about a pretty, technically correct representation, and more about creating something striking. This change in thinking requires time to absorb and adjust to.

Skin tone basics

To begin with, let's look at creating a consistent range of skin colour from six colours. Start with the primaries pyrrole red, cadmium yellow medium and cobalt blue. To these we can add yellow ochre as our earthy light tone, permanent blue violet – useful for both dark and light skin types – and titanium white.

Quantities play a big part and a mixing tray where you can test the colours and have various pools to choose from is essential. It's imperative not to overmix acrylic paint into one flat shade but allow some level of streaking as these will lift the luminosity of the colour mix.

A base mix for skin can be made from red, yellow and ochre. This produces a warm orange tint which looks too artificial, so introduce small shots of green and blue. These colours cool down the mix and create an earthier pigment.

Permanent blue violet is the darkest tone in the palette and can be added to the original mix in various amounts to create options for dark skin colour. The amount of titanium white is reduced and at this stage ochre can be used to soften darks. If the violet proves too domineering, add pure versions of each colour to counteract it.

For lighter skin, we can vary the proportions of the base mix. Less red in the overall mix will produce an olive-skinned colour, while less yellow will make a stronger pink. Reducing most of the warm colours is great for gritty, moody or even zombie portraits. The cooler colours also double up for shaded areas of skin.

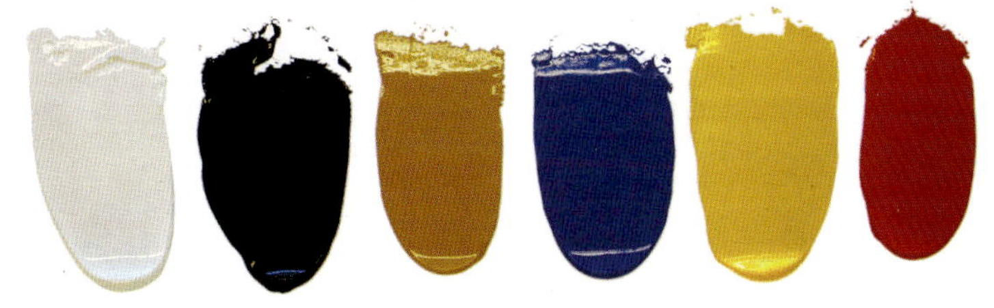

SKIN PALETTE

From left to right: titanium white, permanent blue violet, yellow ochre, cobalt blue, cadmium yellow medium and pyrrole red.

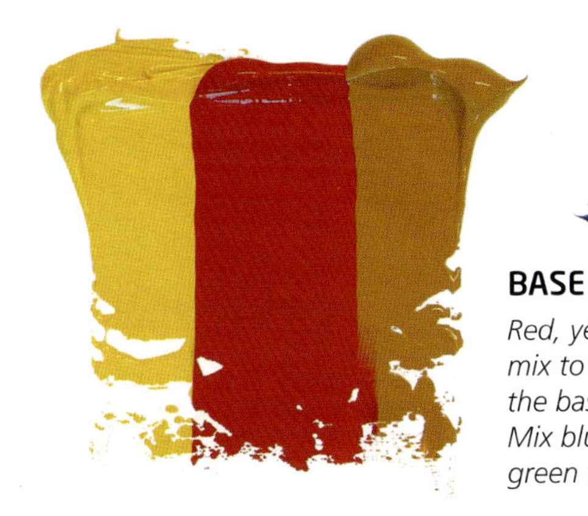
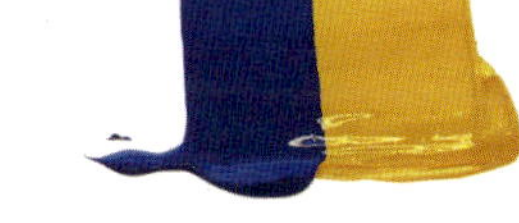

BASE MIX

Red, yellow and ochre (left) will mix to create a colour suitable as the base for almost any skin tone. Mix blue and yellow (above) for a green that will mute vibrancy.

DARK COLOUR MIXES

Adding violet to the base mix allows you to create darker skin tones.

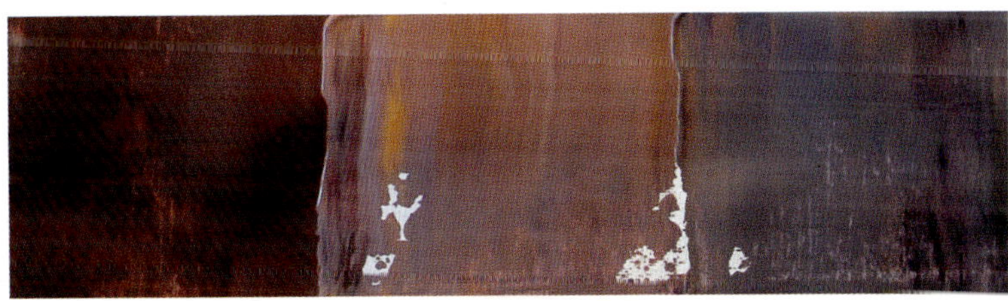

This very dark mix uses a relatively large amount of permanent blue violet.

This addition of titanium white and permanent blue violet gives a mid-dark.

Adding more cobalt blue alongside the permanent blue violet gives a rich warm grey.

LIGHT COLOUR MIXES

Adding titanium white and small dabs of cobalt blue to the base mix will create lighter skin mixes.

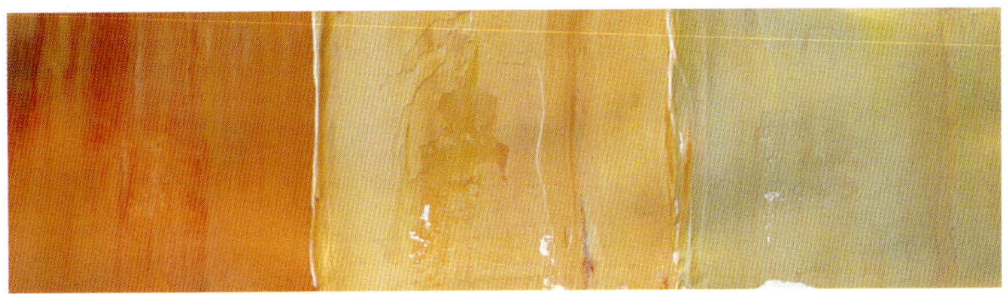

A warm mix that uses only tiny touches of blue and white.

More titanium white gives very pale skin.

More cobalt blue creates grey mixes suitable for shadows and the elderly.

Skin and environment

There are plenty of nuances in painting skin including variation of thickness in different parts of the face. Thin areas of skin such as the ears or the end of the nose can sometimes appear redder.

Beyond physical considerations, complications in painting skin can arise from external factors. Multiple colour light sources which bounce off various parts of the face will create a complex range of shadow colours as well as highlights. In these cases you have to work out what each colour is doing and how it affects the others.

If you get stuck trying to mix any awkward colour, it's worth considering the following; is the colour warm or cool; dark or light? Does a particular colour dominate? A tint or neutral may still contain a bias toward a particular pigment. In addition, pay attention to the surrounding colours or tones in order to see how they relate.

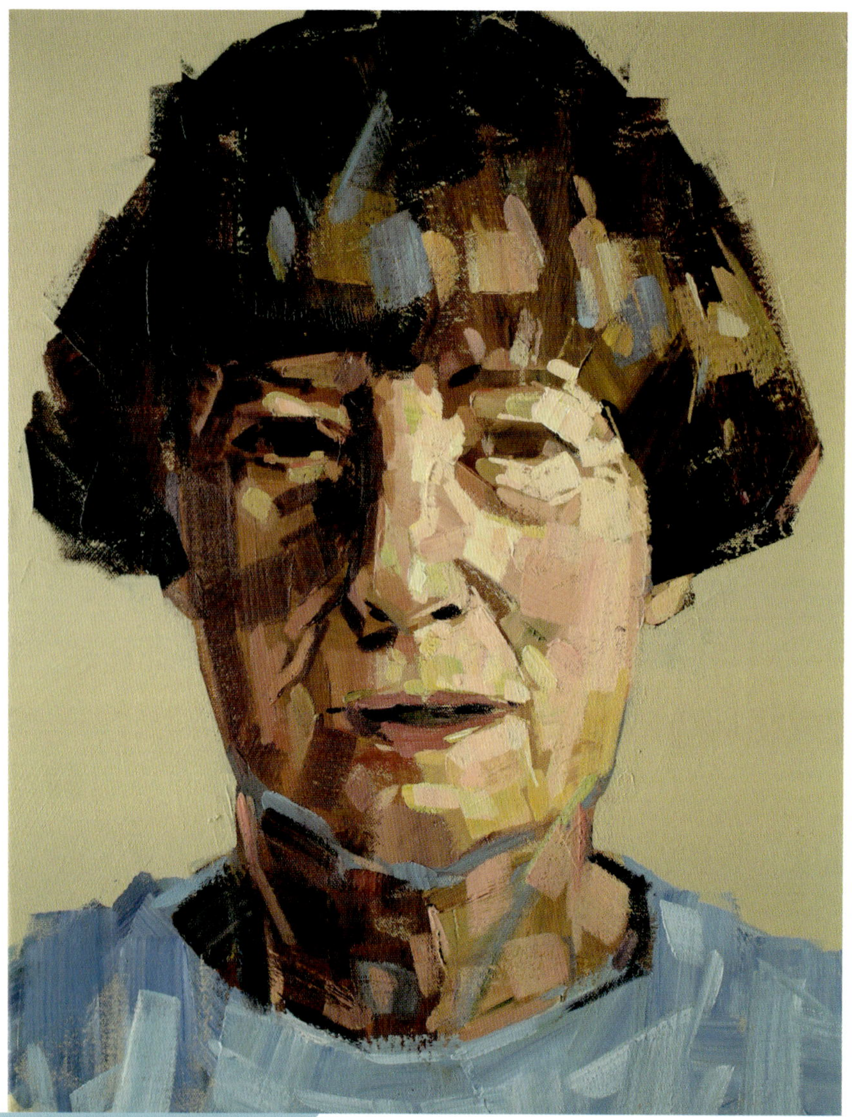

PAT 46×61CM (18×20IN)

The reflective nature of skin picks up on colours around it. Someone wearing a blue top – as here – will reflect some of that colour in their face and arms. In colour mixing terms, this is relatively easy to deal with.

Stark bright light such as daylight can pick up any imperfections of the model, so you may want to explore shading parts of the face to minimize - or emphasize - this effect.

Use of light on skin

The reference photograph for *Elena, Night* (opposite, left) was taken in the street at night; and the resulting portrait relies on the artificial light that envelops the entire figure in a consistent orange glow – great for unifying the painting. Things would be more complicated with multiple coloured lights (see above), but it's worth exploring such environments to provide unusual takes on lighting a portrait.

Daylight, especially that of a strong sunny day, bounces colour all over the place. You can use this to its extreme in order to optimize colour. A good example of this is in *Elena, Day* (opposite, right) where natural daylight streams in, showing the natural colours of the skin and enhancing the golden streaks in the hair. The light illuminates the lower portion of the painting and creates strong darks in the top half. The shadows around the mouth reflect the intense warm glow while the other shadows are blue or a dark, burnt red.

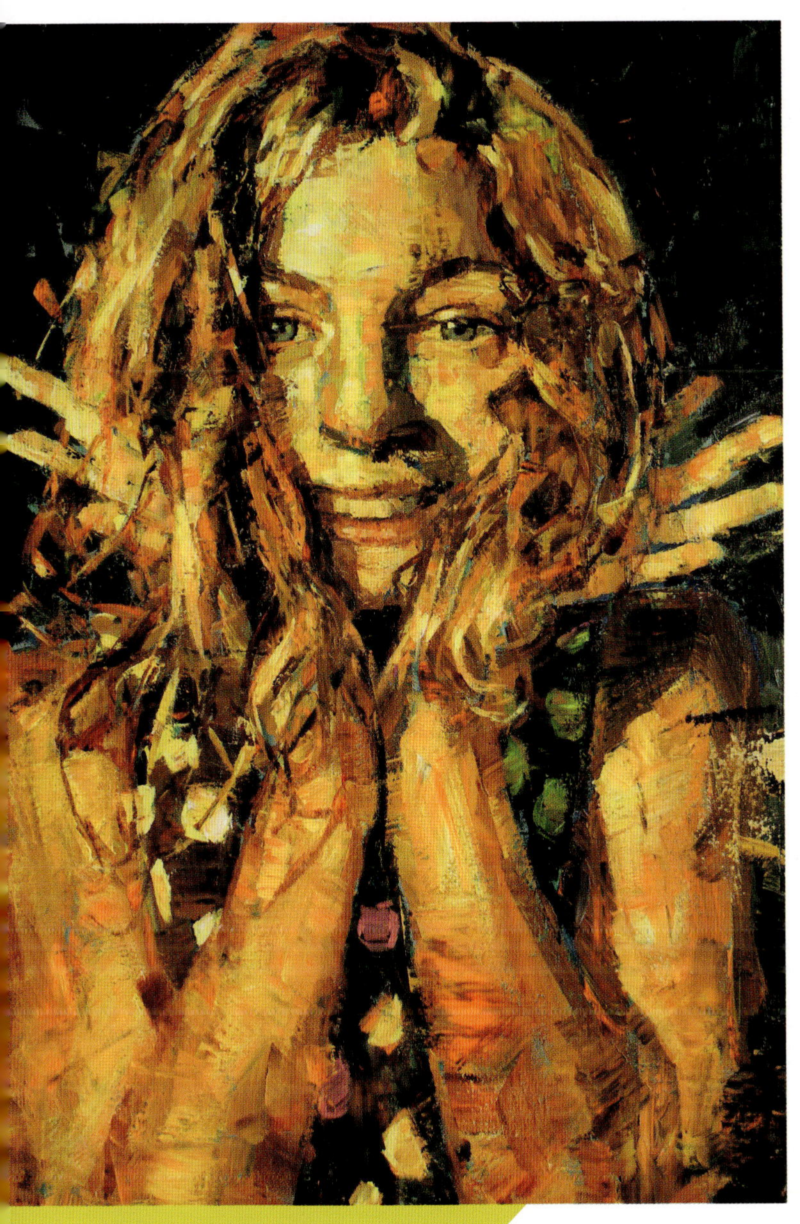

ELENA, NIGHT 51×71CM (20×28IN)

Darks frame the face and the fingers add a diagonal leading in to the face. Small shots of colour from the model's top create a few diversions away from a simple monotone image. The blue-grey in the eyes is a complementary of the orange light that colours the skin, and so creates tiny sparks.

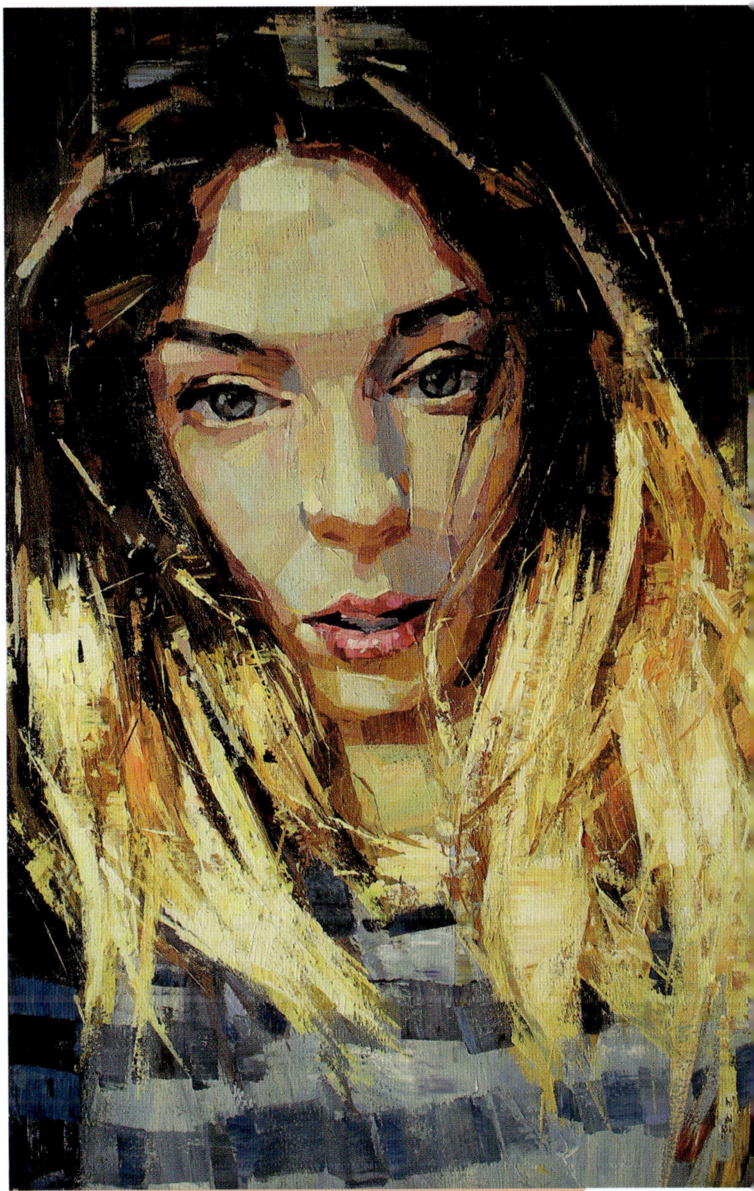

ELENA, DAY 51×76CM (20×30IN)

Again, the blues here are used to play off the shimmering yellow and orange, but the natural daylight means the colours are more balanced.

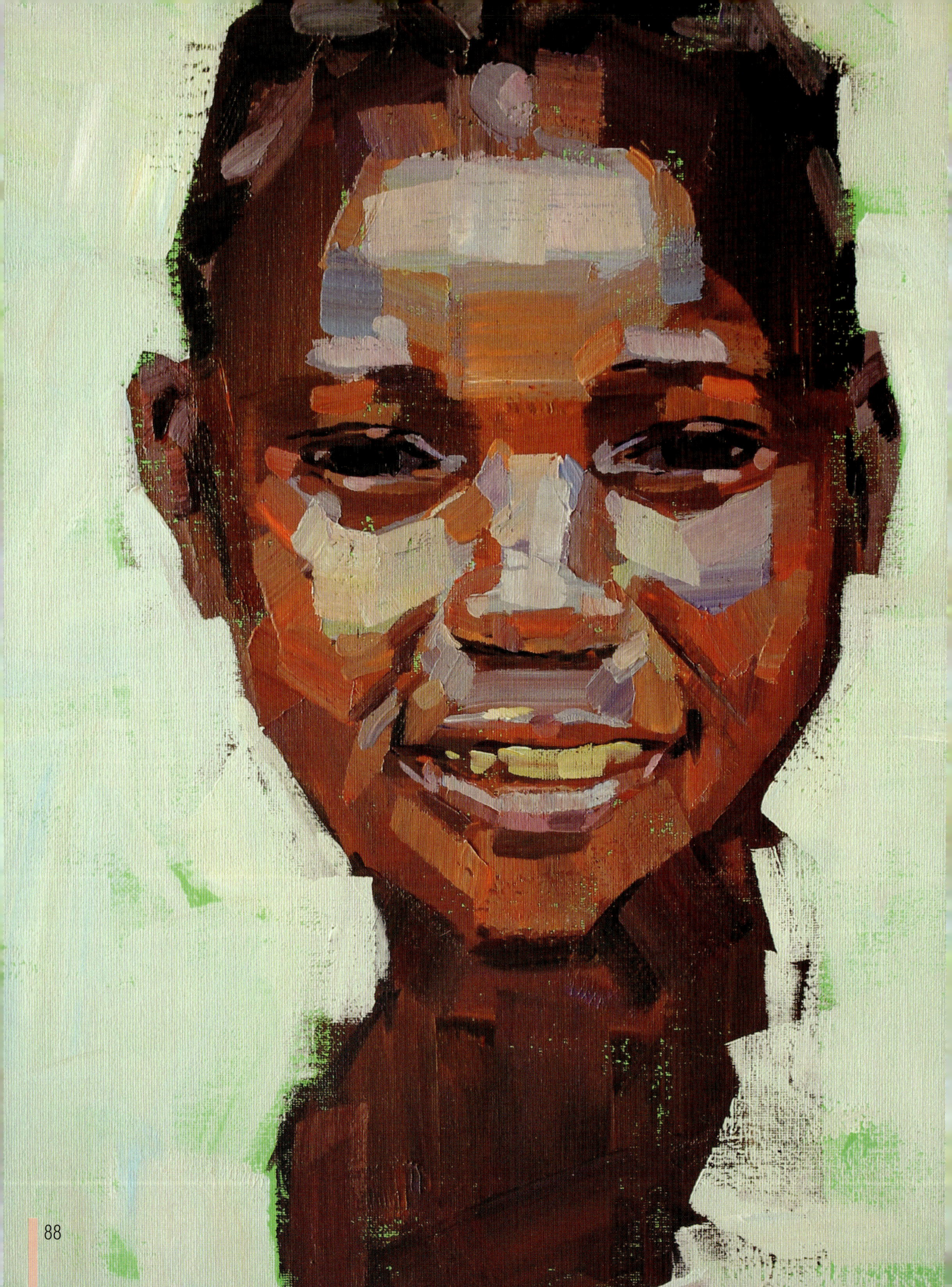

Painting children

Young children are particularly difficult when painting in acrylics as their skin tones are very smooth. Flow improver or retarder can be used to dilute paint for some blending or you could use blocks of subtle colour placed side by side. Youthful faces tend to have plenty of pastel tints, which require balancing colour with white to avoid chalky colour mixes. Children's features are also more delicate than adults, and need a certain amount of accuracy.

Anatomically, babies have rounded faces with gentle curves. They have no visible cheekbones and with less pronounced features than adults. As they get older, children start to show more contouring in their face, with their nose and chin becoming more defined. When they enter their teens, features such as the nose, cheekbones, eyelid folds, and muscle tone become more visible, and hair and eyebrows become fuller.

Vibrancy is important when portraying youthful skin. One of the most common complaints when using acrylics is that the colours get duller than when using oils, the traditional medium for portraits. Some artists try to lift colour by varnishing the finished painting with a gloss varnish or revert to oil painting halfway through. However, using neater applications of acrylic will help to maintain pigment luminosity. Using complementary colours next to each other will make colours appear brighter, too. Another way to improve vibrancy is to use less white in your mixes, as it can result in chalky mixes.

Painting *Girl on White*

Before painting I sketched out the portrait on a light green base colour. Using plenty of violet, red, burnt sienna and a touch of sap green, I began applying dark for hair and skin tones to the sides of the forehead, then added the eye sockets and darks around the neck. I also plotted a few lighter darks around the nose and mouth. The centre of the face glows, so warmer colours including red, ochre, orange and a small amount of buff titanium dominate the dark mix.

To maintain the luminous colour, I did not introduce white at this stage: yellow ochre and buff titanium tint the dark sufficiently. White was only added to the mix later, for the lightest tints. As a result, the vibrant colours maintain a strong hold. The highlighted areas also contain shots of king's blue and light violet to spark off reds and yellows.

A considered amount of detail helps to sharpen up the features. I've used broad strokes throughout but these are applied with confidence and left un fussed. A light cream background emphasizes the portrait shape with flickers of the green base coming through to play off the warm reds.

GIRL ON WHITE 36×46CM (14×18IN)

I began my career painting children's portraits with predictable staged smiles from ear to ear; but it's far more naturalistic to have a relaxed expression and pose.

The colours used for the figure in this project are harmonious: the magenta in the top is reflected in the sunglasses, for example. To add contrast, I've decided to use a light turquoise base colour. It's useful to make these decisions early on as you are guaranteed some kind of reaction.

To achieve the appearance of smooth skin here, you need fewer transitions. To help with this, try mixing the skintone pool up a little more than in the earlier demonstrations in the book. The paint shouldn't be completely homogenous, but you want fewer obvious colours standing out in the pool than when painting an adult's skin.

YOU WILL NEED

Brushes: 37mm (1½in) flat, 25mm (1in) flat, 16mm (¾in) flat

Paints: Turquoise green, quinacridone rose opaque, titanium white, yellow ochre, cadmium orange, yellowish green, sky blue, burnt sienna, permanent blue violet opaque, pyrrole red, turquoise blue, permanent blue violet

Surface: Canvas board, 51×61cm (20×24in)

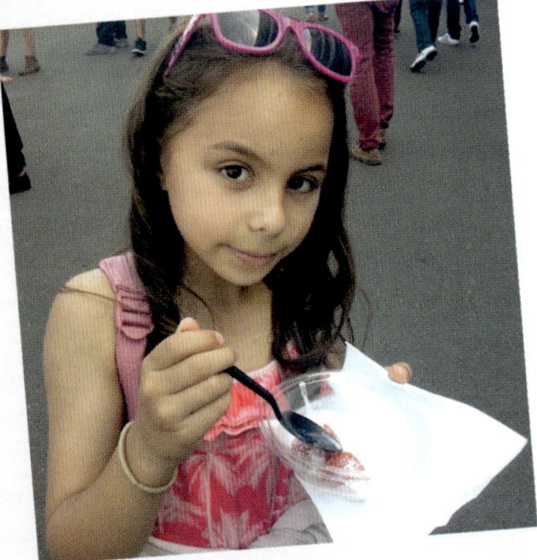

The source photograph.

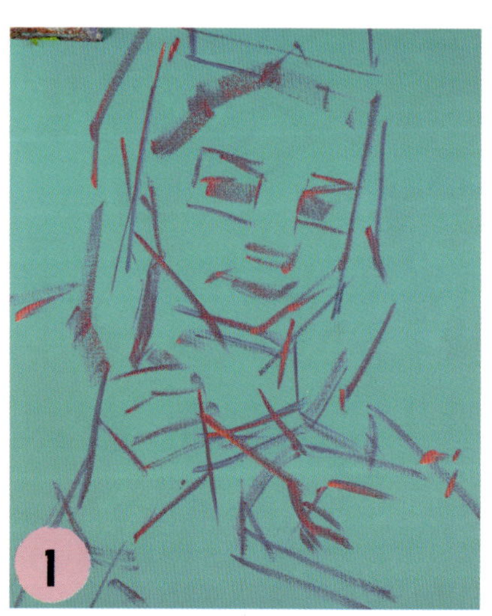

1 Starting from a field of turquoise green, use a 25mm (1in) flat brush to create the basic frame using quinacridone rose opaque.

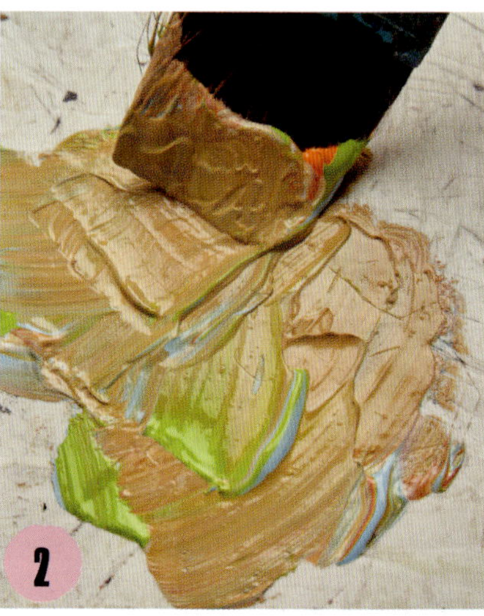

2 Load a 37mm (1½in) flat brush with titanium white, yellow ochre, cadmium orange, quinacridone rose opaque, yellowish green and sky blue for a basic olive skin tone.

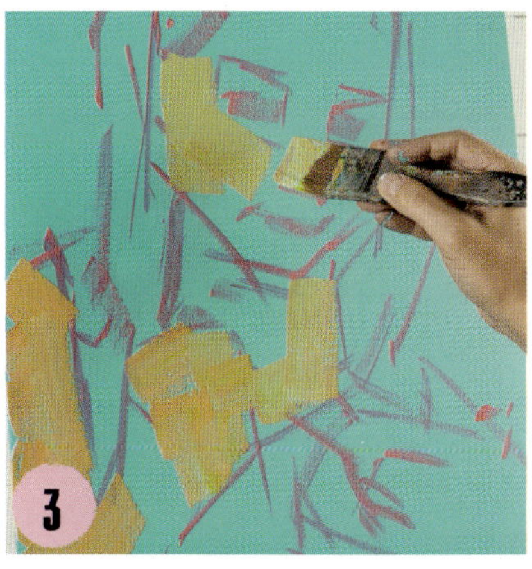

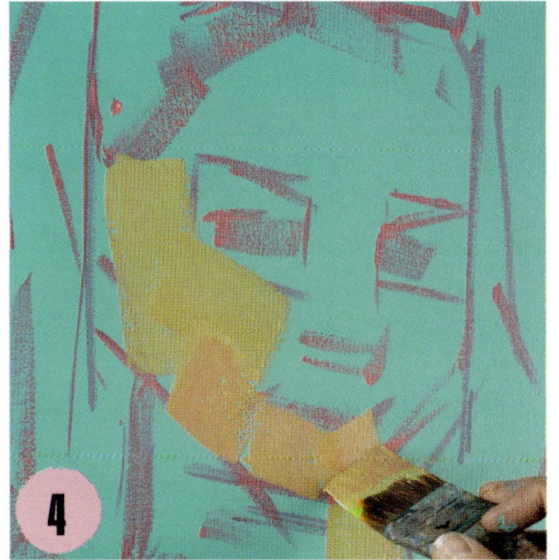

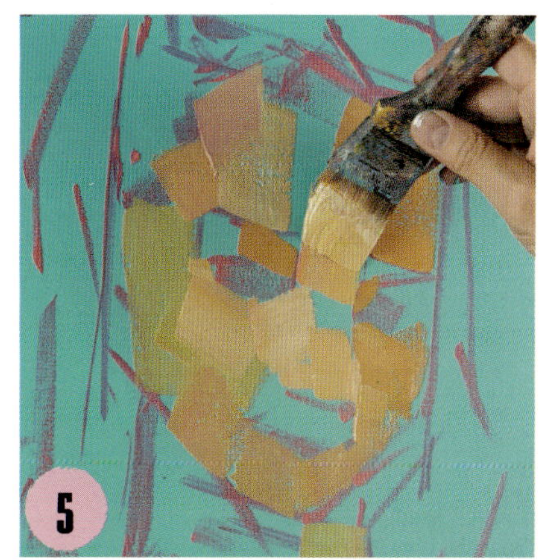

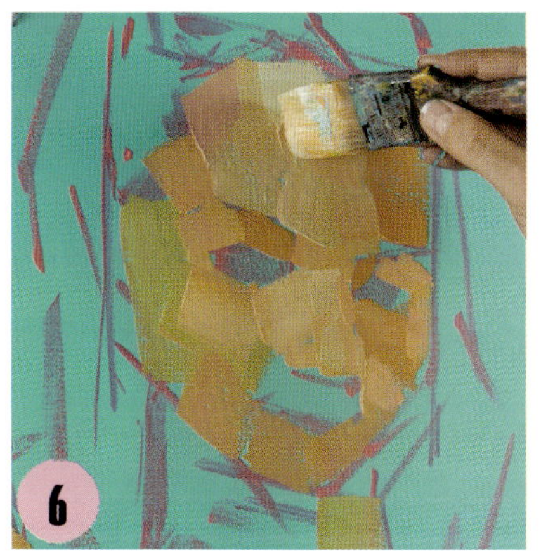

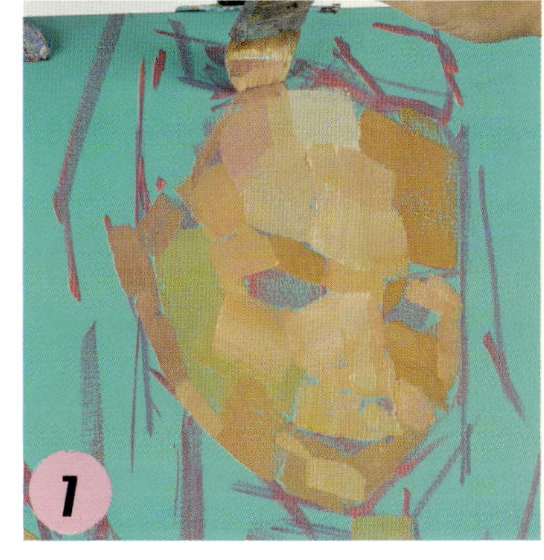

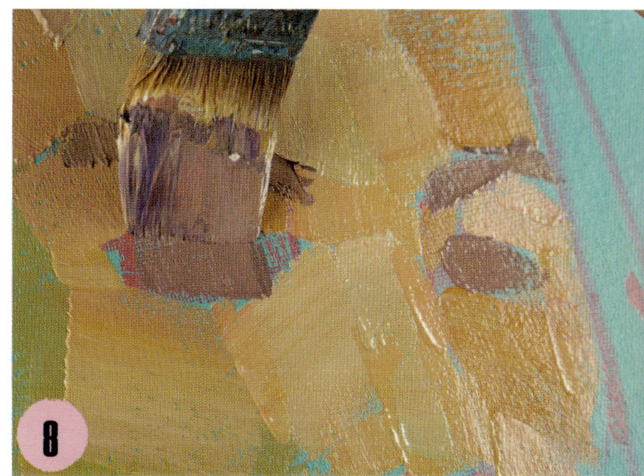

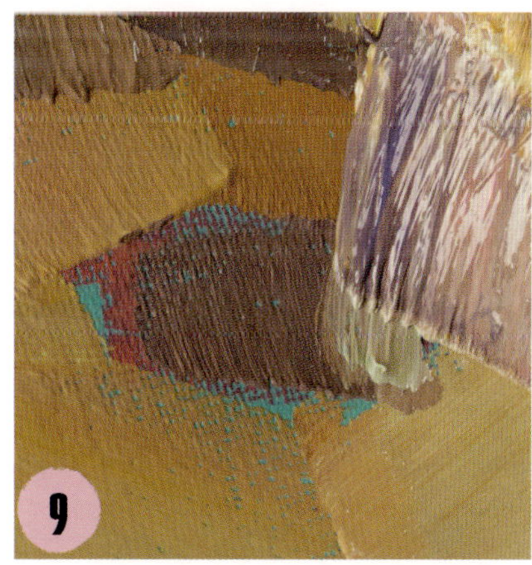

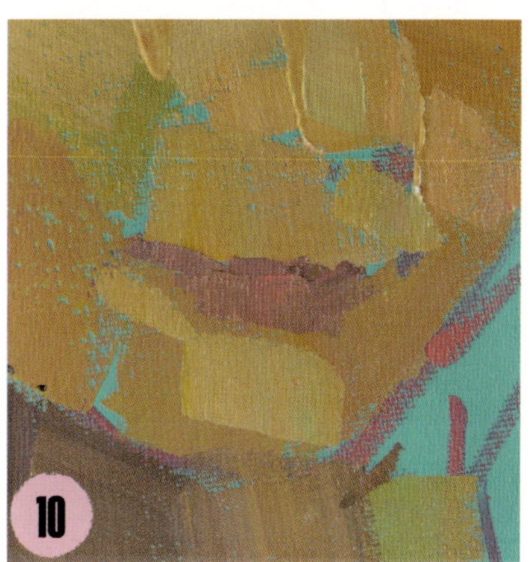

3 Use slightly longer, larger strokes that overlap and intersect to paint the arm and the cheek. Aim for fewer gaps and breaks than in adult skin.

4 Use a little more quinacridone rose opaque for the chin and jawline, aiming for subtlety.

5 Add some burnt sienna and more yellowish green for the side of the areas of the face in shadow.

6 Continue building up the patchwork of colour across the face. You need to strike a balance between smoothness and blandness; aim for interest and variety – just avoid obvious exposed brushstrokes where possible.

7 Add more burnt sienna and quinacridone rose opaque for the ear and left-hand side of the face.

8 Introduce permanent blue violet opaque for the neck in shadow, to establish the position of the eyebrows, and also to fill the eyes.

9 Use the corner of the brush to touch in the whites of the eyes using a light part of the main skin tone pool, adding a hint more sky blue to brighten it.

10 Add some quinacridone rose opaque to the darker area of the pool and paint in the lips.

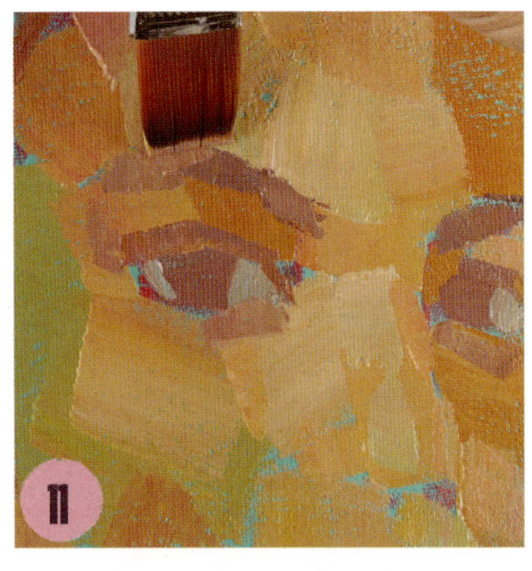

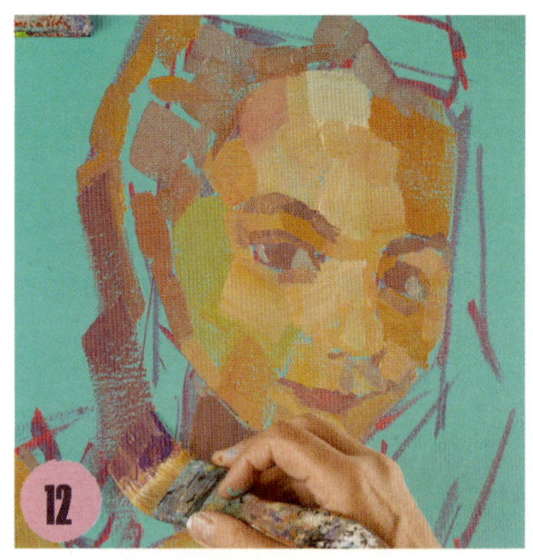

11 Change to a 25mm (1in) flat brush and add in the eyelids and area beneath the eye with the edge of the brush. These marks must be subtle; as should be the variation in colour.

12 Add more sky blue to the main skin tone pool to mute it. Use this neutral to build up the hair.

13 Use some yellow ochre for the top left of the hair, then work in permanent blue violet for the lower part on the left, and the hair in shadow on the right.

14 Incorporate some yellowish green into the same mix and develop the shadow on the hand, picking out the fingers.

15 Create a new pool of pyrrole red, cadmium orange and quinacridone rose opaque.

16 Using a clean 37mm (1½in) fat brush, paint in the strong reds on the top. Add titanium white to make a pink for the backpack straps.

17 Cool the red pool with sky blue for the shadow areas on the top, then add more pyrrole red to the mix for the strawberries in the bowl.

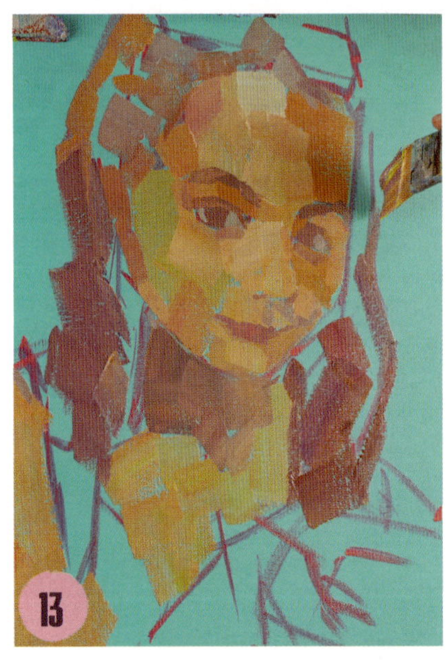

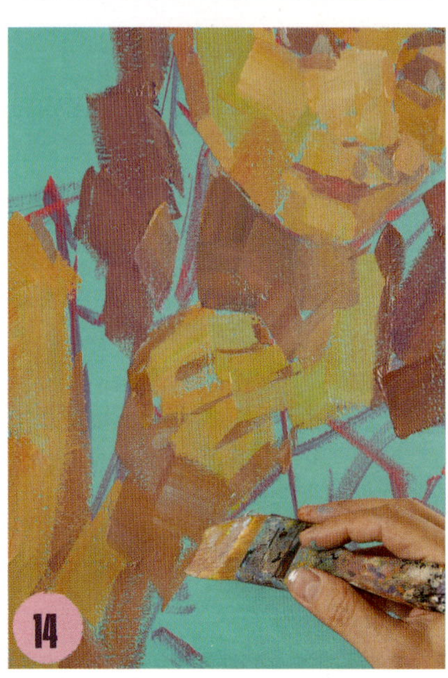

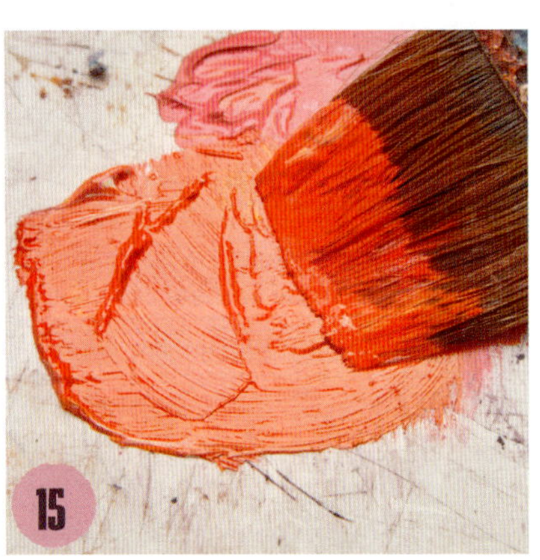

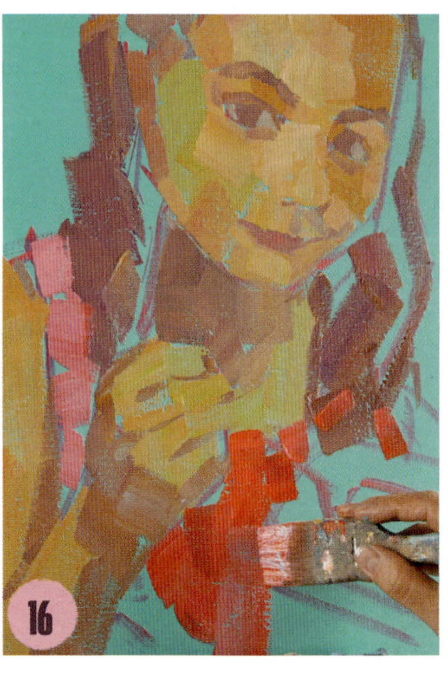

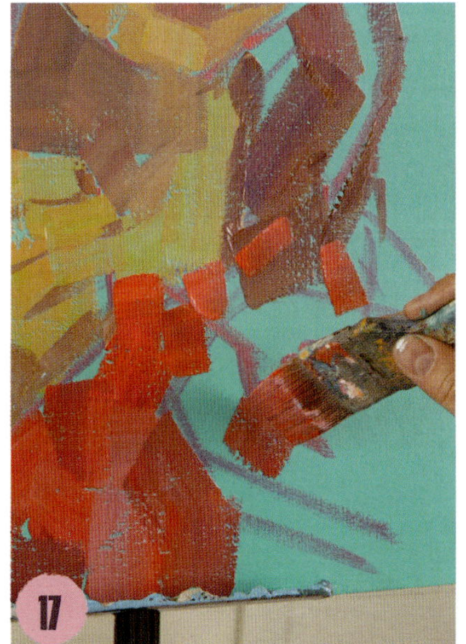

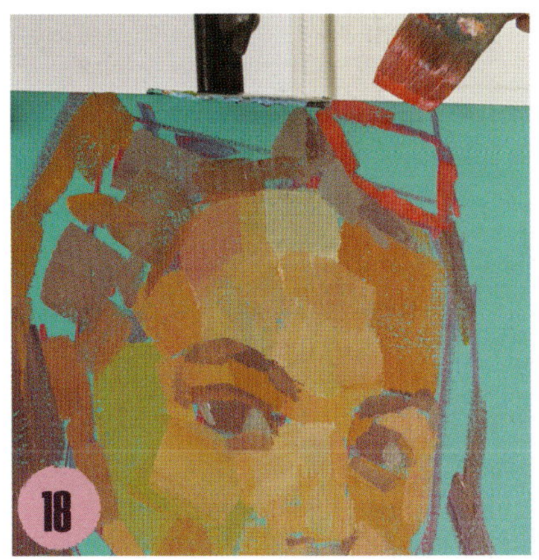

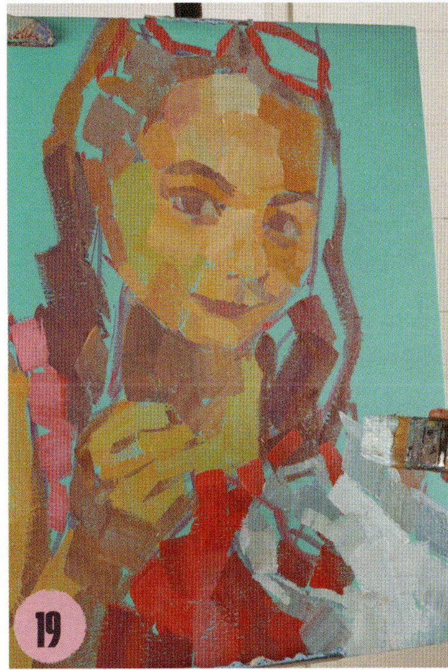

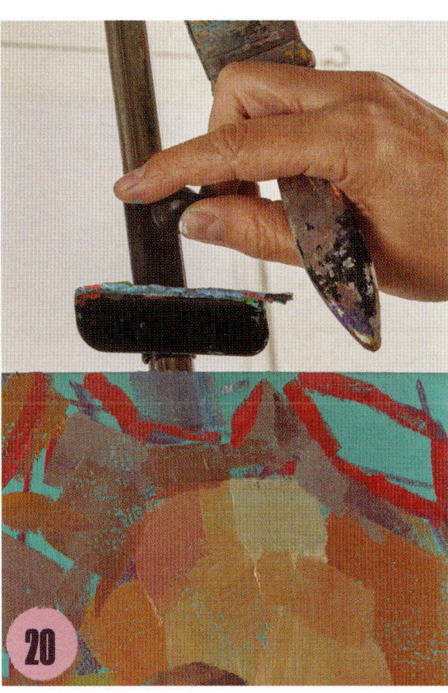

18 Still using the same brush, add the frames of the sunglasses using quinacridone rose opaque.

19 Adapt the skintone pool by adding turquoise blue to the browner areas. This will produce a vibrant, cool blue-grey you can use to develop the napkin and clear bowl on the lower right-hand corner.

20 Use the same mix for the lenses of the sunglasses – if you need to move the securing part of the easel, feel free. Just remember to replace it.

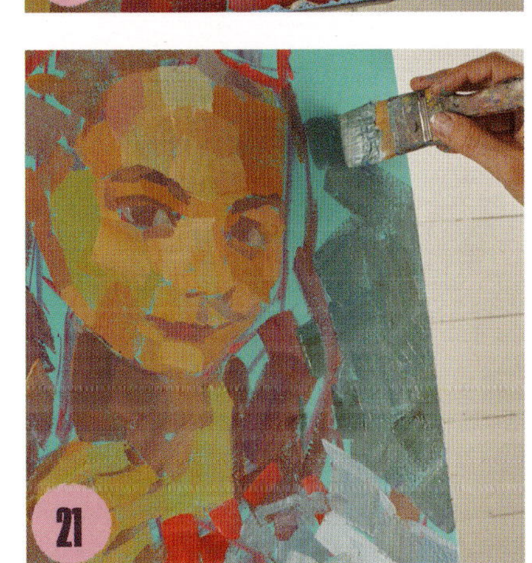

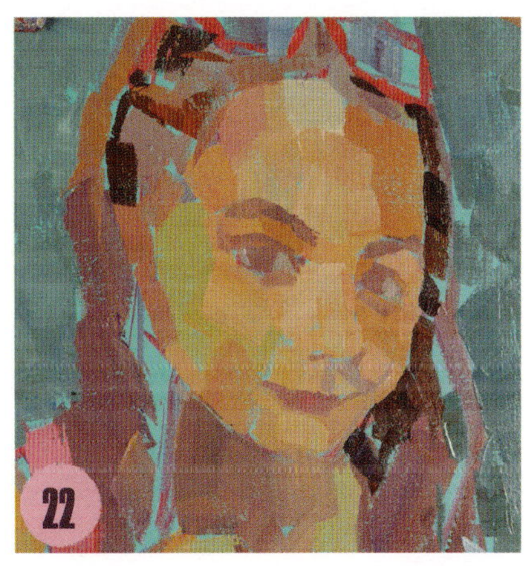

21 Add burnt sienna to the mix to make a darker variation, and use this to quickly block in the background using different directional brushstrokes.

22 Using the 37mm (1½in) brush you used for the reds, begin to block in the darks on the hair; adding permanent blue violet, cadmium orange and a little yellowish green and sky blue to the red pool.

23 Use some of the deeper colours to subtly develop the eyebrows. Be careful not to make them too strong. The deep tone of the eyes and line of the mouth, which will be added later, need to contrast with the surrounding areas.

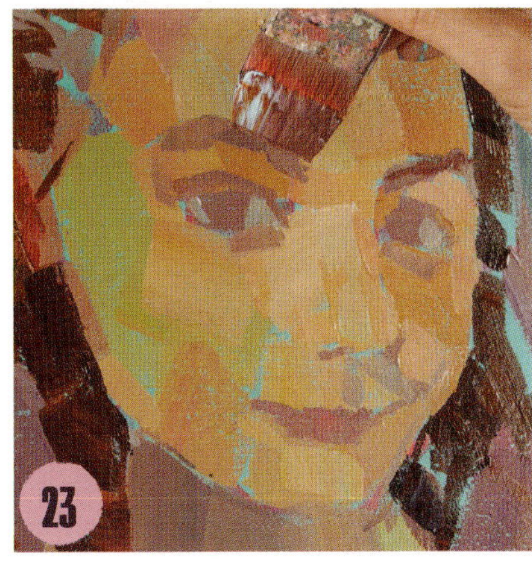

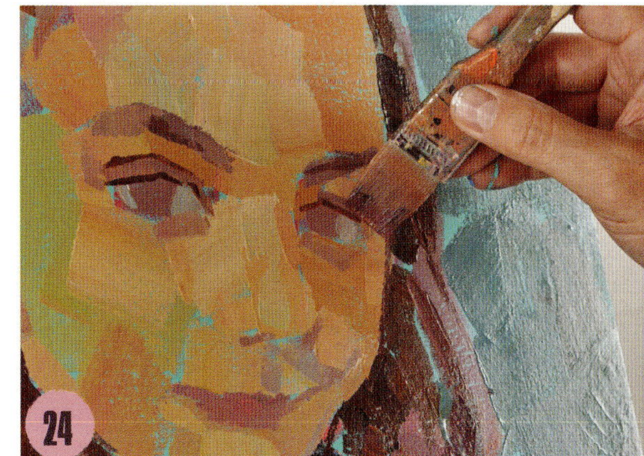

24 Change to a 25mm (1in) flat brush and use the pool of darks (see step 21) to add in the eyelashes and eyelids.

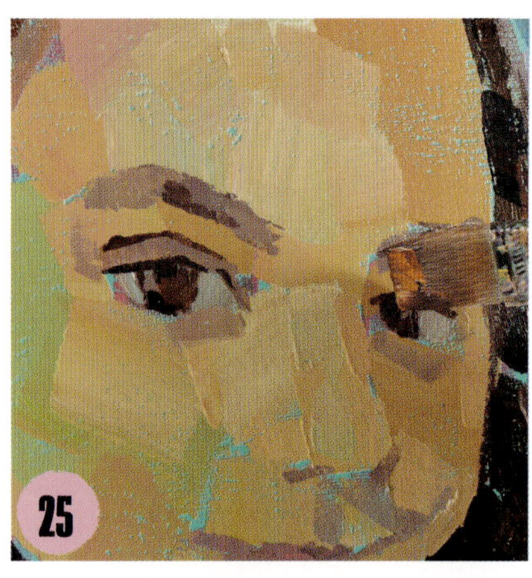

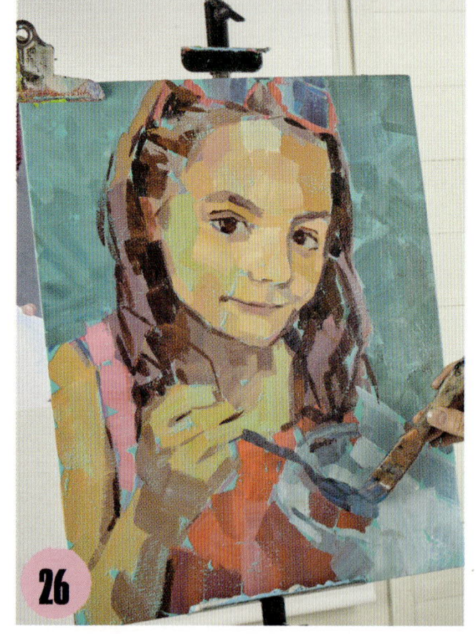

25 With the paint remaining on the brush, touch in the irises and pupils. Make considered marks using the edge of the brush

26 Use the darks on the palette to block in the lenses of the sunglasses and to paint in the spoon.

27 Use a clean 25mm (1in) flat brush to add more titanium white to the basic olive skin tone (titanium white, yellow ochre, cadmium orange, quinacridone rose opaque, yellowish green and sky blue), in order to tint it. When creating a highlight mix for younger skin, aim for slightly less contrast than you would with adult or older skin. This helps to soften the transitions, and avoids disrupting the smoother underlayer you've created. Build up the shoulder and arm.

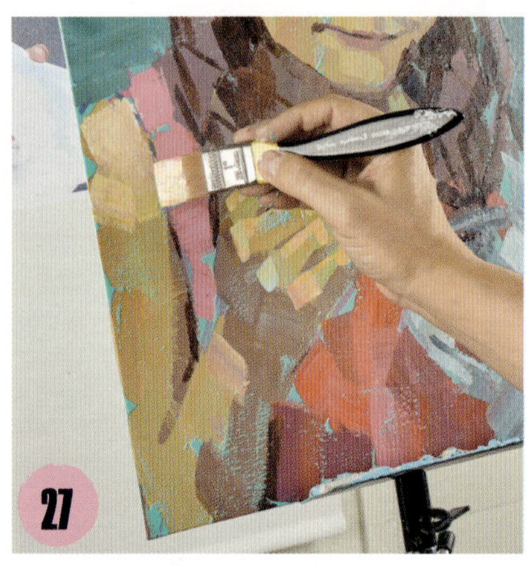

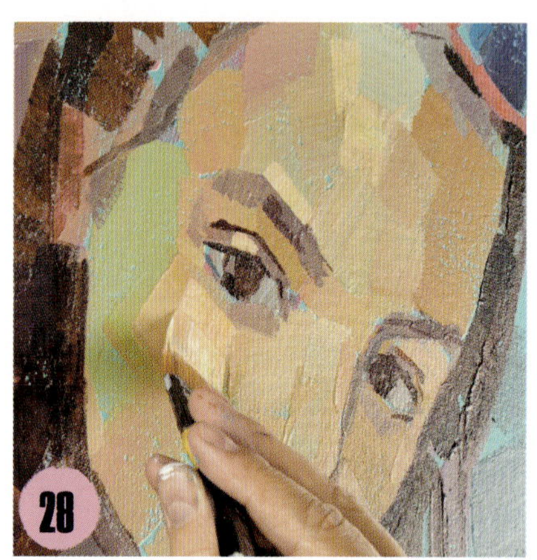

28 Move on to the face, making small adjustments to the cheek, forehead, nose and chin. These should be subtle: perhaps larger in brushstroke size than you might for an adult, but much closer to the underlying skin tone in hue.

29 Add sky blue to the mix and add sharp highlights to the sunglasses (top) and plastic bowl (bottom).

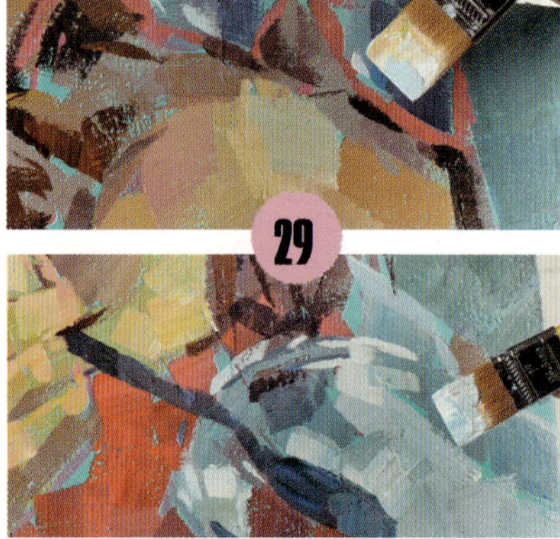

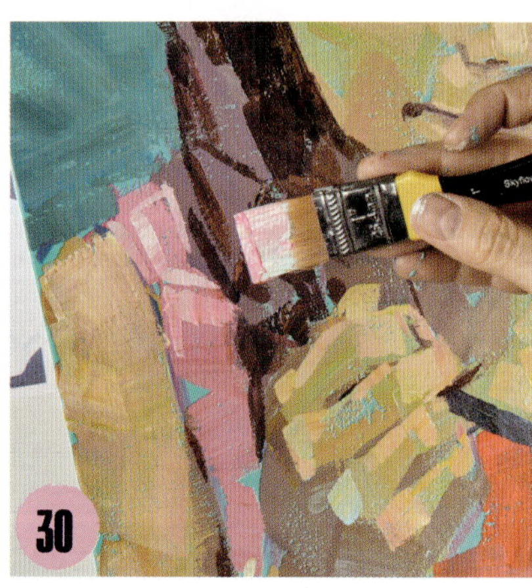

30 Add a simple bracelet with a few marks, then use a light pink pool to add highlights and detail to the backpack strap.

31 Add some more burnt sienna and sky blue to the skin highlight mix and suggest some sunlight caught on the hair on the left-hand side, then make any adjustments you feel necessary to finish.

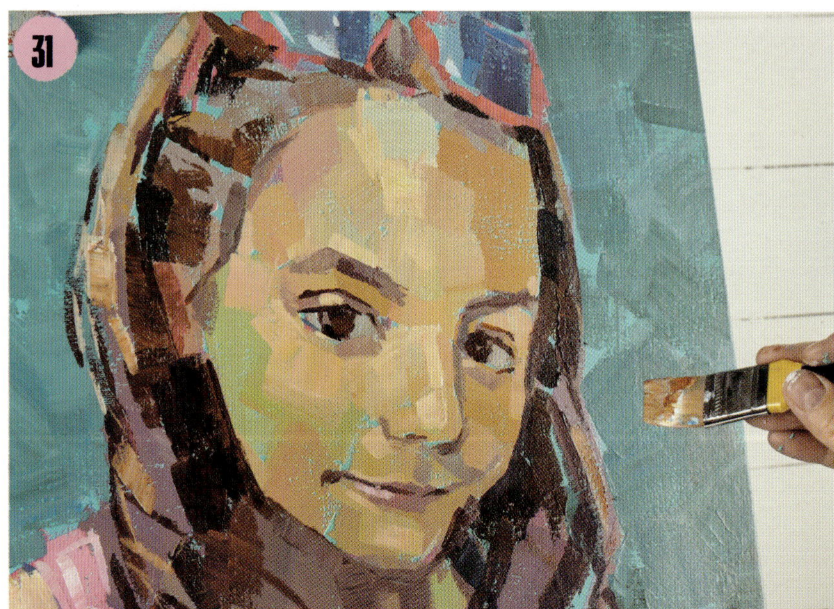

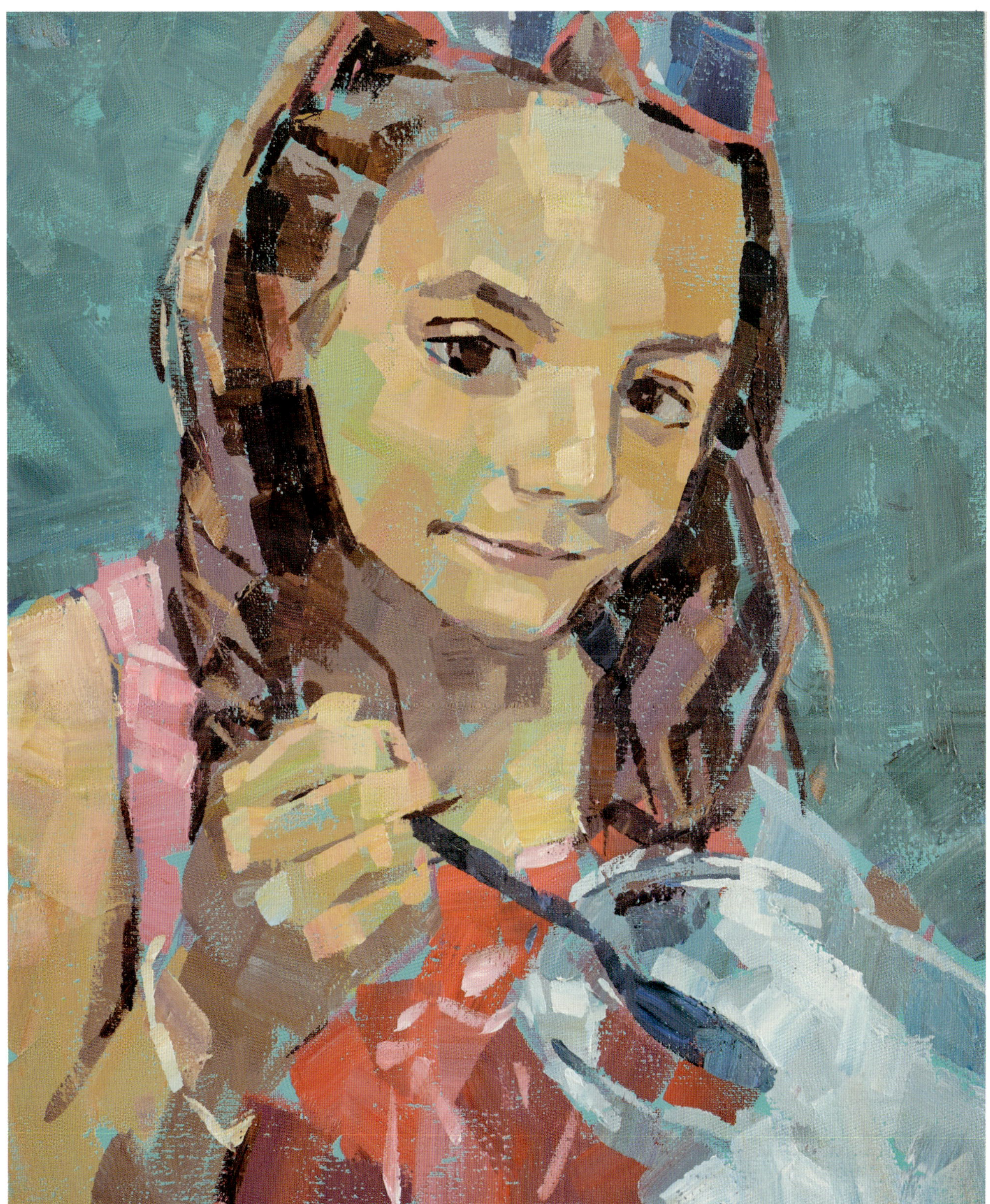

THE FINISHED PORTRAIT.

*Additional highlights – to the lower lip and to add decorations to the top – were
made with the light pink pool. Fine adjustments like this are useful for any portrait,
and particularly handy for painting the smooth skin of children. Just be careful
not to be overly fussy, or you will lose the spontaneity that's equally important.*

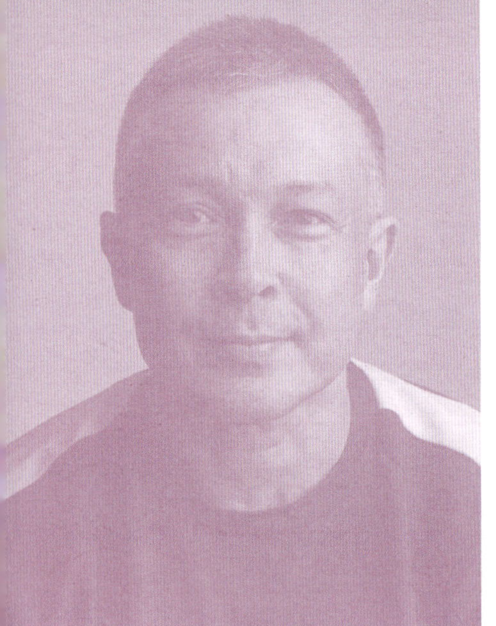

Painting self-portraits

You are your own best model. You're available, you know the nuances of your face intimately, and you know the traits that make up your personality. Self-portraits, whether from photographs or from life, will give you the chance to experiment with all kinds of expressions and poses.

You can get to know bone structure, feel the weight of your head, the texture of skin, the subtle changes of colour in light and – even more intimately – the recognition that a brain and personality are housed underneath the façade. We have an understanding of these facets, but drawing and painting provides time to fully explore them.

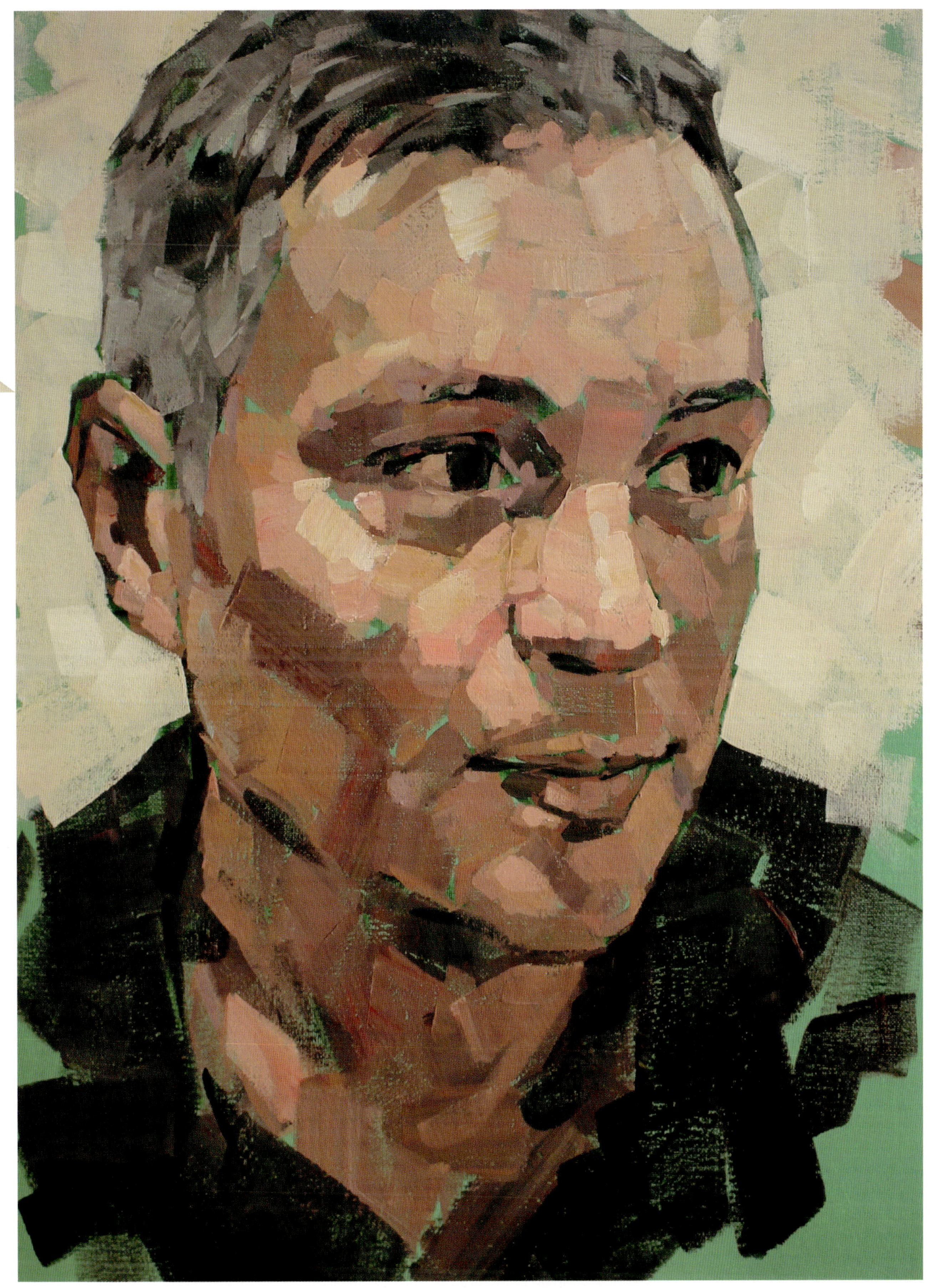

Scale, proportion and measurement

Many traditional art theories on drawing faces can contradict each other. They may be based on classical art techniques, but some of these ideas have proven not entirely accurate for everyone. Ethnic differences, medical conditions or treatments contribute to varying proportions. You may find some symmetry in faces, especially with children, but as we are all different it's difficult to rely on set formulas. Self-portraits provide the opportunity to really examine the scale and proportion of features and see how they correlate.

I avoid thinking of a face in literal terms, as the complexities of illustrating features like eyes, wrinkles and ears can be overwhelming. Instead I start by looking for big, simple shapes that de-clutter the detail, such as the forehead and cheeks. It's only once the foundations are laid that other elements can be defined and the smaller components added and adjusted for accuracy.

If a measurement is off, I generally look for what I consider to be my most accurate part of the drawing, which might be the length of the nose or the width of the chin to the bottom lip. I can then use that measurement as a guide to help me re-draw the inaccurate area.

You may see artists in life-drawing classes holding an upright pencil at arm's length, their thumb at a point on the pencil. This technique makes the distance between the tip of the thumb and the end of the pencil act as the measuring scale; allowing features to be easily compared with each other and, if necessary, adjusted.

As the eyes are generally the most important features I concentrate here more than any other area for accuracy. A measurement I use frequently and find true is that the distance between the eyes is an eye's width: effectively three eyes sat next to each other. Any more or less can make the portrait look inaccurate.

There are plenty of art books and online lectures solely devoted to drawing accurately, but the science can overwhelm the fun. Children dive in and just draw; over time they get better, but stifling their enjoyment by laying down hard and fast rules will kill the creative urge.

Multiple view sketches

Before embarking on a full painting it's a good idea to get to know your face by producing a series of sketches from different angles. It's a great warm-up and will make you consider something other than just a straight head-on pose. You may even find the painting works better as a series of viewpoints, a concept modern-day portraiture embraces quite widely.

SELF-PORTRAIT SKETCHES

I prefer sketching with paint and brushes as the marks and strength are more immediate. I can employ tone in an instant using the width of a large brush, and refinement by using the edge.

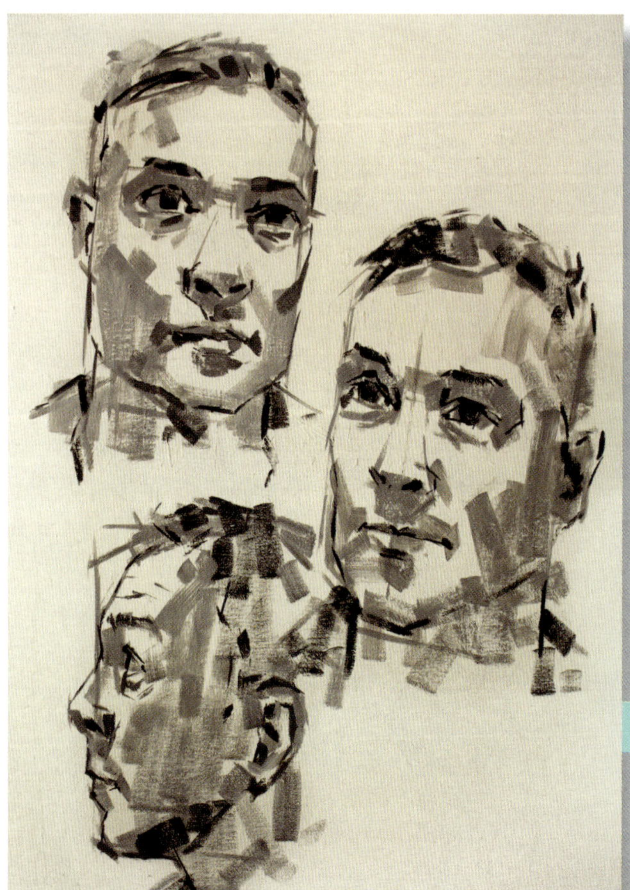

SELF-PORTRAIT FROM SKETCHES 36×46CM (14×18IN)

Starting with sketches always makes you better informed when tackling full -colour paintings. Even the mental notes you make will acclimatize you to the portrait. With this self-portrait I was keen to add some movement to the painting by diffusing edges and exploiting colour in addition to tone.

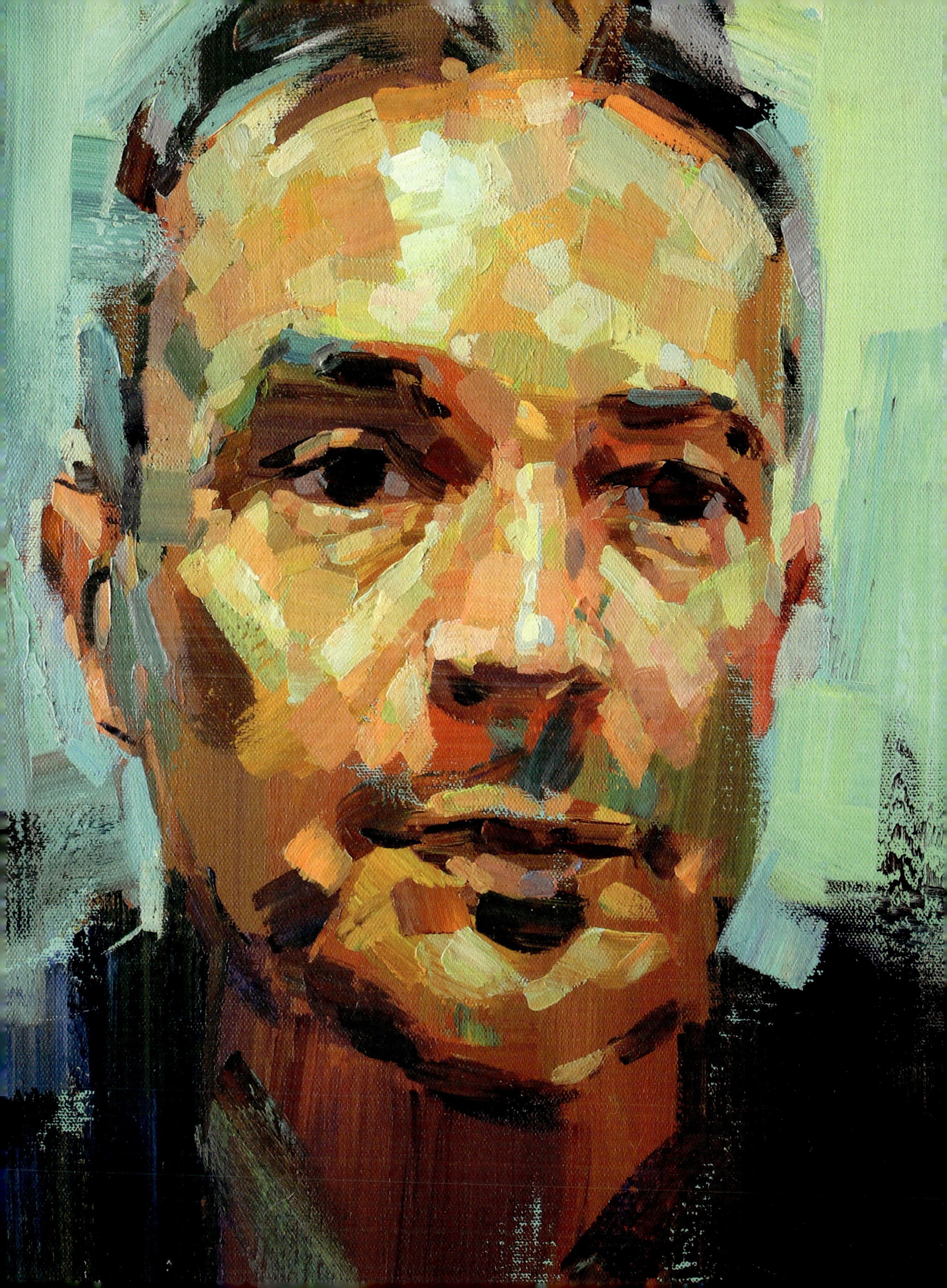

Having completed some preliminary sketches, I feel more adept at tackling a colour portrait, although I will limit the palette. This means that I can be less precise regarding skin colour and concentrate on tonal values. The pose will be an angled head and shoulders and I'll work from a photograph.

This project is about temperature rather than tone; warmth and coolness, rather than light and dark. Since you're familiar with your own face, it's a great chance to work without a framework.

It is worth noting at this point that it is important not to be self-indulgent. Of course we all want a good reflection of ourselves, but occasionally ego can get in the way of being fully objective. I've been around for fifty years and my face reflects this, I have larger than average nostrils, my face is slightly scarred above my right eye and I can't grow a full beard. Drawing your own portrait from a mirror can be quite tense and your facial muscles can tighten so perhaps begin drawing or painting from a few informal photos.

YOU WILL NEED

Brushes: 50mm (2in) flat, 37mm (1½in) flat, 25mm (1in) flat

Paints: Sky blue, permanent yellow medium, lemon yellow, yellow ochre, cadmium orange, pyrrole red, quinacridone rose, quinacridone rose opaque, burnt sienna, yellowish green, permanent blue violet opaque, turquoise blue, king's blue, phthalo blue, sap green, permanent blue violet, titanium white

Surface: Canvas board, 51×61cm (20×24in)

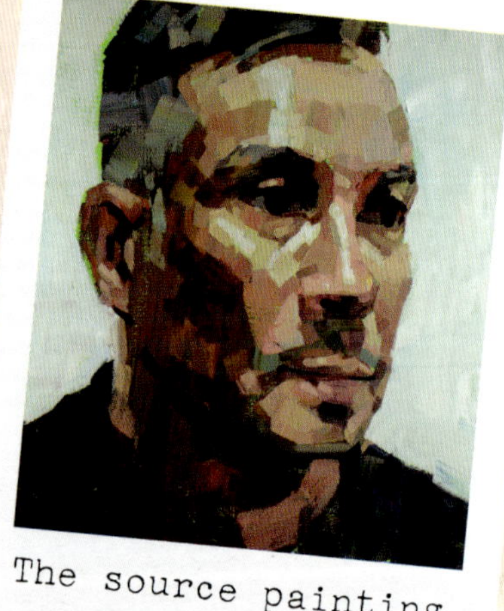

The source painting.

Get your portrait painted

Getting your portrait painted by another artist is an enlightening experience and gives you the chance to experience the sensation from the other side of the easel. You'll feel a greater sense of empathy for individuals who may sit for you and be mindful of your subject's expectations of the painting.

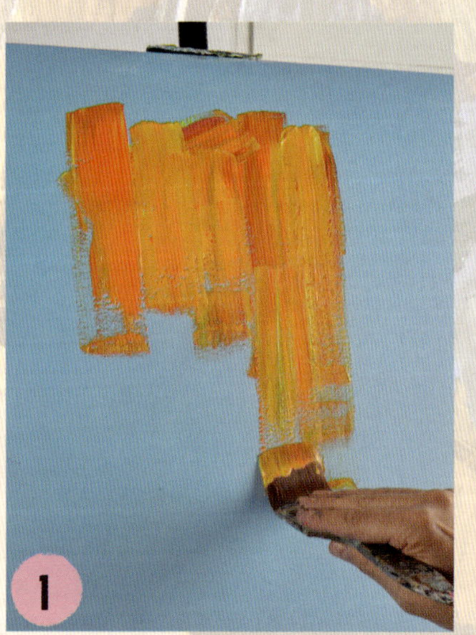

1 Starting from a base of sky blue, load a 50mm (2in) brush with permanent yellow medium, lemon yellow, yellow ochre, cadmium orange, pyrrole red, quinacridone rose, quinacridone rose opaque and a little burnt sienna. Start by making big, bold statements; creating a large area of warmth with the brush. Look for areas where light is hitting your face.

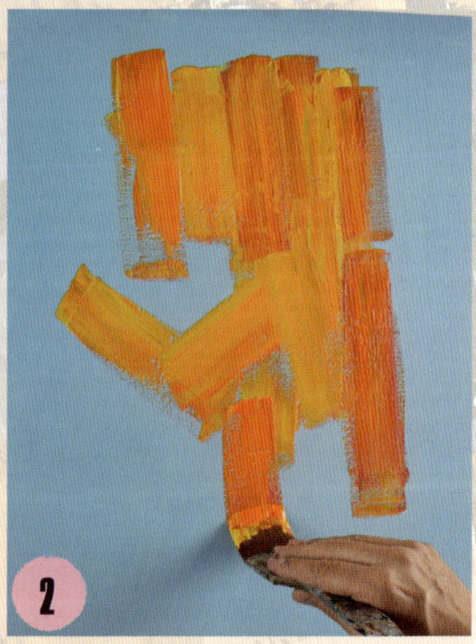

2 Add a hint of yellowish green every so often when you reload the brush for variety, and build up the basic structure of the face – you'll see a cheekbone, hole for an eye and a forehead here.

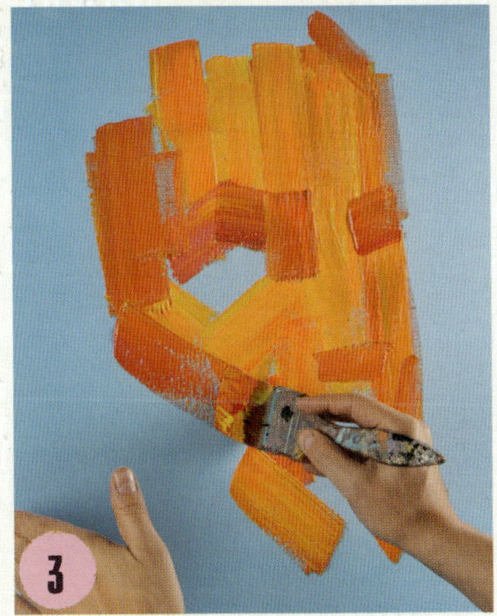

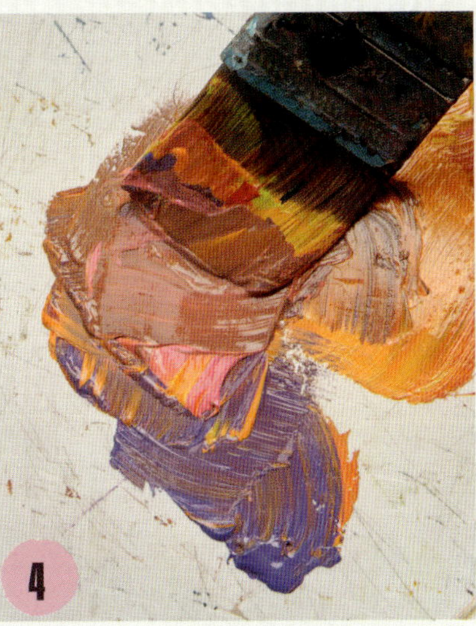

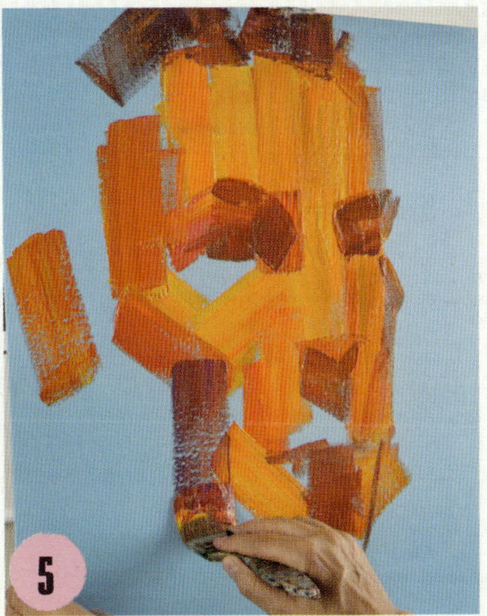

3 Create a pool of the same warm colours, with more pyrrole red, permanent yellow medium, quinacridone rose opaque and yellowish green. Use this to establish the shadows of the nose, eye sockets and cheek.

4 Add permanent blue violet opaque to an area of the pool to darken it further.

5 Establish the hair and shadow of the eye recesses. Hint at the eyes – use big strokes to block in an area for the eye, rather than being tempted to be too detailed. Add the shadows for the mouth, the area below it, and the cheek.

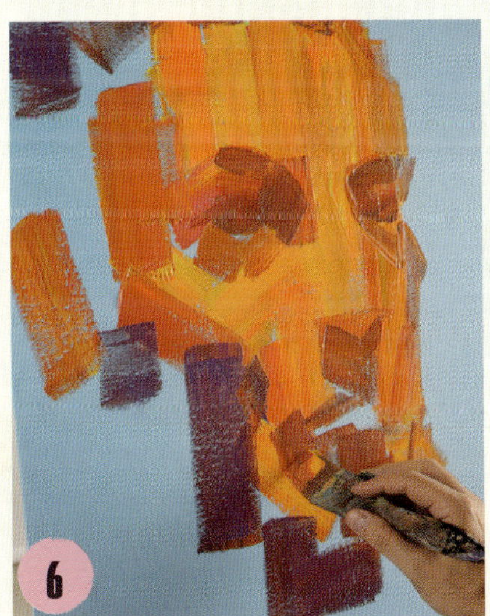

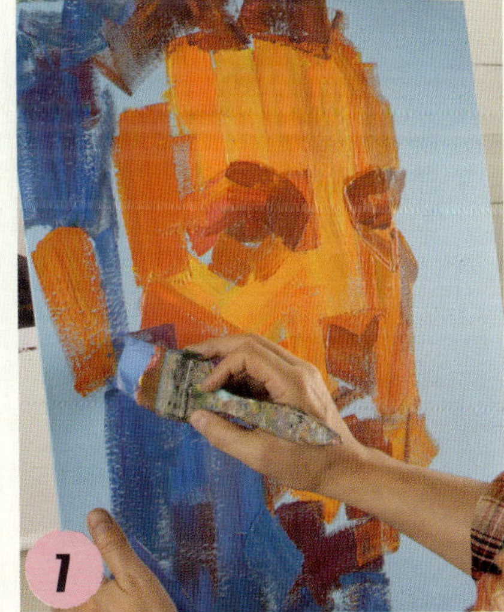

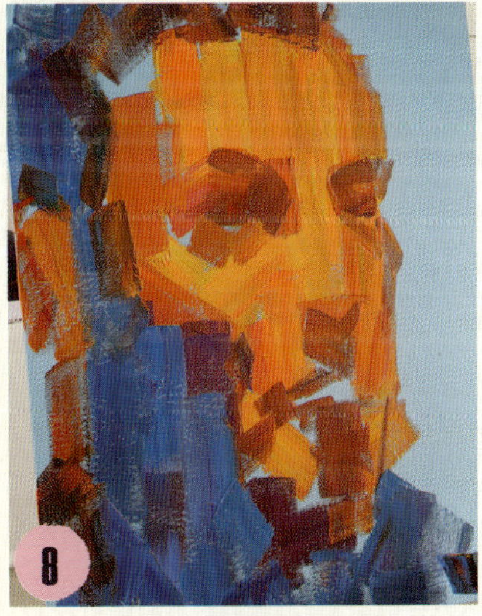

6 Using much more permanent blue violet opaque on your brush, block in the transitional areas like the neck. Change to a 37mm (1½in) flat brush to fill in a few gaps, and build up the areas beneath the eyes, and build up the area around the mouth, chin and jaw.

7 Swapping back to the 50mm (2in) flat (note that it has not been cleaned), pick up turquoise blue, king's blue and phthalo blue. These cool colours are a strong contrast, and will be used for the shadows. Build up the coolest areas in the portrait – the cheek and neck in the lower-left hand corner.

8 As before, swap to the 37mm (1½in) brush to fill in a few gaps; using the new cool pool. Use the cool blues to block in the shoulder. Vary the hue with hints of sap green when you reload.

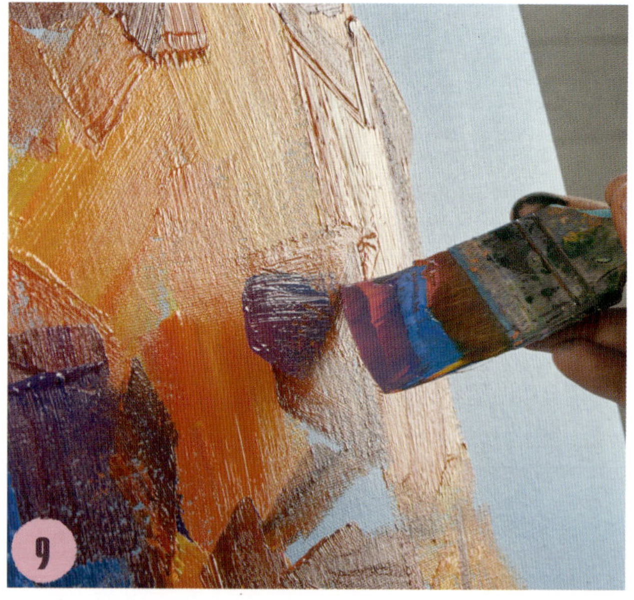

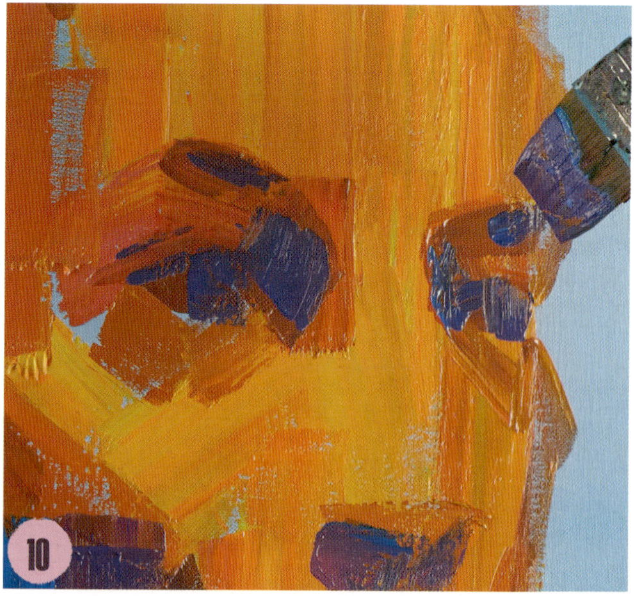

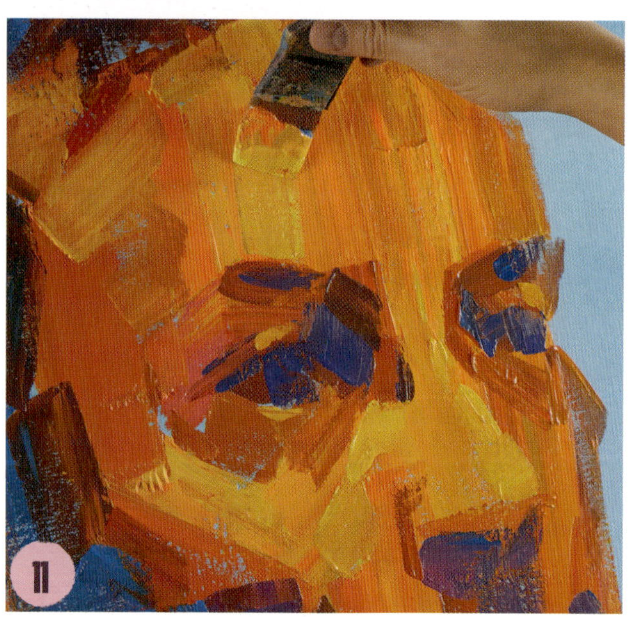

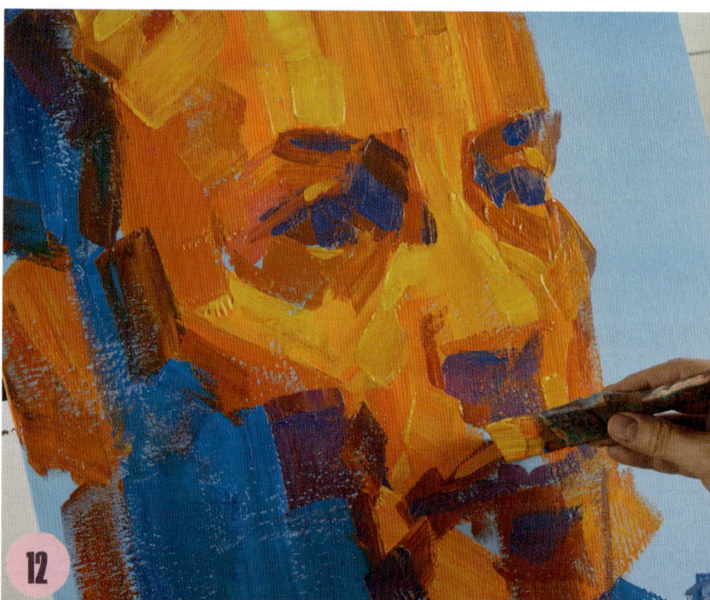

9 With the main shapes established roughly, the immediate quandary is linking the warm and cool areas. Warm an area of the cool blue pool by adding quinacridone rose dark opaque and permanent blue violet dark, and use this to block in the transitional zones, and overlay areas that are incorrectly placed.

10 Make more considered bridging marks, manoeuvring the brush in such a way that you can make smaller marks. Develop the eyes a little – but again, don't overwork them.

11 Use the warm pool to add some descriptive lines. Adding more permanent yellow medium and lemon yellow to the warm pool will help you pick out areas of particular highlight, such as on the bridge of the nose, eyelids and centre of the brow.

12 Bring in some variety to the colour with the addition of more quinacridone rose opaque for the lower lip and around the eye.

Dominant colour

To avoid these transitional colours going muddy, it is important to have a dominant colour that you reload with more than any other. Here, quinacridone rose opaque is that colour, because it has both cool (blue) and warm (red) aspects, and so can work with either of the main pools of colour.

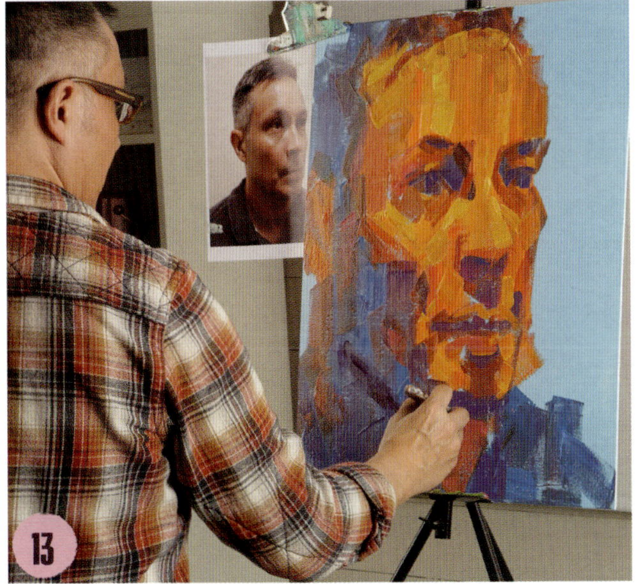

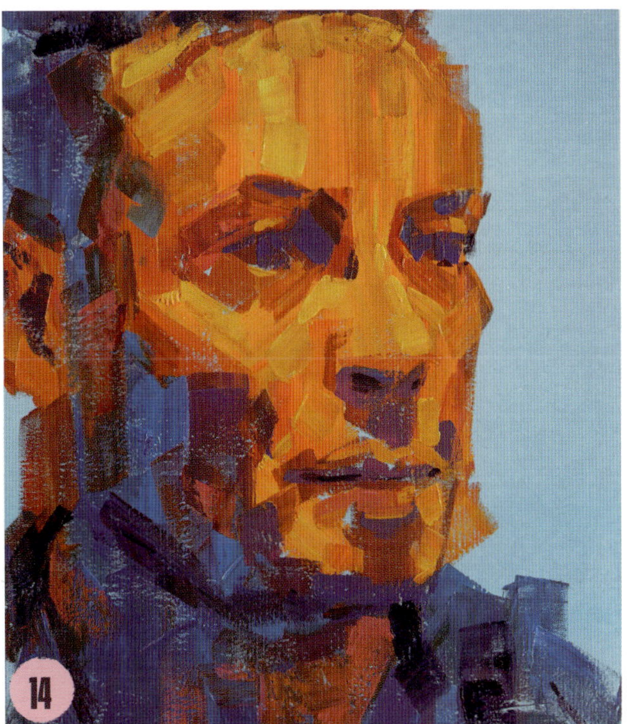

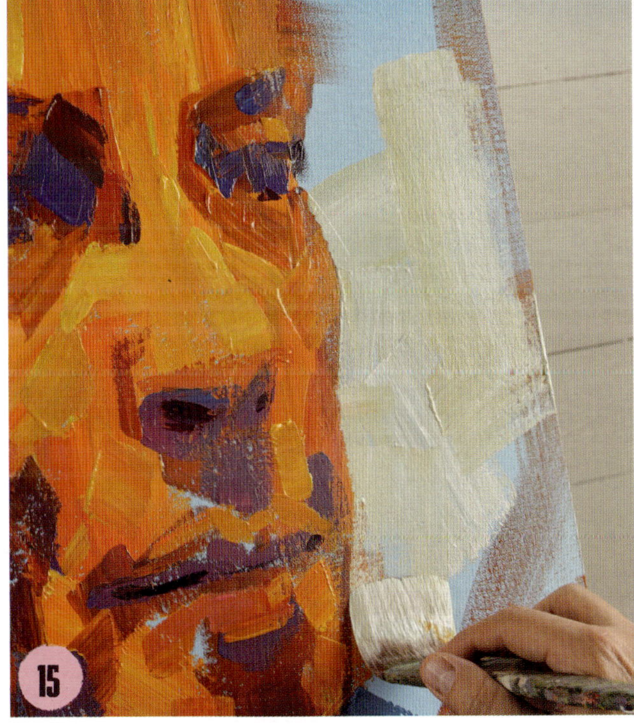

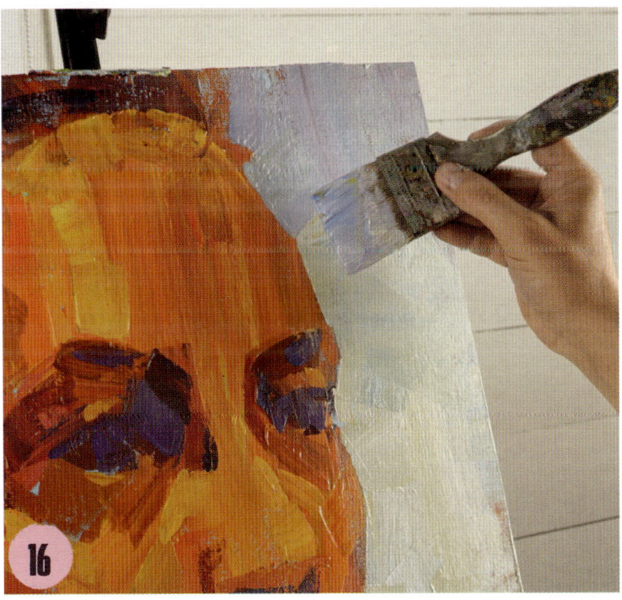

13 Introduce permanent blue violet and sap green for a darker tone. Use this sparingly to bring out the jawline and hair.

14 Add smaller touches of the same mix to create details for the nostrils and the line of the mouth. Allow to dry before moving on.

15 Using the pools on the palette, add some loose marks to the background area. Allow these to dry a little then use a clean damp 50mm (2in) flat brush with titanium white, king's blue and yellow ochre to block in the background. Use this chance to refine the profile of the face.

16 As you build up the background, add some permanent blue violet to darken the tone near the edges and corners of the painting. This acts as a subtle framing device and encourages the eye back into the painting.

'Use this chance to refine the profile of the face.'

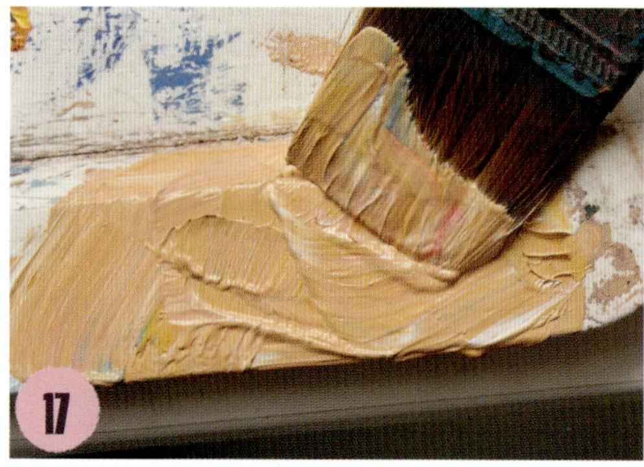

17 Using another clean 50mm (2in) brush, create a pool of colour for a more naturalistic skin – titanium white, yellow ochre, and small amounts of yellowish green and king's blue.

18 Build up the midtones on the skin, overlaying the colour. You're still using the paint fairly thickly and generously, but do leave some intentional gaps. The idea is to let the garish underpainting show through in places and influence the paint on top. I'm starting with the forehead as it's a relatively large area, but you could equally well start with the cheek, for example.

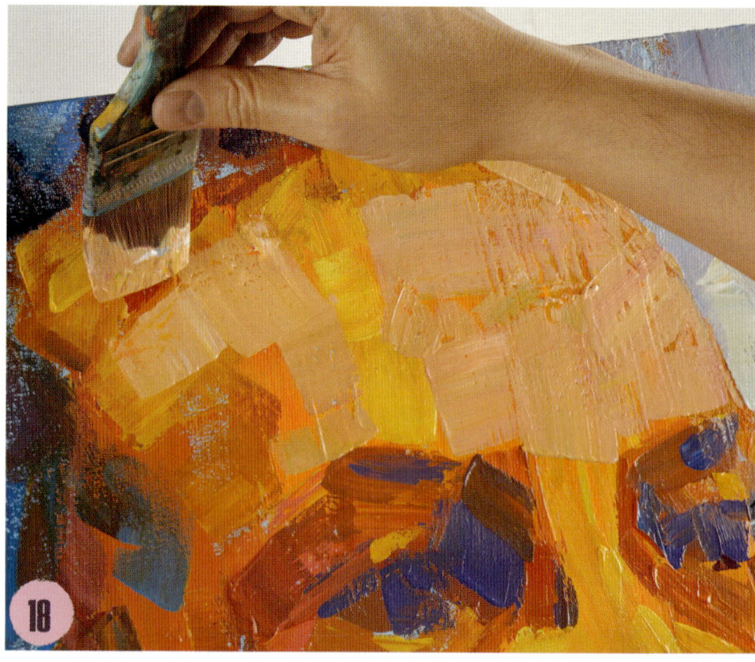

Reserve highlight areas

As you build up the warm region of the face, don't be tempted to work over the highlights - these will come in later; and the eventual mix will 'pop' more against the underlying bright yellow than the naturalistic hue.

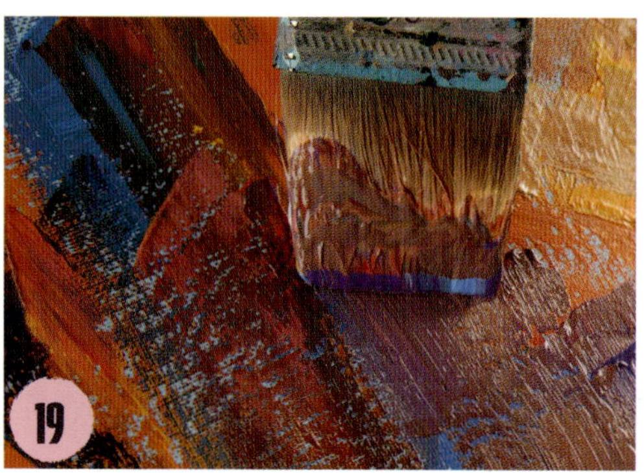

19 Still using the same brush, make a new pool of yellow ochre, burnt sienna, permanent blue violet opaque, yellowish green and king's blue.

20 Use this to begin to smother the blue in the cool shaded areas. As with the midtone skin of the warm areas, leave some of the underlying colour showing through.

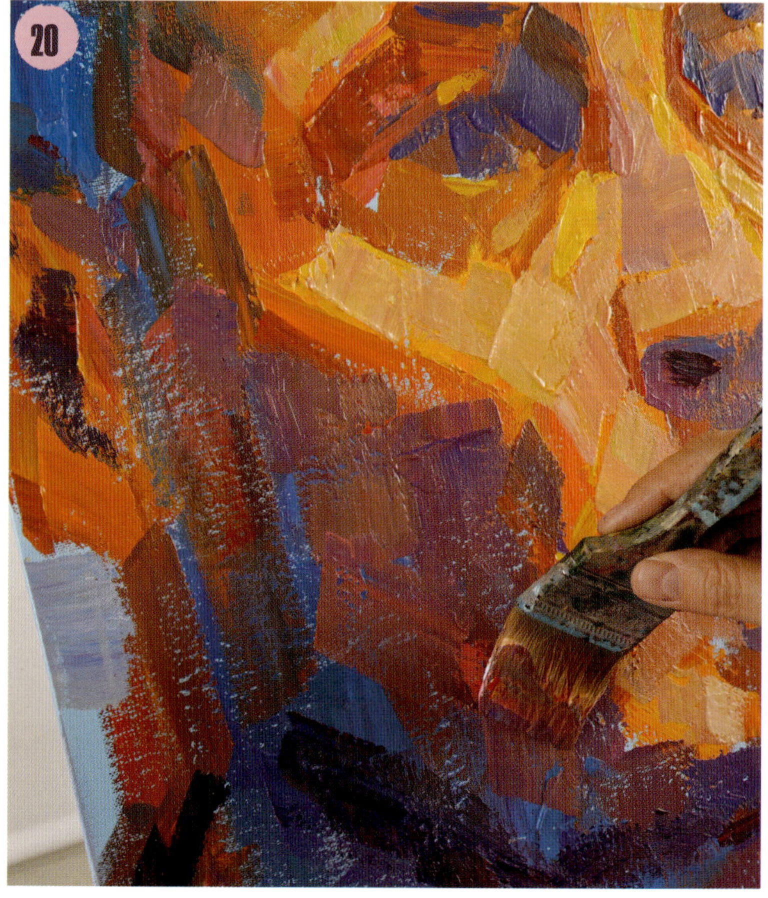

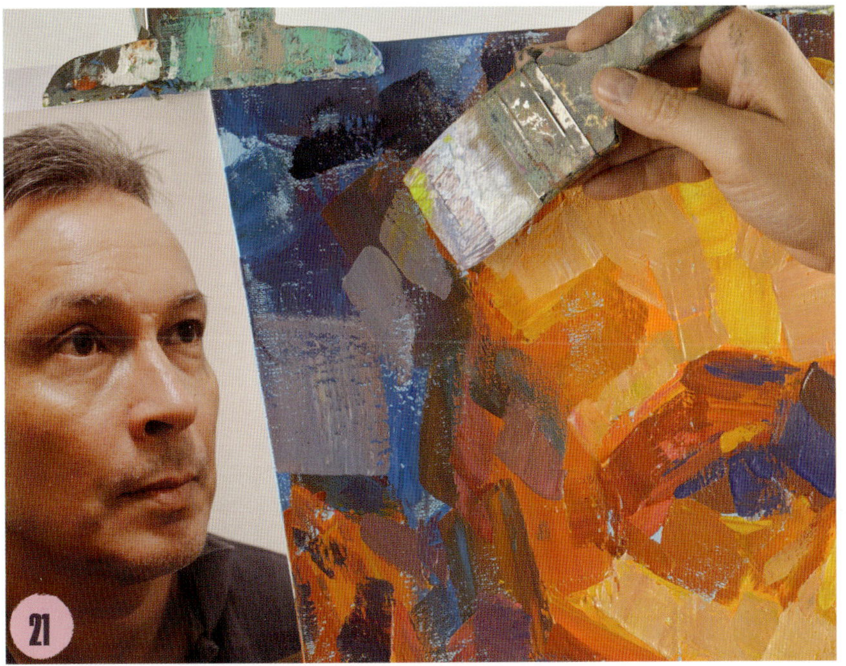

21 Combine a little of this new pool with the background pool (titanium white, king's blue and yellow ochre) to create a neutral grey. Use this to detail the hair on the side of the head.

22 Using the same mix, touch in the eyebrows and stubble using finer marks.

23 Using the corner of the brush, touch in the whites of the eyes with any neutral grey that remains on the brush.

24 For the highlights across the face, load a clean damp 37mm (1½in) brush with titanium white, permanent yellow medium and sky blue, and touch them in.

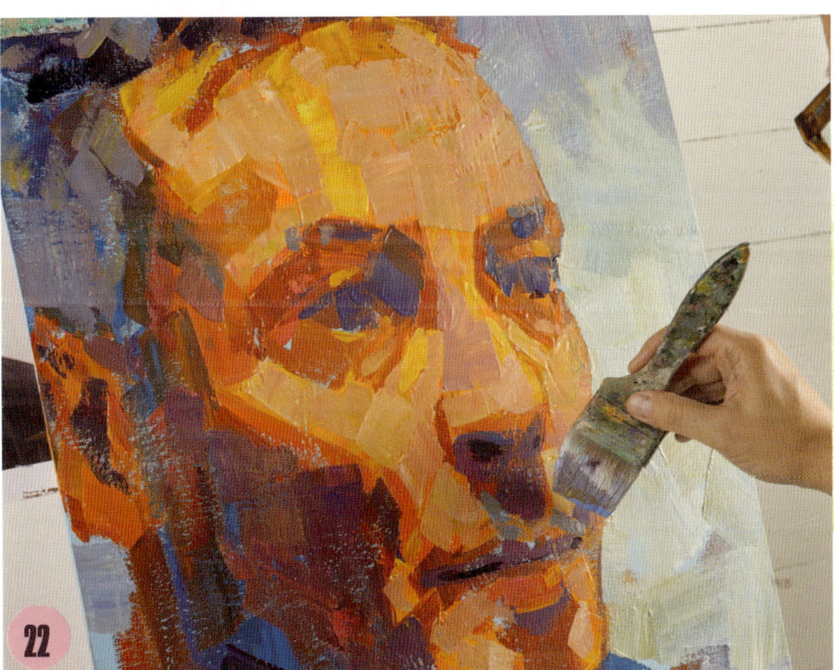

'You're still using the paint fairly thickly and generously, but do leave some intentional gaps. The idea is to let the garish underpainting show through in places and influence the paint on top.'

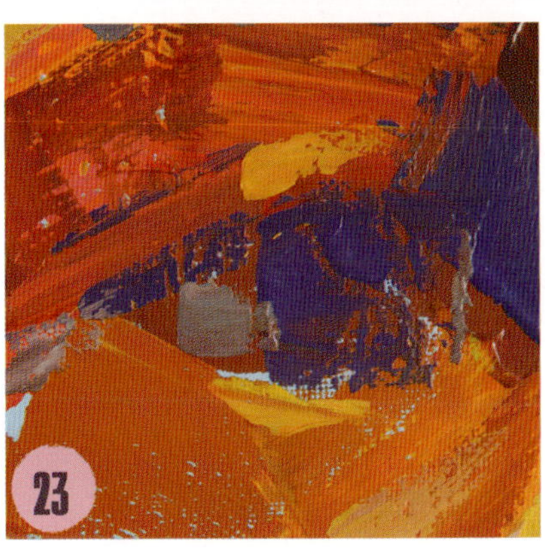

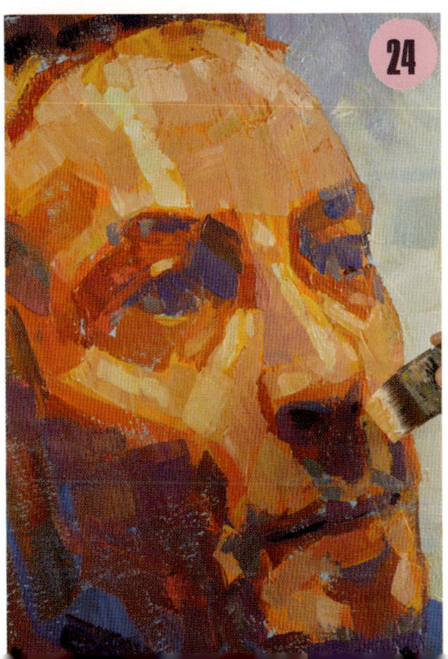

25 If the result is too stark, combine it with the midtone pool used for the warm skin (titanium white, yellow ochre, and small amounts of yellowish green and king's blue). Some pinker hints, added by incorporating your linking colour – quinacridone rose opaque – can be used to sharpen and lift areas.

26 Make a very dark pool of permanent blue violet, sap green and burnt sienna, and add some deep darks with a 25mm (1in) flat. Apply these sparingly; they're here to promote some of the drawing aspects of the painting, but too much will overtighten the painting, and lose some of the appeal of the technique.

27 To finish, refine and soften the area around the eyes using the mixes on your palette and the 37mm (1½in) flat brush. This more detailed area provides a focal point. Like the contrast between the warm and cool areas, the contrast between the more refined areas of the face and the looser, more dynamic parts creates an arresting effect.

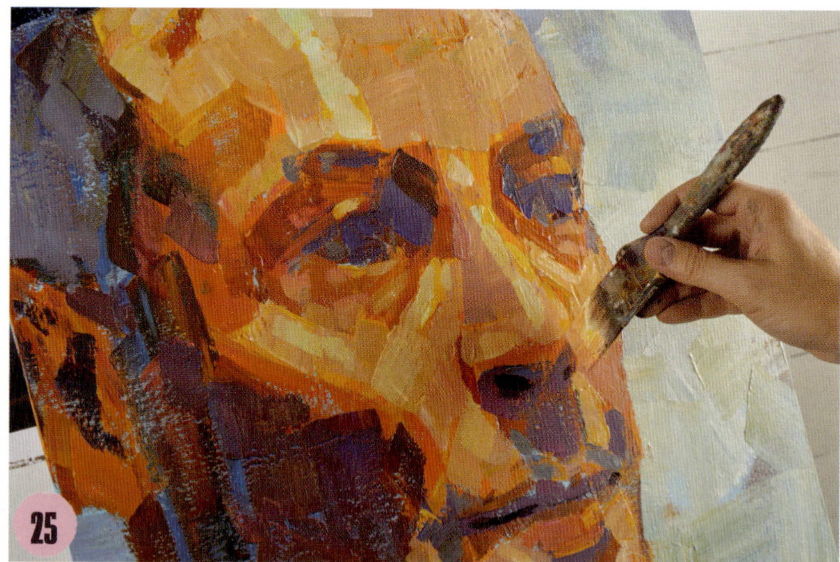

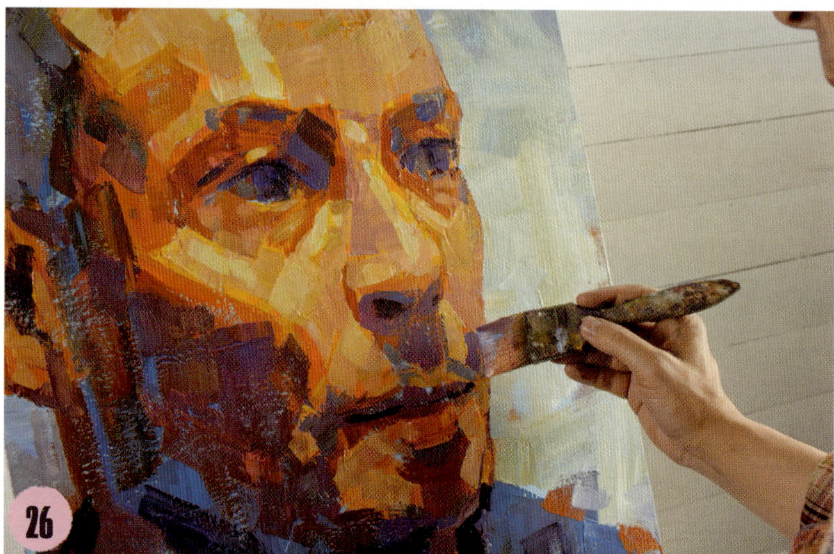

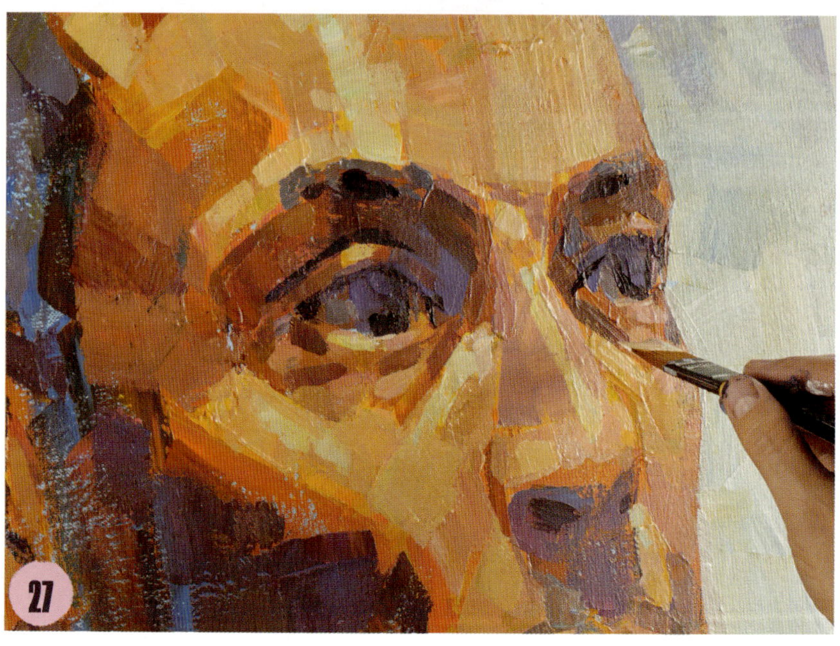

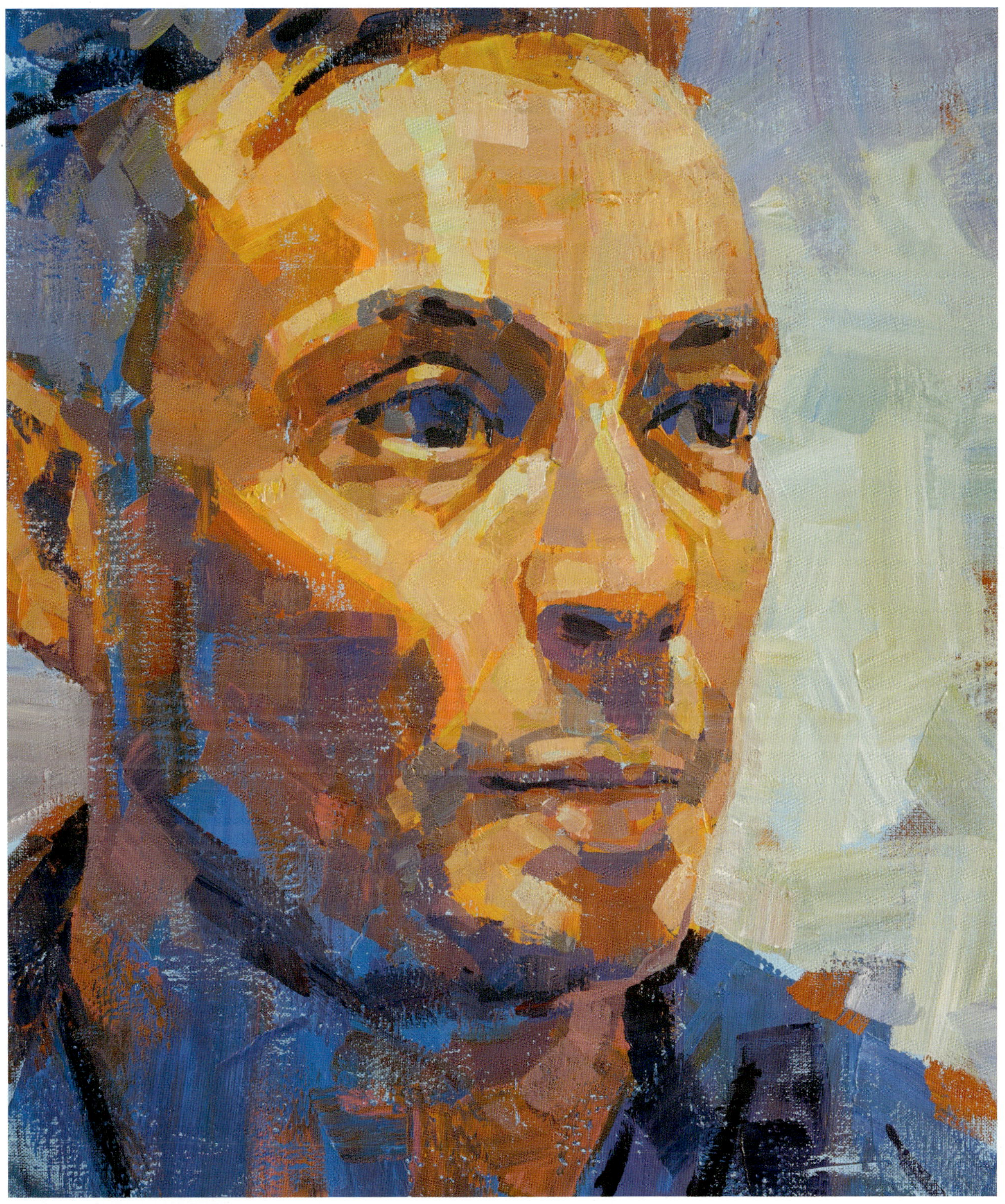

THE FINISHED PORTRAIT.

Feel free to make any further adjustments you feel necessary – but do stand back every so often; it's important not to overwork the painting.

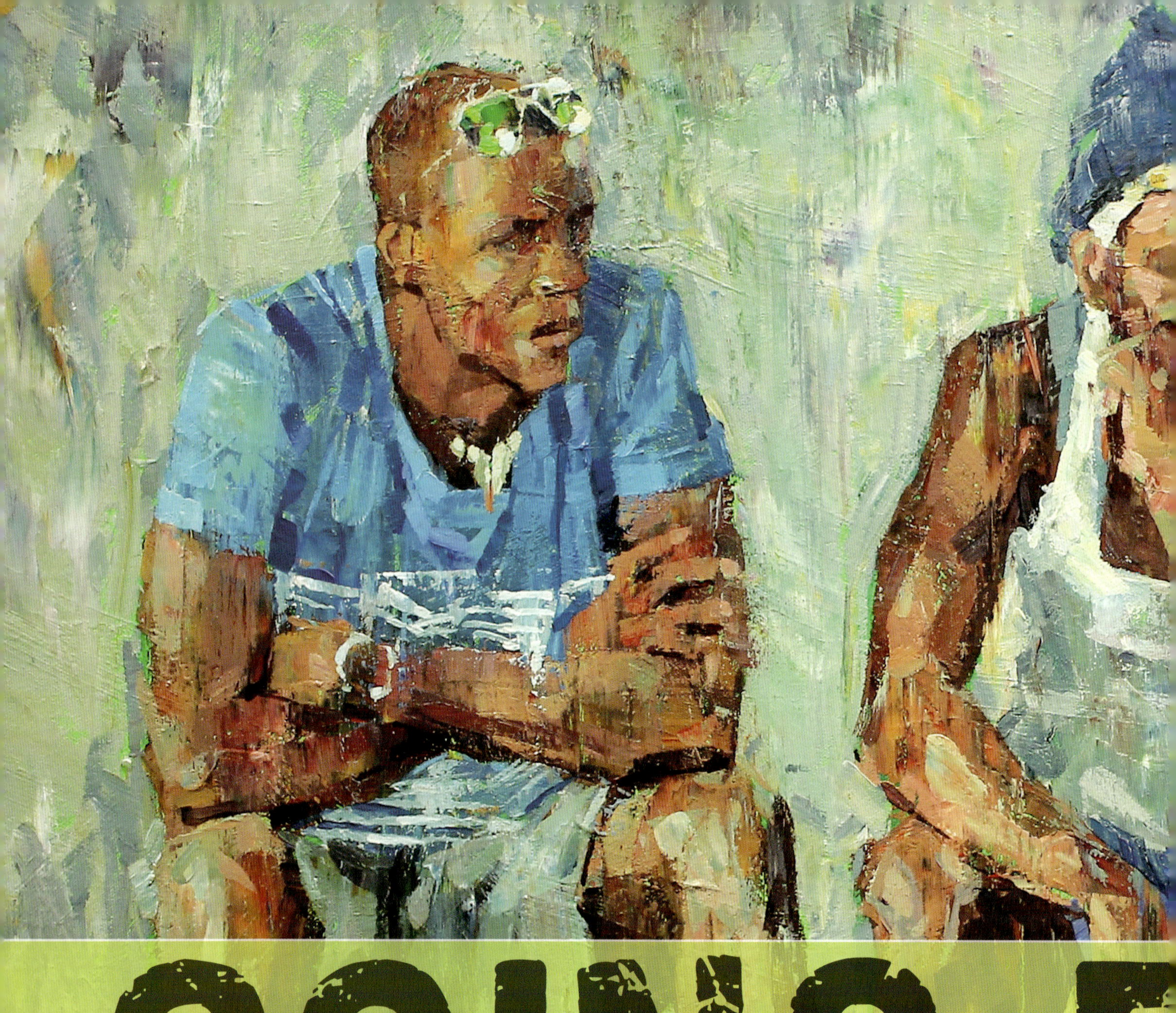
GOING F

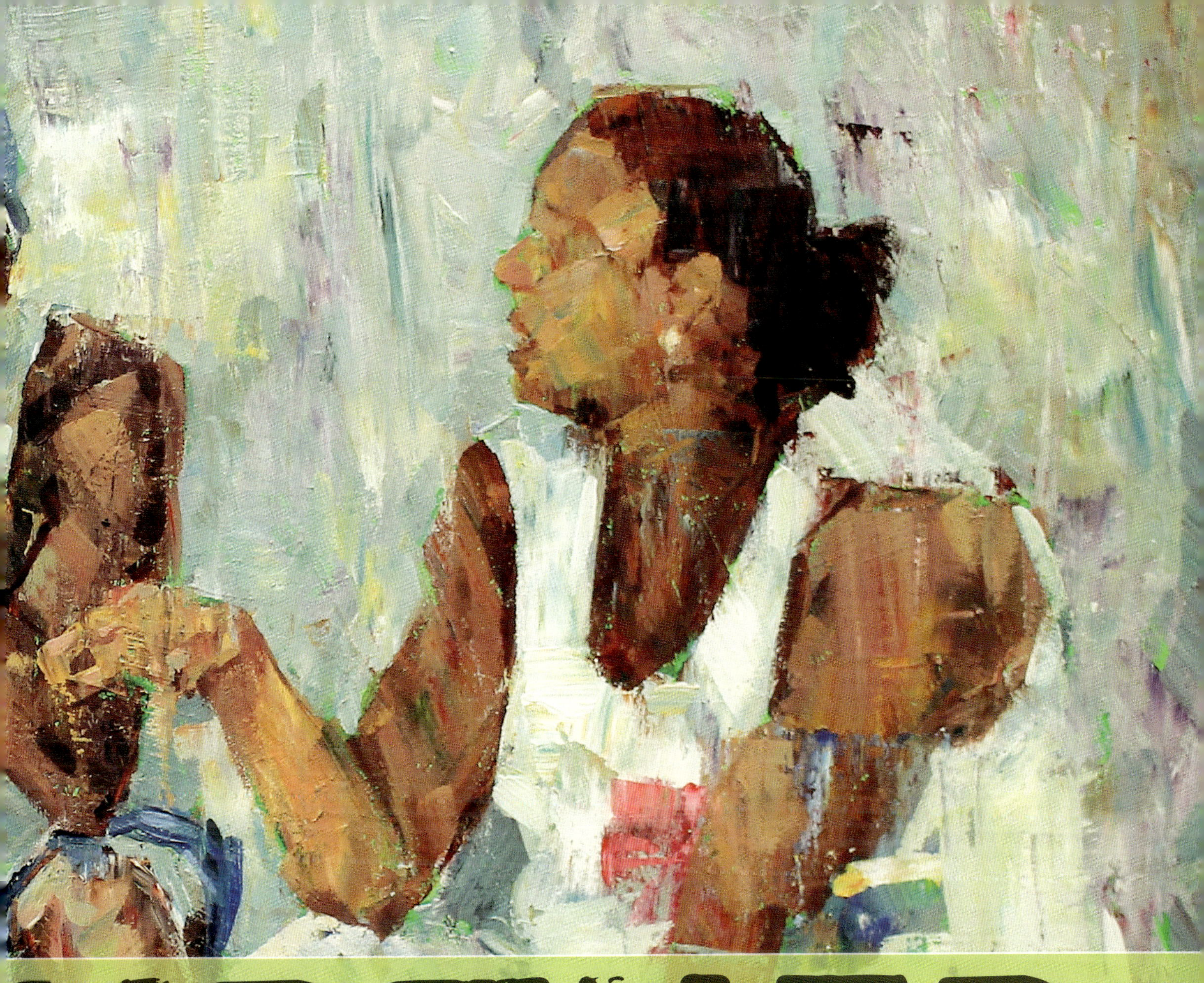

URTHER

Focal points

Focal points are the main areas of interest in a painting. In portraiture, the eyes tend to be natural focal points. Since we each have two eyes, portraits usually have two focal points to choose from, and the viewer will flick between the two.

If you want something else to be the focal point you have to specifically draw attention away from the eyes to something else. You can create greater points of interest if the element is unusual or different: a large mole, rainbow-coloured hair or gold teeth, for example. Any of these would make a great focal point.

Too many points of interest, however, will confuse us and we'll look away. In drawing and painting, this equates to the artist creating areas of quiet, areas which build up or lead the viewer's gaze to the focal points. I always think of this as creating stepping stones: large or small, stepping stones are a fun way of getting to the place we want to be.

The traditional theory in painting is that focal points should have the most contrast. This might be in terms of colour; with primary or complementary colours next to

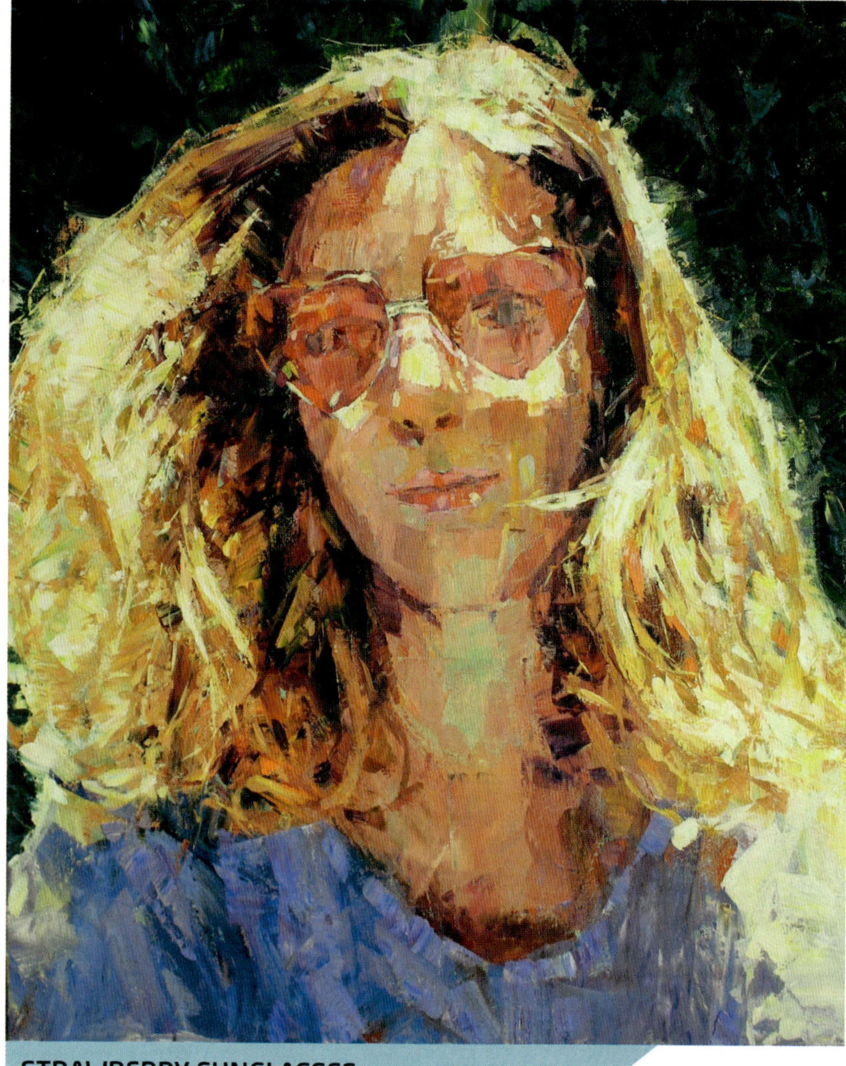

STRAWBERRY SUNGLASSES 61×76CM (24×30IN)

The focal point in this portrait is the eyes, with light streaming down from above. In terms of painting process, however, the hair was far more interesting. As paintings are subjective, you will discover your own points of interest which override the obvious.

each other, or earthy colours next to vibrant ones. It might be through loose drawing contrasted with more refined marks; or through tone, with light next to dark. These contrasts should also be uncontrived clues – don't signpost the interesting bit. There are passive ways to draw attention to – or from – an area. These include expressive brushmarks swirling to the focal point or soft edges leading to harder ones. Look out for underlying elements that create diagonals leading in such as long hair, shadows or folds in clothes.

Compositionally, one of the reasons why you should avoid placing the focal point in the centre of your painting is that it becomes a predictable 'bull's eye' or target, and hogs the attention from the supporting parts.

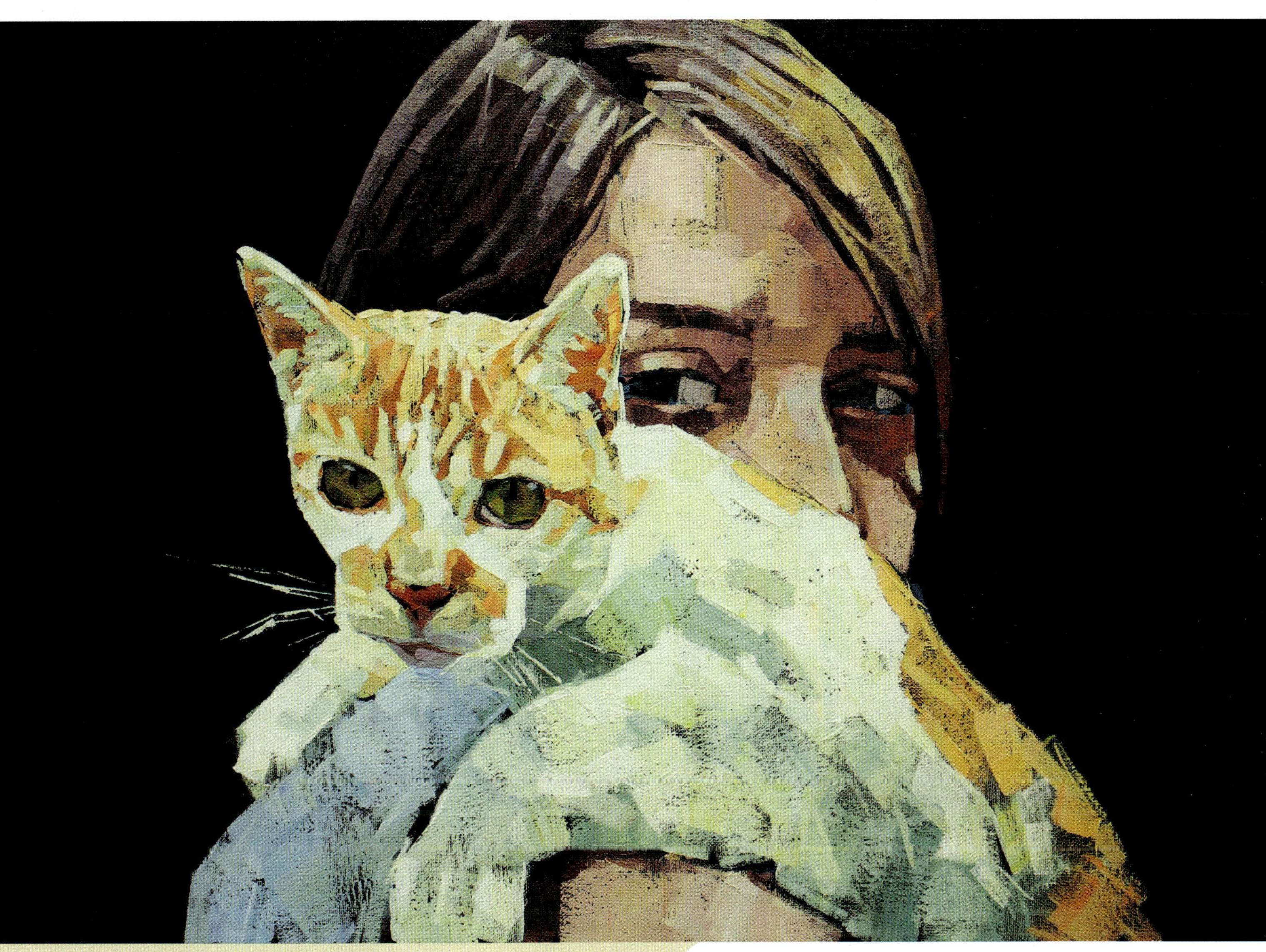

MARIE AND CHARLIE 76×51CM (30×20IN)

This portrait has both figure and animal vying for attention, although Charlie the cat wins out. His patterning of lines on the forehead, vibrant orange colour and light against dark trump the figure, making him the focal point. He's also extremely cute!

Natural poses

Traditional portraiture suffers from poses which look contrived and expressionless, the seriousness of the undertaking etched on the sitter's face.

If I'm asked to pose for a photograph I immediately feel under pressure, and tense up. Holding a smile for more than a few seconds or figuring out what to do with your hands adds to the awkwardness. It's almost always better to aim to catch a moment when the model is completely relaxed, in order to reflect a more authentic natural state.

This is one of the benefits of social media as a library of visual ideas and reference. It provides a great insight as to how people actually are, or would like to view themselves. The pictures are raw and unpolished, and there's a wealth of novel ideas on composition and concepts which aren't automatically overruled or corrected by long-held art theories. While it's good to know the basics, be sure not to spend so much time developing technique that you lose sight of the content of the portrait.

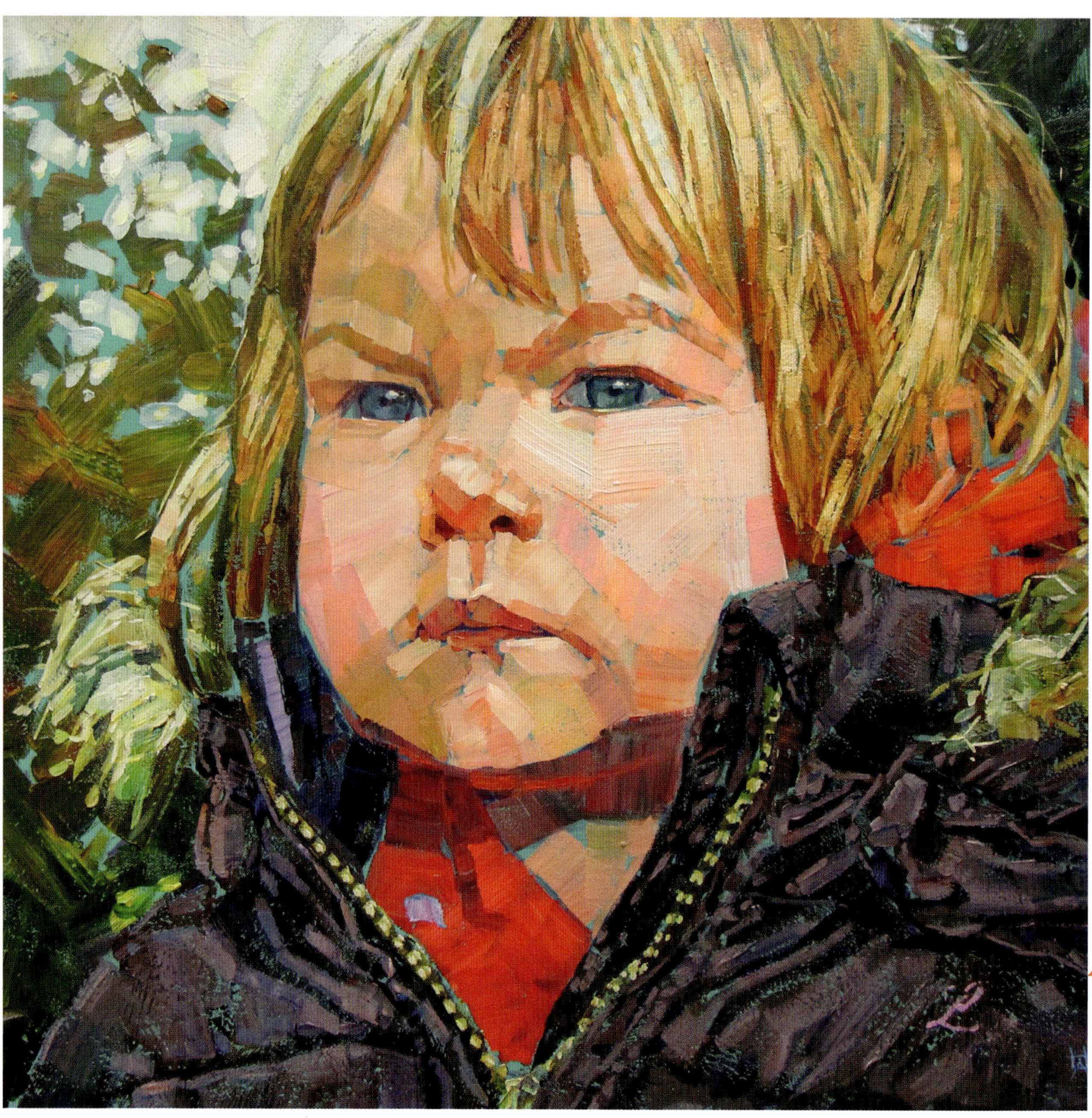

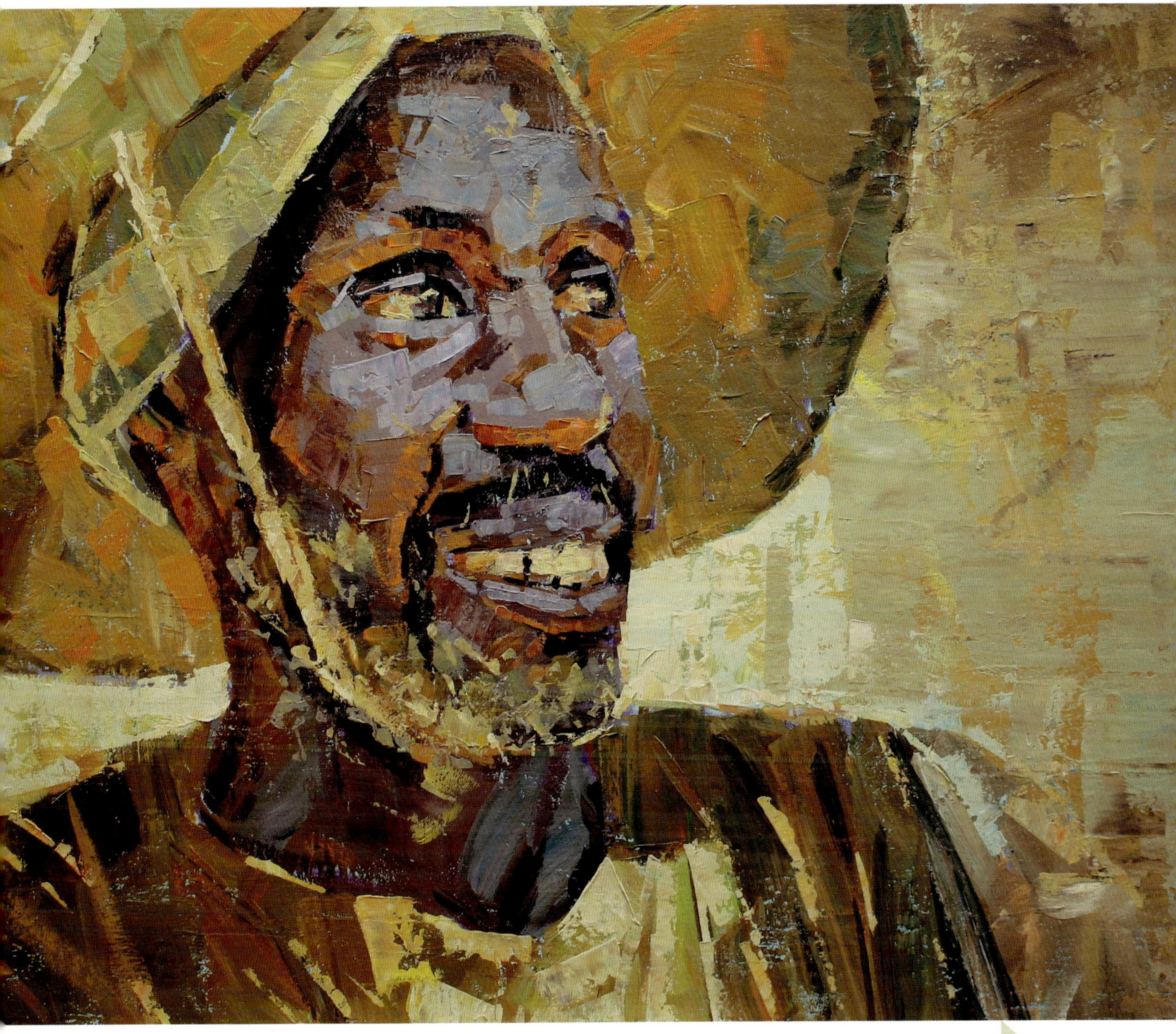

The environment and attire form part of the naturalism of a pose. The more unusual, the better, as it will make an interesting statement. This also goes for props that someone might be carrying or that appear in the picture plane.

MILLA 56×56CM (22×22IN)

When painting or photographing children for reference, the best expressions and poses are often those caught in natural settings rather than posed. Try having them tucking into food, playing or being fascinated by new surroundings.

Backgrounds

Backgrounds offer a wealth of opportunities. They can provide more narrative to a portrait, telling a story of the model's surroundings or environment. It could be a detailed interior or exterior; or you may choose a simple pattern or colour as an addition to decorate rather than illustrate.

A background can be used to add emotion to a static portrait by applying random brushmarks or splattering paint. You could include other figures, animals, collage various landscapes together or use your imagination to create something outlandish or surreal.

Whatever you choose, there are a few things to consider when using a background. Most importantly, does it enhance or detract from the portrait? Ideally, the background should create an interesting journey to the main focal point. The background can also be informative and tell you something about the model; or be used to contrast with the model.

A background with plenty of unwanted elements needs de-cluttering. This is difficult if you're use to following the source material rigidly. Try to avoid reading literal meanings into various elements. Rather than labelling an object as a car, a cloud, or a window, for example, instead look at them as abstract shapes: diagonals leading you in, or circles rotating the eye around.

Background ideas

- Contrast detail in the focal point(s) of the portrait by using looser, sketchier marks in the background.

- Remember that warm colours can lead you in, as can extremes of light and dark.

- Make sure the background connects with the portrait, either by softening edges from one element to the next or by linking colours.

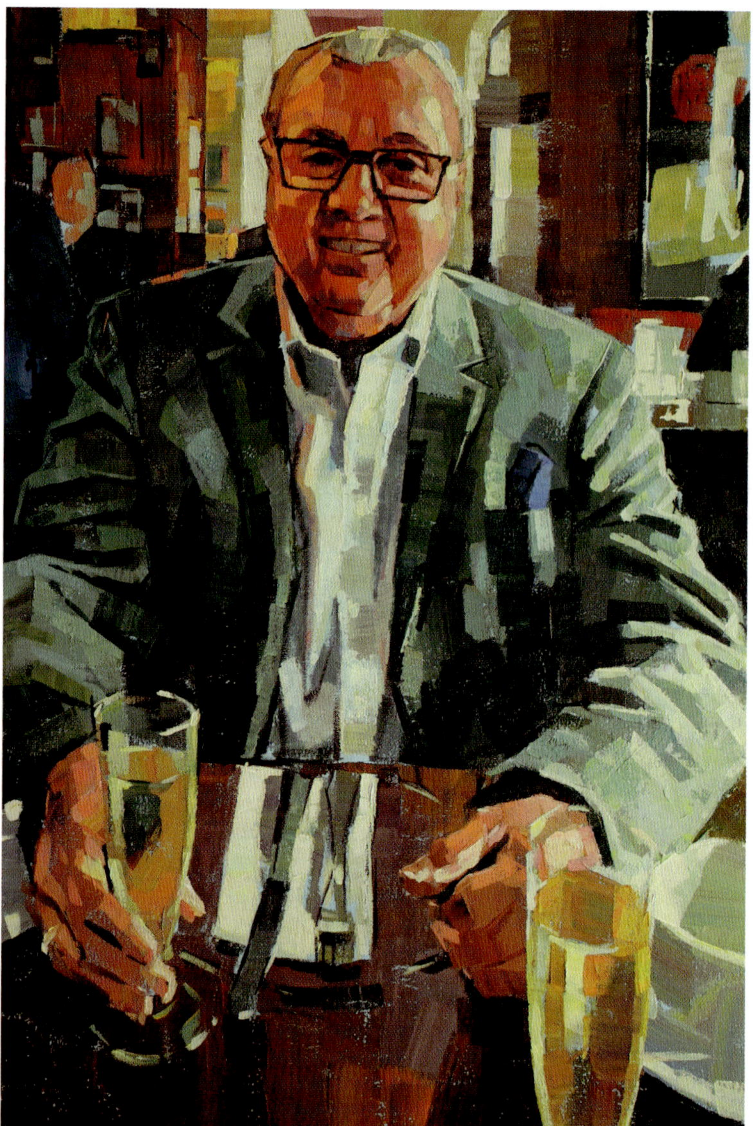

JOHN 51×76cm (20×30in)

This portrait invites you in to join the model; the smile and slightly raised glass are welcoming gestures. The cool colours in the suit make us veer towards the warmer pigments even more, an effect helped by the diagonals in the creases of the suit and arms. The background here is implied rather than defined, but its inclusion is important to the atmosphere, making it clear that the area is public rather than private. The other seated figure creates a sense of scale and softer colours in the distance add depth.

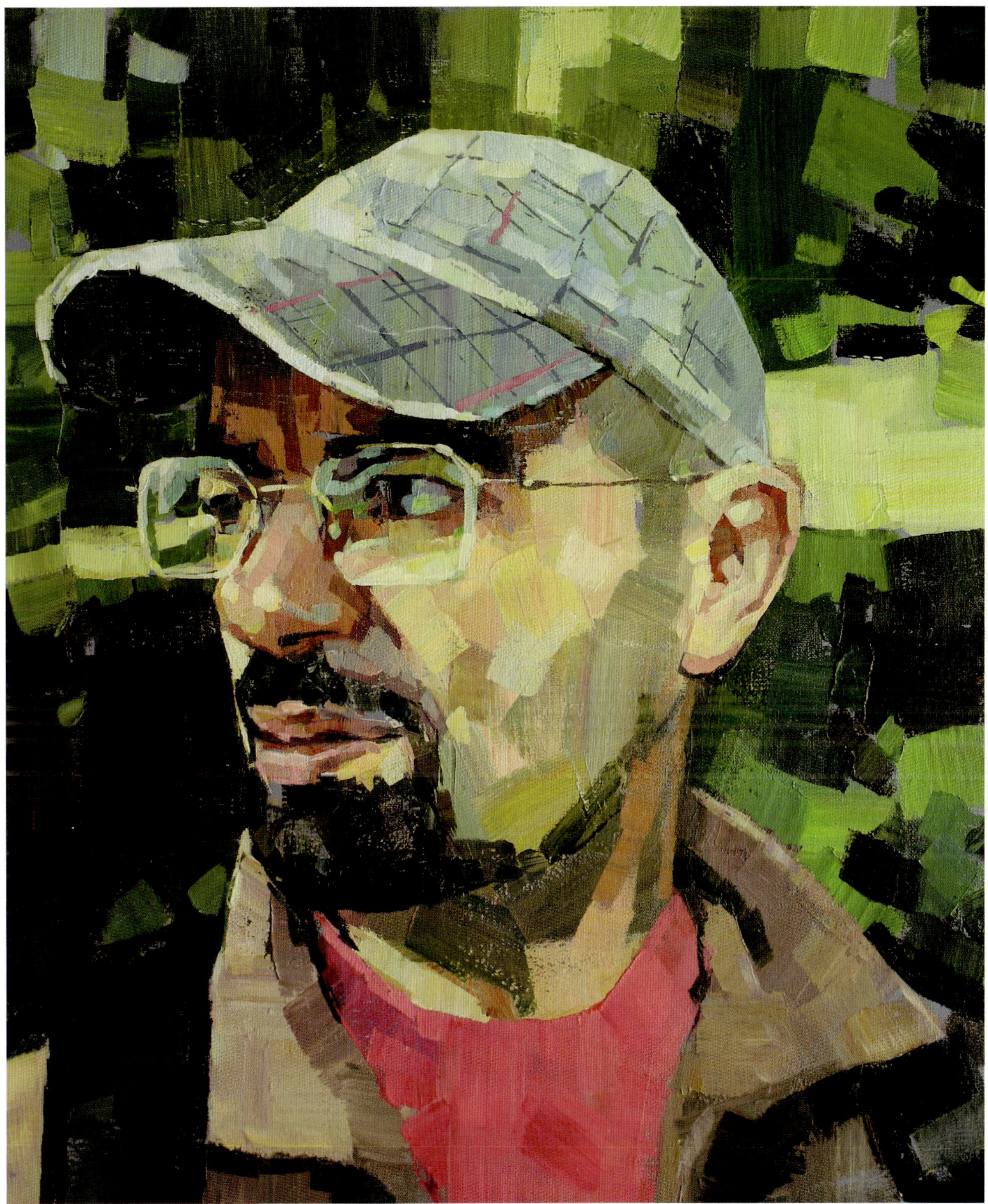

The background in this painting is simply large blocks – an abstract, almost pixelated effect. We can assume it's sunny and the greens signify trees or scrubs. Rather than the detail, it's the colours that spark the main reaction between the figure and background, and the emphasis is firmly on the figure. This idea better reflects how we see things in our peripheral vision, as opposed to the clear, highly defined and even-handed treatment a camera gives to every element of the image.

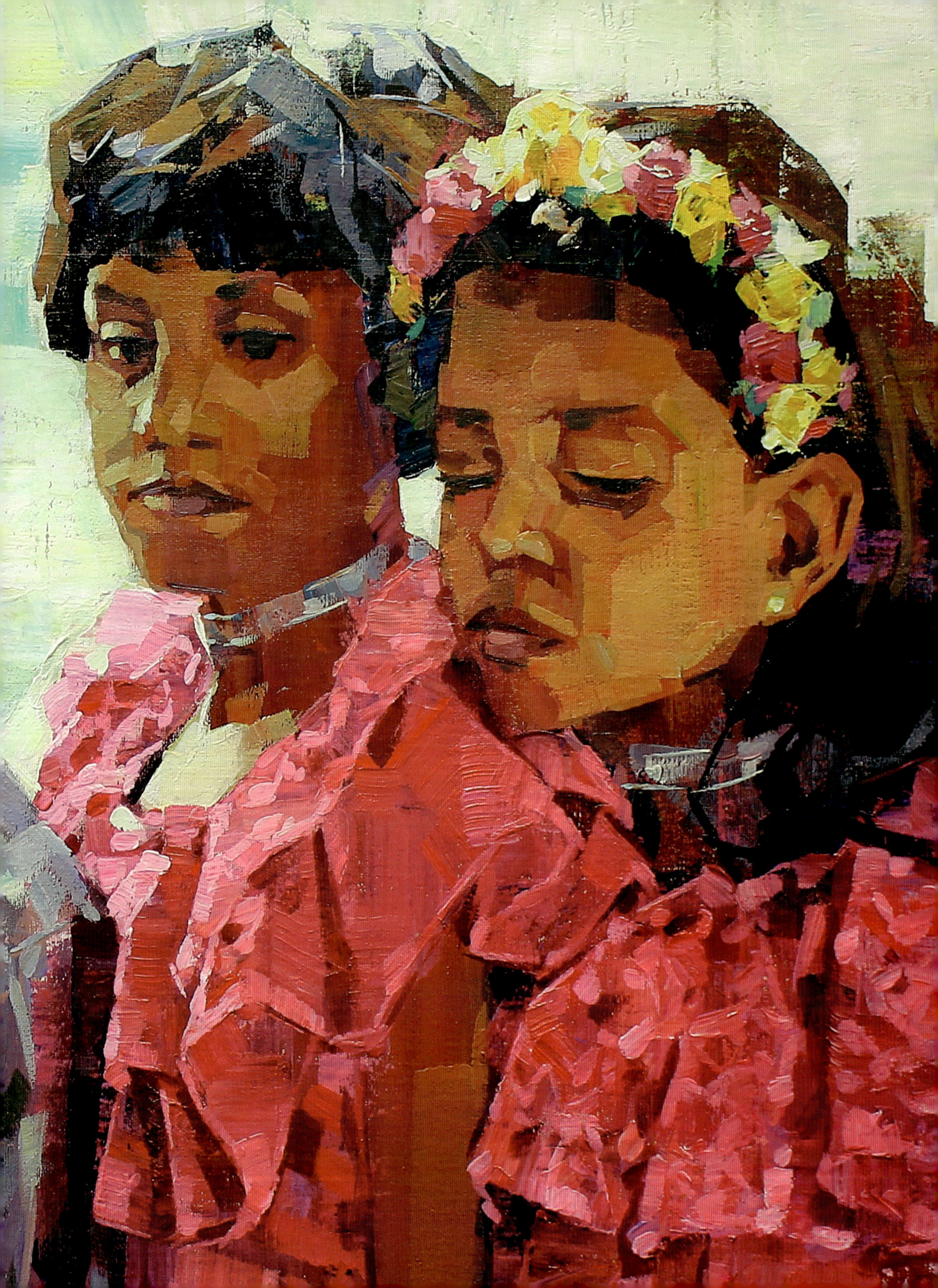

Portraits of more than one figure

When including more than one person, the focal points will be divided between them, unless you decide one should be the main focus. To avoid over-complicating the portrait, treat the whole group of figures as a single element and connect them as much as possible by using similar colours and marks, and avoiding being overly fussy with detail.

Painting *Two Girls*

In *Two Girls*, opposite, the portraits echo each other, forming a mirror image of information. There are slight differences – one figure is slightly taller, the other has a floral headband   but these create interest and serve to draw attention to the similarities.

With this approach the figures merge, creating one singular shape. This is useful for double portraits as your eyes shift effortlessly from one to the other.

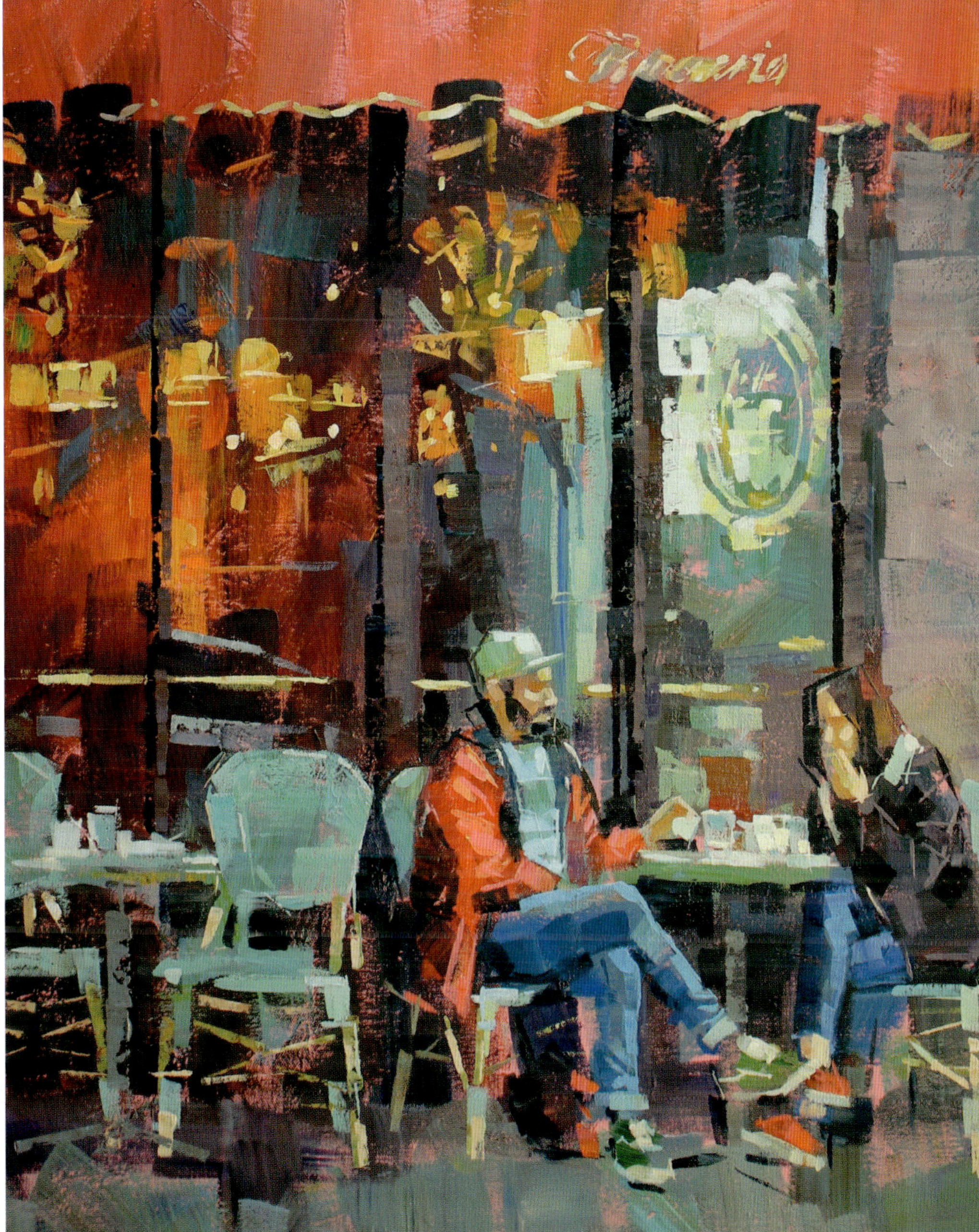

COUPLE AT CAFÉ 61×76cm (24×30in)

For this painting I've included a large part of the café façade, with the figures towards the bottom corner. Although the couple are the main draw, there is a level of importance given to the setting. Figures will generally predominate over a scene like this as they tend to be more animated, so we relate to them more.

TWO GIRLS 41×51cm (16×20in)

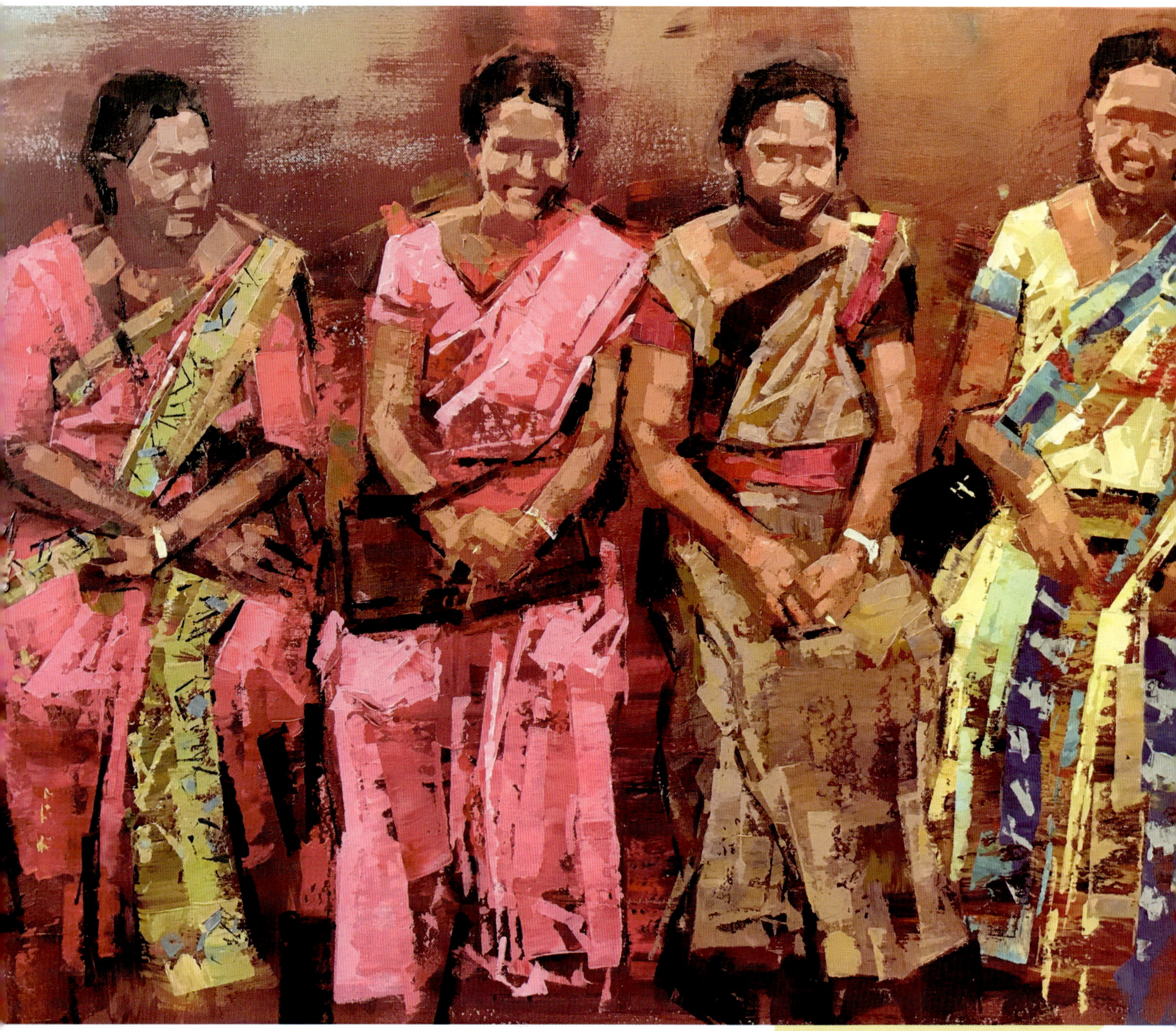

Painting *Sarees*

This painting is less to do with individual portraits and more about colour and patterns. I began with large applications of reddish brown and violet and used my dragging tool for all the folds in the sarees. This adds some interesting crackles to the applications, almost mimicking an old photograph. I'd like to think the figures have unique characteristics without the features being over-described.

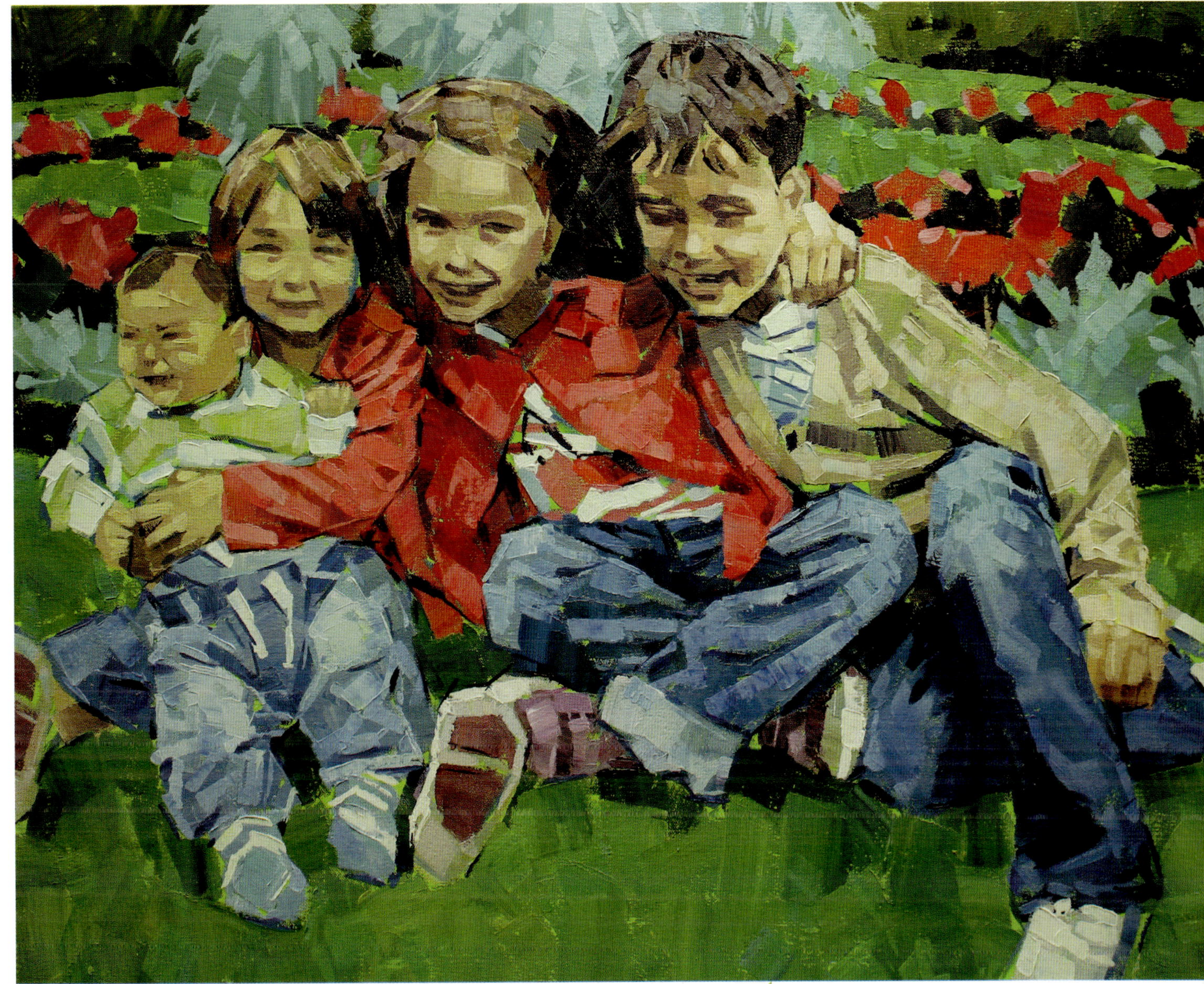

Painting *Elaine's Kids*

This family portrait has lots of areas of interest vying for attention. Four full-figure smiling portraits; arms and legs creating dynamic angles; and an environment with flashes of intense red. I decided early on to use a limited palette and keep the facial features relatively minimal. A sketch is essential to place the figures correctly and gauge the portraits. Most of the initial painting is blocking in colour; all the reds at the same time, similarly with blues and so on. No details are added at this stage as confidence can dip if these go wrong. Blocking in large areas will give you reassurance and valuable thinking time to consider difficult elements.

The first forays into the portraits here were gentle skims of tints looking for eye sockets, shadows and positioning of the mouth. Creases were brought forward in the clothes using tones and tints of the main colours. The features were sharpened and light tints used to contour the faces. I ended the painting with my darkest line work, edging and crisping up the figures.

FULL-LENGTH PORTRAIT

Drawing and painting the entire figure provides the ultimate challenge for the portrait artist. The full figure will also make you look at skin colour – not just for the face, but on arms and legs too.

A key point to look out for is foreshortening as the portrait may be set back and look relatively small in comparison with other parts of the body. If you get the chance to do some life drawing, this will provide valuable experience in seeing the workings of the figure.

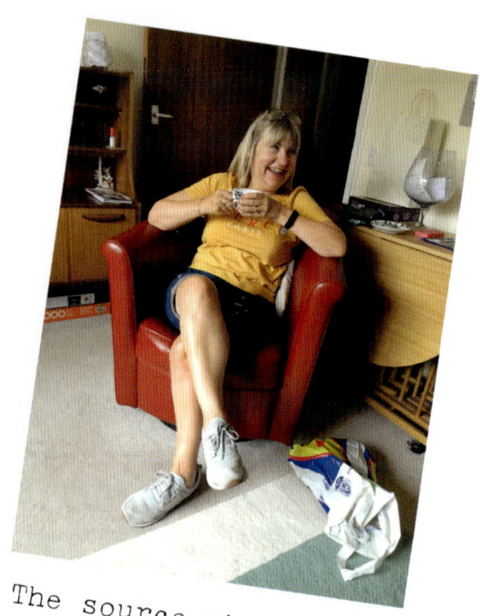

The source photograph.

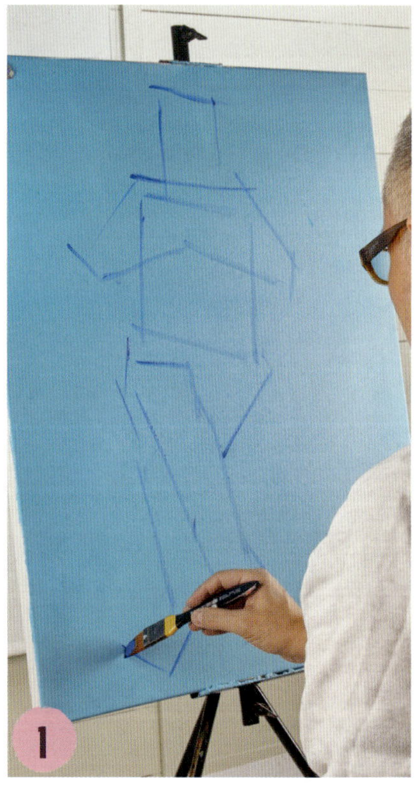

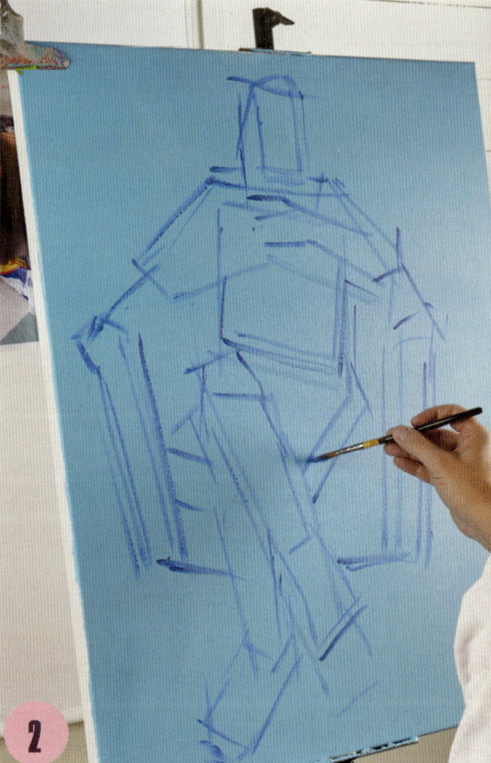

Match the angles

When drawing, look for similar lines and angles – the upper arm on the left and arm of the chair, for example - to help guide you.

1 Start from a base of turquoise blue mixed with titanium white. When making the preparatory drawing, use a 25mm (1in) flat brush. You can use almost any colour for this – I'm using cobalt blue. Start with a box for the head, near the top of the canvas. Add the rest of the body in very simple shapes. Work quickly, and with light pressure.

2 Now work back up, making any adjustments to improve the composition. Here, I want to include both the feet, so I need to reduce the overall size of the figure to fit. There's no need to erase the existing lines; use them to guide you. Remember, these blocks are here to indicate the rough areas that the shapes (head, arms, legs etc.) fill; so they don't need to be particularly precise; nor should you feel constrained by them later.

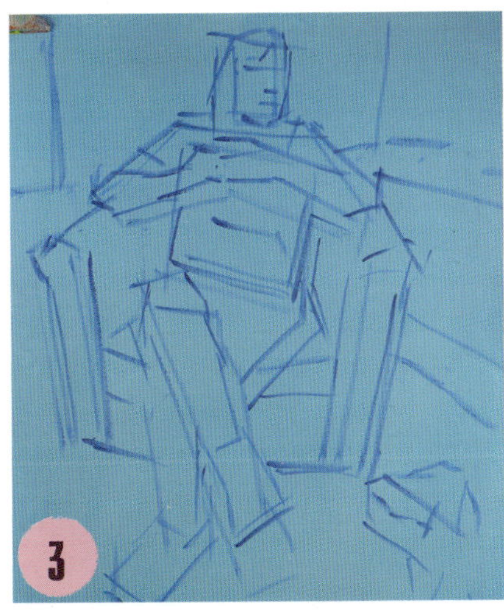

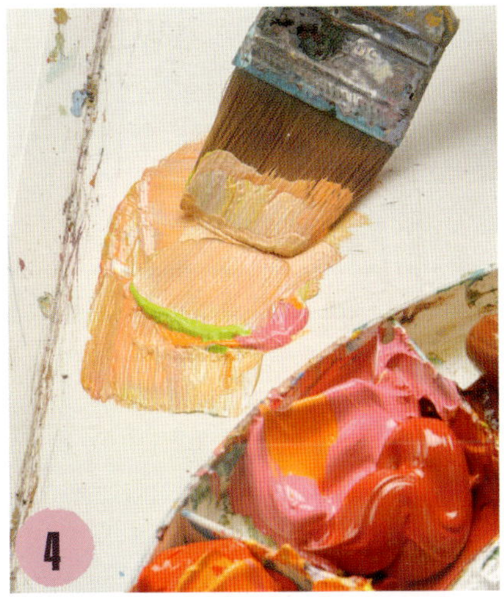

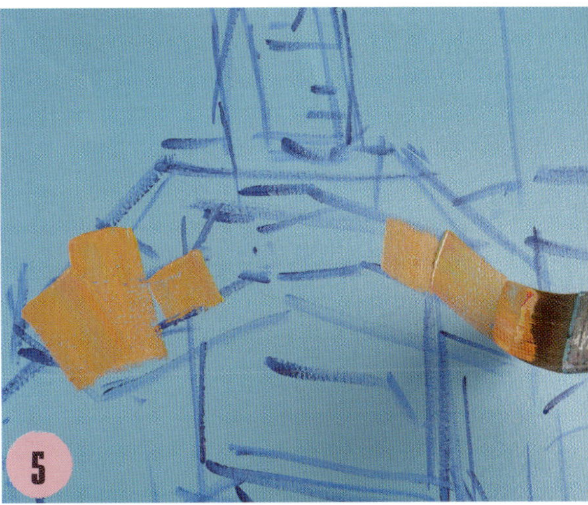

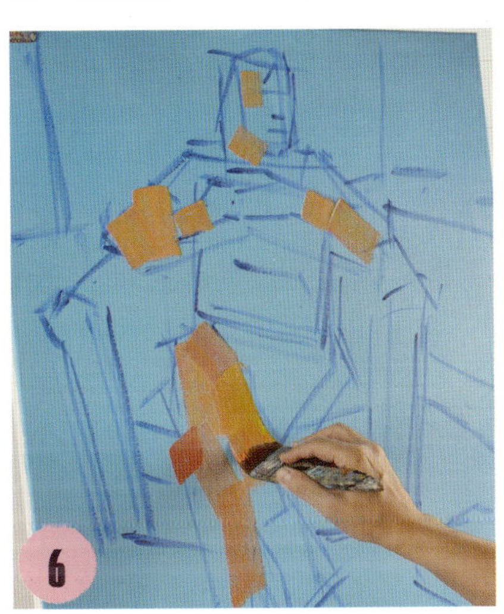

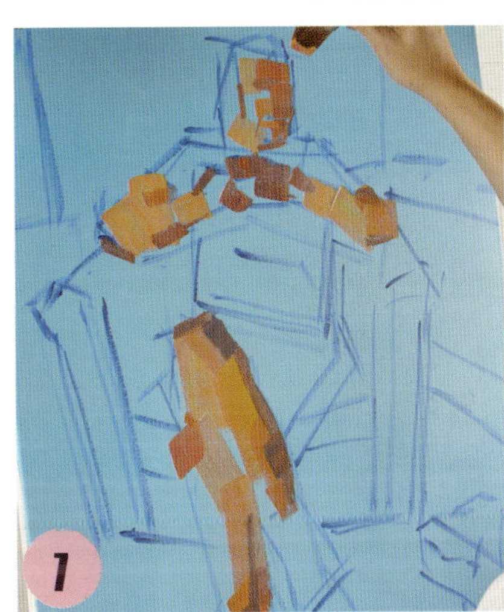

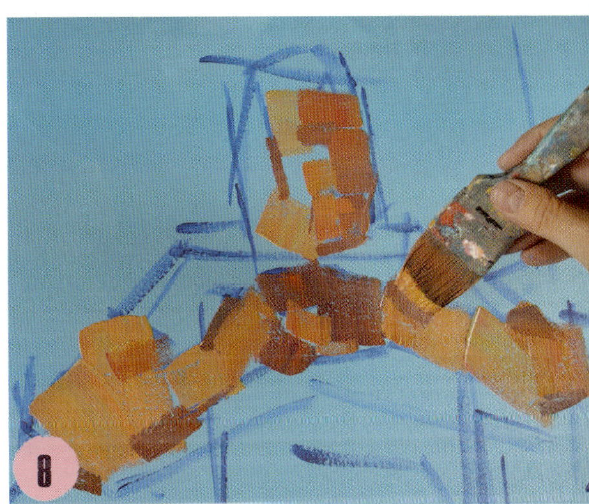

3 With the figure in place, add any surroundings that you want to include. Note that the face is simpler than a full face – you just need an indication of eye line, nose and mouth.

4 Using a damp 50mm (2in) flat brush, create a basic skin pool by loading the brush with titanium white, yellow ochre, cadmium orange, pyrrole red, quinacridone rose opaque, along with a little yellowish green and sap green.

5 When painting the skin, each mark should be a different statement – think about it like building up a mosaic. The colours in each stroke should be very similar, but not identical. To achieve this, keep dipping back into the pool of colour on your palette; and vary the proportions of colour you pick up when reloading. Avoid focussing on one area; jump around across the different skin areas. This will ensure there is an overall harmony across the painting.

6 Try not to study the original photograph too much – glance at the area on your reference, look away, and then paint what your impression was. For example, when painting the legs, I had the impression the knees had a hint more red than the rest of the legs, so I picked up a little extra pyrrole red on the brush when painting these areas.

7 Add touches of quinacridone rose and burnt sienna, along with more sky blue and yellowish green to the pool. Use these cooler, deeper tones to paint in the shadow areas of skin. Introduce cobalt blue for the coolest darks.

8 Change to a 37mm (1½in) flat brush to add smaller marks to fill in some of the gaps between the big blocks. In particular, pay attention to the face and hands – more small shapes here will create interesting contrasts with the rest of the painting.

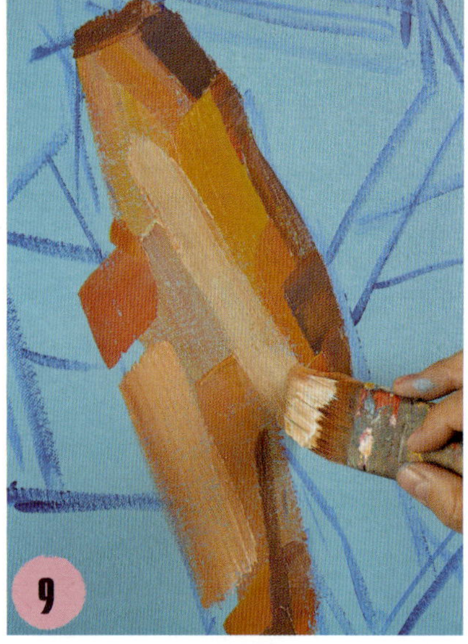

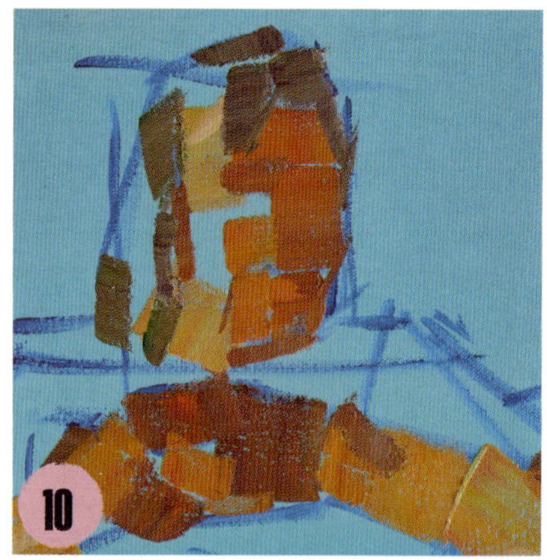

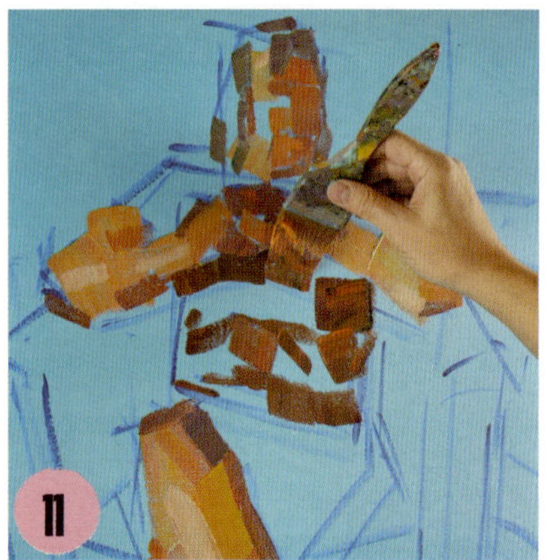

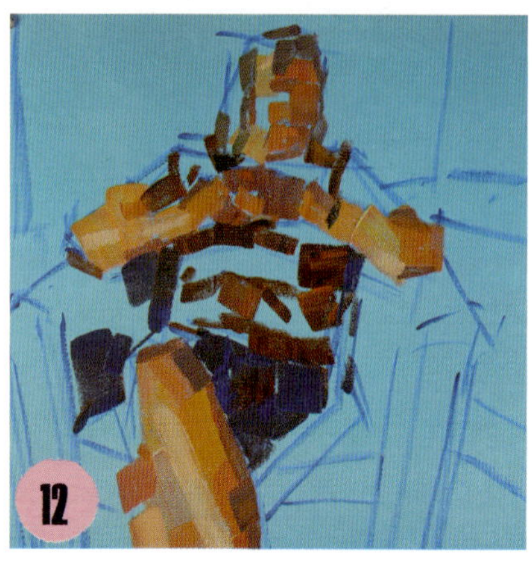

9 Add a little titanium white to the pool and add some highlights to the skin.

10 Add sap green to the dark area of the pool to make a muted brown. This can be used to frame the face by blocking in the hair.

11 Change back to the 50mm (2in) brush used earlier. Pick up a little cadmium orange, permanent blue violet, yellowish green and pyrrole red. Use this along with the muted brown on your palette to paint in the shaded areas of the T-shirt. Aim for a suggestion of texture by picking out only folds and creases that lead the eye; ignore the others.

12 Add a lot more cobalt blue and block in the shorts. Using the same brush ensures that some of the previous colours are included here, helping the different elements to link up. Add the watch strap on the model's arm, then use the same colour to paint in the shaded areas on the chair. Tidy up the outline of the arm where it overlaps here.

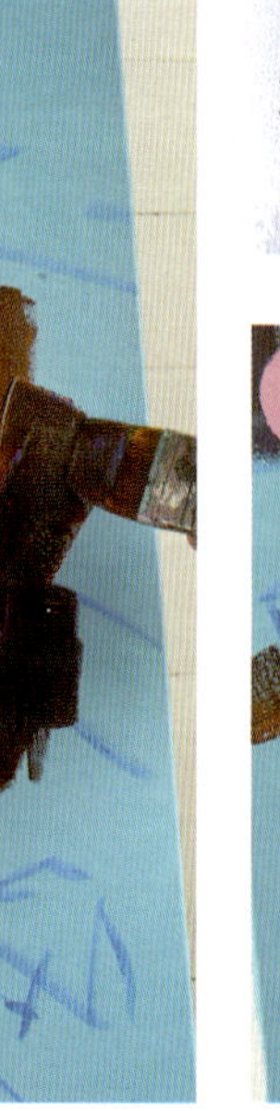

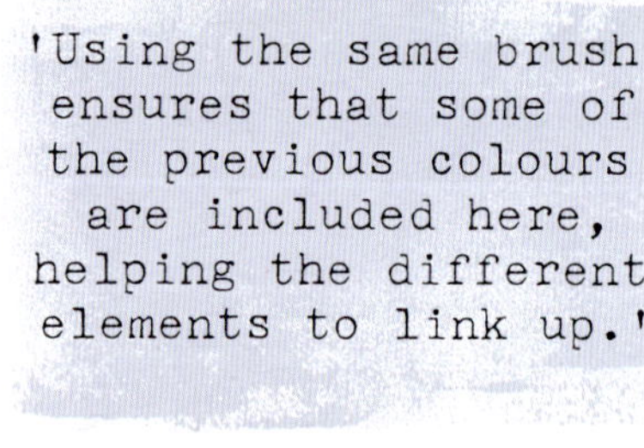

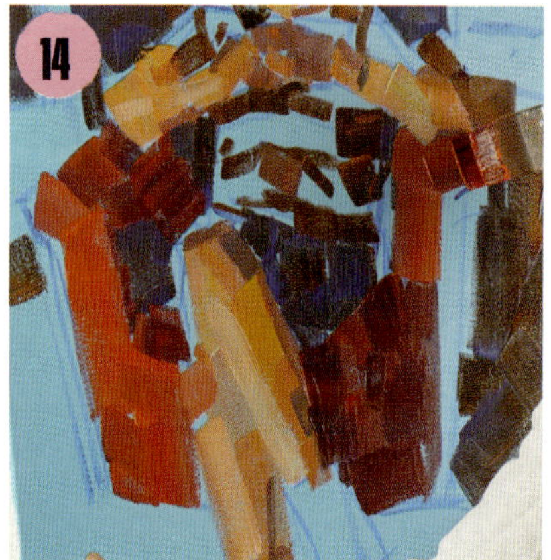

13 Take the opportunity to step back and assess. Take a change of pace and tackle a less important area – in this case the background. Using the same blue-brown pool, paint the area around the head. Add more cadmium orange to the pool and use the resulting neutral hue to paint the wooden furniture.

14 Change to a clean 50mm (2in) flat brush and build up a redder pool with quinacridone rose, cadmium orange, sky blue and yellowish green. Use this alongside some of the neutral pool and block in the chair. Add cobalt blue and more pyrrole red for the midtones on the chair.

15 Using a clean 37mm (1½in) flat brush and a pool of cadmium orange, yellow ochre, permanent yellow medium, yellowish green and sky blue, paint in the main body of the T-shirt. Vary the mix with the browns on your palette for creases and soft shadows, and use the edge of the brush to suggest folds over the underlying shades established earlier.

16 Add some titanium white, sky blue and yellowish green to the pool, and use this for the hair highlights.

17 Change to the 50mm (2in) brush and load it with sap green, cadmium orange, sky blue, burnt sienna. Use this to block in the remaining wooden furniture.

18 Paint the carpet with a grey pool of titanium white, yellow ochre, cobalt blue and yellowish green added to the brown mix used for the furniture. For darker areas, add permanent blue violet. Paint the cushion to the side of the chair and shoes at the same time, with the same mix. Don't worry if they overlap – we can pick them out with highlighting to differentiate them later on.

19 Add more yellowish green, permanent blue violet and sky blue to the mix and paint in the wall at the top right. Add turquoise blue to the pool to paint the blue patch of the carpet.

20 Change to a 25mm (1in) flat brush and detail the plastic bag. This bit of texture breaks up the flat texture of the carpet, and introduces some colour. Use cobalt blue for the blue section, and permanent yellow medium with yellow ochre for the yellow part. Finally, add pyrrole red knocked back with a little burnt sienna to add the red detail (see inset).

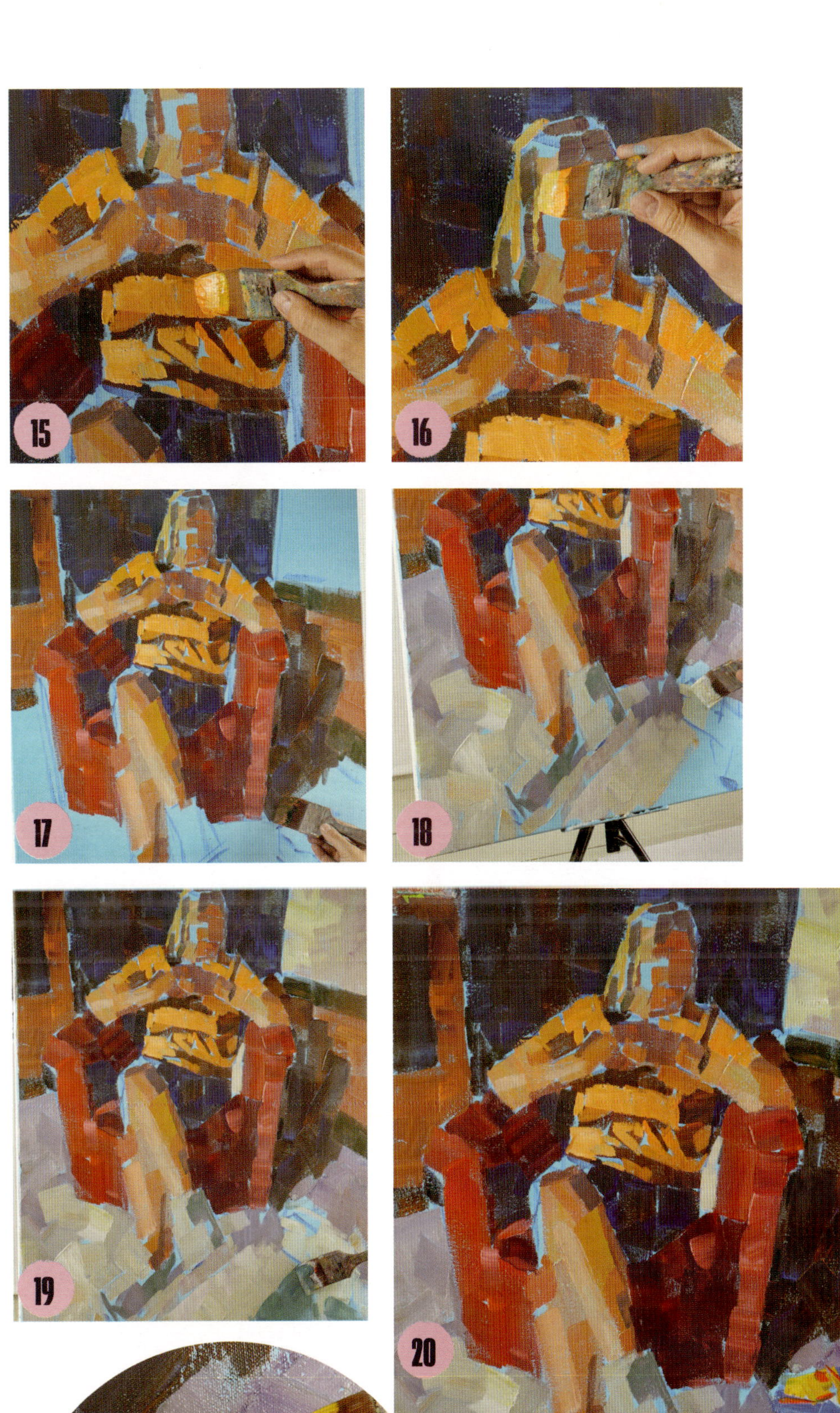

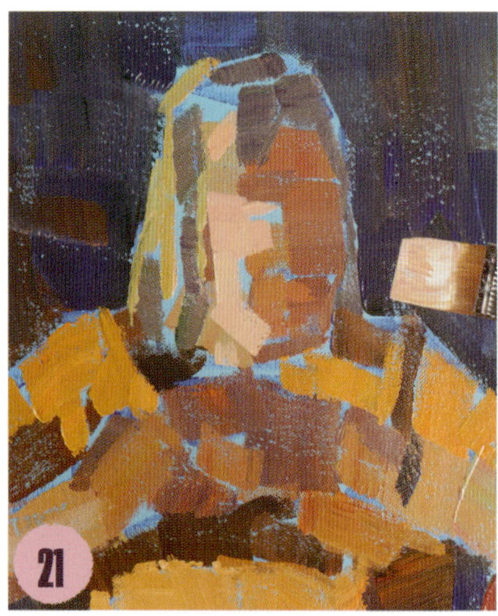

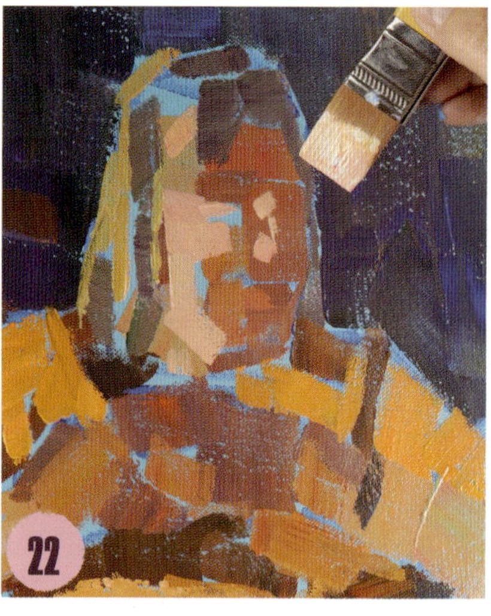

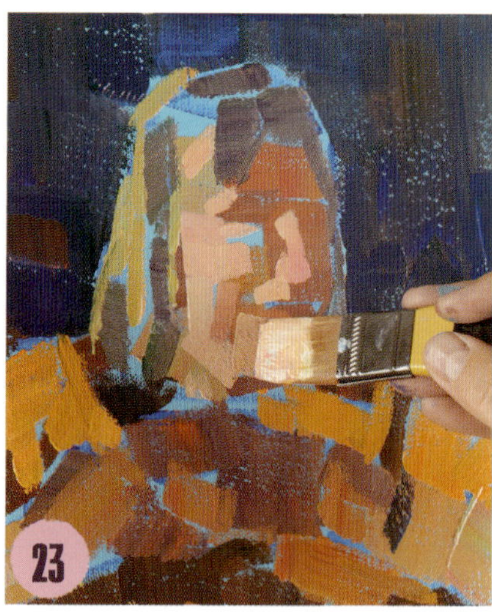

21 Make a highlight mix for the skin – titanium white, cadmium orange, quinacridone rose opaque and a touch of sky blue. Use a clean 25mm (1in) brush to paint the left-hand side of the face.

22 Pick out the nose and right-hand side of the mouth, picking up a little more quinacridone rose opaque for this section.

23 Add as few additional marks as you can to describe the face. When painting a full-length portrait, it's important not to overtighten the face, or you risk losing the sense of animation.

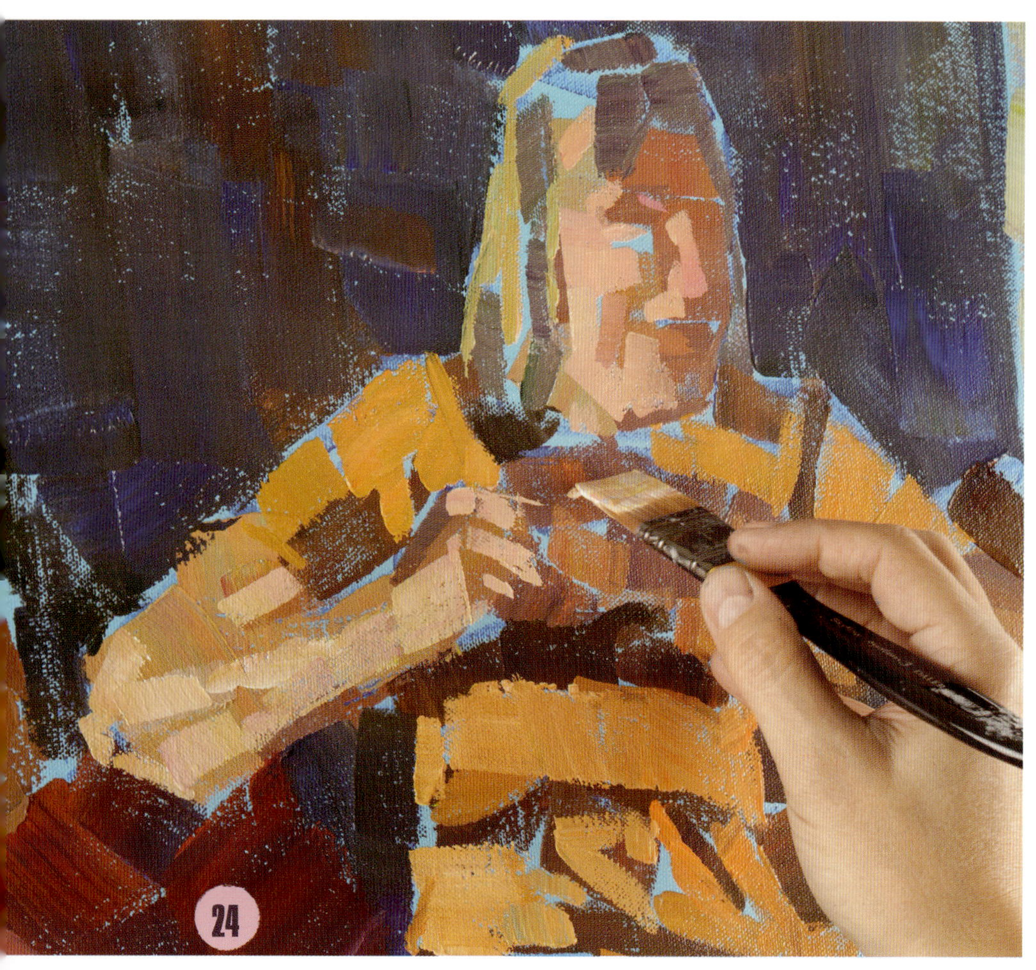

24 Use the same skin highlight mix to develop the arms. Just like the face, avoid the temptation to overdetail the hands.

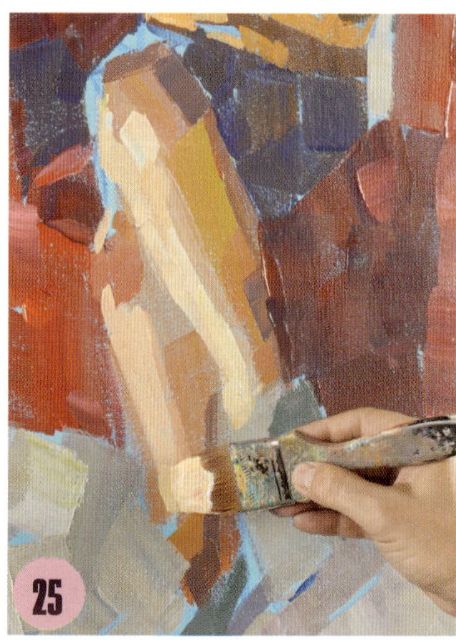

25 Change to a clean 37mm (1½in) flat brush for the legs, using the same pool. Be sparing with the highlights; make sure you balance white against colour, or things will go chalky.

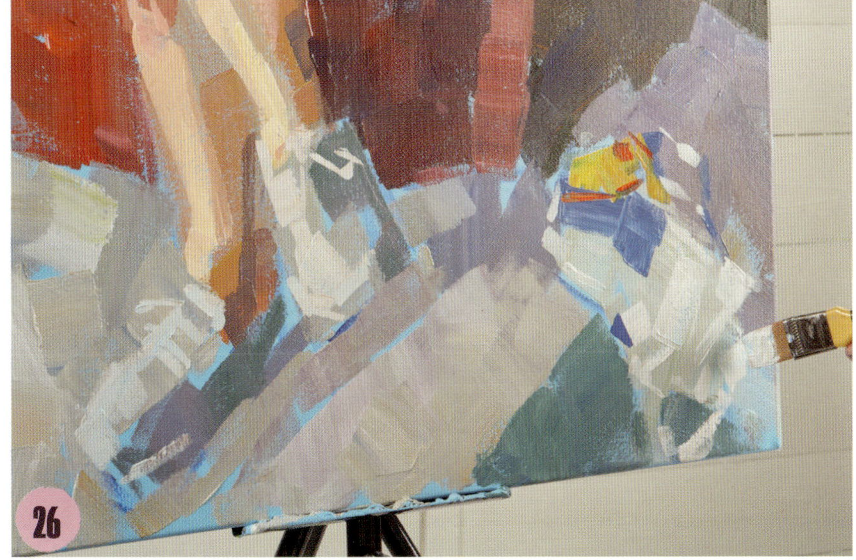

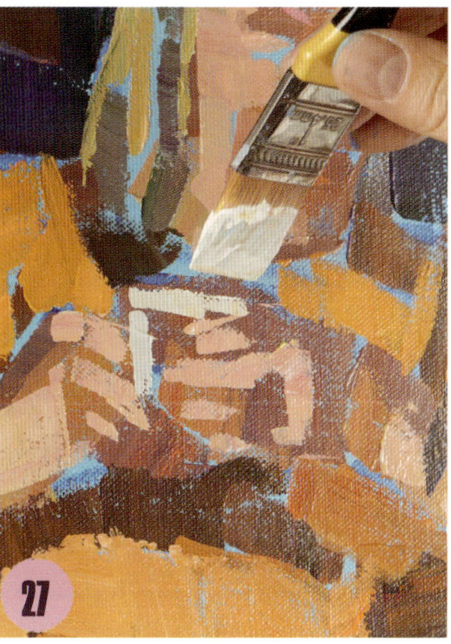

26 Add sky blue, burnt sienna and titanium white to the skin highlight mix and bring out the highlights on the shoes to help differentiate them from the surrounding carpet. Add still more titanium white to bring out the highlights on the plastic bag.

27 This mix can also be used to pick out highlights on the teacup.

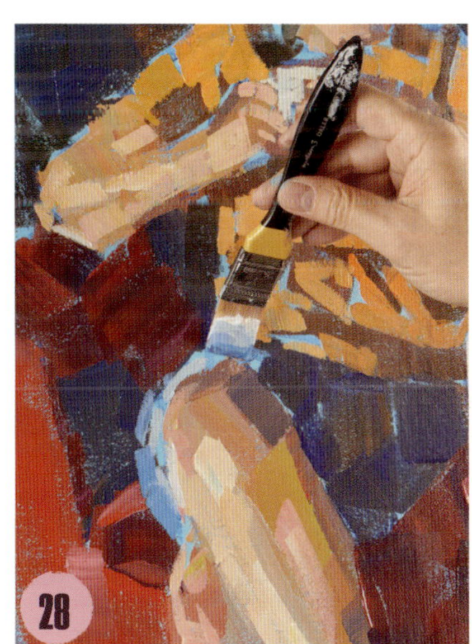

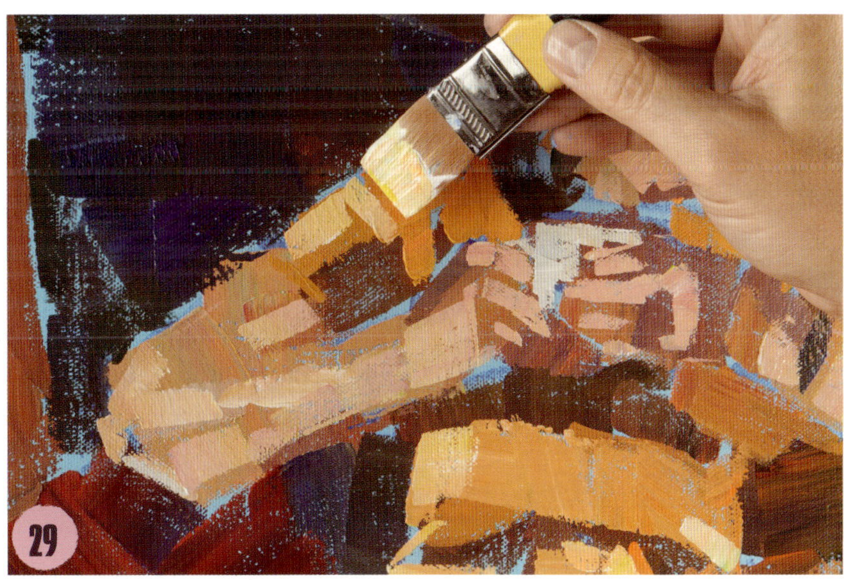

28 Add a little cobalt blue to titanium white, and add some shaping to the shorts.

29 Use a pool of titanium white, permanent yellow medium, sky blue, yellowish green and a hint of cadmium orange to add final highlights to the T-shirt.

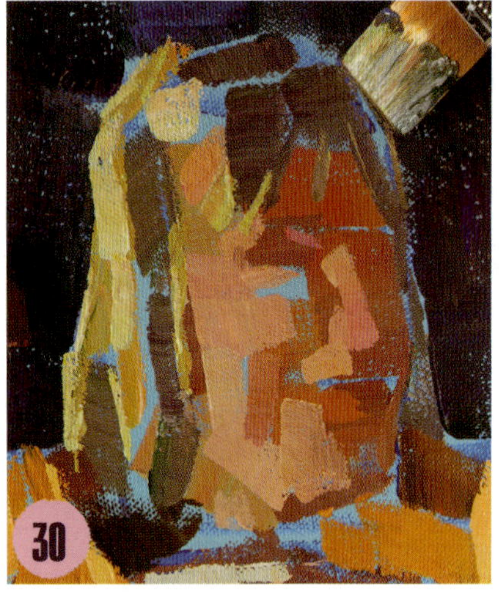

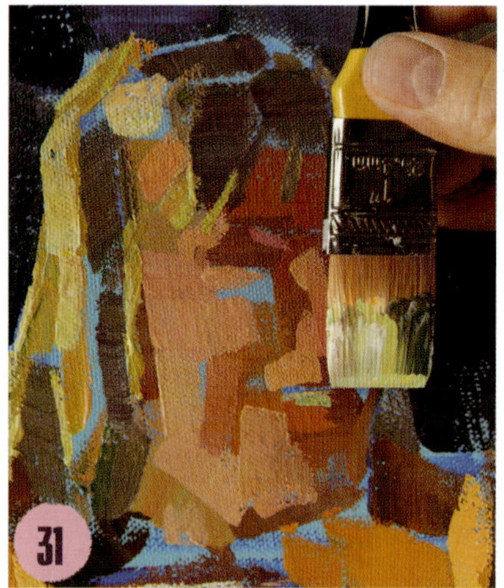

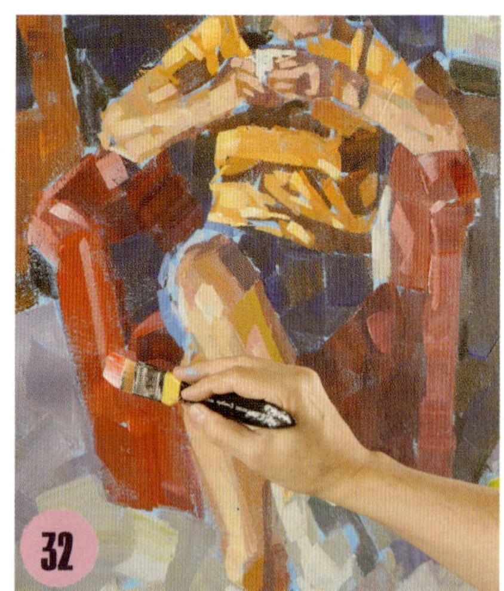

30 Still using the 25mm (1in) flat brush, add more sky blue and titanium white, plus a little yellowish green. Use this to highlight the hair.

31 With the paint remaining on the edge of the brush, add the teeth.

32 Load the brush with pyrrole red, titanium white and sky blue to add the highlights to the chair.

33 Start to sharpen the painting with bridging marks – those touches that fill some of the spaces in the painting – using the mixes on your palette: refine the T-shirt using the midtones of orange on your palette, and the face using the skin tones.

34 Use the bridging marks to sharpen and shape; making any adjustments you feel necessary to finish.

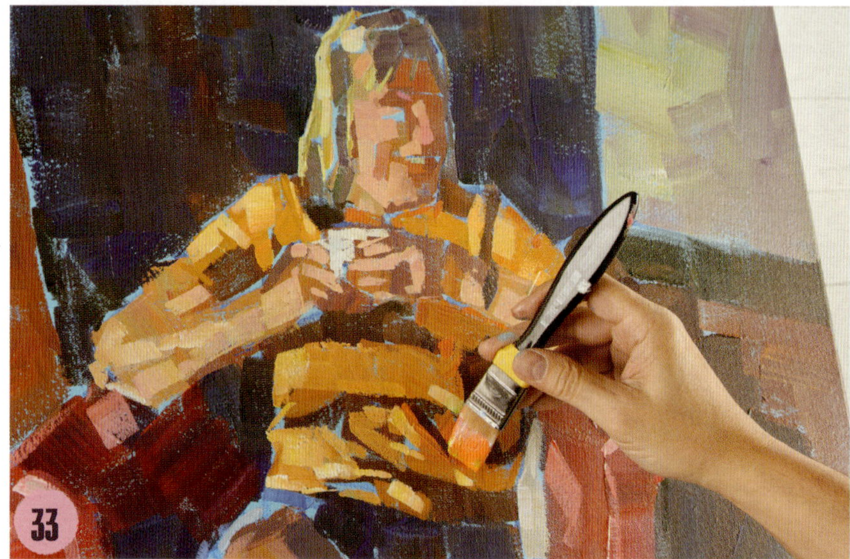

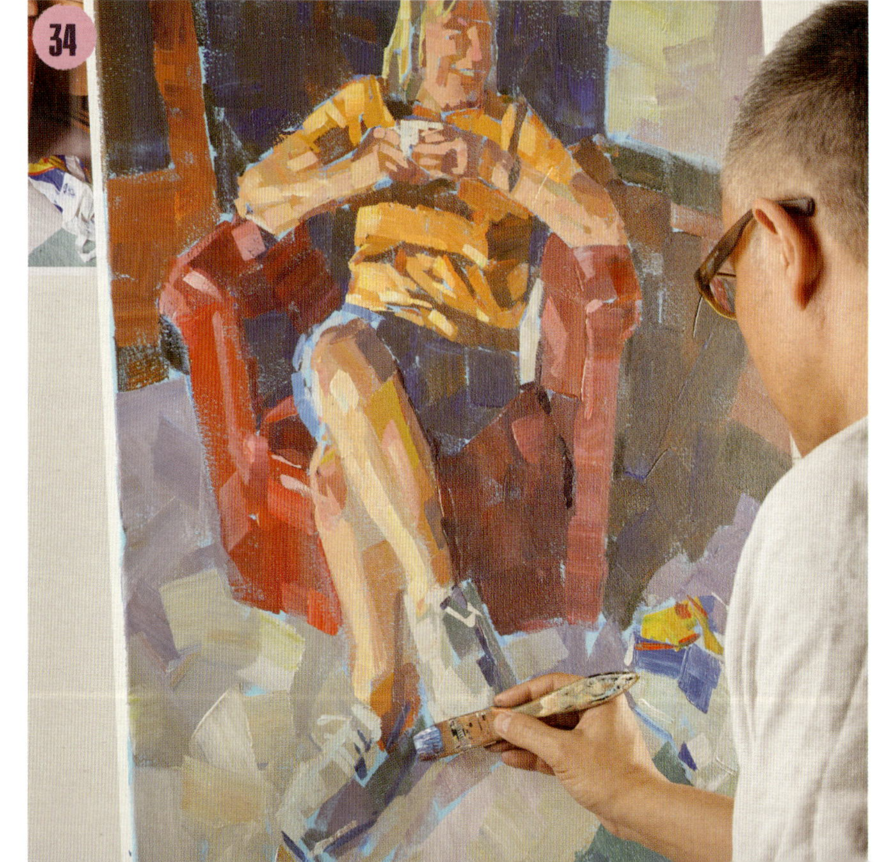

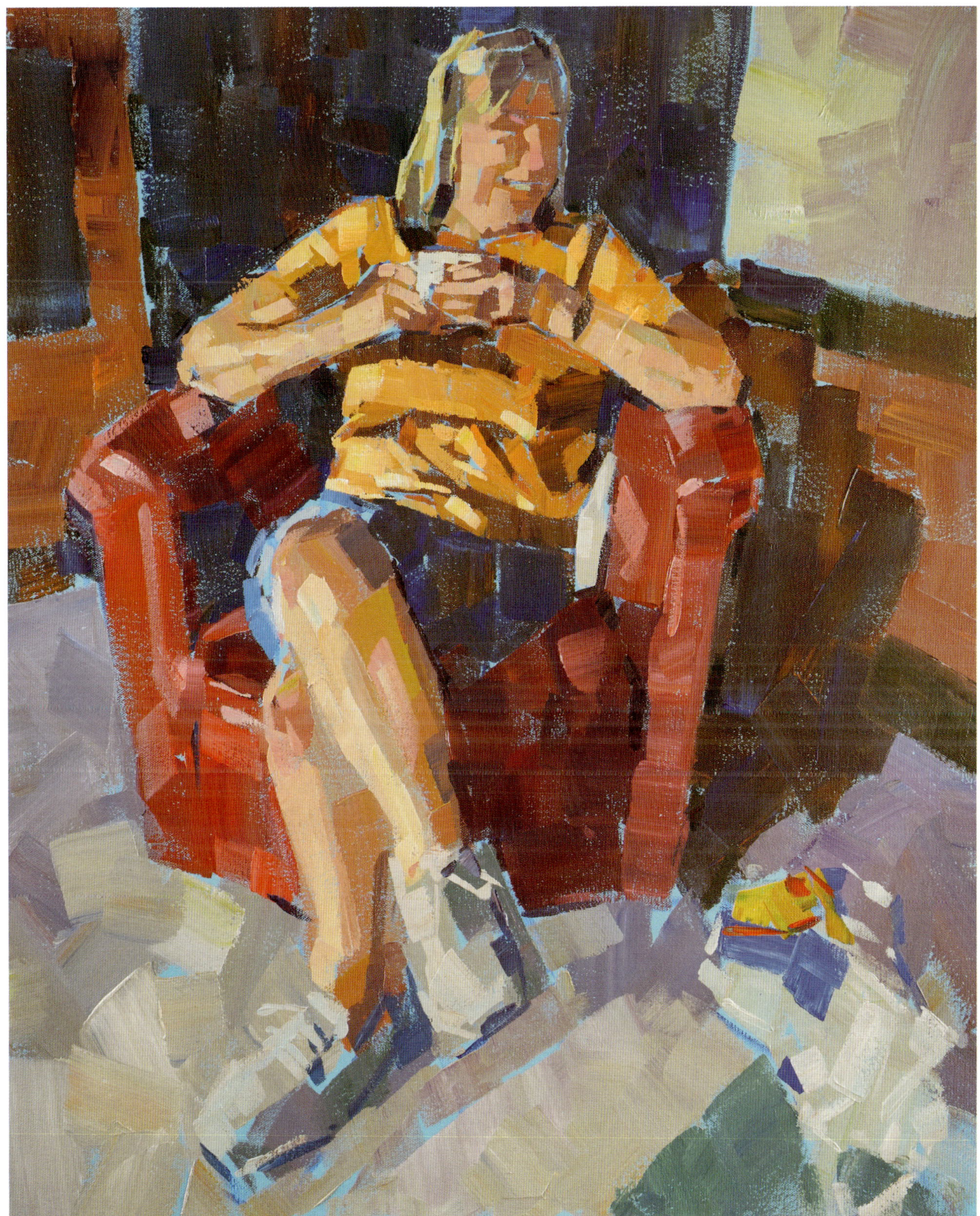

THE FINISHED PORTRAIT.

With any of these exercises in this book, there is the opportunity to develop the paintings further. Refining is a lengthy process, however, and I will stress that a deadline is worth setting to avoid overworking. You can be too close to a painting to judge the finishing so it may be worth leaving it overnight and returning with fresh eyes the next day. For this portrait, I would be keen to strengthen some of the darks to intensify the lights. I would also patch over some of the base colour to focus the blues more in the shorts and plastic bag.

Texture

Acrylics allow for the addition of various enhancers and mediums to change the consistency of the paint. This is just like adding water to thin the paint – in fact, if you think of water as a thinning medium, it can help to understand the effects you can get from other, more specialist, mediums.

These mediums include modelling paste for more pronounced brushwork, and gels which contain grains of sand or lava for subtle variations. These can be used before painting to create a textured surface, or added to pigment while painting.

Acrylic mediums

I use a few mediums which help in some way to enhance the flow, create texture or prolong working times of acrylic. They are not essential, especially for beginners, but as your art improves you may want to consider them.

Flow improver Diluting paint with water dulls the pigment, while employing a medium like flow improver helps the paint to move smoothly while retaining vibrancy. By using it along with water, you can create transparent or diluted washes with very little colour shift. When used neat with pigment, it produces a satin finish.

Retarder Retarder is an additive that extends the painting time of acrylics, allowing for more blends or subtle gradations of colour. It's available as a gel or a liquid and is added in small amounts to the pigment. I use the liquid form in a diffuser bottle so I can spray it over my palette or over layers of paint on my canvas.

Texture gels Texture gels and pastes are added to acrylic to create pronounced, impasto-style brushwork. There are a quite a few variations and thicknesses available. Moulding paste is particularly dramatic and can be used before painting to create texture on the support. Texture gels are usually clear in colour while the pastes are white. Avoid large amounts when mixing with pigment as colours will become dull.

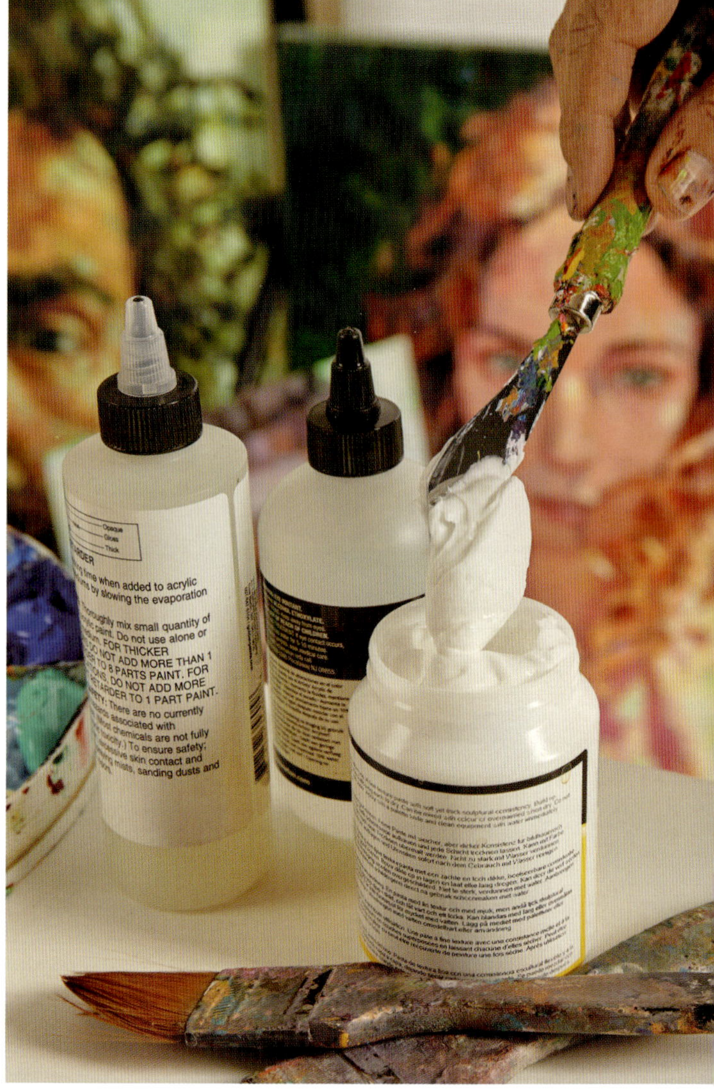

A selection of mediums.

Smooth finishes

For smooth finishes you can use a soft or fluid acrylic, but if you only have heavy body acrylic you can use the mediums described here to dilute and thin out the paint. Such mediums come in gloss, satin and matt finishes, and you can vary the proportions of paint to medium in order to create more or less transparency and fluidity.

I find using too much retarder can make layers a bit tacky, which can spoil smoothness, but this is very much trial-and-error territory.

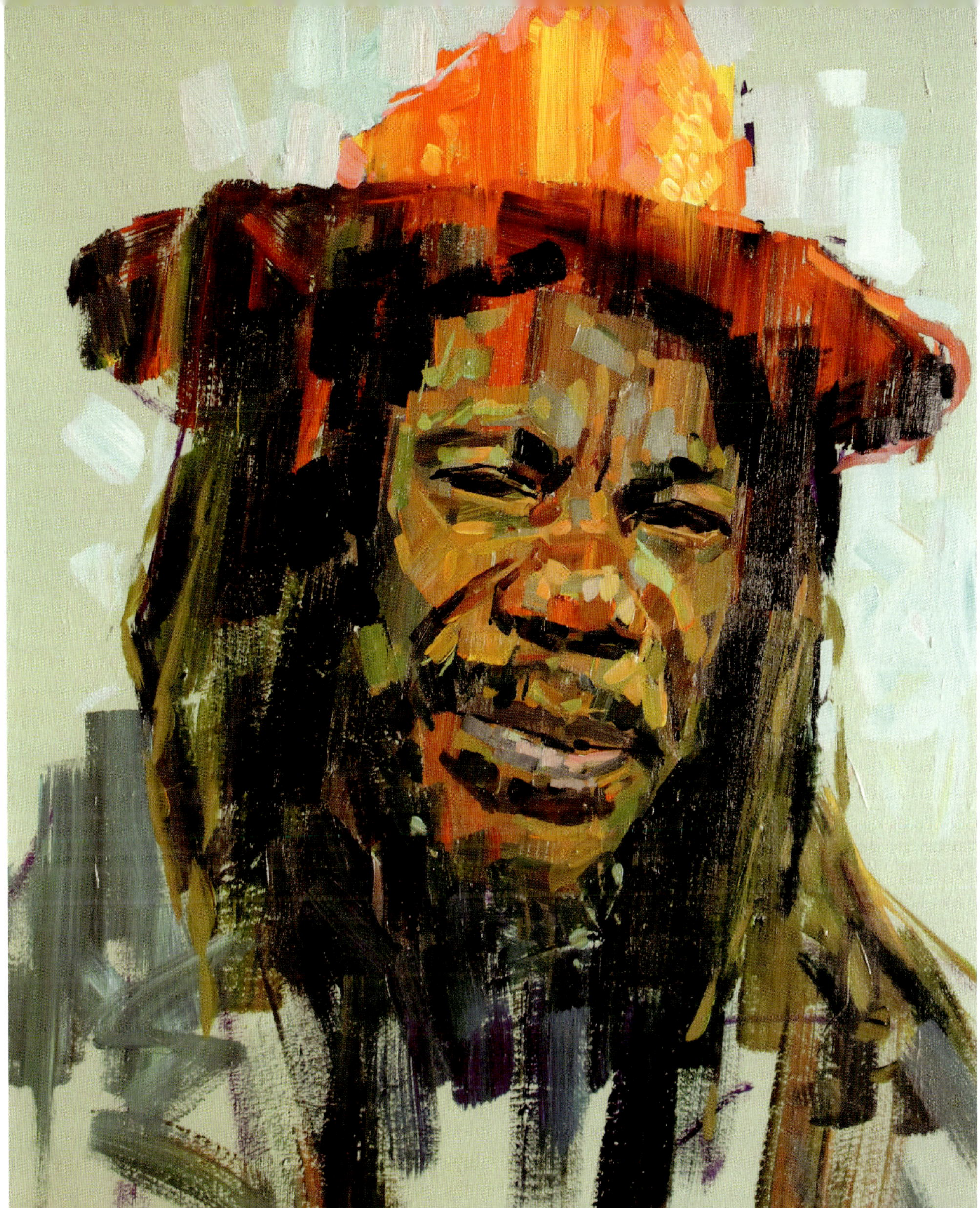

RED HAT 41×51CM (16×20IN)

I occasionally paint over canvases that already have paintings on them – sometimes two or three layers of them. After each one I simply repaint a base colour and it's good to go. This provides a rough texture to work on, especially if you've previously used heavy body acrylic or applied impasto gels or pastes. This portrait has naturally picked up on a previous painting with subtle grains in the beard and surrounding areas. I tried to keep the face full to add more depth.

Texture is a tactile thing, and photographs can't quite pick up on every nuance, but it does add value when seen in the flesh. It allows another one of the senses to participate in the enjoyment of a painting.

There is a limit both to the amount of overpainting a canvas can take and to the amount of texture applied. If you like the directness of a bold brushmark, it may be sensible to keep a base texture to a minimum.

Using texture pastes

If you're painting a very weathered face, texture pastes will do a lot of the work for you. Sketch out the face and apply the paste neat with a palette knife, following the contours of the features. Allow to dry, then paint the portrait as usual; the base texture will come through and create a three-dimensional impression.

If you are using a soft body acrylic, a heavy texture paste will add weight to the paint. Be careful not to add too much gel or paste as this will effect the luminosity of the pigment.

I used texture pastes early on in my career to loosen up – a rough surface or heavy, textured paint makes it difficult to fuss over. You could create an interesting base for any portrait by simply applying random textured layers. The portrait itself could be left smooth and the surrounding areas could be textural. Having applied the paste there is a little shrinkage that takes place once the layers dry.

You can use brushes to spread the paste but these can be easily ruined if allowed to dry on the brush. Wash brushes immediately after use with soap and water.

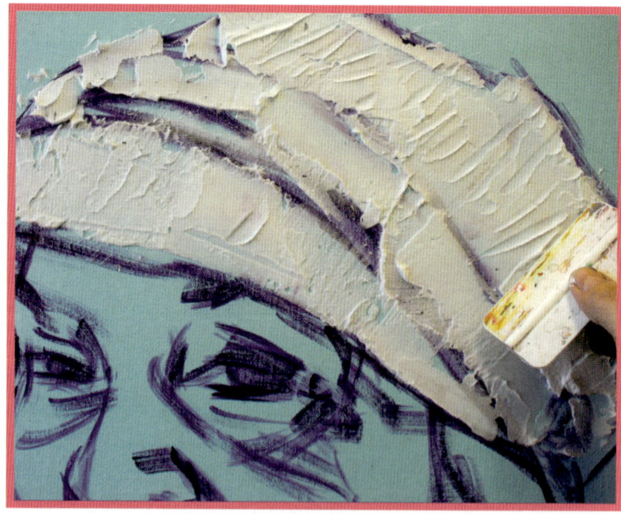

Apply the modelling paste using a scraper to create the ridged effect of the corduroy material.

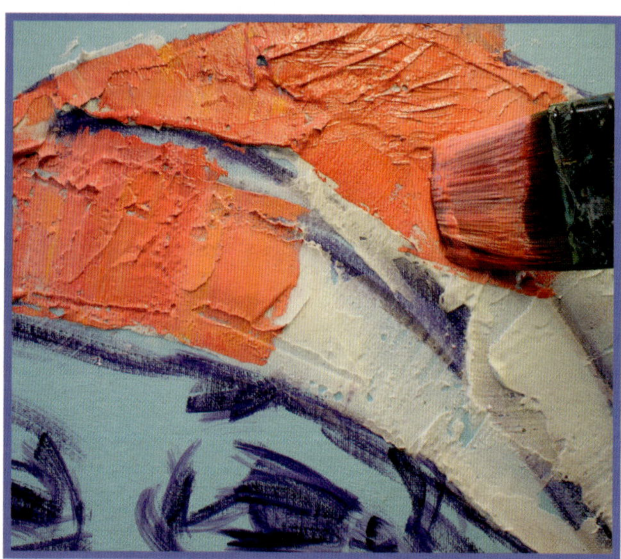

Once dry, the texture can be painted over.

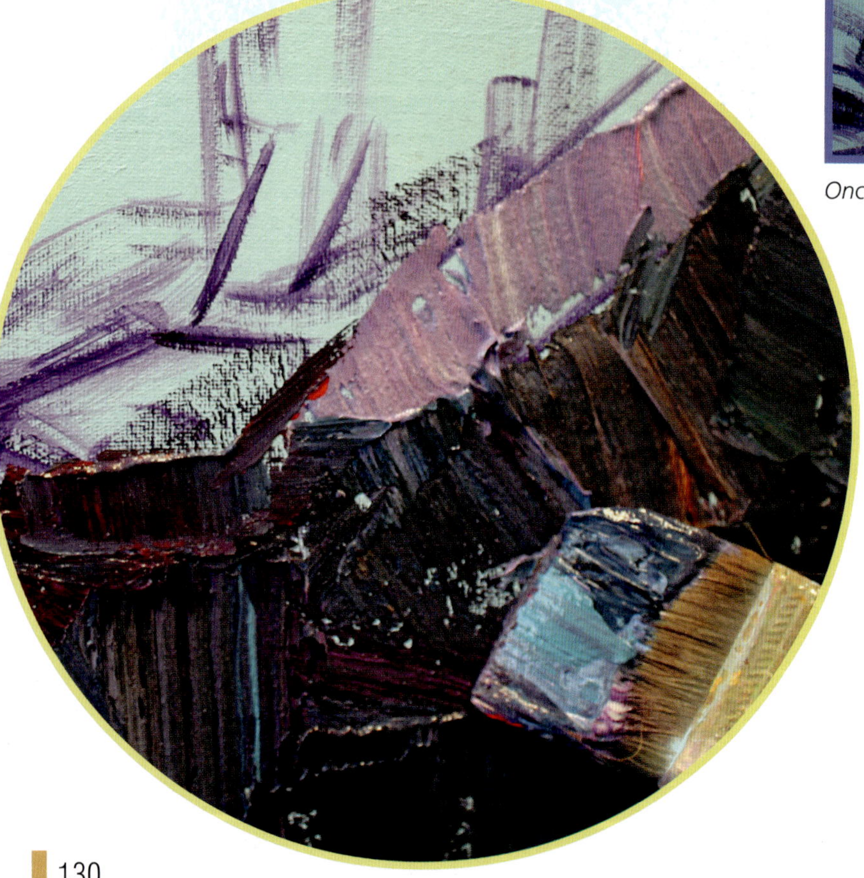

The texture gel can also be mixed in with the paint and applied directly, as shown here.

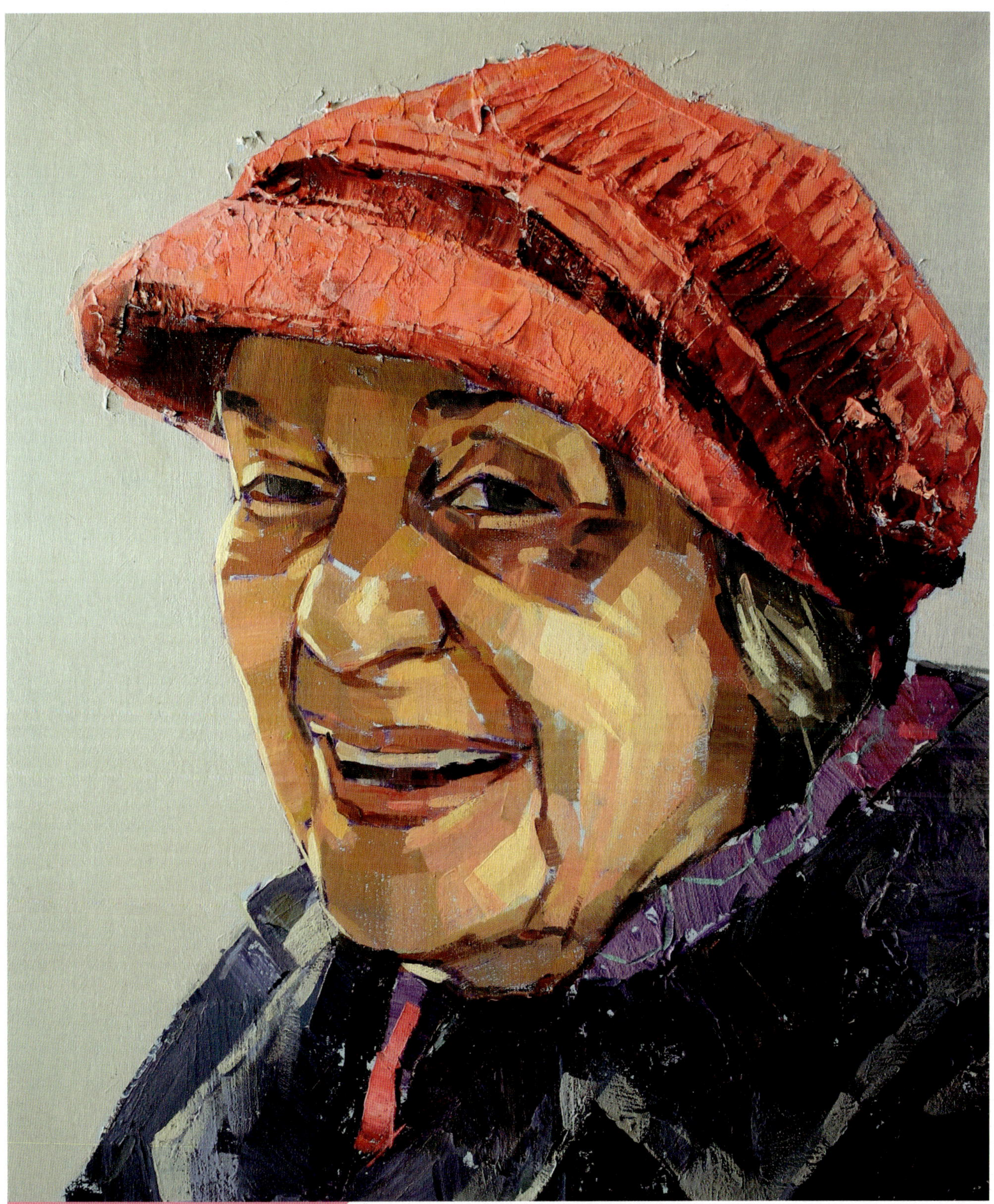

Before any painting, I applied modelling paste to create a texture for the hat. This was allowed to dry before layers of red were painted over it. I also used modelling paste pre-mixed with pigment for the jacket; this allowed marks and colours to merge together at the same time. The face, although applied with blocky brushstrokes, used paint combined with retarding medium, allowing the layers to interact and provide a smooth finish. The background is a pale grey mix diluted with flow improver for greater coverage.

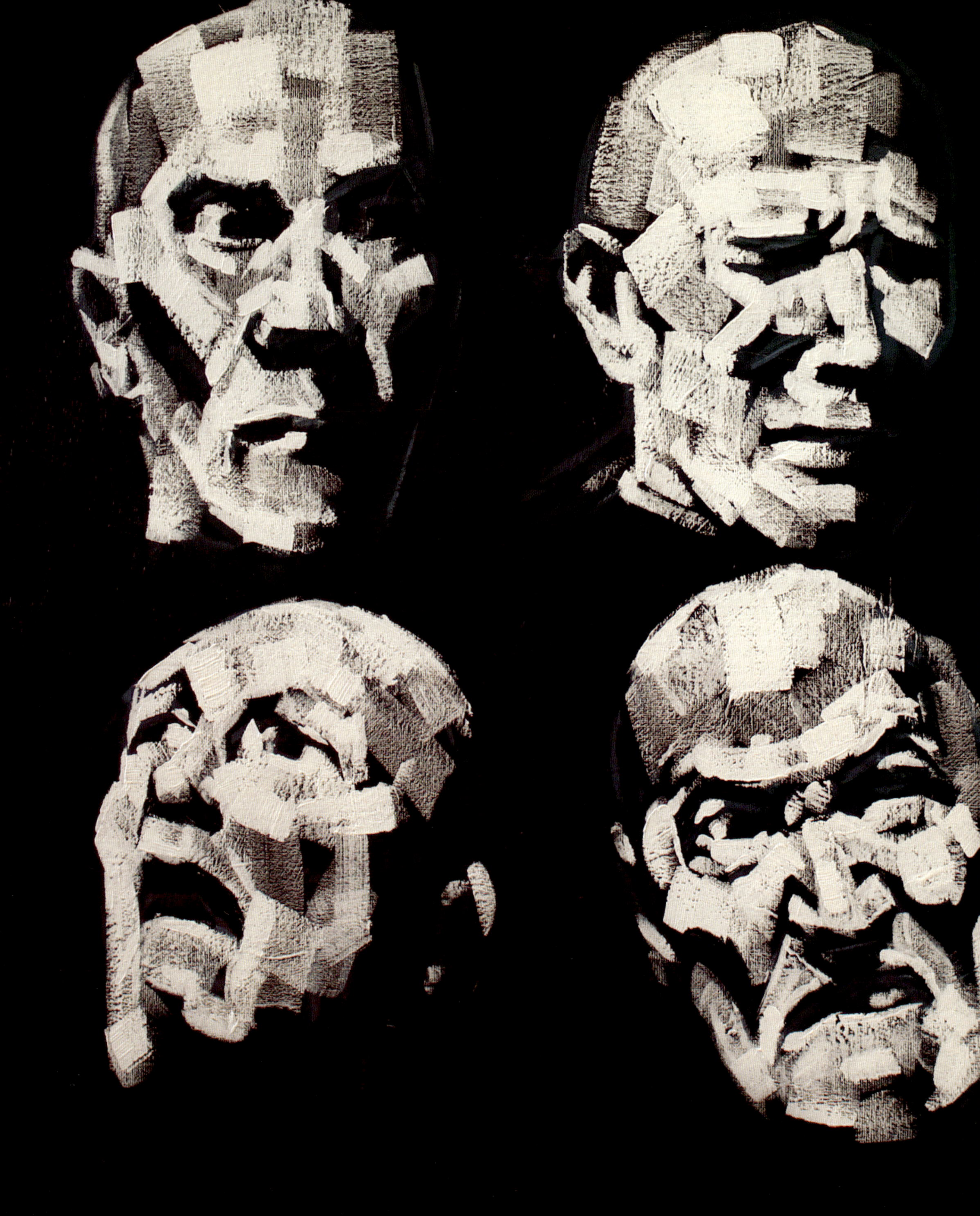

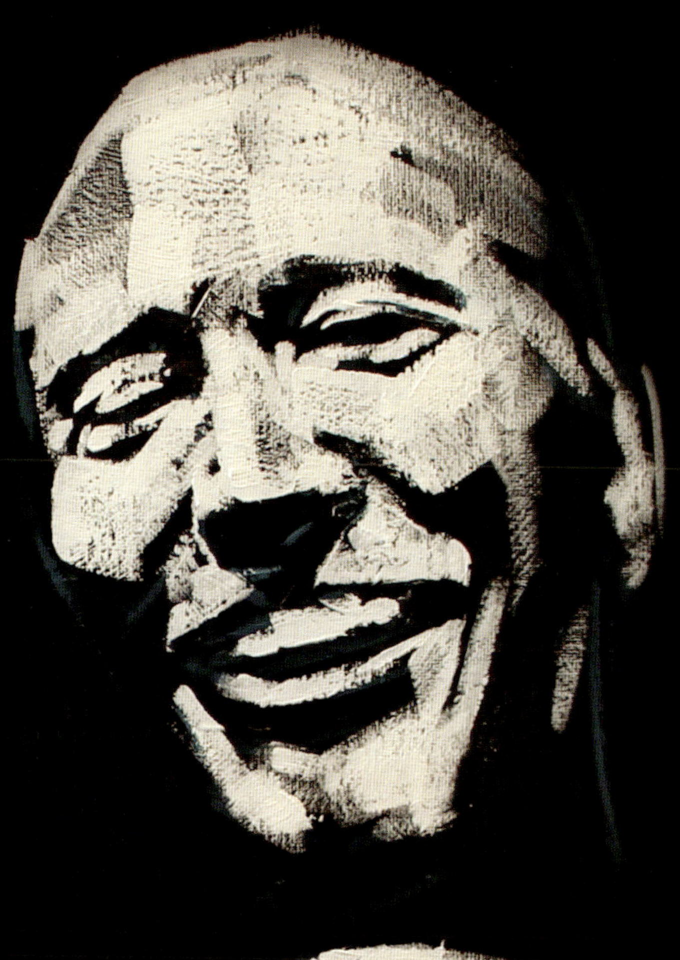

Unusual expressions

Smiling faces in painted portraits tends to be a rarity - teeth can be problematic, and traditional portraiture favours neutral or moody poses. However, traditionally rare or problematic expressions are precisely the kinds of features that create scope for more originality. You could even make a point of making the smile the focal point by overly whitening the teeth.

When drawing or painting different expressions, look for how the face creases up, engaging more diagonal lines. Eyes and nostrils may widen, and the mouth may reveal gritted teeth or a winning smile.

Portraits can be a mirror image of emotions we've all been through, and this can make your portraits more engaging. We are prone to picking up on signals that facial movements make. These movements can be subtle or obvious, and we react accordingly. We warm to a smiling face, feel threatened by an anger-filled visage, and feel empathy if someone looks sad or tearful.

For group portraits, an unusual or dramatic expression can create a very effective focal point. A single angry face really stands out from a group portrait of smiling faces. This is not limited to the face - you can achieve a similar effect with a group of full figure portraits by having one in a more dramatic pose than the others.

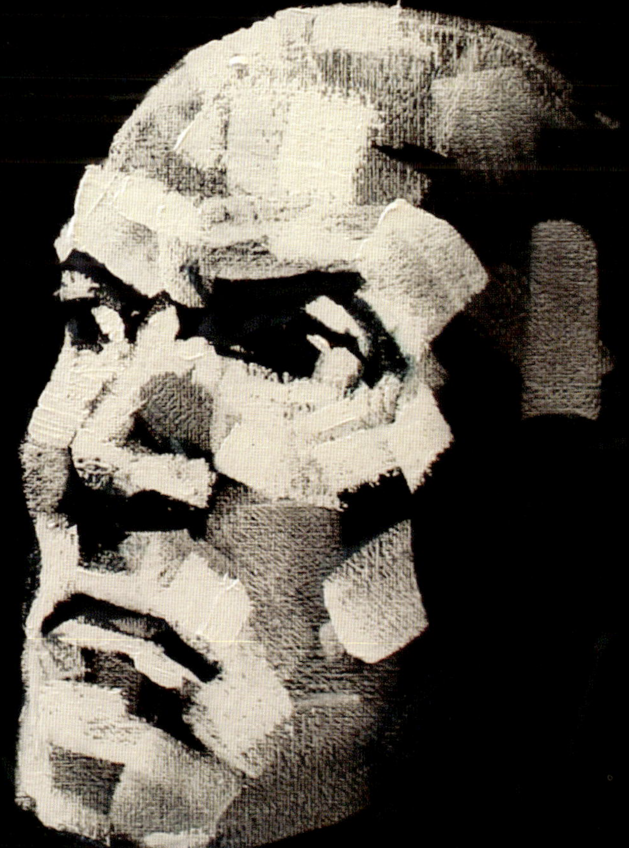

MAKING FACES 76×51cm (30×20in)

Sketches or tonal studies are a great way to get to know the different shapes and folds the face makes when displaying a range of emotions. Look to see what shape the eyebrows or corners of the mouth make; and how tense or relaxed the face is when you're happy, angry, surprised or sad.

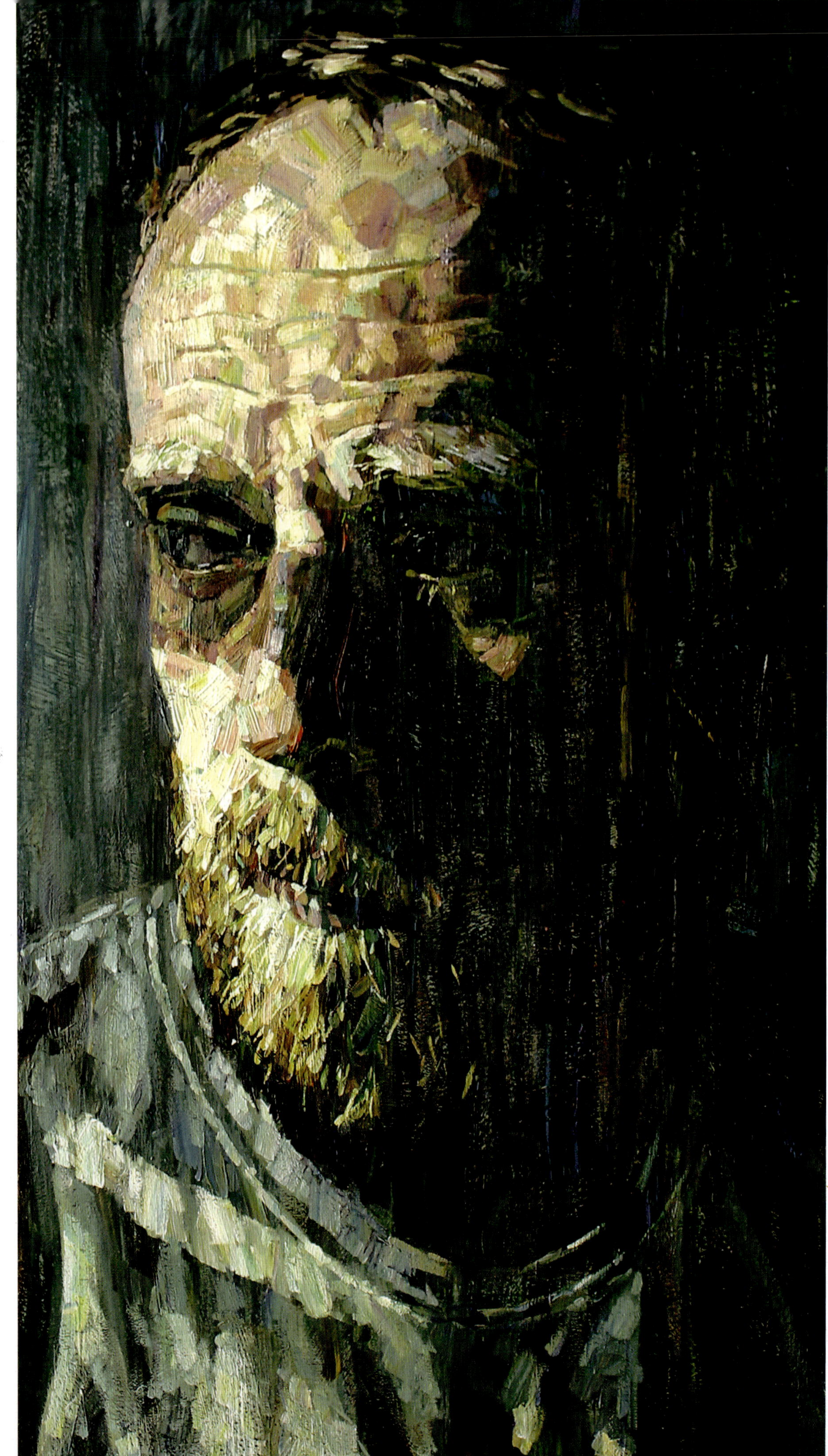

Evoking a mood

We know colours can accentuate a mood, and we can use these to complement the expression of a sitter. However, when using colours to link a mood with an expression you might want to hold off sledgehammering the point. As an example, a moody portrait full of darks, blues and greys might need a shot of optimism with a hint of warmth. Similarly, an overly cheery scene with lots of warm pigments might need a spike of cool colour to stop it becoming saccharine.

These aren't hard and fast rules. Children's portraits, for example, can be particularly vocal and obvious: a big grin unashamedly depicted with bright or pastel colours would work well.

You might try playing with the expectations and perceptions of the viewer, too, by deliberately contradicting the expression with contrasting colours: using vibrant colours for a person who looks sad, for example, or sombre colours twinned with a happy expression.

Expressions can be intensified if the portrait fills more of the painting. This can also be useful to convey intimacy or make a more confrontational piece. Similarly, a portrait set back will create distance, giving you the opportunity to use the surroundings, and make the viewer a more casual observer.

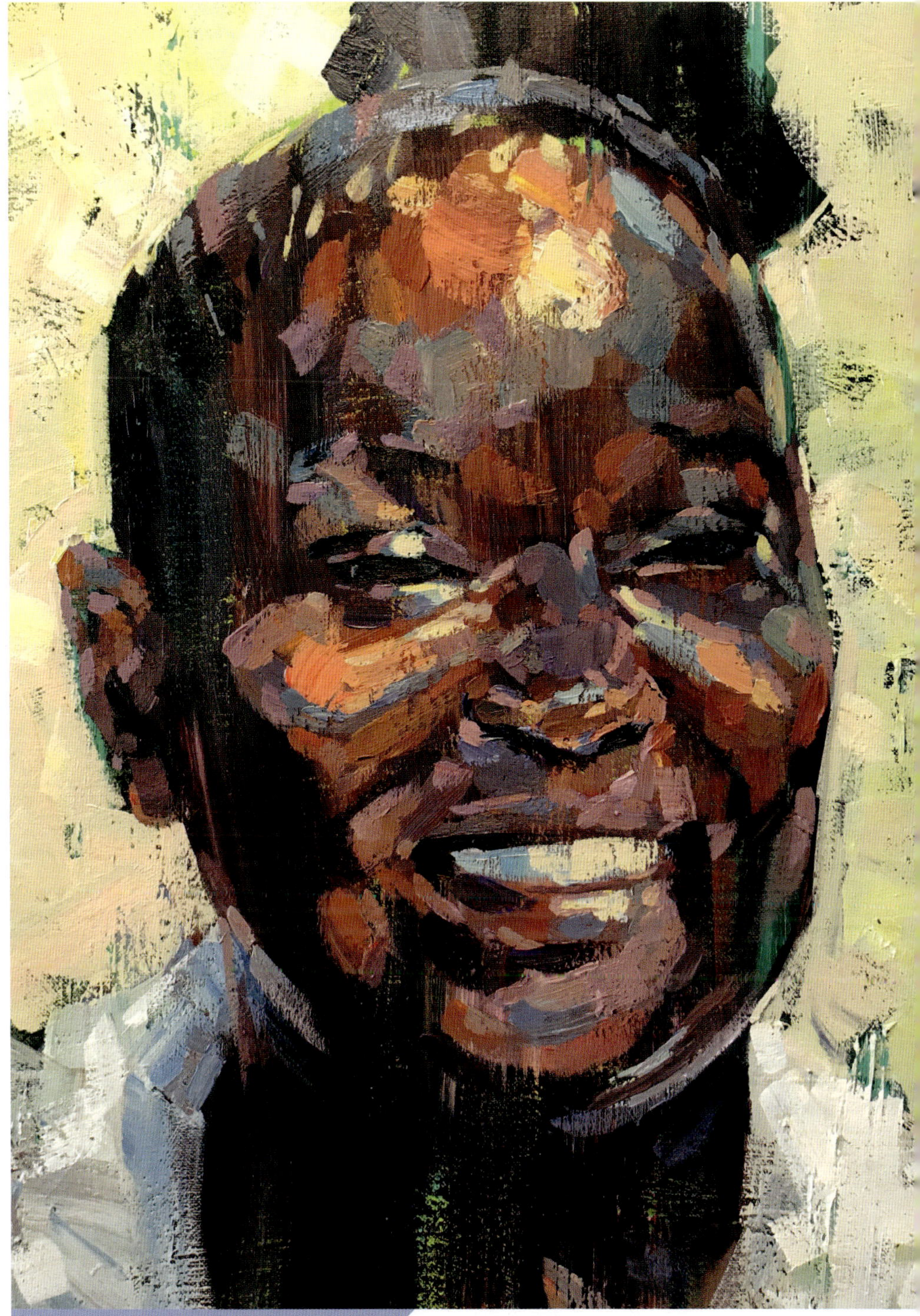

SMILEY 42×61cm (16½×24in)

Smiling faces create pleasing rounded shapes but teeth can be an issue. Try to avoid drawing each one. Instead, treat the teeth as a whole and use subtle shades to darken them in groups, using a couple of subtle lines to separate. Smiling faces can look overly sweet or cheesy, so look to leave a few expressive marks or vary the colour. In this portrait there are lots of warm colours, so I've added blues in the face to counteract the warmth.

J.P. 41×71cm, (16×28in)

Mood can be enhanced by colour as well as the expression. The cool blues, greys and darks reflect the expression, but optimism is found in the warmth of the highlights which have a yellow bias.

Profile portraits tend to be less popular as the sitter is disengaged from the viewer. Lacking the immediate connection of the full-face gaze, the profile does, however, offer other opportunities and challenges.

A profile creates strong, pronounced shapes, and as the main features rest on one half of the canvas, the balance is far more interesting in terms of composition.

Composing the image

The original photograph (see below) with mother and child has everything you're looking for as an artist: colours, tone, and interesting subjects with strong triangular shapes. With that said, I cropped the original photograph for this exercise to concentrate on a single figure. This way there are fewer distractions and I can put all my effort into getting the profile right.

Brushes: 50mm (2in) flat, 37mm (1½in) flat, 25mm (1in) flat, and 16mm (¾in) flat

Paints: Quinacridone rose opaque, turquoise blue, cadmium orange, quinacridone rose, burnt sienna, yellowish green, king's blue, permanent blue violet, permanent blue violet opaque, sap green, yellow ochre

Canvas board, 51×61cm (20×24in)

Large and small plastic scrapers

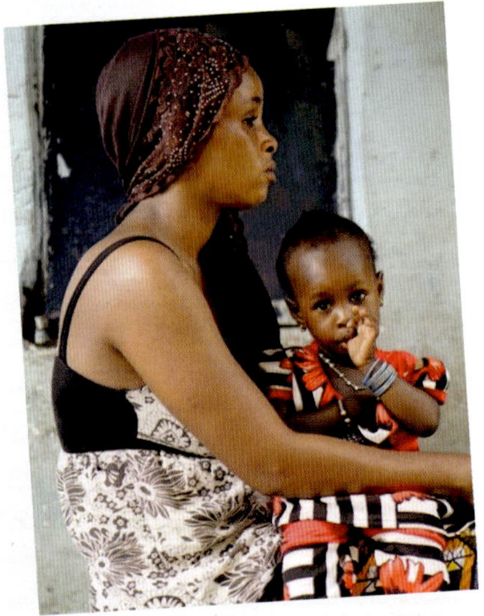

The source photograph.

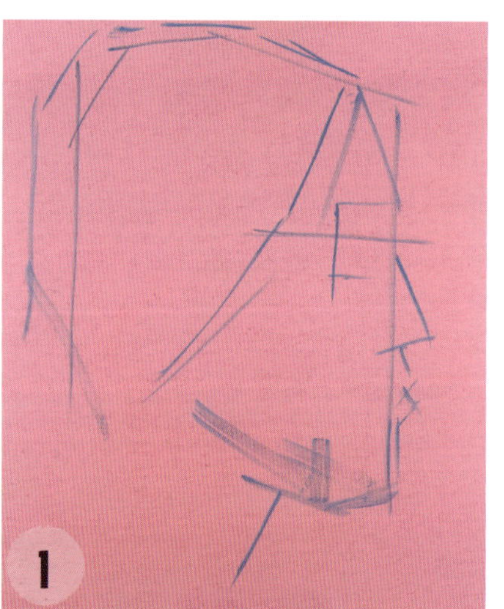

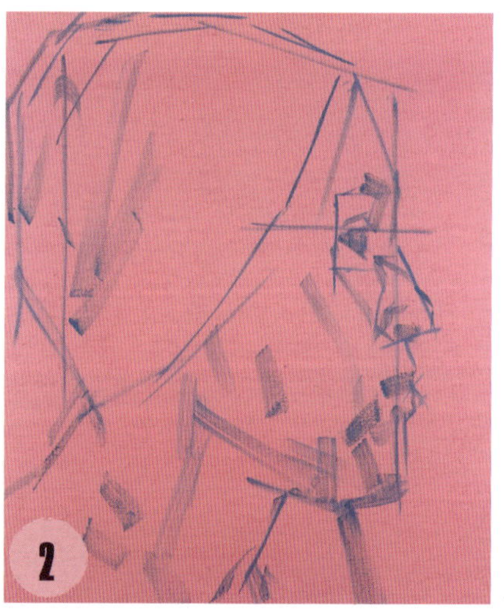

1 Working on a field of quinacridone rose opaque, use a 25mm (1in) flat brush to block in the main shapes of the face. When working in profile, the eyeline is still important, and you still need a box to accommodate the eye. State the structure of the lips and chin, and suggest the jawline.

2 Still using the same brush and colour, begin to refine the drawing. Because it's a profile, there's less face to deal with – it's thus important to make sure it's accurate before you get stuck in. The continuous line from the top of the forehead down to the chin, defining the nose and mouth, is difficult to get right, so take your time.

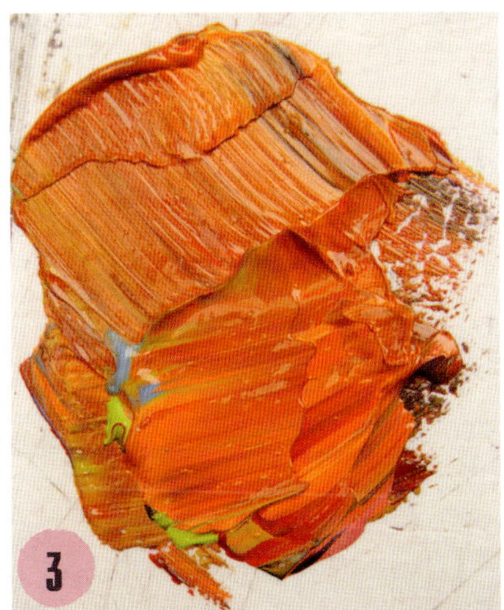

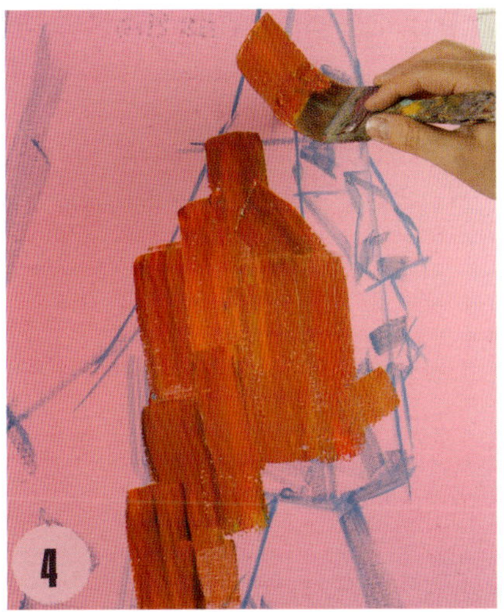

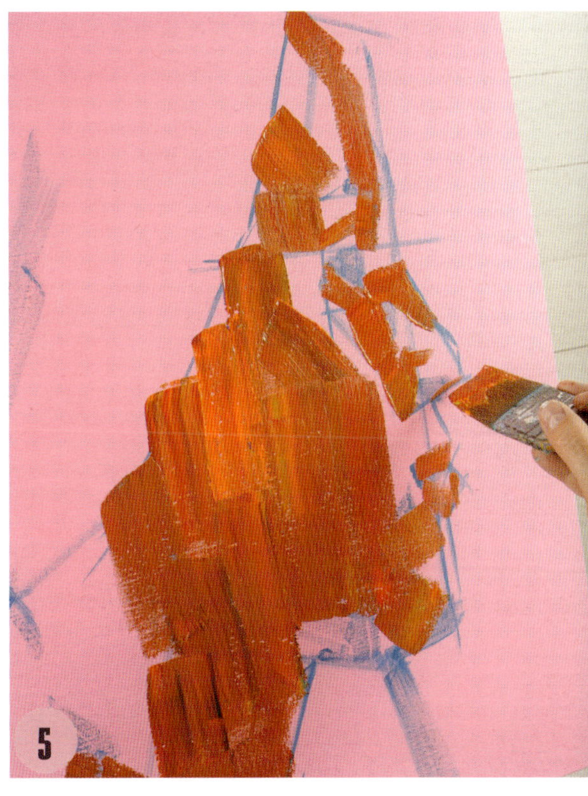

3 Load the 50mm (2in) flat brush with cadmium orange, quinacridone rose, quinacridone rose opaque, burnt sienna, yellowish green, king's blue, permanent blue violet and permanent blue violet opaque; and create a pool of base skin tone.

4 Use this to begin blocking in the cheek with bold strokes. The woman is young, but not a child; so we allow the colour variation to come through (unlike in the child portrait). However, unlike the older portraits, we keep the direction of the brushstrokes relatively uniform. This ensures not too much texture is suggested and the face retains a youthful quality.

5 Still using the 50mm (2in) flat, use the edge to begin to develop the features with short strokes.

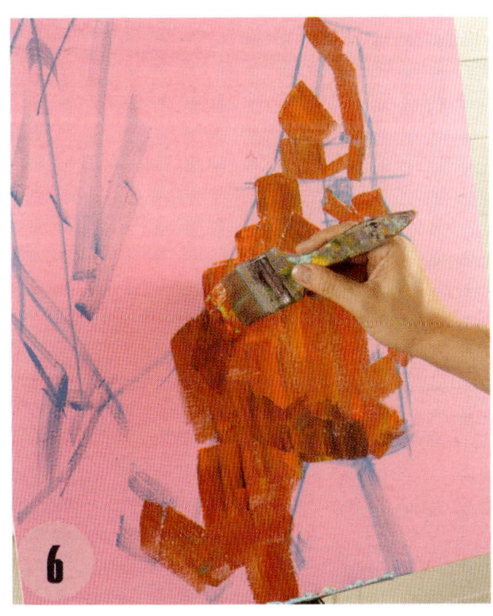

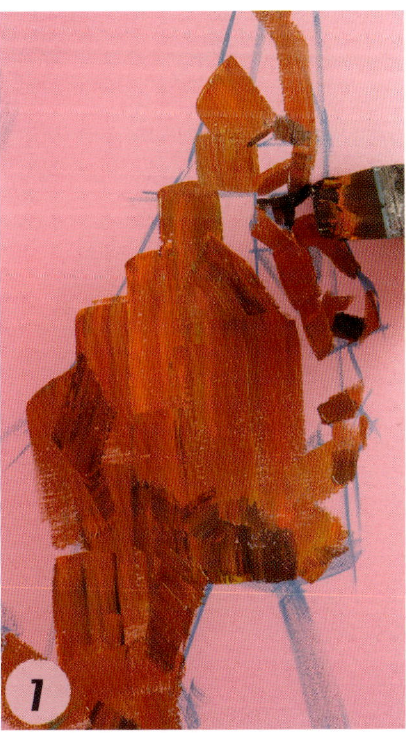

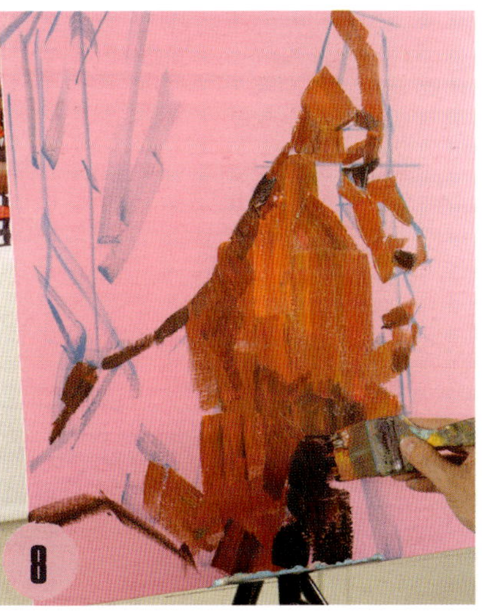

6 Adding more permanent blue violet, permanent blue violet opaque and sap green to the base skin pool, create darker hues for shading under the jaw. Work quickly – if the previously layer is still wet, you will achieve good integration between the layers of paint.

7 Establish the line of the mouth, nostril, brow and eye itself with the same mix.

8 Use the same dark to suggest the shadow of the headscarf. Add more cadmium orange or pyrrole red to enliven the mix. Use the opportunity to cut into and define the neck.

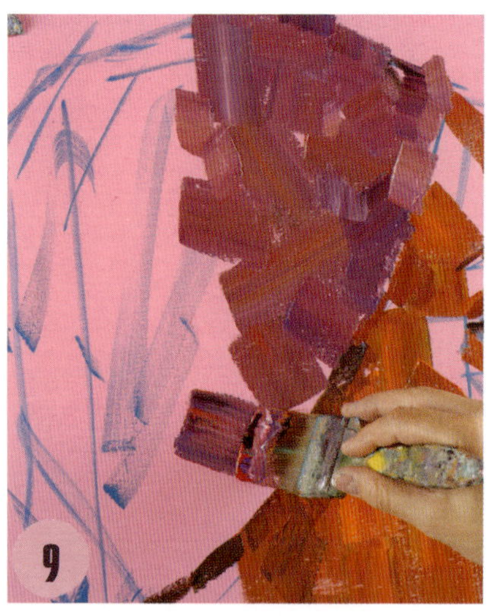

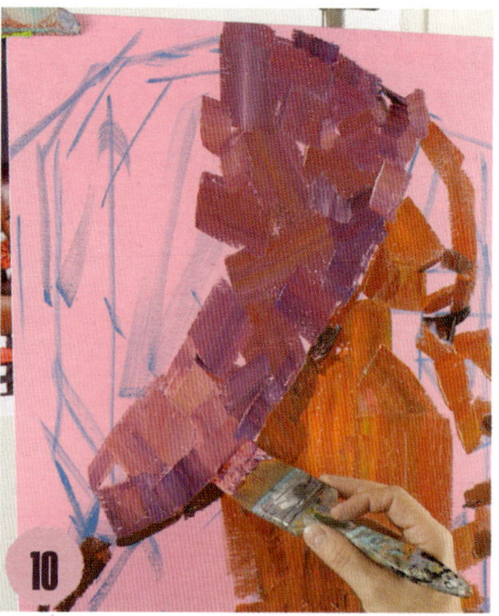

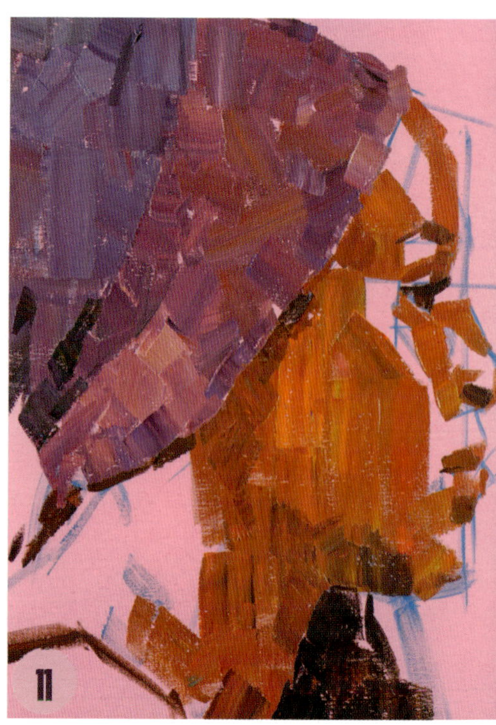

9 Add more quinacridone rose, titanium white and cadmium orange to the base skin to give you a plum-coloured pool for the headscarf. Build up the textured part at the front, using short, choppy brushstrokes.

10 Err towards using more titanium white and cadmium orange on the lower part, where the sunlight is hitting it.

11 Work back up the headscarf with the darker tones, then fill in the smoother area at the back with longer, cleaner strokes. Mix permanent blue violet opaque and sap green into the plum-colour pool to add dark, deep creases.

12 Create a pool of permanent blue violet opaque, cobalt blue, king's blue, and yellow ochre. Use this to establish the background. Work carefully down around the face, reserving a small gap of the pink underpainting showing in front of the figure's face.

13 As you reach the lower part of the portrait, add some king's blue.

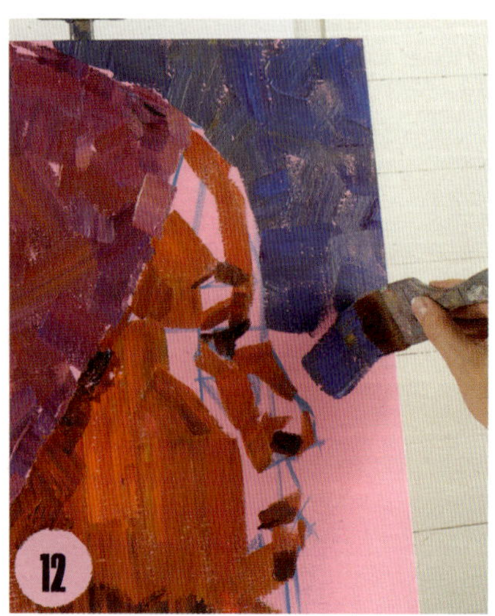

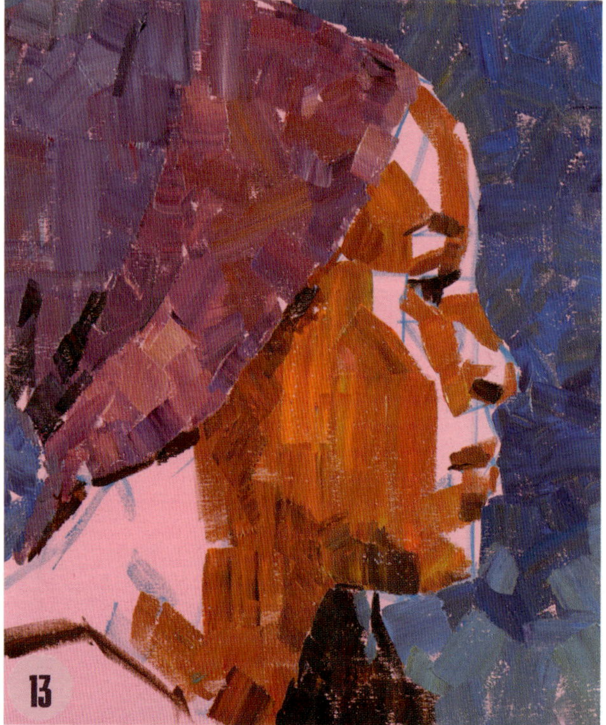

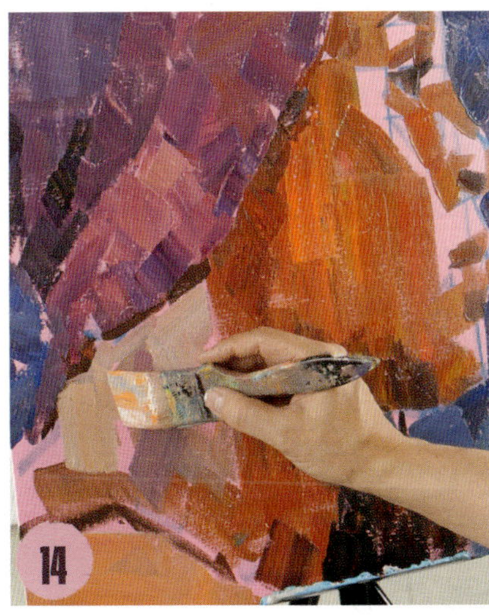

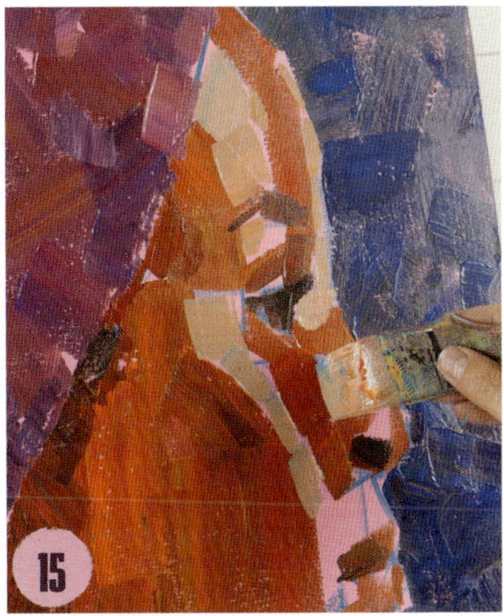

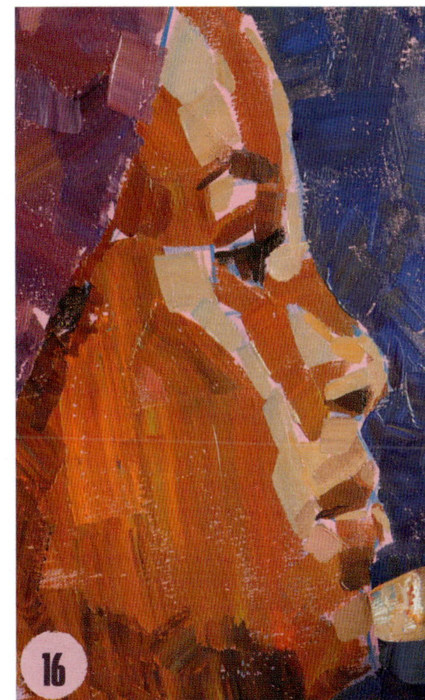

14 Into the basic skin tone pool (cadmium orange, quinacridone rose, quinacridone rose opaque, burnt sienna, yellowish green, king's blue, permanent blue violet and permanent blue violet opaque), add titanium white opaque, along with more cadmium orange and quinacridone rose opaque. Use a clean 37mm (1½in) flat brush to paint the figure's shoulder and back of the neck where the sunlight is hitting. Introduce more king's blue and cadmium orange to the areas in indirect light.

15 Use this mix to pick out the reflected light on the figure's face, including the reserved strip of pink in front of the face.

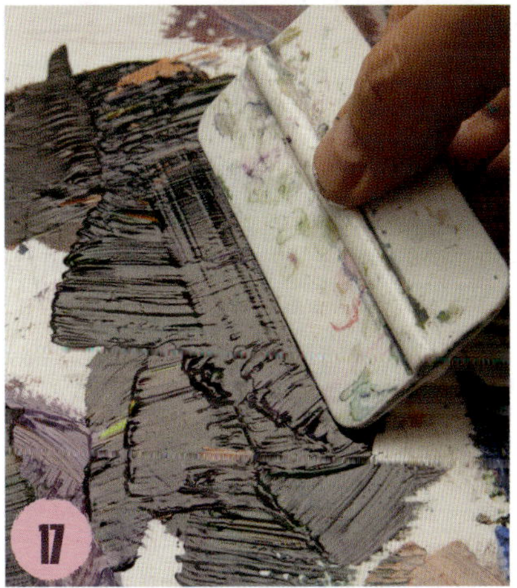

16 Include some quinacridone rose opaque on the loaded brush around the lips.

17 Build up a large, dark pool of permanent blue violet and sap green. Use a scooping motion to load the scraper with paint.

18 Place the loaded edge of the scraper on the headscarf where you want a crease, then draw it a short distance to deposit some of the paint.

19 Continue building up creases and texture on the headscarf in this way, varying the mix with the addition of quinacridone rose.

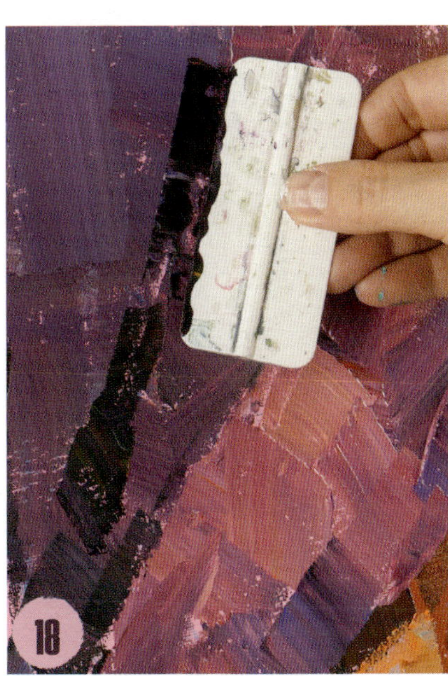

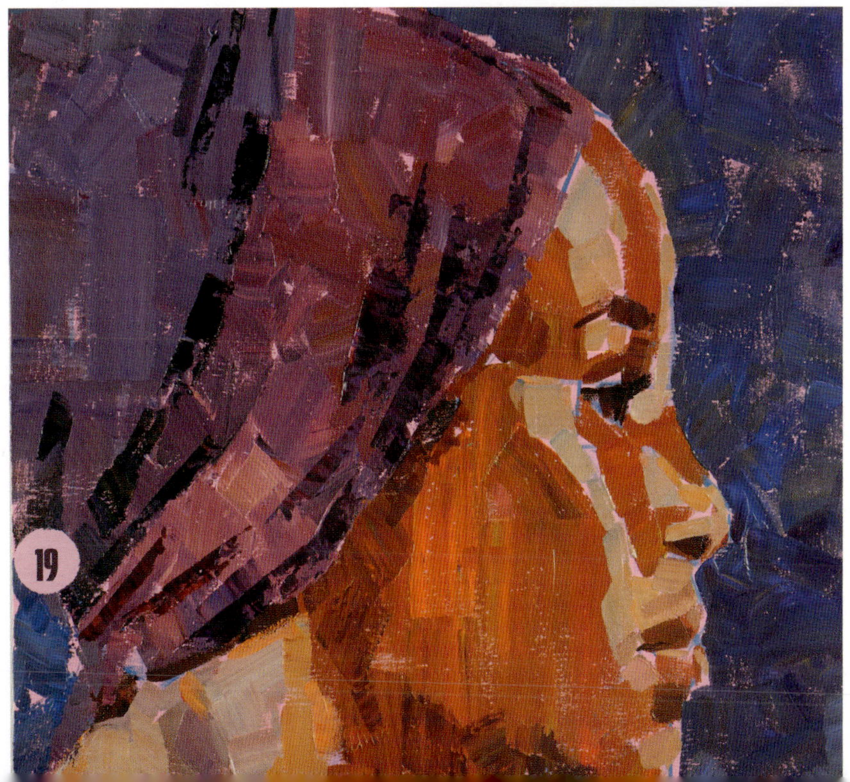

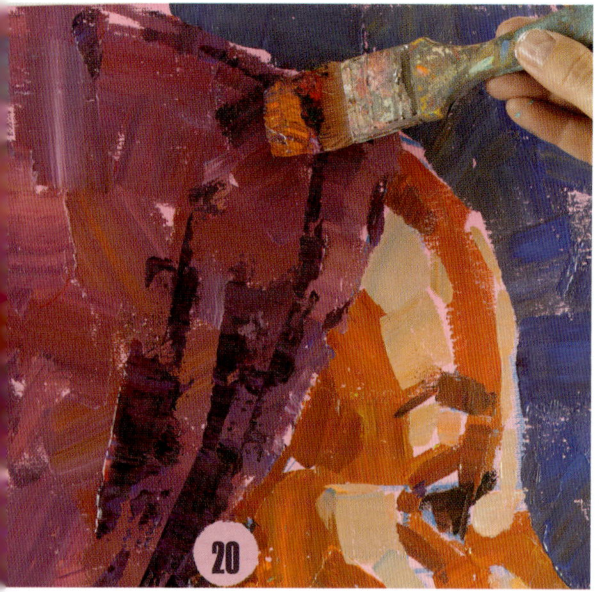

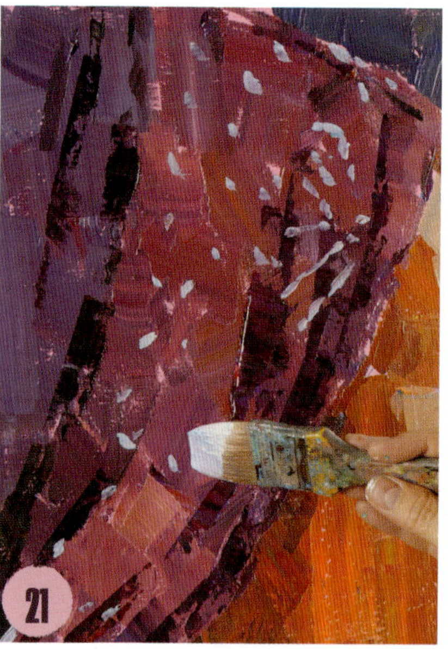

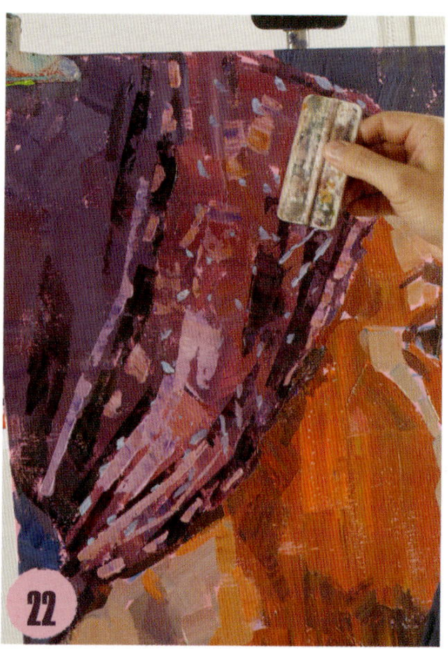

20 Add a few touches of the same mix with the tip of the 37mm (1½in) brush. This helps to integrate the marks made with the scraper.

21 Load a clean 37mm (1½in) brush with titanium white, king's blue and a little of the purple on your palette. Add some light decorative touches across the headscarf as shown.

22 Add some highlights to the left-hand side of the headscarf with a pool of permanent blue violet opaque, titanium white, quinacridone rose opaque and a little burnt sienna. Use a scraper to apply the paint.

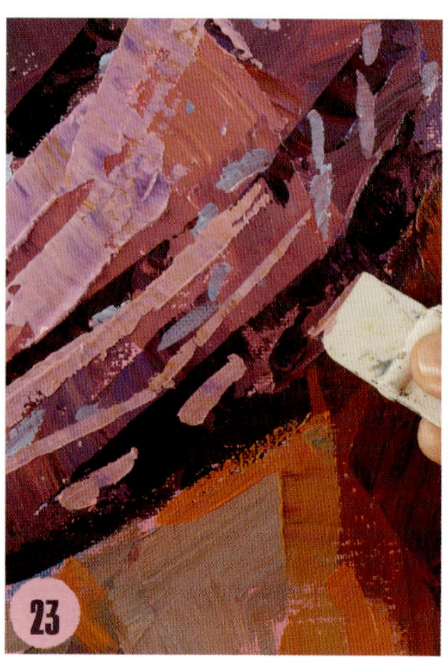

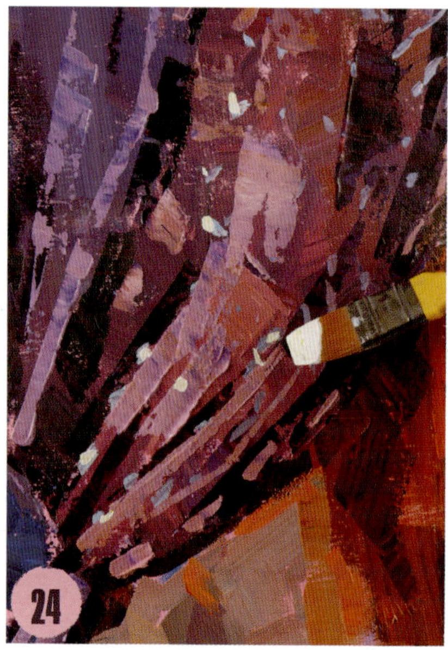

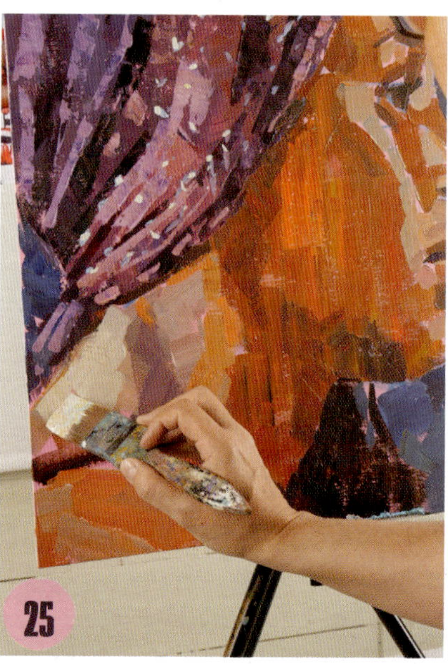

23 Change to a smaller scraper if necessary for finer marks.

24 Switch to a pool of titanium white, sky blue, yellow ochre and yellowish green to pick out the reflections on the headscarf decorations, applying the paint with a 25mm (1in) flat brush.

25 Combine parts of the two pools (the ones used for highlighting the scarf, and for highlighting the decorations) and use the resulting mix to highlight the nape of the neck with a 37mm (1½in) flat brush. Underplay the highlights here slightly to avoid drawing the viewer's eye away from the face.

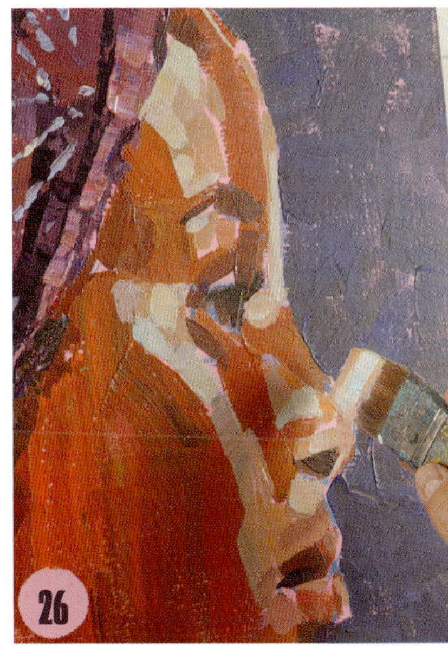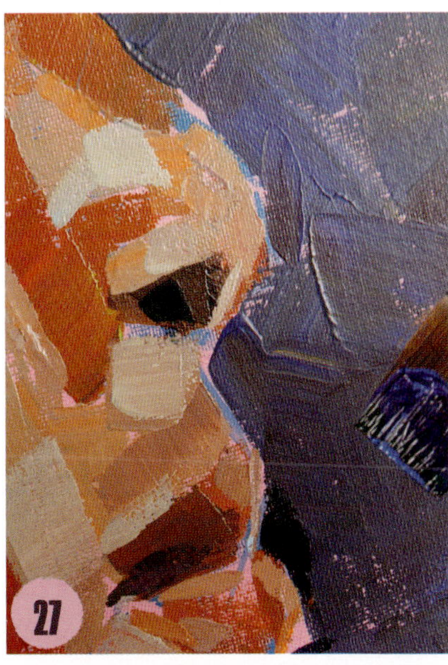

26 Add more titanium white and yellowish green to the pool to brighten the mix. Swapping between the 25mm (1in) and 37mm (1½in) flat brush, add highlights to the face, including the highlight between the edge of the head and the background.

27 Using a clean 25mm (1in) flat brush, mix up a strong dark pool of sap green, cobalt blue, permanent blue violet and burnt sienna. Apply this to refine the edge of the face, if necessary.

THE FINISHED PORTRAIT

The highlights are fairly subtle; close in tone to the underlying paint. They serve to add some final definition, and are a good opportunity to make final adjustments before you step away.

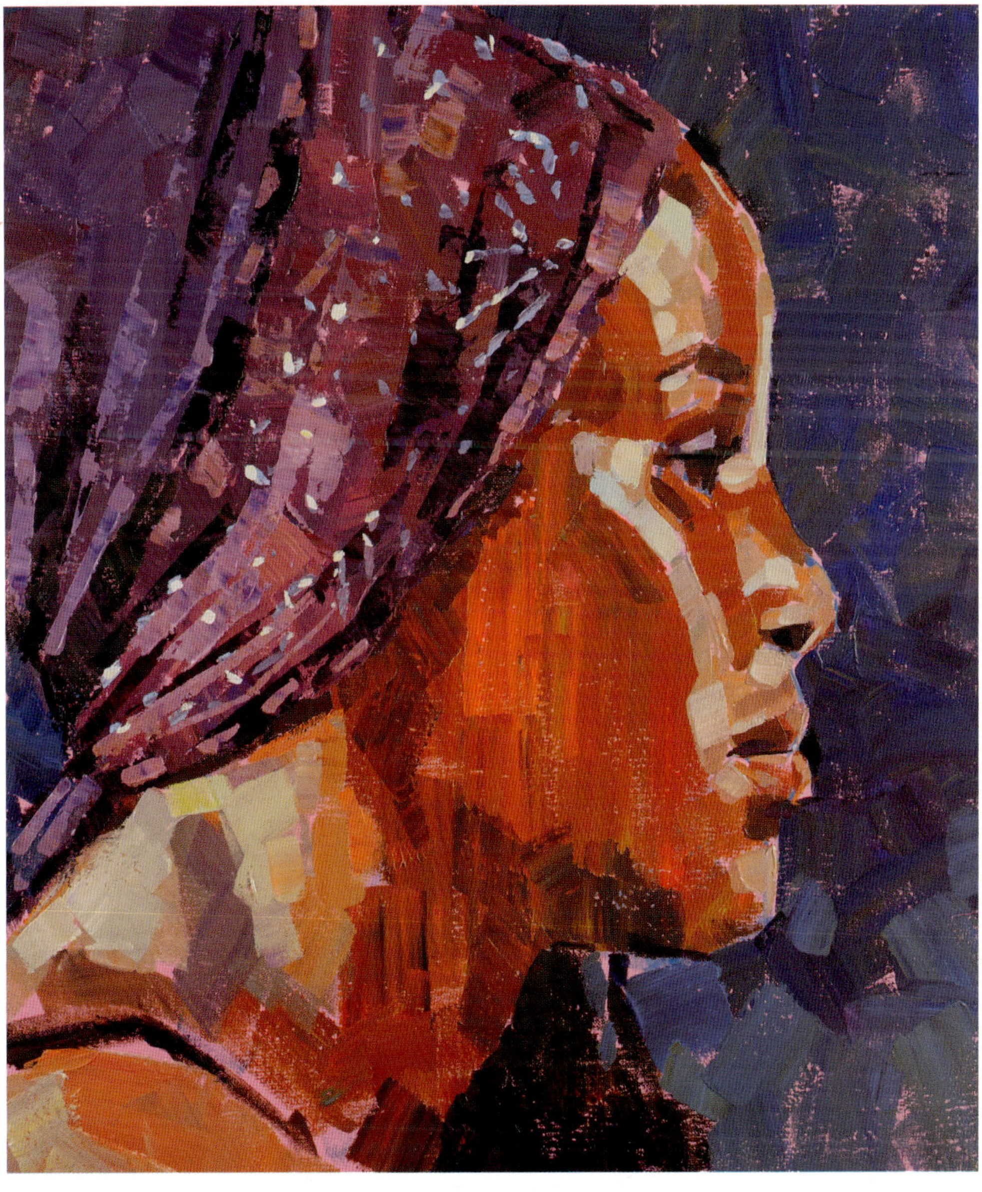

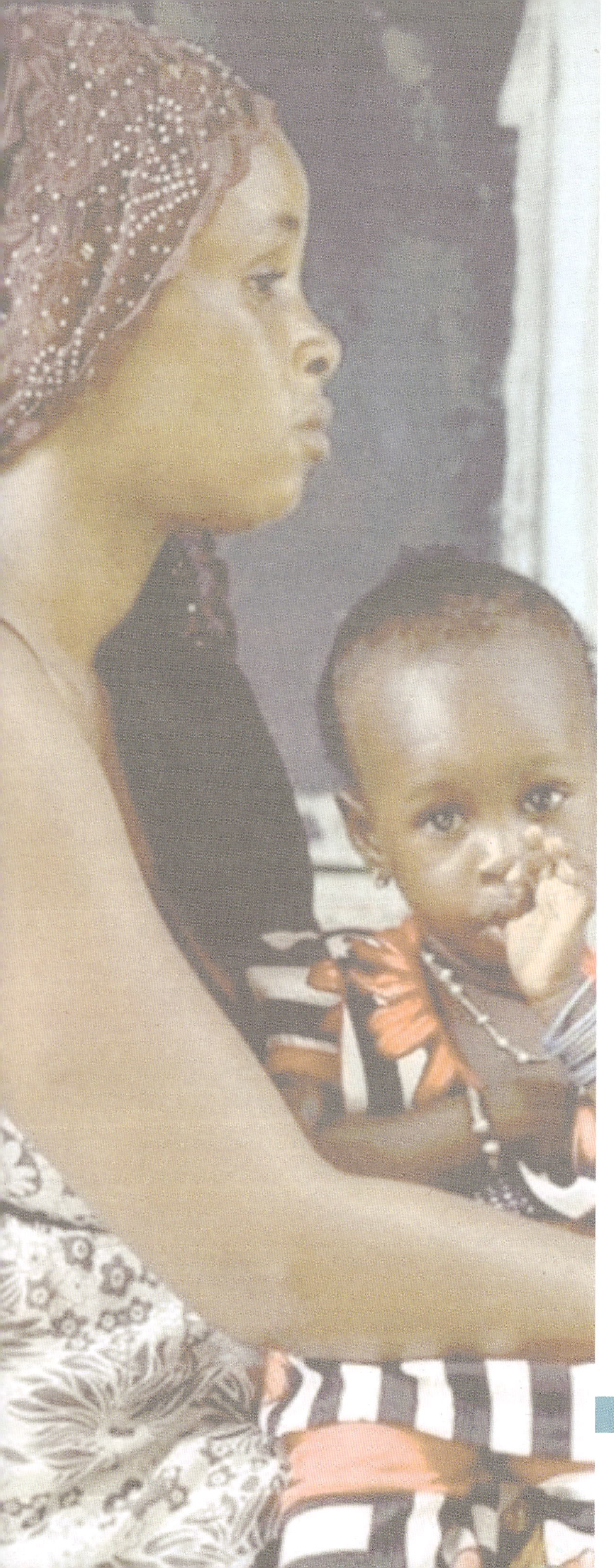

The importance of good reference material

Behind every portrait is a story; perhaps a very different one from how we may live. This portrait is one that immediately resonated and I wanted to include. Hasan Söylemez is the photographer and, as I write this, he is on a seven-year trek cycling through fifty-four countries on the African continent.

Reference material for any painting is important and I've been extremely fortunate to have access to some of his wonderful photographs that have allowed me to paint a number of portraits for this book. I've painted several of his subjects and really wanted to acknowledge his efforts, as his evocative work has made my job of translating them into paint both easier and more enjoyable.

As artists, we should always try to bring our own interpretations. However good the source material, make sure that your painted portraits can be informative, both in terms of representation and artistic interpretation.

Painting *Mother and Child*

As a complement to the demonstration on the previous pages, this painting showcases the full scene with both mother and child. Compositionally, it's interesting to combine both a profile and a full-face pose in the portrait, as we follow's the mother's gaze down to the child who engages with us more directly. It's more common that scenes such as this can be downbeat and contain an earthy palette, so I made the choice to use relatively rich colours, in order to suggest an optimistic and positive outcome.

MOTHER AND CHILD 51×61cm, (20×24in)

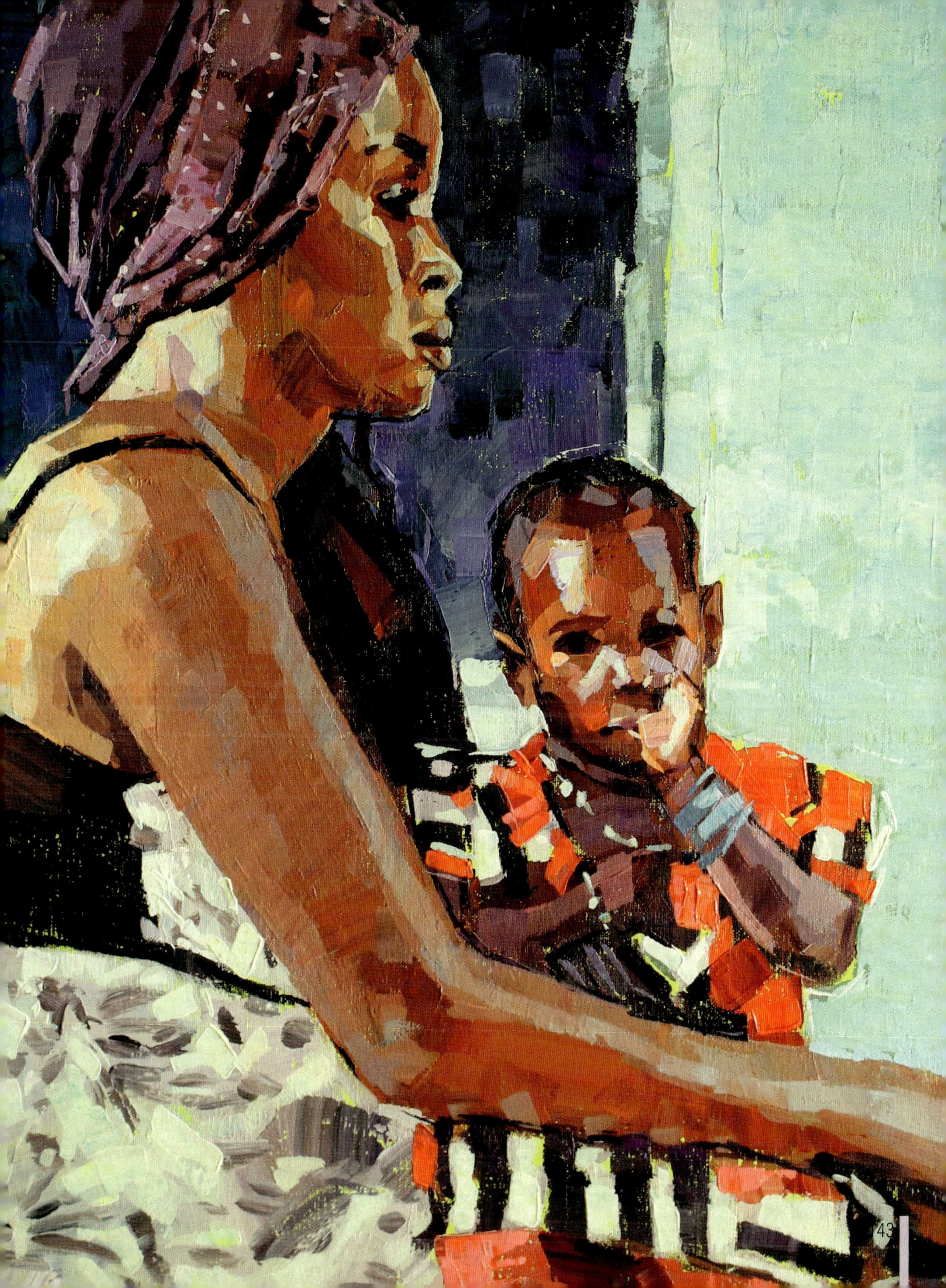